Cornerstone on
Anti-social Behaviour

Second edition

Cornerstone on
Anti-social Behaviour

Second edition

Kuljit Bhogal LLB (Hons) (London)
Barrister, Cornerstone Barristers

Bloomsbury Professional

LONDON · DUBLIN · EDINBURGH · NEW YORK · NEW DELHI · SYDNEY

BLOOMSBURY PROFESSIONAL
Bloomsbury Publishing Plc

41–43 Boltro Road, Haywards Heath, RH16 1BJ, UK

BLOOMSBURY and the Diana logo are trademarks of Bloomsbury Publishing Plc

British Library Cataloguing-in-Publication Data

A catalogue record for this book is available from the British Library.

ISBN:	PB:	978-1-52650-864-5
	ePDF:	978-1-52650-866-9
	ePub:	978-1-52650-865-2

Typeset by Evolution Design & Digital Ltd (Kent)

To find out more about our authors and books visit www.bloomsburyprofessional.com. Here you will find extracts, author information, details of forthcoming events and the option to sign up for our newsletters

About the author

Kuljit is barrister specialising in all aspects of public law.

She studied law at King's College, University of London before being called to the bar in 1998.

She is ranked as a leading lawyer by the legal directories, *Chambers and Partners UK* and *The Legal 500,* for social housing law.

She is also an ambassador for the Women of the Future programme having been specially commended at the Asian Women of Achievement Awards. Recently she participated in the international Leading Women Conversation organised by the University of London.

In her public sector work, she acts predominantly for local authorities, housing associations and health bodies. In her private sector work, she acts for private landlords, housing associations and developers.

Kuljit is able to provide policy and strategic advice at the most senior levels. She has extensive experience of policy and governance issues as well as in relation to individual cases and contracts. She is able to provide advice quickly and efficiently and provides practical solutions whilst working in partnership with her clients.

Her recent work has ranged from governance (and other) issues relating to Public Space Protection Orders, the contracting out of local authority functions (in particular, homelessness functions) and the legality of Part VI Allocation Schemes.

She advises on all aspects of the Anti-Social Behaviour, Crime and Policing Act 2014. Her practice also includes social housing, Court of Protection and community care work. Further information on her experience and details of her cases can be found at www.cornerstonebarristers.com/barrister/kuljit-bhogal/

For Amaya and Arjan

Be fierce
Be bold
Be fearless
Be determined
Be open-minded
Be considerate
Be virtuous
Become the best at whatever you choose to be

Contents

Contents

Preface

Following the publication of the revised Statutory Guidance for Frontline Professionals and some case law (at last!), the requests for a further edition have been overwhelming. It's been a mammoth task but here it is …

Like the first edition this book has been written with both lawyers and non-lawyers in mind. I have created a 'one-stop shop' for the resources that anyone working in the anti-social behaviour field will require.

The contents have been fully revised and whilst some of the material will be familiar to readers, references to new case law and legislation have been added, the text has been updated and there are even more template documents.

In writing this edition there are several people to whom I owe huge thanks. The starting point are my Mathaji, Prakash Kaur and my parents Bhajan Singh and Salinder Kaur Bhogal who support me in everything I do. Words cannot express how much I owe to them. I also thank the rest of the Bhogal, Syan and Karir families.

A special thanks to my husband Indy Syan and our children Amaya and Arjan. As ever, they have provided love, encouragement and humour when it was needed most.

I thank all my clients, many of whom who have provided case studies and invaluable feedback on the first edition. I also thank Stuart McNair (contributor of the sample prohibitions in Appendix E).

Thanks too to all of my colleagues, both members of Chambers and staff, who have helped to forge this book (and the previous edition) and provided encouragement and support. Particular thanks for the input provided by my valued friends and colleagues: Philip Kolvin QC, Ranjit Bhose QC, Jon Holbrook, Catherine Rowlands, Andrew Lane, Shomik Datta, Josef Cannon, Clare Parry, Jennifer Oscroft, Ryan Kohli, Zoe Whittington, Ben de Feu, Tara O'Leary, Richard Hanstock (contributor of the new committals section in Chapter 3), Ruchi Parekh, John Fitzsimons, Dr Alex Williams and Dr Sam Fowles.

I also thank everyone at Bloomsbury, especially Leanne Barrett and Gillian Pickering.

The law is stated as at 15 March 2019 and any errors are my own.

Kuljit Bhogal
Public law barrister
Cornerstone Barristers
kuljitb@cornerstonebarristers.com

Abbreviations and acronyms

ASBA 2003	Anti-Social Behaviour Act 2003
ASBI	Anti-social behaviour injunction
ASBO	Anti-social behaviour order
CPN	Community protection notice
CDA 1998	Crime and Disorder Act 1998
CJPA 2001	Criminal Justice and Police Act 2001
CNEA 2005	Clean Neighbourhoods and Environment Act 2005
CPR	Civil Procedure Rules
CRASBO	Anti-social behaviour order on conviction
Crim PR	Criminal Procedure Rules
DDA 1995	Disability Discrimination Act 1995
DPA 1998	Data Protection Act 1998
EPA 1990	Environmental Protection Act 1990
EA 2010	Equality Act 2010
ECHR	European Convention on Human Rights and Fundamental Freedoms 1950
FPN	Fixed penalty notice
HA 1980	Housing Act 1980
HA 1985	Housing Act 1985
HA 1988	Housing Act 1988
HA 1996	Housing Act 1996
HRA 1998	Human Rights Act 1998
LA 2003	Licensing Act 2003
PSPO	Public space protection order
VCRA 2006	Violent Crime Reduction Act 2006

Table of Statutes

[References are to paragraph numbers]

Table of Statutory Instruments

[References are to paragraph numbers]

Table of Cases

[References are to paragraph numbers]

R

S

CHAPTER 1

Introduction

'It took me 28 months to finally get rid of my antisocial neighbour just before Christmas. The stress and sleep deprivation he caused wrecked my mental and physical health. It was easier for the authorities to just ignore me than do something about him.'

ASB Help (2019), 'The Community Trigger: Where We Are Today'

	What this chapter covers	
A	The Act: a snapshot	1.01
B	The contents of the second edition	1.02
C	Background: Dow and Pilkington	1.04
D	The consultation and passage through Parliament	1.05
E	Ending the arms race	1.08
F	Conclusion	1.09

A THE ACT: A SNAPSHOT

1.01 The Act rationalised a large number of dedicated (but not necessarily effectively used) mechanisms and replaced them with a select few devices which are supposed to be flexible enough to deal with a wide range of anti-social behaviour.

Numerous separate remedies have been replaced with six new powers.

Figure 1.1 Replacement powers introduced by the Act

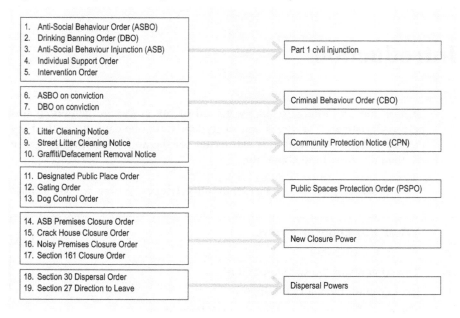

B   THE CONTENTS OF THIS BOOK AND WHAT'S NEW IN THE SECOND EDITION

1.02   All of the content has been re-visited for this second edition. Each chapter has been updated and contains cross-references to the Revised Guidance and relevant cases. Real life case studies have been included wherever possible.

The templates and precedents in Appendix D have also been updated and there are completely new templates for a Community Protection Warning and a Community Protection Notice.

Chapter 2 is of general application to all of the powers. It considers the human rights implications and the Equality Act 2010, including a section on the Public Sector Equality duty which has been a feature of some of the recent case law. There is also a section on hate crime.

Chapter 3 looks at the **civil injunction.** It examines how the injunction differs from the ASBO and ASBI. There is an explanation of the rules on consulting/informing and there is a quick reference textbox on the difference between the two. There is a section on terms to be included in an injunction including how positive requirements can be used. The chapter considers the relevance of existing and new case law when looking at the definition of anti-social behaviour and when deciding which terms to include. There is a completely new section on the committal process for when an injunction is breached. Appendix D contains updated precedents for use when making an application.

Chapter 4 deals with **Criminal Behaviour Orders (CBOs).** It explains when a CBO can be sought, against whom and the test to be met. Much of Chapter 3 will also be of relevance insofar as it relates to the terms of an order and publicity. Part 31 of the Criminal Procedure Rules is cross referenced wherever appropriate.

Chapter 5 examines the **dispersal power** given to the police. The procedure for seeking authorisation and the test for using the new power are explained. There is an assessment of how the new power differs from the old.

Chapter 6 looks at the **Community Protection Notice (CPN)**. There is an explanation of how the CPN differs from the old powers and there are examples of how the powers have been used. The chapter also explains how a CPN may be appealed and considers the extent to which the case law relating to abatement notices will be relevant. Appendix D contains new templates for a CPN warning and a CPN.

Chapter 7 deals with **Public Space Protection Orders (PSPOs)**. This is the principal power to deal with anti-social behaviour in public spaces and allows local authorities to make orders which apply to everyone within a designated space. The statutory requirements to consult, notify and publicise are explained and there is a worked example of how a PSPO might be used. References from the two statutory appeals to reach the High Court are included.

Chapter 8 examines how premises can be closed using a **closure order**. The chapter explains the two-stage closure process, the rules on the contents and service of closure notices and the ability to access premises. Appendix D contains updated templates for a closure notice, an application and a closure order. There is a new case study involving a 'cuckooed' tenant.

Chapter 9 covers the **discretionary and absolute grounds for possession**. The review procedure for the mandatory grounds is explained and there is a section on defences. Appendix D contains Notices of Seeking Possession when mandatory grounds are being relied upon in addition to discretionary grounds (for both secure and assured tenancies) and a template form for requesting a review of the decision to seek possession on a mandatory ground.

Chapter 10 looks at **anti-social behaviour case reviews** which have been created to empower victims. It explains how victims of anti-social behaviour (or someone acting on their behalf), can demand action starting with a review of their case. The chapter explains the need for qualifying complaints and looks at what anti-social behaviour case review policies/procedures should include. The chapter includes a quick reference textbox on information sharing and a case study on how the process has been used effectively.

The Guidance

1.03   In December 2017 the Home Office updated the statutory *Guidance for Frontline Professionals*.[1] The Guidance was issued under ss 19, 32, 41, 73 and 91 of the Act and replaced the guidance issued in July 2014. This book will refer to the updated Guidance as the Revised Guidance. The Revised Guidance

---

1   https://www.gov.uk/government/uploads/system/uploads/attachment_data/file/352562/ASB_Guidance_v8_July2014_final__2_.pdf.

deals with all of the powers covered in this book and a copy can be found in Appendix C.

C BACKGROUND – DOW AND PILKINGTON

1.04   On 3 August 2011, Dr Suzanne Dow sent an email to her housing officer explaining that her neighbour had stones thrown at her open window and that she had been the victim of verbal abuse from him. She explained that her neighbour had shouted 'when I [find] what c**t has called the police they'll be sorry'. She tells her housing officer 'I feel very vulnerable and desperate about this situation'.

The housing officer does not reply to or acknowledge Dr Dow's email. Dr Dow writes to her housing officer again: 'As you know I have been despairing of this situation. Every time I set foot [in my own garden] I am subject to a barrage of abuse. Could you at least acknowledge receipt of my emails?'

Still no response, she writes yet again 'I really don't think I ought to put up with this for any longer'. In other emails Dr Dow says 'I am at my wits end … I do not feel safe in my own house … my life is being made unbearable by this situation and it is having a serious effect on my health, mental and physical'.

Over a year after she first made complaints about her neighbours, Dr Dow took an overdose of pills at her home on 3 October 2011. In the last email before her death she explained how she had been unable to sleep and that she had reached the limits of her tolerance.

An inquest into Dr Dow's death heard how she had been a victim of anti-social behaviour at the hands of her neighbour ever since she moved into her home just over three years before her death.

The local authority did eventually reply to Dr Dow's emails but said it was unaware of her history of mental health problems until the inquest.

The sad reality is that Dr Dow's story is not an isolated one.[2] On 23 October 2007, the bodies of Fiona Pilkington and her 17-year-old daughter Francecca Hardwick were found in a burnt out car in a lay-by on the A47 near Earl Shilton in Leicestershire.

Ms Pilkington's daughter had severe to profound multiple learning difficulties, she had significant developmental delay and was functioning at the level of a three to four year old. Ms Pilkington's son had special educational needs and the family was receiving support from Leicestershire Social Services. They had made numerous complaints to the police about the behaviour of youths living in the local area. Their MP had written to the police on Ms Pilkington's behalf and complaints had also come from her neighbours. The anti-social behaviour they suffered from the local youths was long standing and there had been some extremely serious incidents which warranted a proper response from the enforcement agencies. The youths identified as responsible were living in local authority or housing association properties.

---

2   The details set out in this chapter have been taken from an article by Keith Cooper in *Inside Housing* dated 21 June 2013, 'Driven to despair'.

The police records showed 33 reports to the police between November 1997 and October 2007. On one occasion Ms Pilkington's 13-year-old son was locked in a shed by two boys and had to break his way out. It took the police four days to visit Ms Pilkington to take a statement. During a video interview with her son he explained how he had been physically dragged from a friend's garden to a local youth's house, a knife had been produced and he had been locked in the shed for several hours. He had to physically smash his way out of the shed and he had thought that the youth was going to kill him. Ms Pilkington was able to name several of the offenders and at least one of the youths had admitted that a knife was involved and that he had been present. The incident only resulted in harassment warnings being issued.

The then Independent Police Complaints Commission (IPCC) (now the Independent Office for Police Conduct (IOPC)) published its investigation report into the deaths of Ms Pilkington and her daughter in May 2011. The report detailed 92 findings on the Pilkington family's interaction with the Leicestershire police and on the police's procedures and systems. At the heart of the IPCC's findings was a failure by the police to identify the family as vulnerable. The investigation concluded, inter alia, that:

- officers did not identify a difference in the level of seriousness between general anti-social behaviour and specific harassment of the Pilkington family, and they failed to consider their treatment as hate crime;

- police officers should have picked up on Ms Pilkington's repeated assertion that the situation was 'on-going' and that it was her family in particular being targeted;

- aside from the family's vulnerability, Ms Pilkington was a member of a local community who was reporting incidents of crime and anti-social behaviour and simply asking police to carry out their responsibilities, which they failed to do;

- there was a tendency for incidents to be closed without any record of action having been taken, and without any supervising officer checking that matters had been dealt with satisfactorily;

- Bardon Road, where the family lived, was not considered by the police to be an anti-social behaviour 'hotspot', and was therefore not targeted for a more proactive response; and

- warning letters and 'acceptable behaviour contracts' were being issued by the local authority and police officers without any co-ordinated system in place to share information.

Pilkington and Dow are some of the most serious and tragic examples; but how widespread is the problem? The Crime Survey for England and Wales (CSEW) estimated that 34% of all respondents experienced or witnessed anti-social behaviour in their local area in 2018, an increase from the previous year when the figure was 31%. This is the highest percentage since the data were first collected in the year ending March 2012.

Around 1.6 million incidents of ASB were recorded by the police in the latest year for which data are available, a decrease of 13% from the previous year. These are incidents that may still be crimes in law, such as littering and dog fouling, but which are not severe enough to result in the recording of a notifiable offence and therefore are not included in the main police recorded crime series.

There has been no recent inspection into ASB; however, in 2012 a review by Her Majesty's Inspectorate of Constabulary (HMIC) of police crime and incident reports looked at the quality of crime and incident data and the arrangements in place to ensure standards were maintained and improved.[3] The HMIC report highlighted the wide variation in: (i) the way in which anti-social behaviour was recorded; and (ii) the identification of repeat and vulnerable victims at the first point of contact. The British Crime Survey summarised the findings of the HMIC as follows:

- forces [are] failing to identify crimes, instead wrongly recording them as anti-social behaviour;

- reported anti-social behaviour [is] not being recorded on force systems, for instance if the victim had reported it directly to the neighbourhood team or via email (as opposed to by telephone);

- reported anti-social behaviour [is] being recorded as something else, such as suspicious behaviour; and

- incidents that were not anti-social behaviour were being recorded as anti-social behaviour.[4]

The HMIC report revealed that only 22 forces could effectively identify repeat victims at the point of report, only 16 forces could effectively identify vulnerable and intimidated victims and that only 13 forces could effectively identify both.[5]

All of the above was despite the internal investigation by the Leicestershire police into the Pilkington deaths and the IPCC's report that followed. It is this ongoing failure by the relevant agencies to identify those complainants who are vulnerable or repeatedly suffering from anti-social behaviour that has in large part led to an overhaul of the anti-social behaviour provisions.

A report from the Office of National Statistics[6] suggests that in view of the focus on the quality of crime recording, some incidents of ASB have more recently been recorded as crimes and that this could account for some of the recent rise in public order offences.

The measures introduced by the Anti-Social Behaviour Crime and Policing Act 2014 ('the Act') are intended to provide effective powers for tackling the problems.

---

3   *The crime scene: a review of police crime and incident reports*, HMIC 2012.
4   *British Crime Survey* for the year ending March 2014, p 110.
5   Ibid, p 20.
6   Statistical bulletin, *Crime and England and Wales*, year ending 2018. Crime against households and adults, also including data on crime experienced by children, and crimes against businesses and society.

D THE CONSULTATION AND PASSAGE THROUGH PARLIAMENT

1.05   The Act is in 14 parts, runs to over 330 pages and deals with more than just anti-social behaviour. This section examines the Government's assessment of the previous legislation and why it thought reform was required. It also looks at the various consultation documents and some of the highlights of the Act's passage through Parliament. In this book all references to statutory provisions are to the Anti-Social Behaviour, Crime and Policing Act 2014 unless otherwise stated.

The consultation

1.06   On 7 February 2011 the Coalition Government published a consultation document entitled *More Effective Responses to Anti-Social Behaviour*[7] which set out the conclusions of the Government's review of the anti-social behaviour powers. It said:[8]

- there are simply too many tools, with practitioners tending to stick to the ones they are most familiar with;

- some of the formal tools (particularly Anti-Social Behaviour Orders or 'ASBOs') are bureaucratic, slow and expensive, which puts people off using them;

- the growing number of people who breach their ASBO suggests the potential consequences are not deterring a persistent minority from continuing their anti-social or criminal behaviour; and

- the tools that were designed to help perpetrators deal with underlying causes of their anti-social behaviour are rarely used.

The Government noted that despite the introduction of more than ten separate pieces of legislation and a raft of new powers by the previous Labour Government, the 'bloated' toolkit was confusing for practitioners and the public alike and the incidence of anti-social behaviour remained stubbornly high with over 3.5 million incidents of anti-social behaviour being reported to the police each year.

The consultation placed considerable reliance on the fact that too many ASBOs were being breached and that the breach rate had risen from under 40% in 2003 to 56% by the end of 2009 (with 41% of ABSOs being breached more than once). This was regarded as a problem which required redress in view of the fact that the use of other powers such as Anti-Social Behaviour Injunctions (ASBIs), service of Notices of Seeking Possession (NOSPs) and possession actions was also increasing.

What the Government failed to recognise was that the mere fact that an ASBO had been breached did not reflect whether it was effective and that the

---

7   https://www.gov.uk/government/uploads/system/uploads/attachment_data/file/118297/asb-consultation-document.pdf.

8   *More Effective Responses to Anti-Social Behaviour*, p 5.

true measure of effectiveness was the pattern of anti-social behaviour before and after the ASBO had been made. A number of practitioners report an overall improvement in the incidence of anti-social behaviour caused by defendants who have ASBOs. Contrary to the suggestion that they are a 'badge of honour' many practitioners have reported that defendants do not like ASBOs and did not want to be made subject to one.

In May 2012 the Home Office published a White Paper, *Putting Victims First: More Effective Responses to Anti-Social Behaviour.*[9] The Government's view was that the previous approach was excessively driven by targets, that a 'one size fits all' model was inappropriate and that years of the 'top-down' approach had been ineffective: a more localised approach was required. The White Paper contained four themes:

- **Requiring local agencies to focus on the needs of victims:** this meant identifying high risk and vulnerable victims and ensuring their problems were taken seriously.

- **Supporting people and communities in establishing what is and is not acceptable and supporting them in holding local agencies to account**: this desire has led to the introduction of the anti-social behaviour case review or Community Trigger (see Chapter 10).

- **Ensuring professionals had the powers they need to tackle the problems:** the focus was introducing faster and 'more effective powers' to deal with anti-social behaviour in public places and on speeding up the eviction of anti-social tenants.

- **Focusing on long term solutions:** tackling issues such as binge drinking, drugs use, mental health issues, troubled family backgrounds and irresponsible dog ownership. This has led to the availability of 'positive requirements' which are covered in Chapter 3 (injunctions) and Chapter 4 (Criminal Behaviour Orders (CBOs)).

Passage through Parliament

1.07   The draft Anti-Social Behaviour Bill was published on 13 December 2012 and the Anti-Social Behaviour Act 2014 received Royal Assent on 13 March 2014.

Some of the highlights of the bill's passage through Parliament were:

(i)   The need to have regard to a person's caring responsibilities when imposing prohibitions and positive requirements in the s 1 injunctions[10] and CBOs[11] was added at Committee stage. Although the Minister had argued

---

9   https://www.gov.uk/government/uploads/system/uploads/attachment_data/file/228863/8367. pdf.

10 Revised *Statutory Guidance for Frontline Professionals*, p 20.

11 Revised *Statutory Guidance for Frontline Professionals*, p 28.

against these amendments, the first went through without division, and the Government did not oppose the second one.

(ii)   A further amendment at Committee stage would have allowed head teachers and Further Education College principals to apply for injunctions to prevent nuisance or annoyance (IPNAs[12]). This was in the context of debate about how IPNAs might be used to deal with bullying. This proposal did not make it into the Act as passed.

(iii)   What was originally a non-Government amendment to change the test for seeking an injunction[13] was subsequently adopted in a modified form by the Government in its amendments at the Third Reading of the Bill. The effect of these amendments was to replace the first limb of the test, which had originally required that the relevant conduct must have caused or be capable of causing 'nuisance or annoyance' to any person, with a requirement that the conduct has caused, or is likely to cause, 'harassment, alarm or distress' to any person (the old ASBO test but to be proved to the civil not criminal standard). The amendments provided that the 'nuisance or annoyance' test would still apply where anti-social behaviour occurs in the context of housing.[14]

Point (iii) above attracted the greatest debate in Parliament. From a very early stage there was concern that the definition of anti-social behaviour had been set at an inappropriately low level of conduct causing or likely to cause 'nuisance and annoyance'. Civil liberties organisations and charities had warned that the Act could criminalise any nuisance or annoying behaviour in the streets including peaceful protests, street preachers and even carol singers and church bellringers. The following extract from Lord Hope's speech during the second reading of the Bill in the House of Lords provides an illustrative summary of many of those concerns:[15]

'Let us take first the threshold that appears in subsection (2). Every word used here to describe what the person has been doing, or is threatening to do, is important. We find the words "conduct capable of causing", "nuisance or annoyance" and "to any person". Contrast that phrase "nuisance or annoyance" with "harassment, alarm or distress". Why is the threshold being reduced so much? Will the Minister explain the problem that has led to the decision to do this? It is a very significant reduction, let there be no doubt. I have searched the case law over the past 50 years as much as I can, for some guidance as to what a court would be likely to make of this formula. Most cases where the issue has arisen are about noise: shouting, banging doors, loud quarrels between people. However, it does

---

12   IPNAs were how the injunctions were known before the test was changed from 'nuisance and annoyance' to the test now found in s 2.

13   Found in s 2 s enacted.

14   For further information see the explanatory notes of the Lords amendments issued on 19 November 2013, available at http://www.publications.parliament.uk/pa/bills/cbill/2013-2014/0163/en/14163en.htm.

15   HL debate, 29 October 2013, col 1518.

not have to reach a very high level to fall within the expression "nuisance or annoyance". Those two words, "nuisance" and "annoyance", are put together as if they are a reasonably high threshold. However, the two words mean the same thing; putting the two together does not add anything. That which is a nuisance will annoy, and that which annoys will be a nuisance. Let us face the fact that this clause is simply dealing with people who are thought to be a nuisance.

Mention will be made, no doubt, of judicial discretion. There is a case in the books, from 1958—*Raymond v Cook*—that illustrates the problem. It was a case about an ice-cream man. His chimes disturbed the sleep of two night workers who had to sleep during the day. They complained, and the magistrate found the ice-cream man guilty of causing a nuisance. The Court of Appeal had a look at the case and refused to interfere, as it said that this was a matter of fact for the magistrates. It was not necessary to prove that the inhabitants generally were annoyed. The defence led people from the neighbourhood who said that they were not disturbed at all by the ice-cream van, but that made no difference: those two night workers found it to be a nuisance.

What then of the formula used here, of, "conduct capable of causing nuisance or annoyance", and the words "to any person"? Even the best behaved children are often noisy. Are children whose noise when playing wakes up people who have to sleep during the daytime to be exposed [to] this regime? I cannot believe that the Minister really intends that. If that it is so, surely that should be made clear. Even injecting "serious" into the phrase would help to some extent, but surely it would be far better to retain the ASBO formula unless something is demonstrably wrong with it. Indeed, we find it used in Clause 21(3) for criminal behaviour orders. At the very least, an explanation will be needed in Committee as to exactly why the threshold is being so drastically reduced.'

There is a further discussion of some of the concerns in Chapter 3 (injunctions). The strength of feeling expressed by Lord Hope was shared by many within the Houses of Parliament and across the political divide. Peers voted 306 to 178 in support of an amendment by the crossbench peer Lord Dear which re-introduced (from the ASBO) a test of harassment, alarm or distress.[16] The Government was then forced to table its own amendments to the definition of anti-social behaviour changing the test from nuisance or annoyance to what is now found in s 2 of the Act.[17]

---

16 House of Lords, Report stage, 1st sitting, 8 January 2014.
17 Nuisance and annoyance for housing – related anti-social behaviour, harassment, alarm and distress for everything else.

E ENDING THE ARMS RACE

1.08   The House of Commons Home Affairs Select Committee's report on the Anti-Social, Crime and Policing Bill published in February 2013 said:

> 'Each time successive Governments have amended the anti-social behaviour regime, the definition of anti-social behaviour has grown wider, the standard of proof has fallen lower and the punishment for breach has toughened. This arms race must end. We are not convinced that widening the net to open up more kinds of behaviour to formal intervention will actually help to deal with the problem at hand.'[18]

The arms race is showing no signs of ending. Successive Home Secretaries have made commitments to reduce the levels of crime and anti-social behaviour and an increasing number of measures have been introduced to tackle the problem. However, the simplification of the numerous different measures appears to have been welcomed.

F CONCLUSION

1.09   Resourcing remains a problem and anecdotal evidence suggests that breaches are not being pursued due to a lack of funding. Clearly this has the potential to undermine the work done to obtain an order and the goodwill and cooperation of witnesses. There is also little evidence of positive requirements being used in injunctions and CBOs; again this is partly due to a lack of services following funding cuts.

Despite this there has been widespread use of the powers created by the Act. They have been used to tackle anti-social behaviour effectively and in some cases the powers have been put to innovative use; closure powers have been used to tackle the problem of cuckooed tenants, CPNs have helped to deal with 'County Lines' issues and PSPOs have been utilised for detrimental behaviour far beyond the powers they replaced.

---

18   *The draft Anti-social Behaviour Bill: pre-legislative scrutiny*, p 26.

CHAPTER 2

The human rights implications, the Equality Act 2010 and disability, and hate crime

A INTRODUCTION

2.01   This chapter considers the human rights implications of the legislation, looking at the relevance of the Equality Act 2010 and the definition of hate crime.

B THE HUMAN RIGHTS IMPLICATIONS

2.02   The Act contains some powerful remedies.[1] The civil injunctions can exclude a person from their home where there is the use or threatened use of violence or where there is a significant risk of harm to other people. The closure powers can have the effect of closing a person's home or business for up to six months.

There are various sections within the Act where there is an express reference to human rights:

(a)   in deciding whether to give authorisation for a dispersal, police officers must have particular regard to the Article 10 right of freedom of expression and the Article 11 right of freedom of association/assembly;[2]

---

1   All statutory references in this section are to the Anti-Social Behaviour, Crime and Policing Act 2014 unless otherwise stated.
2   For further information on the dispersal power see Chapter 5.

(b)   in making, seeking to extend, vary or discharge a Public Spaces Protection Order (PSPO) a local authority must have particular regard to Article 10 and Article 11 rights;[3]

(c)   the provisions relating to the mandatory grounds for possession are subject to a defence based on the tenant's convention rights within the meaning of the Human Rights Act 1998.[4] That reflects the position under existing case law.[5]

In addition to the express statutory references listed above, there may also be Article 6 (right to a fair trial) considerations when applications are made to the courts or during the review process relating to the mandatory grounds of possession. Some of the powers may engage Article 9 (right to freedom of religion), for example, in the context of religious gatherings which require dispersal due to anti-social behaviour, or Article 14 (the prohibition on discrimination).

This section sets out some of rights contained in the European Convention on Human Rights and Fundamental Freedoms (ECHR). It addresses the relevance of the Human Rights Act 1998 and the concepts that will be engaged when striking a lawful balance between the respect for and any interference with those rights. This section focusses on Articles 8, 10 and 11 and these rights will be referred to as 'Convention rights'.

The Human Rights Act 1998 (HRA 1998)

2.03   The rights protected under the ECHR are incorporated into domestic law in Sch 1 to the HRA 1998.

The HRA 1998 impacts on the new anti-social behaviour powers in a number of ways:

(a)   The Act and any regulations made under it must be read in a way which is compatible with the Convention rights.[6] This means that the Act must be interpreted in a way which is compatible with the Convention unless this is plainly impossible. Certain courts are given the power to make a declaration of incompatibility if they determine that legislation is either not compatible or incompatible with a Convention right.[7]

(b)   It is unlawful for a public authority to act in a way which is incompatible with a Convention right.[8]

(c)   A person who is a victim of an act which is unlawful (because it is incompatible with a Convention right) may bring proceedings against

---

3   s 72(1).
4   s 94 which inserts s 84A into the Housing Act 1985; further information on the mandatory grounds for possession can be found in Chapter 9.
5   *Manchester City Council v Pinnock* [2011] UKSC 6; [2011] 2 WLR 220; *Hounslow LBC v Powell* [2011] UKSC 8, [2011] 2 AC 186.
6   HRA 1998, s 3.
7   HRA 1998, s 4.
8   HRA 1998, s 6.

the public authority or rely on his/her Convention right(s) in any legal proceedings.[9]

For the purposes of s 6 of the HRA 1998, a 'public authority' includes a court or tribunal and any person whose functions are of a public nature.[10] The consequence of this is that a court hearing a claim for possession or an appeal in respect of a Community Protection Notice[11] (for example), is required to interpret the provisions of the Act in a way which is compatible with the HRA 1998, even where a human rights argument is not raised by a party to the proceedings.

The quality of decision-making

2.04   Under the HRA 1998 the court must decide *for itself* whether, on the basis of the material before it, the interference with a Convention right is proportionate.[12] For this reason it is good practice to record the factors that have been taken into consideration when deciding whether and how to utilise the measures in the Act. This is especially important where the Act specifically requires regard to be had to Convention rights. A formal human rights assessment should be undertaken and be recorded in a file note. That assessment should identify:

(a)   the proposal and the legislation which permits the proposal to be made;

(b)   the objectives of the proposal;

(c)   the Convention rights that may be interfered with by the proposal;

(d)   the people that could be affected by the interference or limitation and how they are affected;

(e)   how the objectives in (b) relate to the permitted legitimate aims identified in 2.07–2.08 below;

(f)   the other measures that have been considered and the reasons why (i) these are thought to be inappropriate; and (ii) the proposal is the preferred course of action. This should include details about the measures which have already been used in an effort to meet the objectives;

(g)   the reasons why the proposal is thought to be proportionate in the context of balancing the rights of the individual against the interests of the wider community.

The human rights assessment could be included in a report to the committee which decides whether to make a PSPO (and the requirements that it should include), or recorded on the housing file when deciding whether to take

---

9   HRA 1998, s 7(1).
10   HRA 1998, s 6(3).
11   Community Protection Notices are considered in more detail in Chapter 6.
12   *R (on the application of SB) v Governors of Denbigh High School* [2006] UKHL 15, [2007] 1 AC 100; *Belfast City Council v Miss Behavin Ltd* [2007] UKHL 19, [2007] 1 WLR 1420.

enforcement action in respect of a tenant, or as part of the reasons for relying on the mandatory grounds of possession.[13]

Decision-makers need to be aware of the human rights implications of their decisions. They will need to be able to demonstrate that they have assessed how a proposal is affected by human rights considerations in order to meet an argument that their decision has breached a person's human rights and is disproportionate.

Where conscientious engagement with the relevant considerations can be demonstrated, the courts will not remake a decision reasonably open to the decision-maker, or make a judgement about the relative advantages and disadvantages of the course selected, or of pure policy choices. On those matters, in determining what weight to give to the evidence, the court is entitled to attach special weight to the judgement of a decision-maker with special institutional competence; see *R (on the application of Lord Carlile of Berriew QC) v Secretary of State for the Home Department.*[14]

Articles 8, 10 and 11 of the ECHR

2.05   Article 8 provides for the right to respect for one's home, private and family life. Article 10 provides for the freedom of expression and Article 11 provides for the freedom of assembly and association. The full text of these Convention rights is as follows:

'ARTICLE 8 – right to respect for private and family life

(1) Everyone has the right to respect for his private and family life, his home and his correspondence.

(2) There shall be no interference by a public authority with the exercise of this right except such as is in accordance with the law and is necessary in a democratic society in the interests of national security, public safety or the economic wellbeing of the country, for the prevention of disorder or crime, for the protection of health or morals, or for the protection of the rights and freedoms of others.

ARTICLE 10 – freedom of expression

(1) Everyone has the right to freedom of expression. This right shall include freedom to hold opinions and to receive and impart information and ideas without interference by public authority and regardless of frontiers. This article shall not prevent States from requiring the licensing of broadcasting, television or cinema enterprises.

(2) The exercise of these freedoms, since it carries with it duties and responsibilities, may be subject to such formalities, conditions, restrictions or penalties as are prescribed by law and are necessary

---

13   Under s 84A of the Housing Act 1985 or Ground 7A of Pt 1 of Sch 2 to the Housing Act 1988.
14   [2014] UKSC 60, per Lord Sumption at [21]–[35].

in a democratic society, in the interests of national security, territorial integrity or public safety, for the prevention of disorder or crime, for the protection of health or morals, for the protection of the reputation or the rights of others, for preventing the disclosure of information received in confidence, or for maintaining the authority and impartiality of the judiciary.

ARTICLE 11 – freedom of assembly and association

(1) Everyone has the right to freedom of peaceful assembly and to freedom of association with others, including the right to form and to join trade unions for the protection of his interests.

(2) No restrictions shall be placed on the exercise of these rights other than such as are prescribed by law and are necessary in a democratic society in the interests of national security or public safety, for the prevention of disorder or crime, for the protection of health or morals or for the protection of the rights and freedoms of others. This article shall not prevent the imposition of lawful restrictions on the exercise of these rights by members of the armed forces, of the police or of the administration of the State.'

Each of the above are 'qualified' rights which means that there are circumstances in which these rights can be lawfully curtailed. This is in contrast to an unqualified right such as Article 3 (which prohibits torture). An interference with an unqualified right is not lawful. The questions to be asked when determining whether there has been an unlawful interference with the qualified Convention rights set out above are:

(a) Is the right engaged?

(b) Has the right been interfered with?

(c) Is the interference in accordance with or prescribed by law?

(d) Is the interference necessary in a democratic society?

Whether the right is engaged and whether it has been interfered with will need to be assessed on a case-by-case basis. There are however, some concepts which are common to all of the Convention rights. The following phrases warrant further consideration.

In accordance with or prescribed by law

2.06   An interference with Convention rights must be in accordance with or prescribed by law. The House of Lords has held that 'in accordance with the law' and 'prescribed by law' bear the same meaning.[15] The two phrases can be

---

15 *R (on the application of Gillan) v Commissioner of Metropolitan Police* [2006] UKHL 12, [2006] 2 AC 307, per Lord Bingham at [31].

summarised as requiring a legal basis for an interference or restriction. Legality means: (i) there must be a rule or regime which authorises the interference; (ii) that the law must be adequately accessible; and (iii) it must be formulated with sufficient precision to enable the citizen to regulate his conduct: *Sunday Times v United Kingdom*.[16] In the context of the anti-social behaviour powers covered in this book, all of the powers are derived from primary legislation. The requirement of legality (in terms of the need for a legal basis for the interference) is satisfied by the existence of the Act.[17] In addition, a power must still be exercised in accordance with the terms or limits of that power, for example, the period for the imposition of a dispersal power must not exceed the time limits in the Act.

Legitimate aims

2.07   In order that the interference is lawful, it has to be for the one of the specified purposes (in the interests of national security, public safety, the economic well-being of the county, for the prevention of disorder or crime, for the protection of health or morals or for the protection of the rights and freedoms of others). In the context of anti-social behaviour all of these justifications could be relevant.

Necessary in a democratic society

2.08   An interference with a qualified right must be 'necessary'. The burden of showing that a measure is necessary rests on the decision-maker. To meet the test of necessity the interference must: (i) correspond to a pressing social need; and (ii) be proportionate to the legitimate aim pursued: *Sunday Times*.[18] In *R v Shayler*[19] Lord Hope said:

> 'The word 'necessary' in art.10(2) introduces the principle of proportionality, although the word as such does not appear anywhere in the Convention'

In assessing whether the interference is proportionate the courts have approved a four stage test. A decision-maker must ask themselves whether:

(i)   the legislative objective is sufficiently important to justify limiting a fundamental right;

(ii)   the measures designed to meet the legislative objective are rationally connected to it;

(iii)   the means used to impair the right or freedom are no more than is necessary to accomplish the objective; and

---

16 (1979-80) 2 EHRR 245 at para 49.
17 *R (on the application of Rottman) v Commissioner of Police of the Metropolis* [2002] UKHL 20, [2002] 2 AC 692.
18 (1979-80) 2 EHRR 245 at para 62.
19 [2002] UKHL 11, [2003] 1 AC 247, per Lord Hope at [57] and [59], see also per Lord Hutton at [99]. And see *Handyside v United Kingdom* (1979-80) 1 EHRR 737.

(iv)   the measures strike a fair balance between the rights of the individual and the interests of the community.[20]

The nature of the inquiry to be undertaken by the courts is wider than the approach adopted in the context of judicial review. In *R (SB) v Governors of Denbigh High School*[21] Lord Bingham of Cornhill said:

> 'it is clear that the court's approach to an issue of proportionality under the Convention must go beyond that traditionally adopted to judicial review in a domestic setting ... There is no shift to a merits review, but the intensity of review is greater than was previously appropriate, and greater even than the heightened scrutiny test ... The domestic court must now make a value judgment, an evaluation, by reference to the circumstances prevailing at the relevant time ... Proportionality must be judged objectively, by the court ...'

Therefore, when reviewing the compatibility of executive decisions with Convention rights, there is no constitutional bar to any inquiry that is relevant and necessary to enable the court to adjudicate.

In *Bank Mellat v Her Majesty's Treasury (No 2)*[22] the Supreme Court considered the concept of 'minimum interference' at length and concluded that the relevant question was 'whether a less intrusive measure could have been used without unacceptably compromising the objective'. Restrictions of rights must be 'reasonable for the legislature to impose', but the courts are 'not called on to substitute judicial opinions for legislative ones as to the place at which to draw a precise line'.[23]

In the PSPO case of *Dulgheriu v Ealing LBC*[24] the High Court confirmed that a court should undertake a 'heightened scrutiny' of the decision under challenge when human rights were engaged. The facts of that case were that Ealing Council had introduced a PSPO to provide for a buffer zone to allow unimpeded access to an abortion clinic situated in a residential street in its area. The PSPO was made necessary due to the presence of pro-life and pro-choice activists outside the gates of the clinic. One of the primary objects of the pro-life groups was to dissuade users of the clinic from going through with their abortions. They employed a variety of strategies, including handing out leaflets, displaying placards and posters illustrating what a foetus looks like at various stages of gestation and attempting to engage the users in dialogue in the hope that they might change their minds. The pro-choice activists engaged in regular counter

---

20   *Huang v Secretary of State for the Home Department* [2007] UKHL 11, [2007] 2 AC 167, per Lord Bingham of Cornhill at [19], adopting the three stage test in *Elloy De Freitas v Permanent Secretary of Ministry of Agriculture, Fisheries, Lands and Housing* [1999] 1 AC 69 and adding the fourth consideration relating to the need to strike a fair balance. The criteria adopted in the 'De Freitas' test have been approved by the House of Lords on numerous occasions including in *R (Daly) v Secretary of State for the Home Department* [2001] UKHL 26, [2001] 2 AC 532 and most recently *R (on the application of Lord Carlile of Berriew QC) v Secretary of State for the Home Department* [2014] UKSC 60.
21   [2007] 1 AC 100, at [30].
22   [2014] AC 700.
23   Ibid, at [20], [74]–[75].
24   [2018] EWHC 1667 (Admin), [2018] All ER 881.

protests outside the clinic. Ealing's PSPO created a 'designated area' for all the activists to continue their activities but away from the gates of the clinic. The pro-life groups argued that the PSPO interfered with their human rights of freedom of expression, assembly and religion. As human rights were engaged, the High Court applied a 'structured proportionality' review higher than the usual intensity of review which applies in judicial reviews. The Court rejected their arguments and the PSPO was upheld. The claimants' appeal to the Court of Appeal will be heard in July 2019.

The court is not entitled to substitute its own view for that of the decision-maker, and the degree of quality of the judicial scrutiny called for depends on the significance of the right, the degree of interference, and the factors capable of justifying the interference: *R (on the application of Lord Carlile of Berriew QC) v Secretary of State for the Home Department.*[25]

As to the first question (sufficiently important objective), the Act's objectives of making provision for tackling crime, disorder and anti-social behaviour are relevant.[26]

The second question (measures are connected to the objective) will be satisfied if the measures taken are connected to furthering the identified objectives.

Question three (that the means used to impair the right or freedom are no more than is necessary to accomplish the objective), requires the decision-maker to undertake a comparison of the alternative options with a view to determining whether it is disproportionate to choose option A over options B or C. The alternative options should be considered even where they are thought to be less effective. The decision-maker should think about whether s/he should utilise measures which are only slightly less effective in achieving the identified objective but have a greater benefit in terms of being far less restrictive than an alternative measure. Good practice would be to undertake a costs and benefits analysis in relation to each of the options. This exercise would be undertaken with a view to determining the least restrictive means of achieving the legitimate aim.

Question four (fair balance) requires the decision-maker to consider whether any of the options are proportionate. This is an overall costs and benefits analysis of whether taking any action is appropriate in view of the restrictions that result.

As stated above, the need to have regard to human rights is expressly recorded in various parts of the Act. In other situations the need to have regard to human rights is imported by the Human Rights Act 1998.

C THE EQUALITY ACT 2010 AND DISABILITY

Introduction

2.09   The Equality Act 2010 (EA 2010) came into force on 1 October 2010 in England, Wales and Scotland, consolidating and in some respects extending the existing disparate provisions of anti-discrimination law. The EA 2010 identifies those characteristics in respect of which it is unlawful to discriminate

---

25 [2014] UKSC 60. See in particular the judgment of Lord Sumption at [1]–[54].
26 See preamble to the Act.

('protected characteristics') and provides a unified approach to discrimination based on simplified concepts. There are certain exceptions to the unified approach. Disability discrimination, for example, has the following distinctive concepts: discrimination arising from disability and the duty to make reasonable adjustments.

The protected characteristics covered by the EA 2010 are:

- age;
- disability;
- gender reassignment;
- marriage and civil partnership;
- race;
- religion or belief;
- sex;
- sexual orientation;
- pregnancy and maternity.

The Act provides protection from discrimination for persons in these situations:

- at work;
- in education;
- as a consumer;
- when using public services;
- when buying or renting property;
- as a member or guest of a private club or association.

The EA 2010 also protects a person from discrimination if they are associated with someone who has a protected characteristic, for example a family member or friend ('associative discrimination') or they have complained about discrimination or supported someone else's claim ('victimisation') or in circumstances in which a person discriminates against another in the mistaken belief that that person has a protected characteristic.

Disability as a protected characteristic

2.10 Particular focus is dedicated in this section to the definition of disability as a protected characteristic because it is often disability which arises as a feature of anti-social behaviour cases, though the other protected characteristics may also be relevant. Victims of anti-social behaviour are sometimes targeted because of a learning disability or a physical condition. In some cases, the perpetrator takes advantage of or targets a person's disability. Victims with a disability are often less able to cope and in greater need of support because of their condition. The

Pilkington case prompted wider concern that many police forces were failing to properly identify hate crimes motivated by disability and thus treating them as low-priority anti-social behaviour. Much of the abuse had been targeted at Fiona Pilkington's children who had learning difficulties which were serious enough to qualify as a 'disability' within the meaning of the EA 2010. Enforcement agencies will need to have regard to victims with a disability, but also perpetrators of abuse who may have mental health conditions or behavioural disorders which may be linked in some way to their conduct. Where enforcement action is taken and defended or challenged, some defendants contend that their behaviour has been caused or contributed to by a disability and that the enforcement action is unlawful discrimination or has been taken without compliance with the public sector equality duty.

What is disability?

2.11   Disability is defined in s 6 of the EA 2010 and has a broad meaning. It is defined as a physical or mental impairment that has a substantial and long-term adverse effect on the ability to carry out normal day-to-day activities.[27] 'Substantial' means more than minor or trivial.[28] 'Impairment' covers, for example, long-term medical conditions such as asthma and diabetes, and fluctuating or progressive conditions such as rheumatoid arthritis or motor neurone disease. A mental impairment includes mental health conditions (such as bipolar disorder or depression), learning difficulties (such as dyslexia) and learning disabilities (such as autism and Down's syndrome).[29] Some people, including those with cancer, multiple sclerosis and HIV/AIDS, are automatically protected as disabled people by the EA 2010.[30] People with severe disfigurement will be protected as disabled without needing to show that it has a substantial adverse effect on day-to-day activities.[31] In the determination (which may be a contested issue) of whether or not a person has

27 What constitutes 'long term effect' and the approach to recurring conditions is set out in EA 2010, Sch 1, Pt 1, para 2.
28 EA 2010, s 212(1).
29 The classification and diagnosis of some mental impairments remains controversial, as illustrated by the debate surrounding the current publication of DSM-V (Diagnostic and Statistical Manual of Mental Disorders, American Psychiatric Association) in 2013. There is no requirement that a person have a diagnosis of a recognised medical condition in order to satisfy the definition of 'disability' within the meaning of the EA 2010 although this may in practice present evidential difficulties.
30 EA 2010, Sch 1, Pt 1, para 6.
31 EA 2010, Sch 1, Pt 1, para 3.

a disability, there is a disregard for medical treatment and other measures to correct or treat an impairment.[32]

Certain conditions are not to be regarded as impairments for the purposes of the EA 2010.[33] These are:

- addiction to, or dependency on, alcohol, nicotine, or any other substance (other than in consequence of the substance being medically prescribed);

- the condition known as seasonal allergic rhinitis (eg hayfever), except where it aggravates the effect of another condition;

- tendency to set fires;

- tendency to steal;

- tendency to physical or sexual abuse of other persons;

- exhibitionism;

- voyeurism.

An example of the quality of medical evidence the court will expect to have available to sustain a determination that a person has a disability within the meaning of s 6 is *Swan Housing Association Ltd v Gill*.[34] In that case, the judge's finding that a housing association's tenant suffered from Asperger's syndrome and was therefore disabled was not supported by evidence. His conclusion, that in proceeding with an application for an anti-social behaviour injunction under the Housing Act 1996, s 153A, the housing association had breached the EA 2010, s 35 and the public sector equality duty under EA 2010, s 149, was therefore flawed.

One difficulty for housing officers and practitioners is that, in a borderline case where it is not clear whether or not a person's symptoms or conditions amount to a disability within the meaning of the EA 2010 (an issue which more frequently arises with mental rather than physical disability) they are not medically qualified to make the judgment themselves. In those cases, officers should therefore: (a) consider what evidence they have of a perpetrator's disability, and

---

32   EA 2010, Sch 1, Pt 1, para 5 which provides:
   '5 Effect of medical treatment
   (1)   An impairment is to be treated as having a substantial adverse effect on the ability of the person concerned to carry out normal day-to-day activities if—
      (a)   measures are being taken to treat or correct it, and
      (b)   but for that, it would be likely to have that effect.
   (2)   "Measures" includes, in particular, medical treatment and the use of a prosthesis or other aid.
   (3)   Sub-paragraph (1) does not apply—
      (a)   in relation to the impairment of a person's sight, to the extent that the impairment is, in the person's case, correctable by spectacles or contact lenses or in such other ways as may be prescribed;
      (b)   in relation to such other impairments as may be prescribed, in such circumstances as are prescribed.'
33   Equality Act 2010 (Disability) Regulations 2010, SI 2010/2128, reg 4.
34   [2013] EWCA Civ 1566, [2014] HLR 18.

make appropriate further enquiries;[35] and (b) even if after those enquiries there is insufficient information to sustain a conclusion either way, make a file note which sets out: (i) whether and why they consider their actions are proportionate; and (ii) that they have had due regard to the public sector equality duty (see 2.24 below), both on the assumed basis that the person against whom enforcement action is taken has a disability. The decision may and should be reviewed in the light of any further enquiries made and information supplied about the person's illness.

Ultimately, if a challenge to enforcement action or possession proceedings is litigated, and the issues of: (a) whether a person has a disability; and (b) the causal connection between the disability and the anti-social conduct relied upon for the enforcement action or possession proceedings, remains contested, expert evidence (usually through the instruction of a single joint expert) will be required and the matter will be determined by the court.

Further references

2.12   The following materials are relevant for those dealing with a case involving disability.

- EA 2010, ss 4, 6 and Sch 1, Pts 1 and 2;

- Equality Act 2010 (Disability) Regulations 2010, SI 2010/2128;

- Statutory Guidance under s 6(5) of the Equality Act 2010: *Guidance on matters to be taken into account in determining questions relating to the definition of disability.*

Prohibited Conduct under Chapter 2 of the Equality Act 2010

2.13   The defined categories of prohibited conduct are:

- direct discrimination;

- indirect discrimination;

- discrimination arising from disability;

- failure to comply with a duty to make reasonable adjustment for disabled persons;

- harassment; and

- victimisation.

Below are some basic summaries of the nature of the prohibited conduct and the identification of the key issues which arise. A detailed review of all of the considerations engaged by a claim or defence of discrimination or a failure to make reasonable adjustments is beyond the scope of this chapter.

---

35   *Pieretti v Enfield LBC* [2010] EWCA Civ 1104, [2011] 2 All ER 642, [2011] PTSR 565.

Direct discrimination

2.14   Section 13(1) of the EA 2010 provides that a person (A) discriminates against another (B), if because of a protected characteristic, A treats B less favourably than A treats or would treat others. To prohibit direct discrimination is to require people to be treated in the same way regardless of their sex, race, gender, disability etc.

To understand whether there has been direct discrimination, a two-stage approach is often adopted by the court:[36]

(1)   to determine whether there been less favourable treatment of B; and

(2)   to enquire how an actual or hypothetical comparator was or would have been treated.

In *Islington London Borough Council v Ladele*, Elias J explained that there may be circumstances in which it is not appropriate to use a comparator:[37]

> 'The concept of direct discrimination is fundamentally a simple one. A claimant suffers some form of detriment (using that term very broadly) and the reason for that detrimental treatment is the prohibited ground. There is implicit in that analysis the fact that someone in a similar position to whom that ground did not apply (the comparator) would not have suffered the detriment. By establishing that the reason for the detrimental treatment is the prohibited reason, the claimant necessarily establishes at one and the same time that he or she is less favourably treated than the comparator who did not share the prohibited characteristic.'

If a comparator is used, the comparison between the claimant and the comparator must be like with like; the relevant circumstances must be the same or at least not materially difference; see EA 2010, s 23(1) and see *Shamoon v Chief Constable of Royal Ulster Constabulary*.[38]

The following example of direct discrimination is given by the Equality and Human Rights Commission (EHRC):[39]

• If a public body refused to investigate a person's complaint because they had a mental health condition.

Indirect discrimination

2.15   Section 19 of the EA 2010 provides that a person (A) discriminates against another (B) if A applies to B a provision, criterion or practice (PCP)

---

36   There is a presumption that a judge will appoint a lay assessor in cases concerning discrimination unless there is a good reason for not doing so: see EA 2010, s 114(7).

37   [2009] ICR 387, per Elias J at para 32.

38   [2003] UKHL 11, [2003] ICR 337, [2003] IRLR 285.

39   EHRC Guidance: *Your rights to equality from local councils, government departments and immigration*.

which is discriminatory in relation to a relevant protected characteristic of B. A PCP is discriminatory in relation to a relevant characteristic of B's if:

(a)   A applies, or would apply, it to persons with whom B does not share the characteristic;

(b)   it puts, or would put, persons with whom B shares the characteristic at a particular disadvantage when compared with persons with whom B does not share it;

(c)   it puts, or would put, B at that disadvantage; and

(d)   A cannot show it to be a proportionate means of achieving a legitimate aim.

Indirect discrimination therefore is different to direct discrimination because it looks beyond formal equality towards a more substantive equality of results: criteria which appear neutral on their face may have a disproportionately adverse impact upon people of a particular colour, race, nationality or ethnic or national origins; see *R (on the application of E) v Governing Body of JFS*.[40] Unlike direct discrimination, indirect discrimination may be justified. It is not necessary to establish that there is no alternative to the PCP, but the PCP has to be justified objectively notwithstanding its discriminatory effect; see *Barry v Midland Bank plc*.[41] The tribunal in that determination will enquire as to whether the proposal is reasonably necessary; see *Hardys & Hansons Plc v Lax*.[42]

The concept of a 'provision', 'criteria', or 'practice' is broad.[43] By way of example in a housing context, a requirement for all tenants or prospective tenants to complete an online application to be considered for a mutual exchange or for an allocation of property, which does not make exception for those whose disability prevents them from using a computer, may constitute indirect discrimination unless it can be justified. The fact that the requirement is not written down, but there is a practice of not offering a paper-based application or an alternative means of eliciting the relevant information, would not prevent the court from concluding that there was a discriminatory PCP.

The following example of indirect discrimination is given by the EHRC:[44]

● A local council decides to apply a 'no hats or other headgear' rule to anyone who enters its buildings. If this rule is applied in exactly the same way to every service user, Sikhs, Jews, Muslims and Rastafarians who may cover their heads as part of their religion will not be allowed to use the council's buildings. Unless the council can objectively justify using the rule, this will be indirect discrimination.

---

40   [2009] UKSC 15, [2010] 2 AC 728, [2010] IRLR 136, per Hale LJ at [56]–[57]..
41   [1999] ICR 859.
42   [2005] EWCA Civ 846, [2005] ICR 1565, per Pill LJ at [32].
43   *British Airways plc v Starmer* [2005] IRLR 863.
44   EHRC Core Guidance: *Local government and central services.*

Disability discrimination

2.16 Under the Disability Discrimination Act 1995,[45] although capable of being justified, detrimental treatment for a disability-related reason was unlawful discrimination. Controversially, the House of Lords, in *Lewisham London Borough Council v Malcolm*,[46] adopted a narrow construction of the law so that the breadth of the protection of discrimination law was significantly limited. The decision in *Malcolm* was a departure from the position which had previously been understood in the Court of Appeal decision in an employment context in *Clark v TDG Ltd (t/a Novacold Ltd)*.[47] The EA 2010 seeks to restore the scope of that protection by reversing the decision in *Malcolm* by s 15(1), which states:

'(1) A person (A) discriminates against a disabled person (B) if—

(a) A treats B unfavourably because of something arising in consequence of B's disability, and

(b) A cannot show that the treatment is a proportionate means of achieving a legitimate aim.

(2) Subsection (1) does not apply if A shows that A did not know, and could not reasonably have been expected to know, that B had the disability.'

Thus, the determination of disability discrimination now engages a three-stage test:

- Has A treated B unfavourably?

- Is the reason for the treatment something arising in consequence of B's disability?

- Can A demonstrate that the treatment is proportionate (see 2.08 above)?

The test found in the EA 2010 therefore is different to the 'less favourable treatment' test in the 1995 Act which was applied in and after *Malcolm*. There is no need for a comparison between the tenant or a person the subject of enforcement action and another comparator to establish whether they would have been treated

---

45 Now repealed and replaced by the EA 2010.
46 [2008] UKHL 43, [2008] 1 AC 1339. In *Malcolm*, the defendant secure tenant had been diagnosed with schizophrenia. He sublet his property, in breach of his tenancy terms, and the local authority issued proceedings for possession. The defendant contended that his conduct in subletting was caused by his schizophrenia. The House of Lords accepted that the defendant was a disabled person and that a breach of the DDA 1995 could amount to a complete defence to a claim for possession. However, applying an objective test, it held that the real reason that the local authority sought possession was because the tenant was not living at the property, a pure housing management decision which was not related to the defendant's mental disability. The right comparator was a person without a mental disability who had sublet the property and left to live elsewhere. On that basis, the defendant was not treated less favourably than other tenants in similar circumstances, but in the same way. The House of Lords also held that a premises provider must know about the disabled person's impairment – and possibly the effects of it – to discriminate for reasons relating to disability.
47 [1999] 2 All ER 977.

differently. There is however a defence based on knowledge.[48] In the context of anti-social behaviour and social housing, a decision to take enforcement action of some kind, to seek an injunction, to serve a notice of seeking possession, a notice to quit, or to issue proceedings to recover possession would all amount to unfavourable treatment which could be discriminatory.

The following example of discrimination arising from disability is given by the EHRC:[49]

• A disabled person with Tourette Syndrome is excluded from a public meeting because the organiser believes the person's vocal tics are distracting to the audience. The person is treated unfavourably because of their vocal tics, which is something arising from their disability. Unless the service provider holding the meeting can show that the decision to exclude the person is objectively justified, this will be discrimination arising from disability.

To take an example of subletting of a secure tenancy therefore, the position under the EA 2010 is as follows. If a local authority landlord of a secure tenant with paranoid schizophrenia discovers that she has been subletting the entire property, notwithstanding the fact that the tenancy ceases by operation of law (Housing Act 1996, s 93(2)) to be secure, the service of a notice to quit and the subsequent pursuit of possession proceedings (the unfavourable treatment) may be unlawful, if the court is satisfied of the following:

(a) the tenant has a disability within the meaning of the EA 2010;

(b) the act of subletting 'arose in consequence' of her disability;

(c) the landlord knew, or could reasonably have been expected to know, that she had a disability (this condition will invariably be satisfied by the stage a defence is filed and served pleading the relevant disability);

(d) the decision to seek to recover possession is not a proportionate means of achieving a legitimate aim.

Thus the unfavourable treatment may still be justified if the court is satisfied that the decision is proportionate. Factors which may be relevant to the court's consideration of proportionality include the following:

(a) The degree of seriousness of the conduct. In the case of subletting, it is recognised as a serious breach of a tenancy agreement because social housing is a limited resource and should be used by those for whom it is intended.

---

48 Social landlords and in particular public authority landlords with the ability to share information with social services departments and mental health teams will unlikely be able to establish a defence based on lack of knowledge at the time of a relevant decision if reasonable enquiries, including of the perpetrator themselves, where not pursued where they were on notice of the possible existence of a physical or mental condition. See, in the context of the public sector equality duty the approach of the court in *Pieretti v Enfield LBC* [2010] EWCA Civ 1104, [2011] 2 All ER 642, [2011] PTSR 565.

49 EHRC Core Guidance: *Local government and central services*.

(b)   The nexus between the disability and the conduct, and the degree of the defendant's ability to have insight into and/or control his or her behaviour. This will often depend on the evidence of an expert and will be highly case specific.

(c)   Whether the court can have confidence it will not happen again with appropriate treatment and support.

(d)   Whether, in the event the landlord is a local authority, the social services team has or will act lawfully and discharge their responsibilities to the defendant.

(e)   Whether the landlord has otherwise acted lawfully and in accordance with its own policies on anti-social behaviour and vulnerable tenants.

(f)   Whether the landlord will continue to comply with its public sector equality duty under EA 2010, s 149 and to act proportionately in the event an order for possession is made.

A recent example of the court's approach to a defence based on discrimination arising from disability is the decision of the Supreme Court in *Akerman-Livingstone v Aster Communities Ltd (formerly Flourish Homes Ltd)*.[50] The facts were as follows. Pursuant to its duty under s 193(2) of the Housing Act 1996 the local housing authority ensured that the defendant, who had severe prolonged duress stress disorder, obtained temporary accommodation with a housing association. When the authority's attempts to persuade the defendant to choose another property as his permanent accommodation failed, it decided that its main housing duty had ended and required the housing association to bring proceedings to evict him so that the property could be made available to another homeless person. The authority issued proceedings and the defendant contended that the bringing of the proceedings amounted to discrimination against him by reason of his disability, in breach of s 15 of the EA 2010. The judge in the county court made a possession order, holding that a court should approach a defence based on disability discrimination in the same way as it would approach a defence based on Article 8 of the ECHR, namely by first considering whether the defendant had a seriously arguable case; that the defendant did not have a seriously arguable case; and that, therefore, there was no need for a full trial.[51] The Supreme Court held that the test as to whether the landlord's treatment of the tenant is a proportionate means of achieving a legitimate aim for the purposes of s 15(1)(b) of the EA 2010 was significantly different from whether it is proportionate to make a possession order for the purposes of Article 8 of the ECHR. Lady Hale said that there may be cases where possession can be ordered summarily when (i) the defendant has no real prospect of showing that he has a disability; (ii) when it is plain that the possession order is not being sought because of something arising in consequence of the disability; or (iii) where granting possession plainly represents a proportionate means of achieving

---

50   [2015] UKSC 15, [2015] AC 1399.
51   For further commentary on the approach to a defence based on Article 8 to a possession claim see Chapter 9 at 9.42.

a legitimate aim, but that each of these issues would usually give rise to disputed facts or assessments so that it would rarely be proportionate to grant possession summarily.

The Supreme Court also said that when a court is asked to look at the proportionality of making a possession order in a claim brought by a social landlord, it should look at whether the landlord has done all that can be reasonably expected of it to accommodate the consequences of the occupier's disability and whether vindication of the landlord's property rights and its need to allocate and manage its housing stock are sufficient to outweigh the effects of eviction on the occupier. It was also said that a landlord was obliged to be more considerate towards a disabled tenant than s/he was to a non-disabled one.

The Supreme Court's judgment in *Akerman-Livingstone* was considered by the High Court in the case of *Eales v Havering LBC*.[52] The facts of *Eales* were that a non-secure tenancy had been granted by the council pursuant to its homelessness duties. Ms Eales was convicted of a racially aggravated public order offence and the council served a notice to quit due to the on-going anti-social behaviour. The council issued possession proceedings which Ms Eales defended on the basis that her anti-social behaviour was due to her psychological problems and, in seeking to evict her, the council was discriminating against her in breach of s 15 of the EA 2010. She argued that (i) an injunction would have been a sufficient alternative remedy and (ii) that the council had failed to follow its policy on vulnerable people. The district judge dismissed her arguments and made a possession order which Ms Eales appealed to the High Court.

In the High Court the judge said that the district judge had been right to make a possession order and that an injunction would not have been a sufficient alternative remedy in view of the fact that the anti-social behaviour was caused by a combination of her psychiatric condition and her drug and alcohol abuse which she had failed to address. The judge also said that the council's failure to follow its vulnerable persons policy was not fatal; the true test was whether the decision to recover possession was one that no reasonable person would consider justifiable.

Reasonable adjustments

2.17   The laws regulating disability discrimination are designed to enable the disabled to enter as fully as possible into everyday life. This requires not merely outlawing discrimination against the disabled; it also needs those who make decisions affecting the disabled to take positive steps to remove or ameliorate, so far as is reasonable, the difficulties which place them at a disadvantage compared with the able bodied. To that extent therefore, the disability law accommodates a measure of positive discrimination.[53]

---

52   [2018] EWHC 2423 (QB), [2018] 7 WLUK 320, [2018] HLR 46.
53   *Archibald v Fife Council* [2004] UKHL 32, [2004] ICR 954, per Baroness Hale of Richmond at [47] and [57].

The EA 2010 recognises that bringing about equality for disabled people may mean changing the way in which services are delivered in practical terms by providing extra equipment and/or the removal of physical barriers.

This is the 'duty to make reasonable adjustments'.

If an organisation providing goods, facilities or services to the public or a section of the public, or carrying out public functions, or running an association finds there are barriers to disabled people in the way it does things, then it must consider making adjustments (in other words, changes). If those adjustments are reasonable for that organisation to make, then it must make them.

The duty is 'anticipatory'. This means an organisation cannot wait until a disabled person wants to use its services, but must think in advance (and on an ongoing basis) about what disabled people with a range of impairments might reasonably need, such as people who have a visual impairment, a hearing impairment, a mobility impairment or a learning disability.

An organisation is not required to do more than it is reasonable for it to do. What is reasonable for an organisation to do depends, among other factors, on its size and nature, and the nature of the goods, facilities or services it provides, or the public functions it carries out, or the association it runs.

Section 20 of the EA 2010 sets out in generic terms the content of the duty to make reasonable adjustments. It identifies three requirements where the duty applies.

The first requirement

2.18   EA 2010, s 20(3): the first requirement is a requirement, where a PCP of A's puts a disabled person at a substantial disadvantage in relation to a relevant matter in comparison with persons who are not disabled, to take such steps as it is reasonable to have to take to avoid the disadvantage.

The second requirement

2.19   EA 2010, s 20(4): the second requirement is a requirement, where a physical feature puts a disabled person at a substantial disadvantage in relation to a relevant matter in comparison with persons who are not disabled, to take such steps as it is reasonable to have to take to avoid the disadvantage.

The third requirement

2.20   EA 2010, s 20(5): the third requirement is a requirement, where a disabled person would, but for the provision of an auxiliary aid, be put at a substantial disadvantage in relation to a relevant matter in comparison with persons who are not disabled, to take such steps as it is reasonable to have to take to provide the auxiliary aid.

The term 'substantial' is defined in s 212(1) as meaning 'more than minor or trivial'. It is not, therefore, a particularly high hurdle to establish substantial disadvantage.

Section 20 of the EA 2010 does not impose the duty to make adjustments; it simply defines what may be required when the duty is imposed. However, not all three requirements are engaged in all cases; the scope varies depending on the circumstance in which the duty arises.

By s 20(13), specific Schedules of the EA 2010 are then applied in the application of the reasonable adjustment duty in various Parts of the EA 2010 to different situations, and Sch 21 is applied to all parts. Specific schedules make provision for the imposition of the duty in relation to transport,[54] or in respect of premises,[55] for example. Section 21 defines the specific discriminatory act of failing to comply with a duty to make reasonable adjustments.

The duty to make reasonable adjustments as it applies to public service providers

2.21   Schedule 2 specifies the nature of the duty with respect to public service providers. It applies and modifies all three requirements of the duty as it applies to the provision of services and public functions. Schedule 2 must therefore be read together with Pt 3 of the 2010 Act which applies to those providing services and exercising public functions.

Section 29(6) provides that a person exercising a public function 'must not … do anything that constitutes discrimination, harassment or victimisation'. The obligation to make reasonable adjustments is applied to persons exercising public functions by s 29(7).

Section 21 provides as follows:

> '(1) A failure to comply with the first, second or third requirement is a failure to comply with a duty to make reasonable adjustments.
>
> (2) A discriminates against a disabled person if A fails to comply with that duty in relation to that person.
>
> (3) A provision of an applicable Schedule which imposes a duty to comply with the first, second or third requirement applies only for the purpose of establishing whether A has contravened this Act by virtue of subsection (2); a failure to comply is, accordingly, not actionable by virtue of another provision of this Act or otherwise.'

To summarise the effect of the statutory provisions therefore in relation to the provision of public service providers: by s 29(6) there is a duty not to discriminate; by s 21(2) discrimination includes, amongst other matters, a failure to make reasonable adjustments; and by s 21(1) this in turn arises where there is a failure to comply with any of the three requirements.

---

54   EA 2010, Pt 3 and Sch 2.
55   EA 2010, Pt 4, Sch 4.

Harassment

2.22   Section 26 of the EA 2010 provides a common definition of harassment, of which there are three forms, defined in s 26(1)–(3).

By s 26(1)–(2), a person (A) harasses another (B) if A engages in:

- unwanted conduct in relation to a relevant protected characteristic; or

- unwanted conduct of a sexual nature; and

the conduct has the purpose or effect of:

- violating B's dignity, or

- creating an intimidating, hostile, degrading, humiliating or offensive environment for B.

By s 26(3), A also harasses B if A or another person engages in unwanted conduct of a sexual nature and or that is related to gender reassignment or sex and the conduct has either the purpose or the effect of either:

- violating B's dignity; or

- creating an intimidating, hostile, degrading, humiliating or offensive environment for B

and because if B's rejection of or submission to the conduct, A treats B less favourably than A would treat B if B had not rejected or submitted to the conduct.

In deciding whether conduct has the effect referred to above, each of the following must be taken into account:

- the perception of B;

- the other circumstances of the case;

- whether it is reasonable for the conduct to have that effect.

Victimisation

2.23   Section 27 of the EA 2010 provides that a person (A) victimises another person (B) if A subjects B to a detriment because B does a protected act, or A believes that B has done, or may do, a protected act.

The following are protected acts:

- bringing proceedings under the EA 2010;

- giving evidence or information in connection with proceedings under the EA 2010;

- doing any other thing for the purposes of or in connection with the EA 2010;

- making an allegation (whether or not express) that A or another person has contravened the EA 2010.

However, giving false evidence or information, or making a false allegation, is not a protected act if the evidence or information is given, or the allegation is made, in bad faith.

Public sector equality duty

2.24   Chapter 1 of Part 11 of the EA 2010 introduced the 'public sector equality duty' under s 149.[56] As part of that duty, public authorities[57] and any person who exercises public functions, must have 'due regard' to the need to: (a) eliminate discrimination, harassment, victimisation and any other conduct that is prohibited by or under the EA 2010; (b) advance equality of opportunity between persons who share a relevant protected characteristic and persons who do not share it; and (c) foster good relations between persons who share a relevant protected characteristic and persons who do not share it.

The duty is a duty to have due regard. It is not to achieve the statutory goals; see Dyson LJ in *R (Baker) v Secretary of State for Communities and Local Government*[58] in relation to the predecessor provision concerning race equality:

> 'is not a duty to achieve a result, namely to eliminate unlawful racial discrimination or to promote equality of opportunity and good relations between persons of different racial groups. It is a duty to have due regard to the need to achieve these goals. The distinction is vital.'

Due regard is the regard that is appropriate in all the circumstances: *R (Baker) v Secretary of State for Communities and Local Government*.[59] In that case Dyson LJ said (at [37]): 'The question is whether the decision-maker has in substance had due regard to the relevant statutory need. It is necessary to turn to the substance of the decision and its reasoning'. The question is therefore one of substance, not of form.[60] As to the balance to be struck by the requirement to have 'due regard', Elias LJ explained in *R (Hurley) v Secretary of State for Business, Innovation and Skills*:[61]

> 'The concept of "due regard" requires the court to ensure there has been a proper and conscientious focus on the statutory criteria, but if that is done, the court cannot interfere with the decision simply because it would have given greater weight to the equality implications of the decision than did the decision-maker. In short, the decision-maker must be clear precisely what the equality implications are when he puts them in the balance, and he must recognise the desirability of achieving them, but ultimately it is for

---

56 The full text of s 149 is in Appendix A.
57 Defined in ss 150(1) and Sch 19, and subject to exception in ss 150(3), (4).
58 [2008] EWCA Civ 141, [2009] PTSR 809, at [31] in relation to Race Relations Act 1976, s 71, the predecessor provision in respect of race to the single equality duty established by EA 2010, s 149.
59 [2008] EWCA Civ 141, [2009] PTSR 809.
60 *McDonald v RBKC* [2011] UKSC 33, [2011] PTSR 1266, per Lord Brown at [23].
61 [2012] EWHC 201 (Admin) at [78].

him to decide what weight they should be given in the light of all relevant factors.'

Some circumstances, such as formulation of policy, or decisions in relation to local authority budget cuts, may point strongly in favour of undertaking a formal equality impact assessment, but that is not a statutory requirement: *R (Brown) v Work and Pensions Secretary.*[62] In that case, at [90]–[96] the Divisional Court identified a number of helpful principles that demonstrate how a public authority should fulfil its duty to have due regard. These included that the due regard duty must be fulfilled before and at the time that a particular policy which might affect relevant persons is being considered; the duty has to be integrated within the discharge of the public functions of the authority; and the duty is a continuing one.

The duty applies not only to the formulation of policies, but also to individual cases. It may require a decision-maker to take steps to establish if a person has a protected characteristic to ensure that the duty can be discharged: *Pieretti v Enfield LBC.*[63] In the context of disability, this assumes particular importance, because those with a disability may not be adept at identifying or communicating that fact as a relevant consideration.[64]

The duty is therefore likely to apply to a public authority decision-maker who is subject to the duty and who is considering whether to exercise their statutory powers to tackle anti-social behaviour, either to enforce against or to protect a person who has a disability, for example, by seeking an injunction or pressing for possession on a mandatory anti-social behaviour ground. An example of reliance by a tenant of a local authority upon breach of that duty as a defence to a claim for possession on the basis of the disability of a member of his household, and of the court's approach to the continuing nature of the duty is *Barnsley MBC v Norton*[65] which is considered at Chapter 9, 9.41.

In *Forward v Aldwyck Housing Group Ltd,*[66] the High Court considered an appeal where it had been argued that the trial judge had erred in her approach to PSED matters when making a possession order on grounds of anti-social behaviour. Mrs Justice Cheema-Grubb DBE confirmed that whilst there had been flaws in the trial judge's approach, that *had* she approached the matter correctly, her conclusion would have been the same; the possession order was ultimately upheld. In her judgment Mrs Cheema-Grubb stated as follows:[67]

> 'There can be no question that a simple proportionality assessment is not what the PSED requires. A rigorous consideration of the impact of the decision to commence eviction proceedings, against the equality objectives encapsulated in the PSED is required. It must be done with an open mind and not as a defensive "sweep-up". This consideration must itself be set in the context of promoting the statutory objectives.

---

62 [2008] EWHC 3158 (Admin), [2009] PTSR 1506 at [89].
63 [2010] EWCA Civ 1104, [2011] HLR 3.
64 *R (Hurley) v Secretary of State for Business, Innovation and Skills*, per Elias LJ at [96].
65 [2011] EWCA Civ 834, [2012] PTSR 56, [2011] Eq LR 1167, [2011] HLR 46.
66 [2019] EWHC 24 (QB).
67 Ibid, at [39]–[40].

A duty of inquiry may well arise: it depends on the context, see *Hurley & Moore v Secretary of State for BIS [2012] EWHC 201 (Admin, Div Court)*. In the current case the appellant was well aware of the necessity to furnish some evidence to establish that he had a mental disability. He failed to provide it. It is still not clear what the respondent could have obtained by further inquiry, albeit Ms Savage did not engage in any, as she could have done.'

Public authorities should therefore ensure that officers have been given training on the meaning of the public sector equality duty and its requirements. Where the decision-maker knows or suspects that a person in relation to whom enforcement action is to be taken, or for whose protection it is to be taken, has a disability, reviews should be conducted and records should be kept demonstrating conscientious consideration of the imperatives set out in s 149 of the EA 2010. Officers should approach such reviews open-minded as to whether, as a consequence of the application of those considerations, a different approach might be justified.

D HATE CRIME

2.25 Practitioners dealing with anti-social behaviour should have an awareness of the definition of hate crime, so that conduct can be properly identified and reported and if appropriate, separate criminal investigations triggered in cases which warrant it.

The Association of Chief Police Officers and the CPS have agreed a common definition of hate crime:

> 'Any criminal offence which is perceived by the victim or any other person, to be motivated by hostility or prejudice, based on a person's disability or perceived disability; race or perceived race; or religion or perceived religion; or sexual orientation or perceived sexual orientation or transgender identity or perceived transgender identity.'

Hate crime therefore encompasses offences motivated by hostility or prejudice based on a belief that a person has one of those protected characteristics.[68] Not all hate incidents will amount to criminal offences, but those that do become hate crimes. Not all five protected characteristics identified by the CPS and the police are protected in the same way by a specific criminal offence or aggravated basic criminal offence, but there is provision for increased sentencing powers in respect of all of them.

It is worth observing that the protected characteristics identified by the CPS and the police in their definition of hate crime are more limited than those which

---

68 There is a growing movement to add a further category to include people from alternative subcultures or lifestyle and dress. The Sophie Lancaster Foundation describes a subculture as: 'a group of people with a culture (whether distinct or hidden) that differentiates them from a larger culture to which they belong. Groups that are described as subcultures often include: Punk Rockers, Ravers, Metalheads, Goths, Emos, Indie, and more …'.

are protected by the discrimination provisions under the EA 2010. Unlike crimes motivated by hostility towards race and religious belief, there is no statutory definition of crimes against a person based on age, for example, nor is it identified specifically as a mandatory aggravating feature justifying an increased sentence.[69]

Existing criminal offences dealing specifically with hate crime do not cover hostility or hatred equally in respect of all five of the protected characteristics identified by the CPS and the police. In October 2018, the Law Commission launched a review into hate crime to explore how to make existing legislation more effective and to consider whether there should be additional protected characteristics such as misogyny and age.[70]

Certain offences listed in the Crime and Disorder Act 1998 (CDA 1998) can be racially or religiously aggravated if the defendant, in committing such an offence, demonstrates, or was motivated by, hostility on the grounds of race or religion.[71] The aggravated offences provide for higher maximum sentences, together with a stigmatising 'label', for example, 'racially aggravated criminal damage'.

A separate set of offences contained in the Public Order Act 1986 (POA 1986) prohibits a range of conduct intended or likely to stir up hatred on grounds of race, or intended to stir up hatred on grounds of religion or sexual orientation.

There are no specific or aggravated offences proscribing conduct motivated by hostility towards persons based on disability or transgender identity.

In addition to the above offences, a statutory sentencing regime applies in the hate crime context. Under ss 146 and 147 of the Criminal Justice Act 2003 (CJA 2003), in any offence other than one prosecuted as an aggravated offence, the sentencing court must treat hostility as an aggravating factor in sentencing the offender. The court must be satisfied that the offender demonstrated or was motivated by hostility. The enhanced sentencing provisions apply to all five protected characteristics.[72] Sections 146 and 147 do not therefore create any new offences; they impose a duty upon courts to increase the sentence for any offence aggravated by hostility based on the relevant protected characteristic or presumed protected characteristic.

---

69 The CPS has a policy dealing with prosecuting crimes against older people: https://www.cps. gov.uk/legal-guidance/older-people-prosecuting-crimes-against, as it does in respect of the other characteristics falling within its definition of hate crime, all of which were updated in August 2018; for disability: https://www.cps.gov.uk/legal-guidance/disability-hate-crime-and-other-crimes-against-disabled-people-prosecution-guidance; race and religious crime: https://www.cps.gov.uk/legal-guidance/racist-and-religious-hate-crime-prosecution-guidance; homophobic, biphobic and transphobic hate crime https://www.cps.gov.uk/legal-guidance/ homophobic-biphobic-and-transphobic-hate-crime-prosecution-guidance.
70 https://www.lawcom.gov.uk/law-commission-review-into-hate-crime-announced/. This follows from its May 2014 report entitled *Hate Crime: Should the Current Offences be Extended?*
71 The CDA 1998 creates separate racially or religiously aggravated versions of certain basic offences; see ss 28–32.
72 CJA 2003, s 145: increase in sentences for racial or religious aggravation; CJA 2003, s 146: increase in sentences for aggravation related to disability, sexual orientation or transgender identity.

E CONCLUSION

2.26   The principles set out in this chapter are directly relevant to the day-to-day decisions that practitioners will be required to make. Decisions which result in an interference with a person's human rights, or which may be indirectly discriminatory, must be necessary and proportionate. There will need to be a willingness to consider alternative methods of dealing with a situation. It will be important to keep an audit trail of how decisions have been made in order to demonstrate how human rights and EA 2010 issues have been taken into account.

CHAPTER 3

The civil injunction to prevent anti-social behaviour

Snapshot

What's out

- ASBOs
- ASBIs
- DBOs
- Intervention and individual support orders

What's in

- Civil injunctions

Key points

- Tenure neutral, no need to be a tenant of social housing
- Two types: nuisance or annoyance (housing related) or harassment, alarm or distress (non-housing related)
- Can apply without notice
- Interim orders, powers of arrest and exclusion from the home all still available
- Respondents must be aged 10 or over
- Applications, including for committal, may be heard by a district judge[1]
- May include positive requirements as well as prohibitions
- Breach is a civil contempt

Templates and resources

See Appendix D for useful updated precedents:

- Injunction forms – county court
    - (a) Draft application for a civil injunction, Form N16A
    - (b) Draft injunction order, Form N16(1)
- Injunction forms – youth court
    - (a) Summons
    - (b) Application for injunction
    - (c) Draft injunction order
- General form of undertaking (Form N117)
- Notice of intention to rely on hearsay evidence

See Appendix E for a list of sample prohibitions.

---

1   Practice Direction 2B – Allocation of Cases to Levels of Judiciary paras 8.1–8.3.

A   THE HISTORY

3.01   The provisions relating to civil injunctions in Part 1 came into force in March 2015.[2]

The Coalition Government felt that new powers were required because anti-social behaviour orders (ASBOs) did not work, far too many were breached and they were treated by some as a 'badge of honour'. Practitioners also saw them as bureaucratic, slow and expensive to obtain. The use of other tools, such as anti-social behaviour injunctions (ASBIs), had increased and these were considered to be more effective. It is against this background that the Government sought to introduce the crime prevention injunction.[3] During the Bill's passage through Parliament the crime prevention injunction became the injunction to prevent nuisance or annoyance (IPNA).[4] The label IPNA had to be abandoned as a result of opposition to the way in which anti-social behaviour had been defined.[5] What one is left with is simply the civil injunction, often referred to as simply the anti-social behaviour injunction or the s 1 injunction.

Of all the measures introduced by the Act, the injunction was the one which attracted the most concern from civil liberties groups, those interested in youth justice and those concerned about the powers of the state.

The Anti-Social Behaviour, Crime and Policing Bill ('the Bill) was described as 'fundamentally flawed' by 24 organisations who wrote a joint letter to the Home Secretary published in the Times.[6] Their principal concern was expressed thus:

> 'Such ill-thought out legislation will sweep up all kinds of non-criminal and non-serious behaviour – wasting police time and clogging up the courts. It threatens to take resources away from genuinely harmful or distressing behaviour, where the police and other services should be focussed.'

Large parts of the Parliamentary debates focused on the definition of 'anti-social behaviour'. The Bill had defined anti-social behaviour as conduct causing or likely to cause 'nuisance or annoyance', regardless of the body making the application, the age of the respondent or whether the behaviour was related to a person's occupation of property.

From a very early stage there was concern that the definition of anti-social behaviour had been set at an inappropriately low level. Civil liberties organisations and charities warned that the Act could criminalise any nuisance or annoying behaviour in the streets, including peaceful protest, street preachers and even carol singers or church bell ringers.

---

2   The delay was caused by the need to amend the Legal Aid, Sentencing and Punishment of Offenders Act 2012 to allow public funding to be available in respect of injunctions.
3   See the Home Office's consultation document *More Effective Responses to Anti-Social Behaviour* (February 2011) and the White Paper *Putting Victims First: More Effective Responses to Anti-Social Behaviour* (May 2012). There is a fuller discussion of the consultation in Chapter 1.
4   In the draft Anti-Social Behaviour, Crime and Policing Bill.
5   For further details see Chapter 1.
6   10 June 2013. They included Liberty, JUSTICE, the Association of Youth Offending Team Managers, Big Brother Watch and the Children's Society, their comments being directed at the whole Bill and not just the proposed injunction.

Lord Hope summarised many of the concerns in an instructive speech during the Parliamentary debates.[7] His concerns struck a chord with the House, peers voting 306 to 178 in support of an amendment by the crossbench peer Lord Dear (a former chief constable of the West Midlands Police) which re-introduced (from the ASBO) a test of conduct causing or likely to cause 'harassment, alarm or distress'.[8] The Government was then forced to table its own amendments to the definition of anti-social behaviour, changing the test from simply nuisance or annoyance to what is now found in s 2 of the Act.[9]

B   THE POWERS WHICH HAVE BEEN REPLACED

3.02   The injunction is created by Part 1 of the Act, ss 1–21.[10]

The following powers have been repealed (subject to the transitional arrangements covered at 3.56 below):

(a)   ASBOs under ss 1 and 1B of the Crime and Disorder Act 1998 (CDA 1998);

(b)   anti-social behaviour injunctions, injunctions against the unlawful use of premises and injunctions against a breach of tenancy agreement (often collectively referred to as 'ASBIs') under ss 153A–153E of the Housing Act 1996 (HA 1996);

(c)   drinking banning orders under ss 1–14 of the Violent Crime Reduction Act 2006 (VCRA 2006);

(d)   intervention orders under s 1AA of the CDA 1998; and

(e)   individual support orders under s 1G of the CDA 1998.

Vandalism, public drunkenness, aggressive begging, irresponsible dog ownership, noisy or abusive behaviour towards neighbours or bullying are all examples of when an injunction could be sought.[11] In practice, the new injunction can be used in almost[12] all of the situations previously covered by ASBIs. The Act does not affect the provisions relating to gang injunctions.[13]

The s 1 injunction combines the ASBO and the ASBI. The tests that were relevant to each of these old orders have survived with the result that many of the concepts covered in this chapter will be familiar to practitioners. However, the s 1 injunction is more than just the old ASBI with a new label. In particular there are now requirements to consult and/or inform, a greater number of bodies able

---

7   Extracts from his speech in the House of Lords can be found in Chapter 1.

8   HoL, Report stage, 1st sitting, 8 January 2014.

9   Nuisance or annoyance for housing-related anti-social behaviour; harassment, alarm or distress for everything else.

10   All statutory references are to the Anti-Social Behaviour, Crime and Policing Act 2014 unless otherwise stated.

11   Revised *Statutory Guidance for Frontline Professionals*, p 23.

12   There may be some terms and conditions of tenancy which could have been relied upon in an ASBI sought under HA 1996, s 153D where the behaviour may not meet the test for the new injunction.

13   Found in the Policing and Crime Act 2009.

to apply and the injunction can include not only prohibitions but also positive requirements.

The s 1 injunction is undoubtedly a powerful remedy which can result in a person (not a child – see 3.22) being excluded from their home in certain circumstances. It can include terms which place significant limitations on a person's ability to, for example, (i) associate with others; (ii) access public places; and/or (iii) leave his own home as a result of a curfew. It can be applied for without notice being given to a respondent and a power of arrest can be attached. Applicants are advised to exercise care in ensuring that they seek injunctions only in those cases which merit them and then always in terms that are necessary and proportionate. Otherwise, as with almost every piece of new legislation in this field in the last 20 years, appeals will be likely.

The transitional arrangements and the enforceability of orders which were obtained prior to the Act coming into force are considered in more detail at 3.56 below.

C WHEN CAN AN INJUNCTION BE OBTAINED?

3.03   A s 1 injunction is available where a court:

(i)   is satisfied that the respondent has engaged or threatens to engage in **anti-social behaviour**; and

(ii)   considers it **just and convenient** to grant the injunction for the purpose of preventing the respondent from engaging in anti-social behaviour.[14]

These will be familiar concepts to practitioners and are considered below.

The Act specifically provides that the existence of anti-social behaviour is to be proved to the civil standard of proof.[15] Unlike with ASBOs, there is no scope for argument on the issue of the burden of proof: even where an injunction contains requirements that are particularly restrictive or especially severe, they do not lose their civil character, as they are fundamentally preventive in nature, not punitive.[16] Breaches of injunction, however, must be proved to the criminal standard of proof, as the court is being invited to punish the offender for breaching the injunction: see 3.44 and 3.54 below.

D WHAT IS ANTI-SOCIAL BEHAVIOUR?

3.04   Anti-social behaviour is defined in three alternative ways in s 2 as:

(a)   conduct that has caused, or is likely to **cause harassment, alarm or distress** to any person;

---

14   s 1(1)–(3).
15   See s 1(2).
16   *Jones v Birmingham City Council* [2018] EWCA Civ 1189, [2018] 3 WLR 1695 per Sir Brian Leveson P.

(b)   conduct capable of causing a **nuisance or annoyance** to a person in relation to that person's occupation of residential premises; or

(c)   conduct capable of causing **housing-related**[17] **nuisance or annoyance** to any person.

The first alternative undoubtedly presents the 'highest' test. It applies irrespective of the identity of the applicant or the nature of the anti-social behaviour alleged. The second and third alternatives present 'lower' tests and only apply in the circumstances set out in the following paragraphs.

The second alternative applies only where the application for an injunction is made by a (social) housing provider,[18] local authority or a chief officer of the police.

The third alternative applies only where the conduct in question is 'housing-related', meaning that it directly or indirectly relates to the housing management functions of a housing provider or local authority.

The reasons for employing a different test for 'housing related' conduct becomes clear from the Parliamentary debates: anti-social behaviour in the context of housing was considered to be of a 'different order' in that 'victims could not be expected to have the same degree of tolerance to anti-social behaviour where it takes place on their doorstep or in the immediate vicinity of their home. It is simply not reasonable to expect victims to move home in such circumstances in the same way as they could walk away from anti-social behaviour in a shopping centre or a public park'.[19]

The statutory definition of anti-social behaviour requires an understanding of the meaning of:

(a)   harassment, alarm or distress;

(b)   nuisance or annoyance; and

(c)   housing related.

These phrases are considered further below.

Harassment, alarm or distress

3.05   Practitioners will recognise the phrase 'harassment, alarm or distress' from the CDA 1998 in relation to ASBOs.

In *R v Jones*[20] the Court of Appeal gave guidance as to the meaning of this phrase:

> '... we do wish to draw a distinction between activity likely to cause harassment, alarm or distress, and activity which merely causes frustration, disappointment, anger, or annoyance. That is plainly not what the Crime

---

17   Defined in s 2(3), see further 3.07 below.
18   See s 20(1).
19   HoL, Third Reading, 27 January 2014, Under-Secretary of State, Home Office, Lord Taylor of Holbeach, col 981.
20   [2006] EWCA Crim 2942.

and Disorder Act 1998 is aimed at. It is aimed at actions likely to cause what might be globally described as "fear for one's own safety"; merely being frustrated at the delay on a train does not come within that meaning, even though in one sense it might be said to cause distress.'

Although there has been a change in the standard of proof[21] the observations set out above remain relevant to defining 'harassment, alarm or distress' for the purposes of the new injunction.

Nuisance or annoyance

3.06   The phrase 'nuisance or annoyance' has appeared in housing statutes for many years, including the discretionary grounds for possession, Housing Act 1985, Sch 2, Ground 2, (secure tenancies) and Housing Act 1988, Sch 2, Ground 14, (assured tenancies). It also appeared in the test for ASBIs.

The case law under those provisions is relevant to an application for an injunction under s 1. Whether conduct is capable of causing nuisance or annoyance is often obvious, may be case-specific and is often a question of fact and degree. It is not restricted, for example, to private or public nuisance as defined by the law of tort. It has been held that nuisance is to be assessed 'according to plain and sober and simple notions'[22]. 'Annoyance' was considered in *Tod-Heatly v Benham*:[23]

> '"Annoyance" is a wider term than nuisance, and if you find a thing which reasonably troubles the mind and pleasure, not of a fanciful person or of a skilled person who knows the truth, but of the ordinary sensible English inhabitant of a house—if you find there is anything which disturbs his reasonable peace of mind, that seems to me to be an annoyance, although it may not appear to amount to physical detriment to comfort. You must take sensible people, you must not take fanciful people on the one side or skilled people on the other … it seems to me there is danger of annoyance, though there may not be a nuisance.'

The courts have held that the following behaviour constitutes nuisance or annoyance:

(a)   playing of loud music, slamming car doors, revving of engines;[24]

(b)   racial abuse;[25]

(c)   repair of motor vehicles;[26]

---

21   For the purposes of ASBOs the existence of harassment, alarm or distress has to be proved to the criminal standard, beyond reasonable doubt: *R (McCann) v Crown Court at Manchester, Clingham v Kensington and Chelsea Royal London Borough Council* [2002] UKHL 39, [2003] 1 AC 787.

22   *Walter v Selfe* (1851) 4 De G & Sm 315. 322, per Bruce-Knight VC.

23   (1888) 40 Ch D 80, 98, per Bowen LJ.

24   *Woking Borough Council v Bistram* (1995) 27 HLR 1, CA.

25   *Kensington & Chelsea Royal London Borough Council v Simmonds* (1997) 29 HLR 507.

26   *West Kent Housing Association Limited v Davies* (1999) 31 HLR 415, CA.

(d)   stone-throwing and spitting;[27]

(e)   supply of drugs and consequent noise and disturbance caused by frequent visitors to premises;

(f)   abuse, harassment and intimidation; [28]

(g)   damage to property;[29]

(h)   setting vehicles alight;[30]

(i)   throwing bricks and iron bars at motor vehicles;[31]

(j)   graffiti.[32]

Other examples of behaviour which is capable of causing nuisance or annoyance include: groups of youths congregating so as to cause obstruction or intimidation, feeding pigeons so that they regularly visit a particular property (with the consequent noise, dust, faeces and feathers), late night DIY activities, regular holding of bonfires, hoarding goods in communal areas/gardens and domestic abuse which can be heard by neighbours.

Housing-related

3.07   Section 2(1)(c) relates to conduct causing 'housing-related' nuisance or annoyance.

This is defined in s 2(3) as 'directly or indirectly related to the housing management functions' of a housing provider or a local authority.

'Housing management functions' are defined in s 2(4) as being those functions conferred by an enactment or the powers and duties of the housing provider or local authority as the holder of an estate or interest in housing accommodation. These would include:

● estate management;

● protecting the physical integrity and sustainability of housing stock and common parts;

● ensuring tenants comply with their obligations;

● tackling anti-social behaviour, maintaining a safe environment for tenants;

● protecting agents and employees in their work.

---

27   Ibid.
28   *Knowsley Housing Trust v McMullen* [2006] EWCA Civ 539, [2006] HLR 43, CA.
29   Ibid.
30   Ibid.
31   Ibid.
32   *R v Brzezinski* [2012] EWCA Crim 198, CA.

In *Swindon BC v Redpath*[33] the Court of Appeal adopted a broad view of housing management functions and made it clear that 'housing-related' in the context of an ASBI was not limited to a local authority's own tenants:

> '55 ... viewed as a whole, I consider that the council's housing management functions easily embrace its sense of responsibility to its continuing tenants and also to owner-occupiers in Warneage Green for the conduct of its former tenant, Mr Redpath, who has pursued his vendetta against his former neighbours irrespective of the loss of his tenancy.

> 56 In this connection, I do not accept Mr Luba's submissions that a local authority would not be acting within its housing management functions if it sought an ASBI to prevent dog-fouling in the vicinity of its tenants' front-doors, irrespective of whether that might or might not affect their rent. Nor does it seem to me to matter whether such fouling takes place on the street, but so as to annoy the authority's tenants, as distinct from within the confined boundaries of a local authority's housing estate. Nor do I accept his submissions about the limited circumstances in which there would be jurisdiction where the defendant to be injuncted puts a brick through someone's window. It seems to me that where, as here, such conduct puts any of the landlord's tenants in fear, there is jurisdiction.'

There is no reason why any more limited approach should be adopted to housing management functions for the purposes of the s 1 injunction.

Just and convenient

3.08   The requirement that the court must consider it 'just and convenient' to grant the injunction for the purpose of preventing the respondent from engaging in anti-social behaviour represents a change from the previous ASBO/ ASBI regime. With the ASBO, the court had to be satisfied that an order was 'necessary'. With the ASBI the court had a general discretion to make an order where satisfied that the alleged anti-social behaviour, unlawful use of premises or breach of tenancy existed.

The extent to which this requirement poses an additional hurdle remains untested and in practice appears to pose little difficulty for applicants if they can prove their factual case. The test may ultimately prove to be a lower standard than 'necessary'. An applicant for a s 1 injunction under the Act is certainly well advised to submit evidence of the steps that have been taken in an attempt to address the behaviour before the application for the injunction was made.

It was established under the previous legislation that, where there were several different tools that a local authority could use to address a particular problem, the applicant authority essentially had a choice: there was no principle of 'closest fit' that restrains judicial discretion to make an order where the statutory preconditions are satisfied.[34]

33 [2009] EWCA Civ 943, [2010] HLR 13.
34 *Birmingham City Council v James* [2014] 1 WLR 23.

This principle could usefully be deployed to meet an argument that a civil injunction is not just or convenient because alternative powers are also available. In practice, applicants should consider each of the various alternative powers in proportionality assessments as part of their decision-making process, having regard to their ASB (and, where appropriate, other) policies.

Conversely, it is also relevant to note that as long ago as February 2000 the Court of Appeal confirmed in *Newcastle City Council v Morrison*[35] that an authority is not required to apply for an injunction to restrain unlawful conduct before they commence possession proceedings:

> 'Thirdly, I think that the recorder was wrong to see the question of reasonableness as turning on the notion that there was an alternative and, as he thought, more appropriate remedy available. In *Sheffield City Council v. Jepson (1993) 25 H.L.R. 299*, it was submitted that the authority landlord ought to have sought an injunction before resorting to possession proceedings. Ralph Gibson L.J. held that, although the authority could have obtained an injunction rather than seeking possession, he saw no reason why a council should be required or expected to take that course. It is in the public interest that necessary and reasonable conditions in tenancy agreements of occupiers of public housing should be enforced fairly and effectively. Mr Holland suggests this a different case where the tenant was personally in breach of a tenancy agreement in relation to the keeping of a dog. It seems to me that what Ralph Gibson L.J. said in the *Sheffield* case clearly applies to the present case.'

E   WHEN DOES THE ANTI-SOCIAL BEHAVIOUR NEED TO HAVE OCCURRED?

3.09   In deciding whether to grant an injunction under s 1 the court can take account of conduct occurring up to six months before the commencement date for Pt 1 of the Act, ie since 23 September 2014.[36] Save for this limitation, there is no statutory requirement that the conduct must have occurred within a particular period of time before the application was made. However, as a matter of common sense, the court is far less likely to grant an injunction where the applicant relies only on stale or aged allegations.

Pre-23 September 2014 evidence may be admissible. Holroyde J held in *Birmingham City Council v Pardoe*[37] that whilst when applying for an injunction under the Act, a local authority had to satisfy the court of the first condition by proving that the respondent had engaged in anti-social behaviour after 23 September 2014, evidence of conduct prior to 23 September 2014 could not, on its own, satisfy the first condition; but the court could take such conduct into account at the first stage where it was relevant to the issue of whether the

---

35   (2000) 32 HLR 891.
36   s 21(7).
37   [2016] EWHC 3119 (QB); [2016] 12 WLUK 95.

respondent had engaged in anti-social behaviour after 23 September 2014. It could also take it into account for the purposes of the second condition.

In the case of applications in the youth court, s 127 of the Magistrates' Courts Act 1980 applies and the complaint must be laid within six months of the behaviour complained of. As long as there is some conduct within this window, a complaint may be laid even if some of the behaviour relied upon occurred more than six months before the application.

F   WHO CAN APPLY?

3.10   The number of bodies that can apply for injunctions has been increased compared with the old ASBOs[38] and ASBIs.[39] This reflects an intention that the burden of making applications should be shared among a greater number of responsible bodies. New to the list of applicants includes, for example, Transport for London and the Environment Agency.

The full list of applicants is as follows:[40]

(a)   a local authority;

(b)   a housing provider (but only where the application concerns anti-social behaviour that directly or indirectly affects its housing management functions);[41]

(c)   the chief officer of police for a police area;

(d)   the chief constable of the British Transport Police Force;

(e)   Transport for London;

(f)   Transport for Greater Manchester;[42]

(g)   the Environment Agency;

(h)   the Natural Resources Body for Wales;

(i)   the Secretary of State exercising security management functions, or a Special Health Authority exercising security management functions on the direction of the Secretary of State;[43] or

---

38   Applicants for ASBOs were limited to the police, the British Transport Police, the local authorities and certain registered providers (non-profit registered providers of social housing, those registered under HA 1996, s 1 as a social landlord and housing action trusts established by order pursuant to s 62 of the Housing Act 1988) (see CDA 1998, s 1(1A)).

39   Applicants for ASBIs were limited to the 'relevant landlord' and included housing action trusts, local authorities, non-profit registered providers of social housing, registered social landlords; charitable housing trusts which did not fall within HA 1996, s 153E(7)(ba) or (c) were also a relevant landlord for the purposes of HA 1996, s 153D.

40   s 5(1).

41   s 5(3).

42   Anti-social Behaviour, Crime and Policing Act 2014 (Amendment) Order 2019 (SI 2019/68).

43   'Security management functions' are defined in s 5(2) as being: (a) the Secretary of State's security management functions within the meaning given by s 195(3) of the National Health Service Act 2006; (b) the functions of the Welsh Ministers corresponding to those functions. These bodies were previously NHS Protect and NHS Protect (Wales), which were abolished in 2017.

(j)   the Welsh Ministers exercising security management functions,[44] or a person or body exercising security management functions on the direction of the Welsh Ministers or under arrangements made between the Welsh Ministers and that person or body.

The Secretary of State has power to amend the list of bodies who may apply for an injunction.[45]

G AGAINST WHOM?

3.11   A s 1 injunction can be sought against any person aged 10 or over. There is no requirement for the respondent to be a social housing tenant or occupant: the injunction is tenure neutral. Applications can also be made in respect of multiple respondents, including persons unknown.[46]

There are specific considerations in respect of youths aged between 10 and 18 which are summarised in the checklist at 3.55 below.

H VULNERABLE RESPONDENTS

3.12   The Government has placed great weight on empowering victims and ensuring that vulnerable victims are identified at an early stage. No doubt this is in part a response to cases like Pilkington and Dow.[47]

However, applicants also need to consider how to deal with vulnerable respondents. A number of issues arise.

Respondents who lack capacity to conduct litigation

3.13   A respondent who lacks the capacity to conduct his defence to the injunction proceedings is a 'protected party' within the meaning of the Civil Procedure Rules (CPR), r 21.1(2)(d). This has three consequences:

(i)   a protected party must have a litigation friend to conduct proceedings on his behalf;[48]

(ii)   the permission of the court is required to do anything other than issuing and serving the claim form or applying for litigation friend to be appointed;[49] and

(iii)   any step taken before a protected party has a litigation friend has no effect unless the court orders otherwise.[50]

---

44   See fn 37.
45   And to amend s 5 or s 20 (in relation to expressions used in s 5): see s 5(5).
46   See for example *Intu Milton Keynes Ltd v Taylor* [2018] 4 WLUK 487.
47   Chapters 1 and 2 contain a discussion of these cases.
48   CPR, r 21.2(1).
49   CPR, r 21.3(2)(b).
50   CPR, r 21.3(4).

The defendant's capacity to conduct litigation is to be assessed in accordance with the test under ss 2 and 3 and the principles under s 1 of the Mental Capacity Act 2005. The issue will be whether the respondent is:

> 'capable of understanding, with the assistance of such proper explanation from legal advisers and experts in other disciplines as the case may require, the issues on which his consent or decision is likely to be necessary in the course of those proceedings. [Whether] he has capacity to understand that which he needs to understand in order to pursue or defend a claim ...'[51]

The capacity assessment may be undertaken, inter alia, by a doctor, social worker or mental health worker. If a respondent is found to lack capacity a litigation friend will need to be appointed in accordance with CPR, Part 21.

CPR, r 21.4 sets out the persons who may be appointed to be a litigation friend without a court order. They are a deputy appointed by the Court of Protection[52] or other persons who can fairly and competently conduct proceedings on behalf of the protected party and have no interest adverse to him.[53] The Official Solicitor may act in an appropriate case, though will need to be satisfied of a number of criteria before accepting the invitation given the pressures on the Official Solicitor's workload. CPR, r 21.5 sets out the procedure to be followed.

CPR, r 21.6 deals with the court's power to appoint a litigation friend. CPR, r 21.6(3) places an obligation on the claimant (ie the applicant for the injunction) to apply to the court for an order appointing a litigation friend where it wishes to take some step in the proceedings. This means that if a respondent lacks capacity and there is no litigation friend, the applicant must apply to the court for the appointment of a litigation friend once proceedings have been issued and served. No other steps, including applying for an interim injunction, can be taken until a litigation friend has been appointed.

Where a respondent is represented, concerns as to capacity will usually be identified by his solicitor who will usually seek a report on capacity. However, it is increasingly the case that respondents are litigants in person. What then? In anti-social behaviour cases, a suspicion of a lack of capacity may arise as a result of the peculiar nature of a respondent's behaviour, because of matters that have arisen in his ongoing dealings with the application or victim or because of his apparent inability to understand the proceedings. Even in cases where there is no known lack of capacity, the court has an obligation to investigate the question of capacity whenever there is a reason to suspect it may be absent.[54] This will usually result in the court ordering the applicant to obtain a report on the respondent's capacity.

---

51 Lord Chadwick at [75] of *Masterman-Lister v Brutton & Co (Nos 1 and 2), Masterman-Lister v Jewell* [2002] EWCA Civ 1889, [2003] 1 WLR 1511, CA.
52 As long as the deputy's power extends to conducting proceedings and the injunction proceedings fall within the scope of his power.
53 CPR, r 21.4(3).
54 *Masterman-Lister v Brutton & Co (Nos 1 and 2), Masterman-Lister v Jewell* [2002] EWCA Civ 1889, [2003] 1 WLR 1511, CA.

Ability to understand and comply with the terms of an injunction

3.14   Capacity has to be considered in relation to the particular decision in question; a person can lack capacity to conduct the litigation but may retain the capacity to understand the terms of an injunction (and vice versa).

Wookey v Wookey[55] concerned a non-molestation order made against a mentally ill respondent who had been diagnosed with early dementia and pathological jealousy.[56] The medical evidence was to the effect that the respondent was not capable of understanding the nature of an injunction. The Court of Appeal was asked to consider whether: (i) it was appropriate to grant an injunction against a person whose mental incapacity meant he was not capable of understanding it; and (ii) it was appropriate to grant an injunction which could not effectively be enforced. The following principles can be derived from *Wookey*:[57]

(a)   an injunction should not be granted to impose an obligation to do something which cannot be enforced;

(b)   the courts expect and assume that orders will be obeyed and an injunction will not normally be refused because a respondent is likely to disobey it;

(c)   the appointment of a litigation friend is not *of itself* a bar to the granting of an injunction or its enforcement because a respondent may be unable to act without a litigation friend but may well be able to understand the order and its consequences;

(d)   if the medical evidence confirms that a respondent is incapable of understanding what he was doing or that it was wrong an injunction should not be granted;

(e)   the judge at the first hearing should consider whether there is sufficient evidence at that stage to appoint a litigation friend.

Wookey concerned the court's inherent jurisdiction to grant injunction relief. Injunctions obtained under the Act are on a statutory footing but the same principles apply, see: *R (on the application of Cooke) v Director of Public Prosecutions.*[58]

In *Cooke* the respondent was an aggressive beggar who had numerous previous convictions and suffered from a borderline personality disorder and post-traumatic stress disorder. He was convicted of a public order offence with a post-conviction ASBO being imposed. He challenged the ASBO and argued on appeal that it had not been necessary because his mental state was such that he was unable to comply with the order. He also argued that it was 'unjust' to make the order and that its effect was to criminalise his mental health problems. The court was referred to *Wookey* and Dyson LJ said as follows:

---

55   *Wookey v Wookey, S (A Minor) (Injunction to Restrain)* [1991] Fam. 121, [1991] 3 WLR 135, CA.
56   The case was listed with another case involving an injunction order in respect of a minor.
57   From the judgment of Butler-Sloss LJ.
58   [2008] EWHC 2703 (Admin).

'12 An ASBO is, of course, not an injunction, but there are obvious similarities, even though an ASBO is a creature of statute. So far as I am aware, there is no previous authority on the question whether an ASBO can, or should, be made against a defendant whose mental health is such that he is incapable of complying with the terms of an order. In my judgment an ASBO should not be granted if the defendant is truly incapable of complying with it. That is because, for the reasons that I have given, an ASBO is not necessary for the protection of the public in such circumstances, and it would, in any event, be a wrong exercise of the court's discretion under subsection (2) to make an order in circumstances where the court knows that the defendant is not capable of complying with it. The justices should not refuse to make an ASBO on such grounds unless the defendant does not have the mental capacity to understand the meaning of the order, or to comply with it. Such an incapacity being a medical matter, evidence should normally be given by a psychiatrist and not by a psychologist or a psychiatric nurse.

13 A defendant who suffers from a personality disorder may on that account be liable to disobey an ASBO. In my judgment, however, that is not a sufficient reason for holding that an order, which is otherwise necessary to protect the public from a defendant's anti-social behaviour, is not necessary for that purpose, or that the court should not exercise its discretion to make an order.'

As can be seen, Dyson LJ drew a distinction between a respondent disobeying an order and being *incapable* of complying with it. Applicants will need to ensure that the medical evidence addresses these issues. Applicants should also note that in cases where the respondent's ability to comply with an order is in issue, evidence should be obtained from a psychiatrist and not a psychologist or psychiatric nurse.

A recent example of the application of the above reasoning is *C v F*.[59] The respondent suffered from an untreated mental disorder (bipolarism), made worse by disposing of his medication. He sent a series of abusive emails in breach of an interim injunction imposed to restrain harassment. It was held that the bipolarism was a significant mitigating factor, but did not come close to excusing the conduct. The respondent was responsible for his conduct at all times, even if the conduct resulted from the bipolar disorder.

Assessment of capacity – the Mental Capacity Act 2005 ('MCA 2005')
Sections 1–3 of the MCA 2005 provide:

1 The principles

(1) The following principles apply for the purposes of this Act.

---

59 [2014] EWHC 3346 (QB).

(2) A person must be **assumed to have capacity** unless it is established that he lacks capacity.

(3) A person is not to be treated as unable to make a decision unless **all practicable steps to help him** to do so have been taken without success.

(4) A person is not to be treated as unable to make a decision merely because he makes an **unwise decision**.

(5) An act done, or decision made, under this Act for or on behalf of a person who lacks capacity must be done, or made, in his best interests.

(6) Before the act is done, or the decision is made, regard must be had to whether the purpose for which it is needed can be as effectively achieved in a way that is less restrictive of the person's rights and freedom of action.

2 People who lack capacity

(1) For the purposes of this Act, a person lacks capacity in relation to a matter if at the material time he is unable to make a decision for himself in relation to the matter because of an **impairment of, or a disturbance in the functioning of, the mind or brain**.

(2) It does not matter whether the impairment or disturbance is **permanent or temporary**.

(3) A lack of capacity cannot be established merely by reference to–

(a) a person's age or appearance, or

(b) a condition of his, or an aspect of his behaviour, which might lead others to make unjustified assumptions about his capacity.

(4) In proceedings under this Act or any other enactment, any question whether a person lacks capacity within the meaning of this Act must be decided on the balance of probabilities ...

3 Inability to make decisions

(1) For the purposes of section 2, a person is **unable** to make a decision for himself if he is unable–

(a) to understand the information relevant to the decision,

(b) to retain that information,

(c) to use or weigh that information as part of the process of making the decision, or

(d) to communicate his decision (whether by talking, using sign language or any other means).

(2) A person is not to be regarded as unable to understand the information relevant to a decision if he is able to **understand an explanation** of it given to him in a way that is appropriate to his circumstances (using simple language, visual aids or any other means).

(3) The fact that a person is able to retain the information relevant to a decision for a short period only does not prevent him from being regarded as able to make the decision.

(4) The information relevant to a decision includes information about the reasonably foreseeable consequences of–

(a) deciding one way or another, or

(b) failing to make the decision.

(emphasis added)

The Code of Practice which supports the MCA refers to a two-stage capacity test comprising:

(i) Stage 1 (the 'diagnostic test'): Does the person have an impairment of, or a disturbance in the functioning of the mind or brain?

(ii) Stage 2 (the 'functional test'): Does the impairment or disturbance mean that the person is unable to make a specific decision when they need to?

Capacity is decided by reference to a person's ability to make a particular decision at a particular moment in time as opposed to his/her ability to make decisions generally.

'in principle, legal capacity depends on understanding rather than wisdom, the quality of the decision is irrelevant as long as the person understands what he is deciding.'[60]

Applicants will need to ensure that the expert who produces the report on capacity is properly instructed on how his/her assessment is to be carried out. The expert should also be made aware of the distinction in *Cooke*[61] between disobedience and the respondent's ability to comply with an order.

---

60   Wright J at para 19 of Masterman-Lister v Jewell [2002] EWHC 417 (QB), [2002] WTLR 563.
61   See 3.14 above.

Protected characteristics and the Equality Act 2010

3.15   Respondents who have a 'protected characteristic'[62] may seek to defend an application for an injunction on the basis that:

(a)   it amounts to discrimination within the meaning of the Equality Act 2010 ('EA 2010'); or

(b)   that a public authority applying for an injunction has not complied with the public sector equality duty under EA 2010, s 149.

Vulnerable respondents may have a 'disability' within the meaning of the EA 2010. Section 6 of the EA 2010 defines as disability as a 'physical or mental impairment' which has a 'substantial and long-term adverse effect' on the respondent's ability to carry out normal day-to-day activities. Expert evidence will be needed on whether the definition is met. The EA 2010 is considered in greater detail in Chapter 2.

In the case of *Forward v Aldwyck Housing Group Ltd*,[63] the High Court dismissed an appeal of a possession order where it had been argued that the trial judge had taken a flawed approach to PSED matters. The High Court confirmed that the PSED requires a 'rigorous consideration' of the impact of the decision to commence eviction proceedings against the equality objectives encapsulated in the PSED and that this must be done with 'an open mind and not as a defensive "sweep-up"'.[64]

Respondents in need of community care services

3.16   Local authorities have a duty under the Care Act 2014[65] to assess any person in their area who appears to require care and support. There may be evidence to suggest that a respondent has mental health problems, is abusing drugs or alcohol or has learning difficulties. Persons who were assessed as eligible for homelessness assistance with a 'priority need' under HA 1996, Part VII may have been allocated temporary or permanent social housing but remain vulnerable and in need of support. Applicants should consider whether the local authority should be invited to assess them. Social services and other support services should be encouraged to engage with the respondent. Applicants may find that a collaborative approach is effective in dealing with some or all of the behaviour and this could be undertaken alongside collecting the evidence needed for enforcement action.

---

62   Section 4 of the Equality Act 2010 provides:
      '4 The protected characteristics
      The following characteristics are protected characteristics—
      age; disability; gender reassignment; marriage and civil partnership; pregnancy and maternity; race; religion or belief; sex; sexual orientation.'
63   [2019] EWHC 24 (QB).
64   See ibid, at [39], per Mrs Justice Cheema-Grubb DBE.
65   Previously under the NHS and Community Care Act 1990.

I   THE TERMS OF AN INJUNCTION – GENERAL CONSIDERATIONS

3.17   An injunction under the Act may *prohibit* the respondent from doing anything described in the injunction.[66] The use of prohibitions will be a familiar concept to those that have experience of seeking ASBIs which were also intended to prohibit certain conduct.[67] The Act creates a new ability to include 'positive requirements' in an injunction; this is considered in more detail below.

Prohibitions – some common terms

- play music that is audible outside a property between the hours of 11pm and 7am;

- engage in swearing, verbal abuse, or threatening or intimidating behaviour;

- enter a defined property, street or area (often with reference to a marked zone on a map);

- use, supply or produce drugs at/from a defined property;

- allow named individual(s) from entering a defined property or block;

- engage in working on or repairing cars, motorbikes or other mechanically propelled vehicles in a defined area;

- enter any A & E department in England and Wales without good cause;

- to call 999 except in case of a genuine emergency.

   Appendix E contains a list of sample prohibitions for a variety of different activities.

Injunctions can require a person not to encourage other people to be involved in a breach of the terms but to do so they must say this expressly.[68]

The Act makes provision for a 'carrot and stick' approach, by permitting injunctions to include terms which *require* the respondent to do the things prescribed in the injunction,[69] for example, a requirement to keep a dog muzzled or on a lead, or a requirement for the respondent to attend a substance misuse or vehicle repair course.

---

66   s 1(4)(a).
67   See HA 1996, s 153A(1) which provided:
       In this section— "anti-social behaviour injunction" means an injunction that **prohibits** the person in respect of whom it is granted from engaging in housing-related anti-social conduct of a kind specified in the injunction; ...'
68   *Circle 33 Housing Trust Ltd v Kathirkmanathan* [2009] EWCA Civ 921; the case concerned an undertaking but the principles are of equal relevance for injunctions.
69   s 1(4)(b).

The ability to include positive obligations set out in s 1(4)(b) of the Act is new. Until the Act was brought into force this type of term was something that could only be sought in an application for a gang injunction[70] or as part of an individual support order[71] attached to an ASBO.[72]

Importantly, positive obligations have effect as requirements of the injunction. This means that an applicant can take enforcement action if the respondent fails to do what was specified in the order. For the first time in the context of injunctions applicants will be able to take committal proceedings if a respondent fails to attend the course or other activity specified in an order. This has the potential to be an effective way of achieving long-term solutions to problems such as alcohol or substance misuse.

The terms of an injunction must be reasonable and, so far as is practicable, avoid any interference with the times when a respondent normally works or attends school or another educational establishment.[73] They should also avoid any conflict with the requirements of any other court order or injunction to which the respondent may be subject.[74]

Additional considerations are set out in the Revised Guidance.[75] The applicant is required to consider the impact of the prohibitions or requirements on any caring responsibilities the perpetrator may have. In cases where the respondent has a disability, the applicant should consider whether the respondent is capable of complying with the prohibition or positive requirement and Equality Act 2010 considerations will be relevant.

The draft Guidance included reference to ensuring, so far as reasonably practicable, that prohibitions or requirements did not 'conflict with the respondent's religious beliefs';[76] this was not reproduced in the approved guidance, nor does it reappear in the 2017 revision. However, any conflict with religious observance is still a relevant consideration. Article 9 of the European Convention on Human Rights (ECHR) provides for freedom of thought, conscience and religion. Interference with Article 9 rights is only permitted where such interference is prescribed by law and is necessary in the interests of national security or public safety, for the prevention of disorder or crime, for the protection of health or morals or for the protection of the rights and freedoms of others. Applicants should also have regard to any conflict between the terms sought and the respondent's religion and seek to avoid such conflict where possible. Human rights are considered in greater detail in Chapter 2.

The injunction should specify the period for which each prohibition or positive requirement is to have effect, though can provide that the order runs until further order.[77] The terms of an injunction can be for differing periods. These provisions

---

70 Made under Pt 4 of the Policing and Crime Act 2009.
71 Made under CDA 1998, s 1AA.
72 There was no effective remedy for breach of the positive requirement as it was not part of the terms of the ASBO itself.
73 s 1(5)(a).
74 s 1(5)(b).
75 Revised *Statutory Guidance for Frontline Professionals*, p 24.
76 Draft Guidance published in October 2013, p 25.
77 s 1(6)(b) – in the case of an injunction granted before the respondent has reached the age of 18, a period must be specified and it must be no more than 12 months.

do not affect the basic proposition of law that injunctions should not generally continue indefinitely unless there is some good reason why they should.

All of the terms of the injunction, whether in the form or a prohibition or positive requirement, will need to satisfy certain basic requirements. Established practice with regards to terms can be summarised as follows:

- using clear, plain and intelligible language;

- avoiding the use of technical words or phrases, particularly for orders in respect of youths;

- be necessary and tailored to the behaviour complained of;

- be a proportionate response to the behaviour complained of.

Further examples of the prohibitions that may be sought for certain types of behaviour can be found in Appendix E.

J   POSITIVE REQUIREMENTS – SPECIFIC CONSIDERATIONS

3.18   An application which includes positive requirements will need to be front-loaded because of the matters the applicant is required to address in the application. This means that all of the evidence required in support of the terms sought within an injunction (as well as the evidence in support of the application itself) will need to be obtained in advance of an application for an injunction. It will require a proper consideration of the terms being sought and specific evidence in relation to the requirements to be included.

The Act has introduced some useful provisions to ensure the effectiveness of positive requirements:

(a)   *Identifying the supervisor*

In order to include a positive requirement in an injunction the applicant must specify who is to be responsible for supervising compliance with the requirement; the supervisor can be an individual or an organisation.[78] The supervisor has a duty to make the necessary arrangements in connection with the positive requirement(s), to promote the respondent's compliance with the requirement(s) and to inform the applicant and the chief officer of the police of the respondent's compliance or failure to comply with the requirement(s).[79]

(b)   *Respondent's responsibilities*

The respondent is required to keep in touch with the supervisor of the requirement and to notify them of any change of address.[80]

---

78   s 3(1).
79   s 3(4).
80   s 5(6).

(c) *Evidence when asking for a positive requirement*

When making the application, the applicant must include evidence of the suitability and enforceability of the positive requirement from the individual who will be supervising the requirement or from an individual representing the organisation that will be supervising the requirement.[81]

The examples of positive requirements given in the Revised Guidance are:[82]

- attendance at alcohol awareness classes for alcohol-related problems;

- irresponsible dog owners attending dog training classes provided by animal welfare charities; or

- the respondent attending mediation sessions with neighbours or victims.

The following examples are taken from the current guidance for gang injunctions[83] and may also be relevant. The respondent may be required to:

- notify the person who applied for the injunction of the respondent's address and of any change to that address;

- be at a particular place between particular times on particular days;

- present himself or herself to a particular person at a place where he or she is required to be between particular times on particular days;

- participate in particular activities between particular times on particular days;

- attend mediation with rival gang members;

- attend anger-management, relationship or other behavioural sessions;

- adhere to a curfew (where there is evidence that problematic behaviour occurs at particular times); or

- undertake job-preparedness or other coaching.

Not all positive requirements will incur a cost. For example, someone may be required to repair something they have broken, but many requirements will need to be funded. Supervisors of the requirements are not expected to provide the funding but no specific funding has been made available. During the Parliamentary debates the Government made clear that there was no additional money for the measures.[84] Funding will be one of the main challenges to the effective use of positive requirements. Practitioners have reported a reduction in availability of diversionary activities that were once available in their areas, largely caused

---

81   s 3(2).

82   Revised *Statutory Guidance for Frontline Professionals*, p 24.

83   *Statutory Guidance: Injunctions to Prevent Gang-Related Violence and Gang-Related Drug Dealing*, May 2016, pp 24–25.

84   HoC Committee stage, 5th sitting, 25 June 13 Minister of State for the Home Department, Mr Browne, col 173. Mr Browne suggested that 'local councils, which have considerable sums of money have to think about how they use that money intelligently on behalf of the taxpayer who funds them. It may well be that some courses offer particularly good value for money and that the cost of adding an additional person is marginal in some circumstances' (col 175).

by a reduction in budgets. One of the consultation documents suggested that a respondent could pay to attend a dog training course. It is unclear how practical this would be in cases where the respondents involved are on benefits or low incomes. The potential benefit of positive requirements will only be tested if there are funds available to allow the requirements to be imposed. Applicants may wish to work with those in the voluntary and charitable sectors to establish whether any assistance can be obtained from them. Ultimately, applicants may find that they will need to fund the positive requirement from their own resources.

K   PROHIBITIONS AND POSITIVE REQUIREMENTS – THE RELEVANCE OF EXISTING CASE LAW

3.19   There is no information in the Act or the Revised Guidance about: (i) the need for a geographical limitation within an injunction; (ii) the inclusion of matters which would also amount to a criminal offence; (iii) the availability of curfews; or (iv) non-association clauses. The current law in relation to ASBOs is set out below and may be used to support arguments about the use of these terms in civil injunctions.

- *Geographical limitation.* It is advisable for all injunctions to specify a geographical limitation if only to demonstrate that the order being sought is a proportionate and necessary one.[85] Injunctions could be limited to 'anywhere in the city of Birmingham' or 'anywhere within the London Borough of XXX' for example. Where nuisance is limited to only a few streets, it is unlikely to be proportionate to draw the geographical area any wider.

- *Criminal offences.* An applicant may wish to include terms which also amount to criminal offences carrying criminal penalties, for example a prohibition 'not to cause harassment, alarm or distress'[86] or 'not to be drunk in a public place'.[87] Under the ASBO regime it had been argued that breach of such a term could give rise to a greater penalty than was available for the offence in the criminal courts. However, the courts have confirmed that there was no bar to the inclusion of a term prohibiting conduct which would also amount to a criminal offence; the key consideration was whether the term sought was necessary: *R v Dean Boness.*[88] Terms should prohibit the particular anti-social behaviour that gave rise to the need for an injunction. A generic prohibition 'not to commit any criminal offence' is too wide.[89]

- *Curfews.* A curfew clause usually requires a respondent to stay indoors during the specified hours. It may be appropriate to provide an exception

---

85   *R v Boness (Dean), R v Bebbington (Shaun Anthony)* [2005] EWCA Crim 2395, [2006] 1 Cr App R (S) 120.
86   Approved in *Boness* but disapproved of in *Heron v Plymouth City Council* [2009] EWHC 3562 (Admin).
87   Approved in *R v Stevens* [2007] EWCA Crim 1128.
88   [2005] EWCA Crim 2395, [2006] 1 Cr App R (S) 120.
89   *W v Director of Public Prosecutions* [2005] EWHC 1333 (Admin).

if the respondent is accompanied by a named responsible adult and/or for emergencies. The use of curfew clauses in ASBOs was approved by the High Court in *R (on the application of Lonergan) v Lewes Crown Court.*[90] These clauses can be useful for those respondents who are responsible for nocturnal anti-social behaviour as a means of ensuring the opportunity to engage in such behaviour is removed. They were frequently imposed in respect of youths.

• *Non-association clauses* are those which prohibit the respondent from associating with named persons or with a specified number of other persons. Non-association clauses can appear extreme but they need not be. Depending on how the clause is drafted the respondents can still be free to see the named individual(s) but in the privacy of their own homes as opposed to in public places.

This type of term can be useful in cases where the anti-social behaviour is being caused by the respondent when he is part of a group. The prohibition is usually on associating in a public place. A term preventing the respondent in an ASBO from 'congregating in groups of people acting in a manner causing or likely to cause any person to fear for their safety or congregating in groups of more than six persons in an outdoor public place' was approved by the Court of Appeal in *Boness.*[91] A non-association clause can name individuals who are not themselves subject to an ASBO: *Hills v Chief Constable of Essex.*[92]

In the event a non-association clause is sought, Articles 8 (private and family life), and 10 (freedom of expression) of the ECHR may be engaged and Article 11 (freedom of association) almost certainly will be. Any interference with those rights must be proportionate. Care will need to be taken when drafting these clauses to avoid the potential for accidental breach (such as when attending a sporting event or queuing for a bus). Consideration will also need to be given to whether the respondent and the prohibited associate attend the same school, workplace or place of worship. In such cases a non-association clause may not be appropriate or specific exceptions may be required. If the court grants a non-association clause, applicants will need to think carefully about how it is enforced and will need to be sensitive to the particular circumstances that gave rise to the breach.

• *Use of the internet.* Social media is increasingly used as a means to intimidate or harass victims. It has also been used to inform others in the group of meet-ups or to boast about the anti-social behaviour in which a respondent has engaged. Applicants may wish to consider a prohibition on using the internet or on using specific websites. In such a case, it would need to be demonstrated that that the prohibition is proportionate and could be properly monitored. Consideration of the proper exercise of powers

90   [2005] EWHC 457 (Admin), [2005] 1 WLR 2570, [2005] 2 All ER 362.
91   [2005] EWCA Crim 2395, [2006] 1 Cr App R (S) 120.
92   [2006] EWHC 2633 (Admin).

under the Regulation of Investigatory Powers Act 2000 and/or Investigatory Powers Act 2016 (and guidance thereunder) may also be required. The case of *Reigate & Banstead Council v Peter Walsh*[93] is an example of the High Court granting an injunction to restrain the defendant from contacting the council by email (or telephone or otherwise) save for a named point of contact who could only be contacted at a specified address and then only in writing,[94] but in view of the increasing use of internet to engage in and promote anti-social activity it is inevitable that the opportunity for judicial consideration will arise soon.

The case of *R v Khan (Kamran)*[95] which involved the making of a Criminal Behaviour Order provides some useful guidance on the ambit of an injunction and is considered in more detail in Chapter 4. *Khan* suggests that it is 'essential' that the guidance provided by the Court of Appeal in *R v Boness (Dean)*[96] is borne in mind.

Terms of injunctions – good practice
Injunction terms should:

- include a geographical limitation and be specific about the area in which the order applies;

- be tailored to the behaviour complained of;

- be necessary;

- be expressed in plain and clear language;

- be of an appropriate length;

- refer to maps to define exclusion zones, include street names and clear boundaries.

L   POWER OF ARREST

3.20   A power of arrest allows a police officer to arrest the respondent without a warrant if he or she has reasonable cause to believe that a breach of the injunction has occurred.

---

93   [2017] EWHC 2221 (QB).
94   See also an unreported example from Norfolk where a district judge granted a term which prohibited 'publishing material which is threatening or abusive, or promotes criminal activity on the internet' (2007). A court in Leeds imposed a term prohibiting the 'posting, or being concerned in the posting of any image or description which encourages or glorifies unlawful activity on the internet'. Sandwell MBC obtained an ASBO which required the defendant to take down a website which was defamatory of a local school.
95   [2018] EWCA Crim 1472, [2018] 1 WLR 5419 at [14].
96   [2006] 1 Cr App R (S) 120.

A power of arrest can be attached to a prohibition or a positive requirement[97] if the court considers that the anti-social behaviour includes the use or threatened use of violence against other persons *or* where it considers that there is a significant risk of harm to other persons from the respondent.[98] Harm can include emotional or psychological harm.

A power of arrest may be a powerful remedy in bringing those who breach orders before the courts quickly with the direct assistance of the police. They also serve to provide comfort to victims who know that if the police attend the scene they will have additional powers to arrest.

Practical considerations

3.21   Once a power of arrest is imposed, applicants may be required to attend hearings (in the first instance often urgently, following an arrest) for a breach of an injunction and to pursue subsequent committal proceedings in circumstances where they would not have issued committal proceedings if the breach had been reported to them. Consider a situation where there is a 'low level' breach of an order, such as a single instance of verbal abuse. If this had been reported to the local authority, it may have resulted in a warning letter and perhaps even several warning letters in the event that the behaviour was repeated. The local authority will take steps to establish what evidence exists (bearing in mind the need to meet the higher criminal standard of beyond reasonable doubt) and may choose to issue committal proceedings only when it is satisfied that the order is not being complied with and evidence of the appropriate quality exists. The power of arrest therefore brings amplified protection, but also extended practical obligation.

In serious and urgent cases, where a power of arrest has been granted at a hearing without notice, the applicant must serve the injunction papers on the respondent before the police are informed about the power of arrest: CPR, r 65.44(3). It appears that this requirement is intended to ensure that the respondent is aware that they could be arrested for behaviour falling short of criminal wrongdoing.

M   EXCLUSION FROM THE HOME

3.22   In cases where anti-social behaviour includes the use or threatened use of violence against other persons, or where there is a significant risk of harm to other persons from the respondent, the court can make an order excluding the respondent from the place where he normally lives.[99] An exclusion clause of this nature could be included in an application for an injunction which is made with or without notice being given to the respondent, although in the latter case the situation would need to be severe for such a clause to be warranted (see further below).

---

97   'Requirement' in this section does not include one which has the effect of requiring the respondent to participate in particular activities.
98   s 4.
99   s 13.

The power of exclusion is only available for respondents aged 18 or over and can only be exercised if the applicant for the injunction is a local authority, chief officer of police, or a housing provider which owns[100] or manages the premises in question.[101]

Article 8 is inevitably engaged when a respondent is to be excluded from her home and the Revised Guidance makes express reference to this consideration.[102] Careful thought needs to be given to whether the circumstances justify seeking a term of this type. In certain circumstances the respondent may be vulnerable and the applicant should consider securing alternative accommodation for the duration of the exclusion.

The use of an exclusion clause in a without notice application for an ASBI was considered by the Court of Appeal in *Moat Housing Group – South Limited v Harris and Hartless*.[103] In that case, the housing association had applied for an ASBI without giving notice to the respondents of their intention to apply for the order. The ASBI included a term requiring the respondents to leave their homes and not return. The district judge made an order in the terms sought and the respondents were required to leave their homes by 6pm the same day. A power of arrest was attached to every term of the injunction including the exclusion clause.[104] The orders were not served until 9pm when officers of the association attended the respondent's home accompanied by the police and asked them to leave immediately. In his judgment, Brooke LJ said as follows:

> 'It is hard to imagine a more intrusive "without notice" order than one which requires a mother and her four children to vacate their home immediately. It is clearly necessary to restate certain principles governing the grant of "without notice" injunctions, and particularly those of an intrusive nature which will be familiar to family law practitioners.[105]

> Nothing in this judgment should be taken as meaning that the court has no power to make an ouster order (associated with an exclusion order) without notice if the facts are sufficiently serious to warrant such a draconian order. If the court is satisfied that there is a risk of significant harm to some person or persons attributable to the defendant's conduct if such an order is not made immediately, and that it is necessary and proportionate to make such a drastic order as a means of avoiding the apprehended harm, then the order may lawfully be made. Very great care is needed, however. The experience of the D family, for instance, shows that the effect of an order like this may be very difficult to reverse, so that it may in practice take

---

100 A housing provider owns a place if—
    (a) the housing provider is a person (other than a mortgagee not in possession) entitled to dispose of the fee simple of the place, whether in possession or in reversion, or
    (b) the housing provider is a person who holds or is entitled to the rents and profits of the place under a lease that (when granted) was for a term of not less than 3 years. (section 13(2))
101 s 13(1)(b).
102 Revised *Statutory Guidance for Frontline Professionals*, at pp 24–25.
103 [2005] EWCA Civ 287, [2005] HLR 33, CA.
104 Powers of arrest are considered in greater detail below.
105 At [62].

effect as a final order. In any event, the judge making such an order should generally be scrupulous to prescribe that the order may only be served at a reasonable time of the day (for example, between 9:00am and 4:30pm on a weekday) …'[106]

The s 1 injunctions are not intended to replace conventional possession proceedings (which are issued on notice and with prior service of a notice of seeking possession) and should not be used to bypass the need to issue formal possession proceedings.

The Revised Guidance states that the power to exclude is not expected to be used often and that applications for such orders should only be made in 'extreme cases' that meet the higher threshold set out in s 13(1)(c) of the Act.[107] This reflects existing case law.

N WITHOUT NOTICE APPLICATIONS AND INTERIM ORDERS

3.23   An application for an injunction can be made without notice being given to the respondent. If an application is made without notice the court must either adjourn the proceedings (with or without granting an interim injunction) or dismiss the application.[108]

The duration of an interim injunction order can be until the final hearing of the application or until 'further order' if the court thinks it 'just' to make such an order.[109] Interim orders made without notice cannot require a respondent to participate in particular activities.[110]

The Revised Guidance suggests that without notice applications can be made in 'exceptional cases to stop serious harm to victims' and states that without notice applications should not be made routinely or in place of inadequate preparation for normal 'with notice' applications.[111]

The guidelines provided by the Court of Appeal in the case of *Hartless*[112] are relevant when deciding whether to make the application without giving notice to the respondent. In addition to the paragraphs set out above it is useful to keep in mind the following passages from the judgment of Brooke LJ:

'63 As a matter of principle no order should be made in civil or family proceedings without notice to the other side unless there is a very good reason for departing from the general rule that notice must be given. Needless to say, the more intrusive the order, the stronger must be the reasons for the departure. It is one thing to restrain a defendant from what would in any event be anti-social behaviour for a short time until a hearing can be arranged at which both sides can be heard. It is quite another thing to make a "without notice" order directing defendants to leave their home

---

106 At [100].
107 Revised *Statutory Guidance for Frontline Professionals*, at p 24.
108 s 6.
109 s 7(2).
110 s 7(3).
111 See p 25.
112 [2005] EWCA Civ 287, [2005] HLR 33.

immediately and banning them from re-entering a large part of the area where they live.

71 It needs to be clearly understood, however, that to grant an injunction without notice is to grant an exceptional remedy ...

72 It would in our judgment be best if judges in the county courts, when deciding whether to exercise their discretion to make an ASBI without notice, followed the guidance given in s.45(2)(a) of the Family Law Act 1996. They should bear in mind:

(1) that to make an order without notice is to depart from the normal rules as to due process and warrants the existence of exceptional circumstances;

(2) that one such exceptional circumstance is that there is a risk of significant harm to some person or persons attributable to conduct of the defendant if the order is not made immediately;

(3) that the order must not be wider than is necessary and proportionate as a means of avoiding the apprehended harm.'

Applicants must therefore ensure that if they make an application without giving notice to the respondent the circumstances warrant this course of action. There may be situations where the behaviour is so serious that an immediate application to the court is required. The test set out above should be applied with rigour given that without notice injunctions are intended to be an exceptional remedy.

A without-notice application may also be justified where the applicant is satisfied that there is a real risk that a respondent could take retaliatory action towards a witness or person implicated in the application. In such a case, an interim injunction would serve to protect the witness or other person against reprisals from the moment that the respondent is served with the application and the evidence. There may be circumstances in which anonymised hearsay evidence could not conceal the identity of an informant, or that redactions are not in any event appropriate. However, if the respondent has already been warned that an application is imminent (and that warning has not resulted in any adverse consequences) it may be difficult to justify taking action without giving notice.

O CONSULTATION

3.24 This is an entirely new concept with regard to injunctions and is set out in s 14 of the Act. Under the old provisions, consultation was only required for ASBOs or gang injunctions and was not necessary for ASBIs. The Government deliberately kept the consultation requirements to the minimum in an effort to reduce bureaucracy and to allow local agencies to act flexibly according to the specific circumstances.[113]

113 HoC, Committee stage, 7th sitting, 27 June 2013, Mr Green, col 222.

Before making an application for an injunction the applicant must 'consult' the local youth offending team ('YOT') if the respondent will be aged under 18 when the application is made and 'inform' any other body or individual the applicant thinks is appropriate.[114]

The need for consultation – the relevance of history

3.25 In the Pilkington report the IPCC found that too many of the incidents were being dealt with in isolation and that both the police and local authority were writing letters or issuing Acceptable Behaviour Contracts without recourse to each other.[115] What was lacking was a coordinated system for sharing information. The requirements to consult and/or inform go some way to addressing this deficiency and are found in various provisions in the Act.[116]

Consultation or informing in practice

3.26 Unlike the consultation that was required for ASBOs there is no *obligation* for local authority applicants to consult the police (or vice versa). The only statutory consultation requirement relates to youths aged under 18 when the application is made.

It should be noted that there is no requirement to obtain the consent of the body being consulted or informed. Despite this, there are some important differences between the duty to consult and the duty to inform.

Most cases are likely to involve information sharing between the housing provider, local authority and police and an applicant should consider informing these bodies of the proposed application for the injunction.

It may be appropriate to inform other bodies or responsible persons, including the respondent's school or other place of education, social worker, support/key worker and probation officer.

Applicants should include evidence of the consultation within the witness statements/bundle in support of the application. There is no prescribed form of record, so a simple letter or pro-forma consultation document will suffice.

There are further consultation requirements if there is an application to vary/discharge.[117]

114 s 14(1).
115 For further details see Chapter 1.
116 There are other steps that enforcement agencies could consider independently of the statutory requirements such as the use of shared IT systems to enable incidents to be recorded on a central database with the ability to search by name or address for example. The use of a common IT system was used by one of the areas which trialled the community trigger.
117 s 14(3).

Consulting v Informing

The case of R v North and East Devon Health Authority, ex p Coughlan[118] provides a useful summary of what constitutes adequate consultation.

The case concerned the closure of a facility for the long term disabled where the occupants had been assured that the facility would be their home for life. One of the arguments in the case related to the adequacy of the consultation which had taken place before the decision to close the facility was made.

The Court of Appeal held[119] that where consultation was a legal requirement it had to be carried out properly and that in order to be 'proper' the consultation must:

(i)   be undertaken at a time when the proposals are still at a formative stage;

(ii)   include sufficient reasons for the particular proposals being made so that the people being consulted could give intelligent consideration and an intelligent response to these; and

(iii) give sufficient time to allow that consideration.

The court also said that the outcome of the consultation must 'be conscientiously taken into account when the ultimate decision was taken'.

Consultation does not therefore amount to a need to obtain the *consent* of the consultee but it does require an applicant to properly consider and grapple with any points that come out of the consultation. The applicant will need to consider whether its proposals need to be modified in light of the consultation process, and to undertake such amendments if necessary.

Example

Consider a situation where the local authority's proposal was to seek an injunction against the son of one of its tenants as a result of anti-social behaviour for which he was responsible in the area.

The proposals include an exclusion zone and a curfew. As the son is aged under 18 the local authority is required to consult with the youth offending team.[120] In consulting with the YOT the local authority should ensure that it makes known the proposed terms of the injunction (in accordance with the need to give sufficient reasons and particulars of the proposals).

During the consultation the YOT points out that both the curfew and the exclusion zone would prevent the son from attending the youth football club of which he is a member (and which is thought to be a positive influence on him).

---

118 [2001] QB 213, CA. The Sedley criteria have recently been endorsed by the Supreme Court in *R (on the application of Moseley (in substitution of Stirling Deceased)) (AP) v London Borough of Haringey [2014] UKSC 56 (29 October 2014)*.

119 Per Lord Woolf MR at [108].

120 s 14(1)(a).

The local authority would need to consider whether to amend its proposals to take account of the son's attendance at the football club, explaining its reasoning in its witness evidence. One solution may be to allow the son to enter the exclusion zone on set days and between defined hours in order to attend the football club and that at those times he must be accompanied by a parent or other responsible adult.

Informing

The local authority has a duty to inform such other individual or body it thinks appropriate.[121] If the son was known to social services (due to special educational needs say), the local authority should inform them of the proposed application.

In addition, whilst there is no requirement in the Act to inform parents, the local authority should inform them in advance of the application being made in the case of an on-notice application.

Without notice applications

3.27 The requirement to consult does not apply to a without-notice application. However, there is a requirement to consult/inform before the first on-notice hearing if a without-notice application is adjourned.[122]

P WHERE TO APPLY

Adults

3.28 Applications for injunctions in respect of those aged over 18 can be made in the county court or the High Court.[123]

The Act does not define the circumstances in which an application to the High Court might be appropriate and in reality the vast majority of applications in respect of those aged 18 or over will be made in the county court. Examples of when an application may be made to the High Court could be where an urgent out of hours hearing is required or the application relates to a combination of adults and youths and the youth court has declined to hear the applications together (see further 3.30 below). It is difficult to envisage other situations where an application would need to be made to the High Court.

121 s 14(1)(b).
122 s 14(1) and (2).
123 s 1(8)(b).

Youths

3.29   Applications in respect of those aged 10 or over but under 18 are made in the Youth Court.[124]

Multiple respondents where there is a combination of adults and youths

3.30   Where there are multiple respondents aged above and below 18 the applicant should apply to the youth court to have the applications heard together. Joint applications cannot be heard in the county court. In order to hear the application the youth court must be satisfied that it is in the interests of justice to hear the case.[125]

Cases involving youths and adults – joint hearings

There is no information in the Act or the Revised Guidance as to when a joint application involving both youths and adults should be heard by the Youth Court. Some suggested examples are:

(a)   a case in which there is a large overlap in the matters alleged in respect of each respondent such that it would be a more effective use of court time to deal with each individual together;

(b)   a desire to avoid lay witnesses having to attend court, give evidence and be cross examined on more than one occasion – in many cases it can be difficult to persuade witness to attend court at all and it cannot be in the interests of justice to require them to go through the ordeal repeatedly;

(c)   cases where there is a dispute between the respondents as to who is responsible, if they are blaming each other it would be helpful for a court to hear each of their cases presented (and tested) at the same hearing.

---

124 s 1(8)(a).
125 Revised *Statutory Guidance for Frontline Professionals*, p 23.

Q HOW TO APPLY

County court

3.31   The vast majority of applications in respect of adults will be made in the county court and will follow the CPR, Part 8 procedure.[126] The rules set down in CPR, Part 65[127] and the corresponding practice direction will apply.

The application can be made in any county court hearing centre by virtue of CPR, r 65.43(2)(b). After the application is issued, it will be sent to the hearing centre serving the address where the respondent resides or carries on business (or where the applicant resides or carries on business): see CPR, r 65.43(2A). If the application is for a without notice injunction, the issuing court can hear the application before transferring the case, CPR, r 65.43(4).

In practice, applicants are advised to have a good reason before issuing at a different hearing centre to that which will ultimately hear the case. Despite amendments to CPR, r 65.43, judicial and administrative sympathies to requests to transfer have been somewhat mixed – not least because transfers can create difficulties with listing an on-notice return date at the other hearing centre on short notice. Therefore, applicants should strive wherever possible to issue applications in the hearing centre local to the respondent; even CPR PD65 warns of the possibility of delay if proceedings must be transferred. Where issuing elsewhere is unavoidable, applicants should be ready to explain why this would not have been practicable: for example, where that hearing centre was not able to hear an urgent application on that day, and delay would have left the complainants exposed to unacceptable risk. Mere convenience for the applicant (or its lawyers) might not be well-received by the issuing court, even though this is not prohibited by the CPR.

Forms

3.32   The forms used for ASBIs continue to be used for injunction applications under the Act. These forms are:

(a) **N16A** Application for injunction (general form). There is no need for a separate claim form or details of claim, Form N16A will suffice;[128]*

(b) **N16** Injunction order.*

In cases in which a power of arrest is also sought, this should be drafted on Form **N110A**.

Suggested examples of those documents marked with a (*) can be found in Appendix D.

126 The 75th update to the CPR made amendments to the Practice Direction for Part 65 to ensure it made reference to the Act and not the old provisions.
127 CPR, Part 65 at rr 65.42–49.
128 CPR PD65, para 1.1(1).

Draft orders

3.33   It is good practice to include a draft order (ideally on Form N16) so that if the injunction is granted as asked (or with minor amendments), the court has the option of making amendments to the draft before it is sealed and the order can be given to the parties at the end of the hearing. This serves to remove any delay between the order being made by the court and being drawn up by the court office. It also enables the applicant to invite the court to dispense with the requirement for personal service by recording the presence of (and service upon) the respondent in the order.

Where the injunction contains more than one prohibition or positive requirement it is good practice to set these out in separate numbered paragraphs. Where a power of arrest is being sought, each provision to which a power of arrest is attached must be set out in a separate paragraph of the injunction.[129]

It is good practice to file a draft of the order sought on a disk in a format compatible with the software used by the court.[130] Applicants may find that they are able to email the draft order to a member of court staff in advance of the hearing and/or have it available on a memory stick.

In practice, where an order falls to be drawn up by court staff on the same day (typically to effect service of an interim injunction immediately after a without-notice hearing), the order should be carefully checked before it is served, as mistakes are sometimes made which could render the injunction difficult or impossible to enforce. Common errors include: missing penal notices; spelling mistakes in names (people or places); maps not attached or poorly photocopied; missing court seal; and incorrect dates. Errors such as these are much easier to remedy before the order leaves the court counter: otherwise, it might be necessary to make a formal application to the court to correct the error or to waive a procedural requirement, causing avoidable delay and uncertainty for victims.

Evidence

3.34   All applications must be supported by written evidence[131] which must be filed with the claim form and state the terms of the injunction applied for.[132]

If the application is made without notice being given to the respondent it must be supported by a witness statement which sets out the reasons why notice has not been given.[133] Judges are often reluctant to hear any further oral evidence from witnesses at the first hearing of without notice applications so that the basis of the exercise of their discretion for an interim order is recorded in and justified by reference to the application documents to be served on the respondent.

Applications must be made on two days' notice to the respondent.[134] The two exceptions to the notice requirement are:

129 CPR, r 65.4(2)(a).
130 CPR, PD25A – Interim Injunctions, para 2.4.
131 CPR, r 65.43(2)(c).
132 CPR, r 65.43(3)(b).
133 CPR, r 65.43(4)(a).
134 CPR, r 65.43(6)(a).

(a)   where the court has directed a shorter period of notice is acceptable; or

(b)   where the application is being made without notice being given to the respondent (in cases of urgency or where the facts justify a without notice application being made, see 3.23 above).

Evidence can take many forms and applicants are encouraged to think about the most appropriate way in which the anti-social behaviour and its consequences can be communicated to the court. The following forms of evidence may be appropriate:

(a)   witness statements from the direct witnesses to the behaviour (ideally where the witnesses are identified; hearsay evidence is considered in the textbox at 3.36 below);

(b)   witness statements from the police, the chair of the residents' association or community leaders about the problems in the area generally and how this individual is considered to be a ringleader or how a particular property attracts numerous visitors;

(c)   documents in the form of diaries and contemporaneous notes;

(d)   photographs;

(e)   sound and video recordings from mobile phones or CCTV;

(f)   certificates of conviction;

(g)   maps to identify areas and 'hot spots'.

Service

3.35   Every application for an injunction which is made on notice to the respondent must be personally served together with a copy of the evidence in support.[135] There is further information on service at 3.42.

Youth court

3.36   Unlike applications for ASBOs there are no rules (as yet) as to the format of an application to the youth court. Whilst there is no prescribed format, the local court may have an approved form in which application should be made and applicants should consult their local court to establish its particular requirements.[136] A number of documents will need to be prepared and these are listed below:

(a)   summons*;

(b)   injunction application*;

---

135   CPR, r 65.43(5).

136   It is arguable that the form of complaint for an order should be at least 'to the like effect' of Form 98 at Sch 2 to the Magistrates' Courts (Forms) Rules 1981, pursuant to rule 2 thereof. This form is seldom used in practice, and is not well-suited to applications of this nature.

(c)   draft injunction order to include any terms sought*;

(d)   evidence in support of the application including:

   (i)   hearsay notices where relevant*;

   (ii)   certificate of consultation;

(e)   case summary for cases where there are numerous witness statements or voluminous documents.

Suggested examples of those documents marked with a (*) can be found in Appendix D.

Evidence – good practice

Applicants will need to ensure that the evidence in support of the application covers the following issues:

(a)   A description of the incidents complained of; any diary sheets or other contemporaneous records should be summarised in the body of the statement. Copies of the diaries or contemporaneous documents should be exhibited.

(b)   The reasons for making the application without notice being given to the defendant.

(c)   The reasons for making an urgent application if an urgent application has been made requesting immediate judicial attention.

(d)   The reasons for seeking a power of arrest and details of which clauses it should be attached to.

(e)   Information about what steps have been taken to deal with the anti-social behaviour (warning letters, meetings, Acceptable Behaviour Contracts). The letters and file notes should be exhibited to the witness statement.

(f)   An explanation of why particular terms are being sought if this is not obvious from the evidence, for example, why a particular area has been chosen as the exclusion zone.

(g)   If the respondent is known to social services, what information is known about their current treatment and/or engagement with services.

(h)   Where the respondent is vulnerable, details of the steps that have been taken to ensure he is referred for the correct support/services and details of what consideration was given to whether the application is necessary and proportionate.

(i)   Evidence of which individuals/bodies have been consulted/informed.

Hearsay evidence

The best evidence is from the direct witnesses to the behaviour. Witnesses should be encouraged to come to court and have their evidence tested to allow judges to place appropriate weight on what they say. This should always be the starting point. Note that it will not usually be necessary for witnesses to attend court on the first occasion, which is likely to take place as a case management hearing; however, this should be verified with the court administration.

There will be situations in which witnesses cannot come to court or are not even prepared to be identified. This may be where they fear reprisals if it becomes known that they have given information to the applicant. If a witness is not prepared to be identified his evidence will be anonymised hearsay.[137]

Hearsay evidence is defined as any statement made by a person whether made orally or in writing other than one made by a witness giving oral evidence which is being relied upon for the truth of its contents.[138] Hearsay evidence is admissible in civil proceedings but notice must be given of the intention to rely on hearsay evidence under s 2 of the Civil Evidence Act 1995. In the county court, these notices are regulated by CPR r 33.2; in the Youth Court, the Magistrates' Courts (Hearsay Evidence in Civil Proceedings) Rules 1999[139] applies.

Section 4 of the 1995 Act governs the weight to be afforded to hearsay evidence:

'(1) In estimating the weight (if any) to be given to hearsay evidence in civil proceedings the court shall have regard to any circumstances from which any inference can reasonably be drawn as to the reliability or otherwise of the evidence.

(2) Regard may be had, in particular, to the following—

(a) whether it would have been reasonable and practicable for the party by whom the evidence was adduced to have produced the maker of the original statement as a witness;

(b) whether the original statement was made contemporaneously with the occurrence or existence of the matters stated;

(c) whether the evidence involves multiple hearsay;

(d) whether any person involved had any motive to conceal or misrepresent matters;

---

137 See *Solon South West Housing Association Ltd v James* [2004] EWCA Civ 1847, [2005] HLR 24 for an example of the appropriate application of the s 2 criteria to hearsay evidence.

138 *R v Sharp (Colin)* [1988] 1 WLR 7, HL.

139 SI 1999/681.

(e) whether the original statement was an edited account, or was made in collaboration with another or for a particular purpose;

(f) whether the circumstances in which the evidence is adduced as hearsay are such as to suggest an attempt to prevent proper evaluation of its weight.'

If a witness cannot attend court to give direct evidence, the next best form of evidence is a witness statement accompanied by a hearsay certificate. That witness statement can be filed in its own right or be exhibited to the witness statement of a person giving direct evidence, such as the housing officer. The housing officer's statement should include an explanation of why the witness could not attend so that the court may apply the considerations in s 2. A hearsay certificate would still be required.

If a witness is not prepared to attend court, nor to identify themselves, a witness statement should be prepared and their personal details (name, address and signature) redacted. The statements should be as detailed as possible and set out the actual words used where there has been swearing or verbal abuse (even though many witnesses will not want to repeat the language). Diaries and other contemporaneous records should be exhibited to the statement with personal details redacted. The witness statements can be exhibited to a witness statement from the housing officer. A hearsay certificate would still be required.

The evidence of anonymous witnesses could be included within a statement from a housing officer with appropriate notice being given of the intention to rely on that hearsay evidence; however, it is preferable for the witnesses to produce formal statements which are redacted.

Note that, in the county court, the requirement to give a hearsay notice does not apply to evidence at hearings other than trials.[140] This means that it is not necessary to serve hearsay notices before a first hearing of an application for an injunction, even where the court is considering at that hearing whether to grant an interim injunction. For this reason, those representing respondents will wish to ascertain at an early stage of proceedings whether the applicant intends to call live evidence from each of their witnesses. There is no such exemption for proceedings in the youth court, which is empowered to curtail the minimum period of notice, but (it appears) not to waive the requirement altogether.[141]

See also CPR, Part 33.

R   VARIATION AND DISCHARGE

3.37   By s 8 of the Act an order made under s 1 can be varied or discharged on the application of the person who applied for the injunction or the respondent.

---

140 CPR, r 33.3(a).
141 Magistrates' Courts (Hearsay Evidence in Civil Proceedings) Rules 1999, r 3(2).

The application to vary/discharge should be made to the court which granted the injunction or to the county court where the injunction was granted by the youth court but the respondent is now aged 18 or over. The application should be made in accordance with CPR, Part 23 on Form N244.[142]

The court's power to vary includes the power to include additional prohibitions or requirements and to extend the period for which a prohibition or requirement has effect.[143]

In addition, the court may attach a power of arrest or extend the period for which an existing power of arrest has effect.[144]

If an application under s 8 is dismissed, the party who made the application may not make any further applications under that section unless it obtains the consent of the court or the agreement of the other party.[145]

Further consultation requirements apply when an application for variation/discharge is made. The applicant must consult the local youth offending team where the respondent will be aged under 18 when the application is made and inform any other person it thinks appropriate.[146]

S PUBLICITY

3.38   The publicity rules for injunctions are the same as they were for ASBOs. Despite this there was considerable concern expressed during the debates in the House of Lords about publicising orders involving young people. This concern was heightened by the fact that an injunction can be made relying on the lower test of 'nuisance or annoyance' and yet still be publicised in the way that an ASBO (which had to be proved to a higher test of anti-social behaviour and to a higher standard of proof) could.

Lord Paddick observed that there had been a tendency amongst some local authorities to publish a rogues' gallery of photographs of people against whom ASBOs has been granted. He said that this had been done for political purposes and not in pursuit of justice.[147] Lord Hope said that powers were being taken away from the courts and entrusted to local authorities and the police and this was of some concern, particularly when an injunction could be applied for without notice being given to a respondent.[148]

Lord Taylor responded on behalf of the Government to the effect that publicity allowed for effective enforcement of an order and should be used for cases where it was necessary and proportionate. He also spoke of how publicity can provide reassurance to the public and be an effective deterrent against other individuals behaving in a similar way.[149]

---

142 CPR, r 65.45(1).
143 s 8(3)(a).
144 s 8(3)(b).
145 s 8(4).
146 s 14(3).
147 HoL, Committee stage, 3rd sitting, 20 November 2013, col 983.
148 HoL, Committee stage, 3rd sitting, 20 November 2013, col 983.
149 HoL, Committee stage, 3rd sitting, 20 November 2013, col 985.

Publicising orders gives rise to some interesting issues which are considered in more depth in Chapter 4 at 4.16–4.19. Chapter 4 also contains a textbox with a publicity checklist.

Adults

3.39   There is no restriction on the reporting of an injunction where the respondent is an adult. Any publicity should be tailored to the requirements of each individual case and should make clear whether an order is an interim order or a final order. Some cases will require only the specific victims to be notified that an injunction has been made; others may require leaflets to be distributed in an estate or an article in the local newspaper/residents newsletter. Publicity can often be justified on the basis that it furthers the proper enforcement of the order: the more people who know about it, the more likely they are to complain if they notice a breach.

Youths

3.40   Section 49 of the Children and Young Persons Act 1933 ('CYPA 1933') imposes reporting restrictions on certain proceedings including those in the youth court (or on appeal from the youth court). Under CYPA 1933, s 49 no report can be published which reveals the name, address or school of any child or young person concerned in the proceedings or which includes any particulars likely to lead to the identification of any child or young person concerned in the proceedings. In addition, no picture can be published of any child or young person concerned in the proceedings. This makes it much harder to monitor compliance with an injunction because it inhibits the ability to inform the community, and in particular those affected by the behaviour, of its existence.

For this reason, the usual automatic reporting restrictions in respect of a respondent under 18 do not apply for injunctions orders by virtue of s 17 of the Act. The Revised Guidance states:[150]

> 'When deciding whether to publicise the injunction, public authorities (including the courts) must consider that it is necessary and proportionate to interfere with the young person's right to privacy, and the likely impact on a young person's behaviour. This will need to be balanced against the need to provide re-assurance to the victims and the wider community as well as providing them with information so that they can report any breaches. Each case should be decided carefully on its own facts.'

The court still has the power make an order under s 39 of the CYPA 1933 to prohibit publication in a newspaper of the picture, name, address or school, or any particulars calculated to lead to the identification, of any child or young person concerned in the proceedings.

---

150 At p 25.

T   AFTER AN INJUNCTION IS MADE

The penal notice

3.41   When the injunction order has been drawn by the court, applicants should ensure that it contains a penal notice warning the respondent of the consequences of breaching the order. The penal notice is required by CPR, r 81.9 in order that the injunction can be enforced by way of committal proceedings. If the order is drawn on Form N16 the penal notice should be included as standard but there have been cases where the penal notice has been omitted resulting in committal proceedings for breach being undermined.[151]

Service

3.42   Proper service of the order is vital to ensuring compliance with it; a respondent cannot be asked to do (or refrain from doing something) unless he has had notice of it. It will also be necessary to demonstrate good service in the event that proceedings need to be taken for a breach of the order.

A copy of the injunction order (and any power of arrest if this is in a separate document) will need to be served on a respondent. Service should normally be effected by personally serving the respondent with a copy of the injunction: CPR, r 81.5.

The court has the power to dispense with personal service if the order contains prohibitions (only) and it considers it just to do so. For prohibitory orders the court can dispense with service where it is satisfied that the respondent had notice of it either because he was present when the order was made or because he was notified of it be telephone, email or otherwise: CPR, r 81.8(1). Service cannot be dispensed with where the order includes positive requirements. Where a copy of the injunction order is given to the respondent directly after the hearing of the application, Applicants are advised to ask the judge/court clerk to record the fact that the respondent has been served on the court file. Any dispensation under CPR, r 81.8(1) should be recorded in the order itself so that it is clear that dispensation has been granted.

If an injunction includes a power of arrest the applicant must deliver a copy of the relevant provisions to any police station for the area where the conduct occurred.[152] If the order containing a power of arrest has been made without notice being given to the respondent, he must be served with a copy of the order before it is delivered to the police station.[153] Where a term containing a power of arrest is varied or discharged the applicant is required immediately to inform the

---

151   The failure to include a penal notice cannot necessarily be corrected as a 'procedural defect' under PD81, para 16.2, it will depend on the facts of the case and upon the court being satisfied that no injustice has been caused to the respondent by the defect.
152   CPR, r 65.44(2)(b).
153   CPR, r 65.44(3).

police station to which a copy of the order has been delivered[154] and to deliver a copy of the varied order to the police station.[155]

U   WHAT TO DO IF AN INJUNCTION IS BREACHED

Who decides whether to pursue a breach and in what circumstances?

3.43   Like ASBIs, the decision whether to pursue a breach of an injunction rests with the applicant. The CPS will no longer need to be involved as they were with breaches of ASBOs.[156]

There is no obligation on an applicant to take action in respect of a breach unless a respondent is arrested under a power of arrest. Applicants may wish to consult with other agencies such as social services or the youth offending team when deciding whether a breach should be pursued. In cases where a respondent has complied with most of the terms of an injunction it may be prudent to send a warning letter rather than institute formal enforcement action. The following considerations will be relevant when deciding whether to take formal enforcement action:

(a)   the fact that a court order with penal notice attached has been breached;

(b)   the need to ensure that a respondent understands that there are consequences attached to his conduct and that court orders are not made to be ignored;

(c)   the seriousness of the breach;

(d)   the impact of the breach on the victim;

(e)   whether there have been previous breaches;

(f)   the quality of the evidence available to support any enforcement action;

(g)   whether criminal charges are being pursued for the same breach;

(h)   the extent to which the respondent is otherwise complying with the injunction.

Both informal and formal responses are available. Informal responses might include a written or verbal warning letter to the defendant. If a formal response is deemed appropriate, this would be by way of proceedings for contempt of court.

---

154 CPR, r 65.44(4)(a).
155 CPR, r 65.44(4)(b).
156 Local authorities were given the power to prosecute breaches of ASBOs but very few seem to have made use of this power.

V CONTEMPT OF COURT

3.44 CPR, Part 81 applies and applications for committal are made in accordance with CPR, Part 23. In summary the application must set out the grounds on which the committal application is made, each breach must be identified separately and numerically and include the date of the breach if it is known: CPR, r 81.10(3). By CPR, r 81.10(4), the application must be supported by affidavit evidence which contains all of the evidence relied upon and must be personally served upon the respondent, unless service is dispensed with or substituted under CPR, r 81.10(5).

A defendant who breaches a civil injunction has defied the will of the court that imposed it. This places him in contempt of court. Contemnors are liable to be punished in a range of ways, to 'discharge' their contempt: imprisonment for a period of up to two years, or an unlimited fine.

Breach of a civil injunction is not, of itself, a criminal offence, though the conduct constituting the breach may also be prosecuted if it amounts to a crime. Owing to the fact that the court has the power to imprison an alleged contemnor, contempt proceedings take on a special legal character, borrowing certain features from the criminal process to minimise the risk of prejudice to the defendant. In particular, the criminal burden and standard of proof applies in committal proceedings, and special rules of procedure are engaged. To mark the solemnity of the proceedings, formal court dress is observed.

Breach proceedings take the form of an application to 'commit' the defendant to prison – though the ultimate sentence if the breach is proven is entirely a matter for the court. These 'committal proceedings' have two stages:

(i) establishing whether a breach has in fact occurred; and if it has

(ii) sentencing the defendant.

Beginning the proceedings

3.45 CPR, Part 81 applies and applications for committal are made in accordance with CPR, Part 23. In summary the application must set out the grounds on which the committal application is made, each breach must be identified separately and numerically and include the date of the breach if it is known: CPR, r 81.10(3).

By CPR, r 81.10(4), the application must be supported by affidavit evidence which contains all of the evidence relied upon and must be personally served upon the respondent, unless service is dispensed with or substituted under CPR, r 81.10(5). If a defendant fails to attend the first hearing, a warrant can be sought for their arrest.[157]

Unlike in other committal proceedings, proceedings in this context can be heard by a district judge: CPR, r 65.47(5).

---

157 s 10.

Arrest and remand

3.46   Where a defendant is arrested in connection with a suspected breach, he or she must be brought before the relevant court within 24 hours.[158] CPR, r 65.30 empowers the judge to 'deal with the matter' there and then, or to adjourn the proceedings (in practice, with case management directions). It is suggested that the power to 'deal with the matter' confers a jurisdiction to proceed to commit the defendant to prison in the absence of a formal committal application, but this would confine the proceedings to the matter for which the defendant was arrested. This initiative jurisdiction must be exercised 'within 28 days' of the first appearance in court (CPR, r 65.47(3)(a)). This is not a fixed limitation period: courts will often extend this period where there is good reason to do so, and CPR, r 65.47(4) provides that expiry does not preclude a separate committal application for the same breach.

The courts may remand an arrested defendant in custody or on bail, either to secure their attendance at a subsequent hearing or for the purposes of a mental health assessment. Strict time limits apply to these remands, which may necessitate multiple review hearings: see Sch 1 to the 2014 Act.

Often, in practice, when an arrest is made for one breach, allegations will emerge regarding other breaches. In order for these other breaches to be taken into account, a separate committal application must be made. Further, some judges are sceptical of the initiative power to proceed to commit in the absence of a formal application so to do: therefore, applicants should assume that it will often be appropriate to make such an application.

Legal aid and representation

3.47   Civil courts in this context should be anxious to avoid committing absent or unrepresented defendants to prison. Criminal legal aid is available to those whose liberty is at risk in these civil committal proceedings: *Brown v LB Haringey*.[159] Before proceeding with a case for committal, the court must satisfy itself that the defendant is aware of this, allowing time for him to make an application for support if he wishes to do so. This applies as much to the question of proving any breaches against the defendant as it does to hearing a plea in mitigation before passing sentence.

Particular difficulties arise with these enquiries where a defendant is absent, or where mental health or other difficulties tend against co-operation with judicial enquiries. The applicant will be expected to be in a position to inform the court of any material matters relating to the defendant's intentions regarding the

---

158   s 9(3). Section 9(2) requires the police to inform the applicant of the arrest as soon as possible. In practice, civil courts often lack the facilities to receive prisoners, and there is a risk that police officers might assume that defendants are to be brought before the magistrates' court. This can cause delay beyond the 24-hour period. Applicants should ensure that arrangements are in place with local custody suites and county courts to ensure that evidence is shared at an early stage, for example through the provision of an out-of-hours telephone number and e-mail address.

159   [2015] EWCA Civ 483.

proceedings or the extent of their mental capacity or vulnerabilities. Applicants should remember that powers of arrest and remand for assessment are available.

Proving the breach(es)

3.48   In the proceedings in which the injunction was obtained, disputed facts needed to be proved on the balance of probabilities (more likely than not). However, in the committal context, the need to observe the criminal standard of proof (beyond reasonable doubt) is usually the most significant obstacle. Applicants should ensure that they have enough evidence to prove the breach before bringing the case to court, without assuming that the defendant will accept the breaches or fail to challenge them. This part of the process is similar to the evidential review stage of the decision whether to bring a criminal prosecution.

To prove a breach, it must be shown that the defendant was aware of the terms of the injunction, that he acted (or failed to act) in a manner which breached the order, and that he knew of the facts that made the conduct a breach. It is not necessary to show that the defendant appreciated that what he was doing would place him in breach of the injunction; however, this will affect his culpability for sentencing purposes: see *Westwood v Knight*.[160]

Giving the defendant the benefit of any reasonable doubt in this context means that hearsay evidence presents greater difficulties than in the proceedings that led to the injunction. As the absence of a witness means that their account cannot be tested in evidence, this can provide a source of reasonable doubt. Applicants enforcing injunctions should be alive to the importance of encouraging witnesses to attend court, and to corroborate their hearsay evidence where their attendance cannot be secured.

Unless the court otherwise orders, written evidence in committal proceedings must be by way of affidavit, which is a sworn form of witness statement: see CPR, rr 81.10(1)(b), 32.16 and PD32, paras 2–16. These formal requirements stand in stark contrast to the defendant's right to call evidence without serving any form of statement: CPR, r 81.28(2). It should be noted that CPR PD81, para 16.2 provides that the court 'may waive any procedural defect in the commencement or conduct of a committal application if satisfied that no injustice has been caused to the respondent by the defect', but this power is sparingly exercised in practice. Applicants may wish to seek to waive the affidavit requirement when obtaining directions to trial where this would entail practical difficulties, for example in requiring witnesses with mobility impairments to attend a solicitor or notary to swear an affidavit at short notice.

Disclosure

3.49   Applicants should pay special regard to their duties of disclosure and candour in committal proceedings. Evidence should be disclosed even where it is harmful to the defence case or might undermine that of the applicant.

---

160 [2012] EWPCC 14 at [38].

Officers in all cases should understand their duties of disclosure and be prepared to face questions about the scope of their investigation into any alleged breach. Disclosure matters should be kept under review throughout the proceedings. Condensed timetables, late or lacking legal representation, and disorganised or inconsistent defendants can all mean that the issues in the case may not become known until very late in the proceedings, which can complicate assessments about relevance of material held by an applicant authority.

To inform assessments of what material held by the authority might be relevant to the issues in the proceedings, those responsible for disclosure should be provided with all pleadings and papers provided by the defence, should strive to be present in court during the committal proceedings, and should document their decisions in a manner similar to that required in criminal proceedings. Practitioners should treat with caution proposals to agree that no further disclosure is required or that disclosure of the full housing file will suffice: such matters are unlikely to contain material relevant to the investigation of an alleged breach.

Sentencing

3.50   The courts can punish any proven breach with a sentence of imprisonment of up to two years, which can be suspended for up to two years ('on such terms or conditions as it may specify': CPR, r 81.29), or an unlimited fine. It may also choose to impose no penalty at all. Sentencing options typical in criminal proceedings, such as community orders and unpaid work, are not available.

Case law confirms that when the court sentences a respondent for breach of an ASBI the court should consider the guidance issued by the Sentencing Guidelines Council in relation to breaches of ASBOs.[161] The Sentencing Guidelines state that:

(a)   the main aim of sentencing for breach of a court order is to achieve the purpose of the order;[162]

(b)   the assessment of the seriousness of an individual offence must take into account not only the harm caused by an offence but also any harm that was intended or might foreseeably have been caused;[163]

(c)   the harm caused may range from no harassment, alarm or distress being caused to serious harassment, alarm or distress and the sentencing increases accordingly:[164]

    (i)   where serious harassment, alarm or distress was caused by the breach, the starting point is 26 weeks' imprisonment;

    (ii)   in less serious cases causing harassment, alarm or distress, the starting point is six weeks' imprisonment; and

---

161 *Amicus Horizon Ltd v Thorley* [2012] EWCA Civ 817, [2012] HLR 43 and *Islington LBC v Doey* [2012] EWCA Civ 1825, [2013] HLR 13.

162 Sentencing Guidelines Council: *Breach of an Anti-Social Behaviour Order, Definitive Guideline*, December 2008, p 2, para 6.

163 Ibid, p 3, para 13.

164 Ibid, p 9.

(iii)   imprisonment will not usually be appropriate where no harassment, alarm or distress was caused by the breach.

Youths

3.51   Breach of an injunction by a respondent who is under 18 is dealt with in the youth court and could result in a supervision, curfew or activity requirement. Detention orders are also available for youths aged between 14 and 17. The powers of the court in relation to breach of an injunction by a youth are set out in Sch 2 to the Act.

Sentencing guidelines published for the criminal courts dealing with breaches of (now defunct) ASBOs can be taken into account by the civil courts upon sentencing a breach of a civil injunction: *Amicus Horizon v Thorley.*[165]

Costs

3.52   Where a committal application has been made, the usual costs principles apply. Courts are generally willing to recognise that an applicant in committal proceedings is doing a civic duty in enforcing an injunction of this nature but may still be penalised in costs if their conduct is unreasonable.

Publicity

3.53   Practitioners should be aware of the Practice Direction and complementary Practice Guidance on committal applications, issued by Thomas LCJ in March and June 2015 respectively. The Practice Direction provides that committal hearings must be placed in the public court list, conferring a right on the public to obtain copies of committal applications in all but exceptional circumstances, and limiting the discretion of the court to hear committal applications in private. It obliges the court to provide a summary of its decision with reasons for publication on the gov.uk website.[166] A proforma is provided in the Practice Guidance which practitioners should draw to the attention of the committing judge.

Committal and other proceedings

3.54   A finding that an injunction has been breached can have important consequences in possession proceedings against a defendant who is also a tenant in social housing. A finding of breach (including by admission) may give rise to a mandatory ground for possession: see Part 5 of the 2014 Act.

---

165 [2012] EWCA Civ 817.
166 A repository of committal decisions is available at https://www.judiciary.uk/subject/contempt-of-court/.

For this reason, defendants are often keen to avoid a finding of breach by offering an undertaking to observe the injunction in the future, or by obtaining an undertaking that the mandatory ground will not be relied upon in separate proceedings. Any proven breach should be recorded on the face of any draft order, including any order adjourning the proceedings for sentence, to avoid delay in obtaining an official record of the finding of a breach to be deployed in possession proceedings.

Where a breach leads to both civil contempt and criminal proceedings, the rule is that the first court to impose a sentence must not presuppose a punishment that has yet to be imposed by the second court, but the second court must take account of the punishment imposed by the first: *Gill v Birmingham City Council.*[167]

X   YOUTHS – CHECKLIST

3.55   Applications where the respondent is under 18 have particular requirements. Below is a checklist of the relevant considerations:

(a)   applicants must consult the local youth offending team (in addition to informing anybody else they think is appropriate)[168];

(b)   applications are to be made in the youth court;[169]

(c)   youths cannot be excluded from the place they usually live;[170]

(d)   injunctions in respect of youths cannot be open ended and cannot last longer than 12 months;[171]

(e)   breach of an injunction is dealt with by the youth court and not by way of a civil contempt;[172]

(f)   an application can rely on behaviour occurring in the six months prior to the complaint being laid.[173]

Applicants are encouraged to work with the parents of the young person in seeking to deal with the problem. Efforts should be made to ascertain whether there are any underlying issues that need to be addressed such as learning difficulties or mental health problems. In many cases it will be appropriate to *consult* the young person's parents despite the absence of a statutory requirement to do so. In every case the parents should be *informed* of the intention to make an order in respect of a young person even though there is no statutory requirement to do so.

---

167 [2016] EWCA Civ 608.
168 s 14(1).
169 s 1(8)(a).
170 s 13(1)(a).
171 s 1(6).
172 Sch 2.
173 Magistrates' Courts Act 1980, s 127.

Many applicants[174] will have duties under s 11 of the Children Act 2004 to 'safeguard and promote the welfare of children'.[175] This reinforces the need to ensure that alternative forms of managing the behaviour are considered and any underlying needs are assessed and addressed.

Y EXISTING ASBOS, ASBIS ETC

3.56 Section 21 of the Act sets out the transitional provisions for 'existing orders'. Existing orders are defined as:

(a) an anti-social behaviour injunction under HA 1996, s 153A;

(b) an injunction under HA 1996, s 153B (injunction against unlawful use of premises);

(c) an injunction in which anything is included by virtue of HA 1996, s 153D(3) or (4) (power to include provision banning person from premises or area, or to include power of arrest, in injunction against breach of tenancy agreement);

(d) an order under CDA 1998, s 1 or 1B (anti-social behaviour orders etc);

(e) an individual support order under CDA 1998, s 1AA made in connection with an order under CDA 1998, s 1 or 1B;

(f) an intervention order under CDA 1998, s 1G;

(g) a drinking banning order under VCRA 2006, s 3 or 4.

The repeals and amendments introduced by the Act do not apply in relation to any application made **before 20 October 2014** for an existing order, or anything done in connection with an existing order or application.

If an existing order is still in force as at 20 October 2019 it will be treated as if the provisions of the existing order were a provision of an injunction made under s 1 of the Act.[176] This will mean that the enforcement of the existing order will change to become consistent with enforcement of injunctions made under Part 1 of the Act.

Z CONCLUSION

3.57 Part 1 of the Act contains a powerful set of provisions which should be deployed with caution. There are clearly human rights implications in their use and there are a number of other important considerations too, especially where

---

174 Children Act 2004, s 11 applies, inter alia, to: local authorities, an NHS trust all or most of whose hospitals, establishments and facilities are situated in England, an NHS foundation trust, the local policing body and chief officer of police for a police area in England, the British Transport Police Authority, so far as exercising functions in relation to England, and a youth offending team for an area in England.

175 Children Act 2004, s 11(2)(a).

176 s 21(5).

vulnerable perpetrators and victims are part of the picture. It remains unclear how far county court judges in particular are prepared to use curfews and non-association clauses; these are concepts which the criminal courts are already familiar with but sometimes reluctant to use. Robust advocacy and clear evidence will be required in support of applications to impose these types of terms.

The ability to control when enforcement action is taken is a welcome improvement on the previous ASBO position. Applicants will now retain control of the enforcement decision instead of relying on the CPS where there was a breach of an ASBO. However, there are a number of practical considerations relating to the use of injunctions. The vast majority of cases are heard in the county court (both for the initial application and for breach). There are increasingly long waiting times for court listings and reduced court centres, and the inevitable additional workload caused by injunctions serve to put greater pressure on the court service. There is the potential for an increase in the number of prison terms being imposed for breach and most county courts do not have the facilities to hold those who are given custodial sentences.

In early 2018, the Civil Justice Council noted that there was growing concern about the way the s 1 injunctions were being sought and/or used, the powers afforded to the courts, the limited powers available to the county court on breach, whether third parties should be involved in the process, and whether breaches of these orders were then a shortcut to mandatory (absolute ground) possession orders.

The still new injunctions are certainly far more than a re-modelled version of the old ASBI. Their true practical use will only be worked out in the fullness of time and will continue to be considered further in future editions of this book.

CHAPTER 4

Criminal behaviour orders

Snapshot

What's out
- ASBOs on conviction
- Drink banning orders on conviction

What's in
- Criminal Behaviour Orders ('CBOs')

Key points
- Minimum term of two years (one year for youths)
- Interim orders are available
- Positive requirements can be imposed as well as prohibitions
- Breach is a criminal offence

> **Resources**
> See Appendix E for a list of sample prohibitions for use in a CBO.

A   INTRODUCTION: THE POWERS WHICH HAVE BEEN REPLACED

4.01   The criminal behaviour order (CBO) is the post-conviction order created by Part 2 of the Act. A CBO can be sought when an offender has been convicted of an offence. It is in effect the old ASBO on conviction or 'CRASBO' as it was sometimes known. The relevant sections of the Act are ss 22 to 33.[1]

CBOs replace the following powers:

(a)   anti-social behaviour orders under s 1C of the Crime and Disorder Act 1998 (CDA 1998); and

(b)   drink banning orders under s 6 of the Violent Crime Reduction Act 2006 (VCRA 2006).

There is a real opportunity available to enforcement agencies to obtain CBOs through partnership working with the police and Crown Prosecution Service (CPS). In many cases CBOs could prove to be a quicker and more cost effective route to obtaining restrictions and/or prohibitions of a type that would ordinarily be sought in a civil injunction under Part 1 of the Act.

The Revised Guidance suggests that CBOs can be used to deal with a wide range of anti-social behaviour including threatened violence against others in the community, persistent drunk and aggressive behaviour in public or to deal with anti-social behaviour associated with a more serious conviction such as burglary or street robbery.[2]

The Revised Guidance also highlights the ability to use CBOs to tackle gang-related problems by preventing gang members from associating with named individuals, or to require them to attend a job readiness course to help them obtain employment.[3]

B   WHEN CAN A CBO BE SOUGHT?

4.02   A CBO can only be made in addition to:

(i)   a sentence in respect of an offence; or

(ii)   an order discharging the offender conditionally.[4]

---

1   All statutory references are to the Anti-Social Behaviour, Crime and Policing Act 2014 unless otherwise stated.
2   Revised *Statutory Guidance for Frontline Professionals*, p 30.
3   Revised *Statutory Guidance for Frontline Professionals*, p 30.
4   s 22(6).

The test

4.03   The court can make a CBO in respect of an offender if:

(i)   it is satisfied that the offender has engaged in conduct that caused, or was likely to cause harassment, alarm or distress to any person; and

(ii)   it considers that the making of the CBO will help in preventing the offender from engaging in such behaviour in the future.[5]

Unlike injunctions under Part 1 of the Act where the behaviour must be proved to the civil standard, the existence of behaviour that caused or was likely to cause harassment, alarm or distress must be proved to the criminal standard, ie beyond reasonable doubt.[6]

As to the second part of the test, namely whether the making of the CBO will help in preventing further behaviour, the Court of Appeal has held that it is not necessary to prove this beyond reasonable doubt but that this was a matter of judgement for the court: *R v Browne-Morgan*[7] cited with approval in *R v Khan (Kamran)*,[8] the latest significant decision on CBOs.

Example of when an application for a CBO could be made

The behaviour
Graffiti has been painted on a housing estate which encompasses an area known as Hestone Park. The estate is situated in the London Borough of Hounslow. Large numbers of youths are congregating in the children's play area in the Park late at night. They are noisy and have been drinking and taking drugs. They are also responsible for leaving the area covered in bottles, cigarette ends, plastic bags and empty takeaway food containers. A number of the residents have complained that they find the graffiti unsightly and that the content is often rude or offensive. The behaviour meets the definition of conduct likely to cause harassment, alarm or distress.

Conviction
Limited to the criminal damage caused by the graffiti.

Apply for a CBO
In addition to any sentence imposed in respect of the offence, the court could be asked to make a CBO to include the following prohibitions:

(1)   not to carry a spray can in Hestone park;

---

5   s 22(1)–(4).
6   s 22(3).
7   [2016] EWCA Crim 1903, [2017] 4 WLR 118, at [15].
8   [2018] EWCA Crim 1472, [2018] 1 WLR 5419, at [12]–[14].

(2)   not to enter the children's play area in Hestone park as defined by the red border on the attached map [that being the area in which the defendant was found on conviction to have painted graffiti].

Local authority provides evidence that problem is more widespread

The local authority could provide evidence that the graffiti by the defendant was not limited to the children's play area but extended to areas on its estate. It could also provide evidence of the large numbers of youths congregating in the children's play area and/or evidence that the convicted defendant's presence was attracting other youths to the estate.

Outcome

Prohibitions in the CBO that relate to a broader area or which exclude the defendant from the whole of the affected area, eg:

(1)   not to carry a spray can in any public place anywhere in the London Borough of Hounslow;

(2)   not to enter the Hestone Park estate as defined by the red border on the attached map.

There is no need to apply for a free standing injunction.

C WHAT IS HARASSMENT, ALARM OR DISTRESS?

4.04   This phrase was used in relation to ASBOs and appears in the Act in the context of both CBOs and non-housing related applications for civil injunctions.

Existing case law in relation to this phrase will be relevant to applications for CBOs and is considered in further detail in Chapter 3 at 3.05.

D WHO CAN APPLY?

4.05   A CBO can only be applied for by the prosecution.[9] This means that the vast majority of applications will be made by the CPS. A local authority will be able to apply for a CBO where it is the prosecutor, for example when it is the prosecuting authority under the Environmental Protection Act 1990.

The CPS can make an application for a CBO of its own initiative or at the request of another. Where complaints have been made to enforcement agencies (other than the police), the agencies should seek to work closely with the police and/or the CPS in order to ensure they have the information they require to decide whether to apply for a CBO.

---

9   s 22(7).

Effective co-ordination between agencies has the potential to save resources and to avoid a duplication of work. Existing procedures for sharing information should allow the various agencies to supply information to the police and/or the CPS in a timely manner with a view to securing a CBO.

E   HOW TO APPLY

Criminal Procedure Rules Part 31 [10]

4.06   Part 31 of the Criminal Procedure Rules ('Crim PR') applies to orders made under s 22 of the Act.[11] A final CBO cannot be made until the defendant has had an opportunity to:[12]

(a)   consider what order is proposed and why and the evidence in support;

(b)   make representations at a hearing.

The above restrictions do not apply to an interim order.[13] An interim order will be of no effect unless the defendant was present when the order was made[14] or is handed a document recording the order not more than seven days after it is made.[15]

A notice of intention to apply for a CBO must be served on the court, the defendant and any person on whom the order would be likely to have a significant adverse effect.[16] The notice must be served as soon as possible and without waiting for the verdict.

The notice of intention to apply must:[17]

(a)   summarise the relevant facts;

(b)   identify the evidence on which the prosecutor relies in support;

(c)   attach any written statement that the prosecutor has not already served; and

(d)   specify the order that the prosecutor wants the court to make.

A defendant who is served with a notice of intention must serve written notice of any evidence on which he relies as soon as possible (and without waiting for the verdict). In that notice the defendant must identify the evidence on which he relies and attach any written statement that has not already been served.[18]

---

10   October 2015 as amended October 2016 and April 2017.
11   Crim PR, r 30.1(3)(a)(vii).
12   Crim PR r 30.2.
13   Crim PR, r 31.2(2).
14   Crim PR, r 31.2(2)(a)(i).
15   Crim PR, r 31.2(2)(a)(ii).
16   Crim PR, r 31.3(2).
17   Crim PR, r 31.3(3).
18   Crim PR, r 31.3(4).

If the prosecutor seeks special measures to assist the defendant or any of the witnesses to give evidence he must apply when serving the notice of intention to apply for a CBO.[19]

A CBO takes effect on the day it is made.[20] The court has the power to delay the date when the CBO takes effect if the offender is already subject to a CBO. In this situation the court can decide that the new order is to take effect when the existing order ceases to have effect.[21] The language of s 25(2) of the Act appears to allow more than one CBO to run concurrently and checks should be made to establish whether the defendant is already subject to a CBO for two reasons: (i) there may be scope to vary an existing order; or (ii) the existing order may need to be brought to a premature end if a new CBO is made.

Evidence

4.07   In deciding whether to make a CBO the court may consider evidence from both the prosecution and the offender and it does not matter that the evidence is of a type that would have been inadmissible in the proceedings in which the offender was convicted.[22]

This means that the prosecution can rely on evidence of anti-social behaviour which is broader than the offence for which the offender was convicted; this would be with a view to securing a CBO which covers all aspects of the offender's anti-social behaviour.

Evidence that would otherwise have been inadmissible (for example, by reason of it being hearsay) can also be used in support of a CBO.

Written notice of the intention to rely on hearsay must be served on the court and every other party directly affected.[23] The notice must explain: (i) that it is a notice of hearsay evidence; (ii) identify that evidence; (iii) identify the person who made the statement or explain why that person is not identified; and (iv) explain why that person will not be called to give oral evidence.[24]

A party can apply to the court for permission to cross-examine a person who made a statement which another party wishes to introduce as hearsay. Any such application must be made in writing and not more than seven days after the service of the notice of hearsay evidence.[25]

19   Crim PR, r 31.3(7); the time limits in Crim PR, r 18.3(a) do not apply.
20   s 25(1).
21   s 25(2).
22   s 23(1) and (2).
23   Crim PR, r 31.6.
24   Crim PR, r 31.6(b).
25   Crim PR, r 31.7, which also contains further rules about who the application must be served on and how the application can be dealt with by the court.

Example – using hearsay evidence

Behaviour
Verbal abuse and threats towards a named neighbour who lives in a block of flats where other neighbours have also been subjected to verbal abuse and anti-social behaviour.

Conviction
Public Order Act 1986, s 5 offence of using threatening words or behaviour towards the named neighbour.

Apply for a CBO
The CBO could prevent the defendant from using threatening words or behaviour to *any* of the residents of a particular block of flats and not just the named victim.

How to do this – using hearsay evidence
The CPS could adduce evidence from a housing officer which details the complaints made by *other* residents who have been victims of verbal abuse by the defendant but who are unwilling to be identified for fear of reprisal. The evidence could take the form of a witness statement signed by the housing officer which explains that the residents are fearful of giving evidence and which exhibits the anonymised witness statements of residents A, B and C. Criminal charges could not be pursued for the behaviour in respect of these witnesses because they are unwilling to be identified, and even if they were identified the court would not be likely to admit their written evidence unless they were willing to come to court. Any evidence that is not oral evidence would not normally be admissible in a criminal prosecution.[26] However, the

---

26   There are some exceptions, for example in relation to business documents, see s 117 of the Criminal Justice Act 2003 (CJA 2003). In addition, s 116 of the CJA 2003 makes provision for evidence that would otherwise be inadmissible to be admitted if the witness is unavailable (through fear for example: CJA 2003, s 116(2)(e)) and the court has given leave to adduce the evidence. In many cases the CPS decides not to pursue a prosecution where live evidence is not available. The full text of s 116 is as follows:

    '116 Cases where a witness is unavailable

    (1) In criminal proceedings a statement not made in oral evidence in the proceedings is admissible as evidence of any matter stated if—

        (a) oral evidence given in the proceedings by the person who made the statement would be admissible as evidence of that matter,

        (b) the person who made the statement (the relevant person) is identified to the court's satisfaction, and

        (c) any of the five conditions mentioned in subsection (2) is satisfied.

    (2) The conditions are—

        (a) that the relevant person is dead;

        (b) that the relevant person is unfit to be a witness because of his bodily or mental condition;

        (c) that the relevant person is outside the United Kingdom and it is not reasonably practicable to secure his attendance;

evidence could be sufficient to form the basis of a CBO with terms which protect all of the residents. None of the anonymous residents would need to be identified or attend court.

A notice of intention to rely on hearsay evidence would need to be served in accordance with Crim PR, r 31.6.

There is a textbox on the use of hearsay evidence in Chapter 3: see 3.36.

F   ADJOURNMENTS AND ABSENT DEFENDANTS

4.08   The court has the power to adjourn an application for a CBO even after sentencing the offender. If the offender does not appear for an adjourned hearing the court can further adjourn the proceedings, issue a warrant for the offender's arrest or hear the proceedings in the offender's absence.[27]

If the court decides to proceed in the offender's absence it must be satisfied that the offender has had adequate notice of the time and place of the adjourned hearing and has been informed that if s/he does not appear the court may hear the proceedings in his/her absence.[28] The rules which apply to applications for CBOs are set out in 4.06 above.

Personal service of the order should be effected as soon as if practicable if a CBO is made in the offender's absence.

(d)   that the relevant person cannot be found although such steps as it is reasonably practicable to take to find him have been taken;

(e)   that through fear the relevant person does not give (or does not continue to give) oral evidence in the proceedings, either at all or in connection with the subject matter of the statement, and the court gives leave for the statement to be given in evidence.

(3)   For the purposes of subsection (2)(e) "fear" is to be widely construed and (for example) includes fear of the death or injury of another person or of financial loss.

(4)   Leave may be given under subsection (2)(e) only if the court considers that the statement ought to be admitted in the interests of justice, having regard—

(a)   to the statement's contents,

(b)   to any risk that its admission or exclusion will result in unfairness to any party to the proceedings (and in particular to how difficult it will be to challenge the statement if the relevant person does not give oral evidence),

(c)   in appropriate cases, to the fact that a direction under section 19 of the Youth Justice and Criminal Evidence Act 1999 (c. 23) (special measures for the giving of evidence by fearful witnesses etc) could be made in relation to the relevant person, and

(d)   to any other relevant circumstances.

(5)   A condition set out in any paragraph of subsection (2) which is in fact satisfied is to be treated as not satisfied if it is shown that the circumstances described in that paragraph are caused—

(a)   by the person in support of whose case it is sought to give the statement in evidence, or

(b)   by a person acting on his behalf, in order to prevent the relevant person giving oral evidence in the proceedings (whether at all or in connection with **the subject matter of the statement**).'

27   s 23(4).
28   s 23(6).

G   THE TERMS OF A CBO – PROHIBITIONS AND POSITIVE REQUIREMENTS

4.09   A CBO can *prohibit* the offender from doing anything described in the order. In addition, it can include terms which *require* the offender to do anything described in the order.[29] Readers are referred for more detail to Chapter 3 on injunctions which contains a section on positive requirements and the evidence required to obtain them: see 3.18–3.19, and Appendix E for a list of sample prohibitions.

The Revised Guidance gives the following examples of positive requirements:[30]

- attendance at an anger management course where an offender finds it difficult to respond without violence;

- youth mentoring;

- attendance at substance misuse awareness sessions where an offender's behaviour occurs when they have been drinking or using drugs; or

- a job readiness course to help an offender get employment and move away from the circumstances that cause them to commit anti-social behaviour.

As with applications for positive requirements within Part 1 injunctions, the court must receive evidence about the suitability and enforceability of any requirement from the person or organisation responsible for supervising the requirement.[31]

In *R v John James*[32] the Court of Appeal gave some guidance on a CBO which would have interfered with a person's usual place of work. The facts of that case were that the defendant was targeting the old and vulnerable and overcharging them for gardening and home improvements. A CBO was made following two convictions for fraud contrary to s 1 of the Fraud Act 2006. The CBO prevented the defendant from 'approaching or entering, directly or indirectly any address within the United Kingdom…'. He argued that the CBO was disproportionate and prevented him from working to provide for himself and his family in his usual occupation. The Court of Appeal gave guidance on the interpretation of s 22(9) which prevents the court from making a CBO which interferes with a person's usual place of work; it held that where the conduct derives from the very performance of the work, there was no *a priori* reason not to make a CBO in an appropriate case.

The Court of Appeal gave further guidance in the case of *R v Khan (Kamran)*[33] and confirmed that the observations of the Court in *Boness* continue to apply to CBOs. The facts in *Khan* were that the defendant had appealed a sentence imposed as a result of convictions for dangerous driving and the supply and possession of a controlled drug. In addition, the sentencing court had made a

29   s 22(5).
30   Revised *Statutory Guidance for Frontline Professionals*, p 31.
31   s 24.
32   [2016] EWCA Crim 676.
33   [2018] EWCA Crim 1472, [2018] 1 WLR 5419.

CBO prohibiting the defendant from associating with his co-defendant in a public place or a place to which the public had access (including inside a mechanically propelled vehicle) for a period of three years. The order applied to the whole of England and Wales. The Court of Appeal stated that:[34]

> 'a court should ask itself before making an order "Are the terms of this order clear so that the offender will know precisely what it is that he is prohibited from doing?" Prohibitions should be reasonable and proportionate; realistic and practical; and be in terms which make it easy to determine and prosecute a breach. Exclusion zones should be clearly delineated (generally with the use of clearly marked maps, although we do not consider that there is a problem of definition in an order extending to Greater Manchester) and individuals whom the defendant is prohibited from contacting or associating with should be clearly identified. In the case of a foreign national, consideration should be given to the need for the order to be translated.'

The following should be borne in mind:[35]

- a CBO must contain precise terms that are capable of being understood by the offender;

- the findings of fact giving rise to the order must be recorded;

- the order must be explained to the offender; and

- the exact terms of the order must be pronounced in open court and the written order must accurately reflect the order as pronounced.

H   DURATION

4.10   The CBO must state the period for which it is to have effect.[36] Different prohibitions and requirements may have effect for differing periods.[37]

Section 27 of the Act allows the defendant or the prosecution to apply to vary or discharge a CBO. This is dealt with in greater detail at 4.15 below. It is worth noting that there is nothing to prevent an application to discharge the order being made before the one or two years has expired. If an application is successful the order could end up lasting for less than the minimum term.[38]

---

34   Ibid at [15].
35   Ibid at [14].
36   s 25(3).
37   s 25(6).
38   Unlike the position with ASBOs where there was a statutory prohibition on an ASBO being discharged before the end of the minimum two year term (unless the parties consented): CDA 1998, s 1(9).

Adults

4.11   Where the offender is aged 18 or above a CBO must last for a fixed period of not less than two years' duration or until 'further order',[39] but individual terms may be shorter than two years, see 4.10 above.

In *R v Nasser Asfi*[40]a 10-year CBO was reduced to seven years by the Court of Appeal which thought this was an appropriate length of time to ensure that the public would be adequately protected.

Youths

4.12   For offenders under 18 the CBO must be for a fixed period of not less than one year and no more than three years.[41] See also 4.21–4.23 on the need to review CBOs made in respect of youths.

I   INTERIM ORDERS

4.13   The court has the power to adjourn an application for a CBO even after sentencing an offender.[42] The requirement to serve a notice of intention to apply for a CBO does not apply to interim orders. As set out above, an interim order will be of no effect unless the defendant was present when the order was made[43] or is handed a document recording the order not more than seven days after it was made.[44]

Section 26 of the Act allows the court to make an interim CBO where the hearing of the main application has been adjourned.

Unlike interim ASBOs which had to be for a fixed term, interim CBOs can last until a fixed date or until 'further order'.[45]

J   CONSULTATION

4.14   The consultation requirements are minimal: the prosecution must 'seek the views' of the local youth offending team where an offender will be under 18 when the application is made.[46] There are no consultation requirements in respect of adults. There is a textbox on the duty to consult in Chapter 3: see 3.26.

---

39   s 25(5).
40   [2016] EWCA Crim 1236.
41   s 25(4).
42   s 23(3).
43   Crim PR, r 31.2(2)(a)(i).
44   Crim PR, r 31.2(2)(a)(ii).
45   Interim ASBOs had to be a for a fixed period: CDA 1998, s 1D(4)(a).
46   s 22(8). See s 22(10) for the meaning of 'youth offending team'.

K VARIATION AND DISCHARGE

4.15   A CBO may be varied or discharged by the court which made it. Both the prosecution and the offender can apply to vary or discharge under s 27 of the Act.

The court's power to vary includes the power to include additional prohibitions or requirements and to extend the period for which a prohibition or requirement has effect.[47]

If an application under s 27 is dismissed, the party who made the application may not make any further applications under that section unless it obtains the consent of the court or the agreement of the other party.[48]

It is notable that the provisions do not prevent an application to discharge an order before the minimum term. This differs from the position with ASBOs where there was a statutory prohibition on an ASBO being discharged before the end of the minimum two-year term (unless the parties consented).[49]

L PUBLICITY

4.16   In many cases the making of a CBO will be publicised. It is difficult to envisage a situation where no publicity will be warranted, even if the information sharing is limited to the witnesses who provided information to support the application for the order. The desire (and need) to publicise an order gives rise to some interesting issues which are considered below under the heading 'general considerations'.

Adults

4.17   There is no restriction on the reporting of a CBO where the defendant is an adult. Established practice with regard to publicity is that it should be tailored to the requirements of each individual case and should make clear whether an order is an interim order or a final order. In some cases only the victims will need to be notified that an order has been made, in other cases it may be appropriate to circulate leaflets on an estate or publish an article in a residents' newsletter. Wider publicity may be required where there is a risk that the behaviour may be displaced to another area.

Youths

4.18   Section 49 of the Children and Young Persons Act 1933 (CYPA 1933) imposes reporting restrictions on certain proceedings including those in the youth court (or on appeal from the youth court). Under CYPA 1933, s 49 no

---

47   s 27(4).
48   s 27(2) and (3).
49   CDA 1998, s 1(9).

report can be published which reveals the name, address or school of any child or young person concerned in the proceedings or which includes any particulars likely to lead to the identification of any child or young person concerned in the proceedings. In addition, no picture can be published of any child or young person concerned in the proceedings. Clearly this would make the ability to monitor compliance with a CBO extremely difficult because it inhibits the ability to inform the community (in particular those affected by the behaviour) of its existence or terms.

For this reason, the usual automatic reporting restrictions in respect of an offender under 18 do not apply for CBOs by virtue of s 23(8)(a) of the Act. The Guidance states[50]:

> 'Publicising a CBO issued to a young person: Making the public aware of the offender and the terms of the order can be an important part of the process in dealing with anti-social behaviour. It can provide reassurance to communities that action is being taken and it will provide the information local people need to identify and report breaches. The decision to publicise a CBO will be taken by the police or council unless the court has made a section 39 order (Children and Young Persons Act 1933) prohibiting publication. When deciding whether to publicise a CBO, public authorities (including the courts) must consider that it is necessary and proportionate to interfere with the young person's right to privacy, and the likely impact on a young person's behaviour. This will need to be balanced against the need to provide re-assurance to the victims and the wider community as well as providing them with information so that they can report any breaches. Each case should be considered carefully on its own facts'

It is important to note that the lifting of the automatic reporting restrictions does not apply to the criminal offence of which the youth has been convicted and care must be taken to ensure that the publicity of the CBO does not reveal this information.

The court still has the *power* make an order under s 39 of the CYPA 1933 to prohibit publication in a newspaper of the picture, name, address or school, or any particulars calculated to lead to the identification, of any child or young person concerned in the proceedings.[51]

Similar publicity rules apply to a proven breach of a CBO except that the power to restrict the reporting of criminal proceedings involving young persons (in the event that a court decides such restrictions are necessary) is found in s 45 of the Youth Justice and Criminal Evidence Act 1999.

General considerations

4.19   Publicising an order can be vital in ensuring the order is effectively enforced. Publicity can give a great deal of comfort to local communities and

---

50   Revised *Statutory Guidance for Frontline Professionals* p 30.
51   s 23(8)(b).

can provide reassurance that the problems in the area are being monitored and addressed. Knowing that the local authority or police are actively monitoring a particular type of behaviour and taking action where warranted can improve confidence in local services and act as an effective deterrent to those engaged in such behaviour.

In many cases it is only when local residents and businesses are made aware of the existence of an order that they can ensure the relevant authorities are informed if they witness a breach. In other cases the publicity can prompt parents to take a greater interest in the behaviour of their children. Publicity can also trigger a greater deal of engagement with housing officers when it comes to compliance with terms and conditions of a tenancy.

A relevant and competing consideration is the risk of an order being regarded as a 'badge of honour' to be desired rather than avoided. After the introduction of ASBOs and the implementation of the Labour Government's 'Respect' agenda, it was widely reported that some youths enjoyed the notoriety which they gained by behaviour singled out as particularly serious. The research which was undertaken delivered a more nuanced picture, but nonetheless there remained a clear evidence base for the concern about glamorising anti-social behaviour, which will likely endure where orders are publicised, whatever the name of the mechanism used to restrict anti-social behaviour.[52]

Publicising an order engages the Article 8[53] rights of both the defendant and potentially the victims of the behaviour. Article 8 provides that everyone has a right to 'respect for their private and family life' and that interference with this right must be 'in accordance with the law' and 'necessary in a democratic society in the interests of … public safety … for the prevention of disorder or crime, for the protection of health or morals, or for the protection of the rights and freedoms of others'.

The Article 8 rights of a defendant were considered by the High Court in *R (on the application of Stanley) v Metropolitan Police Commissioner, Brent LBC v Secretary of State for the Home Department.*[54] The facts of the case were that the local authority and police obtained interim ASBOs in respect of youths who been terrorising the neighbourhood by verbally abusing and threatening residents, drugs use, graffiti and throwing rubbish. The local authority and police decided to publicise the interim ASBOs by distributing leaflets which named the youths and included their addresses and photographs. The local authority put the details on its website and in its residents' newsletter and the orders were widely reported in the local and national media.

Three of the defendants sought to judicially review the decision to publicise and argued that the publicity was unlawful and in breach of their Article 8 rights. In particular, the defendants argued that it was not necessary or proportionate to include their photographs and personal details and that the material should not have been distributed outside the exclusion zone specified in the ASBOs.

---

52   See, for example, the Youth Justice Board research into ASBOs: 'A summary of research into Anti-Social Behaviour Orders given to young people between January 2004 and January 2005'.

53   Article 8 of the European Convention on Human Rights.

54   [2004] EWHC 2229 (Admin), [2005] HLR 8.

The High Court dismissed the application. The following points come out of the judgment of Kennedy J:

(a) informing residents of the existence of an ASBO can be invaluable in enforcing the order;

(b) the publicity was unlikely to be effective unless it contained photographs, names and at least partial addresses; there must be no room for mis-identification;

(c) there was no case for contending that the publicity should be confined to the exclusion zone;

(d) the wider publicity which was intended to provide information and reassurance could not be criticised.[55]

The judge reinforced the need for publicity to be considered on a case-by-case basis and that the Article 8 rights of those against whom orders have been made should be taken into consideration when deciding what form the publicity should take.

An audit trail should be kept about how decisions on publicity have been made. The records should demonstrate that the decision makers have considered whether the form(s) of publicity chosen are necessary and proportionate on the facts of the particular case.

Publicising orders is also considered in Chapter 3 at 3.38.

Decisions about publicity – checklist
The judge in *Stanley* suggested that those considering post-order publicity should record their decision-making process and the factors that have been taken into consideration. Decision-makers may wish to use the following checklist as a prompt for the factors to be taken into account and recorded. Particular care should be taken when dealing with young people:

(a) What is the purpose of the publicity? Informing the community, reassurance and/or deterrent or a combination of these?

(b) What form should the publicity take? Consider leaflets, press release, newsletter.

(c) Should a photograph be included?

(d) How widely should the publicity material be distributed?

(e) Do you want to publicise an interim order or will you wait for the final order?[56]

---

55 Paragraphs 40–41 of the judgment of Kennedy J.
56 In Keating v Knowsley Metropolitan Borough Council [2004] EWHC 1933 (Admin), [2005] HLR 3 it was held that interim orders could be publicised.

(f) What information will you include? As a minimum the publicity must say if the order is an interim one to avoid giving the impression that a final order has been made.

(g) Is it appropriate to publicise all the terms of the order or only some?

(h) Will the publicity create a risk to the victims or to the defendant? Can this be mitigated, and if so how?

(i) The Article 8 rights of the defendant and of the wider community.

The overriding considerations are that the publicity must be necessary and proportionate.[57]

M BREACH

4.20 By virtue of s 30(1) of the Act breach of either a prohibition or positive requirement in a CBO is a criminal offence and any breach would need to be proved to the criminal standard of proof, beyond reasonable doubt.

If a breach is proved the defendant is liable:

(a) on summary conviction, to imprisonment for a period not exceeding six months or to a fine, or to both;[58] and

(b) on conviction on indictment, to imprisonment for a period not exceeding five years or to a fine, or to both.[59]

Where a person is convicted of an offence under s 30 the court cannot make an order for a conditional discharge.[60]

N REVIEW REQUIREMENTS

4.21 CBOs made in respect of those that are under the age of 18 at the end of a 'review period' must be reviewed every 12 months if they have not been discharged.[61]

The review must be carried out before the end of the 'review period' which is defined in s 28(2) of the Act as the period of 12 months beginning with the day

---

57   At the time of writing specific guidance relating to the publicising of the powers under the Act had not been published. The guidance issued by the Home Office, Publicising Anti-Social Behaviour Orders, March 2005 contains some useful further information and is available at http://webarchive.nationalarchives.gov.uk/20100405140447/http:/asb.homeoffice.gov.uk/uploadedFiles/Members_site/Documents_and_images/Enforcement_tools_and_powers/ASBOs_PublicisingGuidance_0031.pdf.

58   s 30(2)(a).

59   s 30(2)(b).

60   s 30(3).

61   s 28(1).

on which the order takes effect (or the date the CBO was varied under s 27) or beginning with the day after the end of the previous review period.

Who carries out the review?

4.22   A review under s 28 must be carried out by the chief officer of police of the police force for the area in which the offender lives or appears to be living.[62]

Although the primary review obligation rests on the police, the chief officer of police 'must act in co-operation with the council for the local government area in which the offender lives or appears to be living and the council must co-operate in that review'.[63]

The chief officer of police may invite other individuals or organisations to take part in the review.[64] The individuals or organisations which may be relevant include the youth's parents or legal guardian, the school, GP, any support/key workers and the landlord of premises where the youth resides.

Matters to be considered in a review

4.23   A review under s 28 must include a consideration of:[65]

(a)   the extent to which the offender has complied with the order;

(b)   the adequacy of any support available to the offender to help him or her comply with it;

(c)   any matters relevant to the question whether an application should be made for the order to be varied or discharged.

O YOUTHS – CHECKLIST

4.24   Applications where the defendant is under 18 have particular requirements. Below is a checklist of the relevant considerations:

(a)   the prosecution must 'find out the views' the local youth offending team;[66]

(b)   CBOs must last for a minimum of one year and no more than three years;[67]

(c)   CBOs must be reviewed every 12 months where the defendant is under the age of 18 at the end of a review period.[68]

---

62   s 29(1).
63   s 29(2).
64   s 29(3).
65   s 28(3).
66   s 22(8).
67   s 25(4).
68   s 28.

P EXISTING ORDERS

4.25   Section 33 of the Act sets out the transitional provisions for 'existing orders'. Existing orders are defined as:

(a)   an order under s 1C of the CDA 1998 (orders on conviction in criminal proceedings);

(b)   an individual support order under s 1AA of that Act made in connection with an order under s 1C of that Act;

(c)   a drinking banning order under s 6 of the VCRA 2006 (orders on conviction in criminal proceedings).

The repeals and amendments introduced by the Act do not apply in relation to anything done in connection with existing orders save that there can be no variation of an existing order which has the effect of extending the order or any of its provisions. The Act does not prevent a CBO being made even where an order under the old rules still exists and one could have a situation where the old and new orders are running concurrently.

If an existing order is still in force as at 20 October 2019 it will be treated as if its provisions were provisions of a CBO made under s 22 of the Act.[69]

Q CONCLUSION

4.26   CBOs allow anti-social behaviour to be managed at the same time as a court deals with a criminal offence. They provide a real opportunity to achieve results through partnership working.

There appears to have been a good take up of this power with large numbers of CBOs having been made by the courts. The CPS website contains guidance and useful forms although as at the date of writing it still refers to the previous version of the Criminal Procedure Rules. It includes guides for both the police and local authorities as well as information about the approach the CPS will take to such applications.

---

69   s 33(4).

Dispersal powers for the police

Snapshot

What's out

- Authorisations under s 30(2) of the Anti-Social Behaviour Act 2003
- Directions under s 27 of the Violent Crime Reduction Act 2006

What's in

- Single power to direct a person to leave an area
- A power to require a person to surrender property

Key points

- Available for those aged 10 and over
- Maximum timeframe for exclusion is 48 hours
- To be used by the police and PCSOs if so designated
- Prior authorisation required

A INTRODUCTION: THE POWERS WHICH HAVE BEEN REPLACED

5.01 The dispersal power is created by Part 3 of the Act, ss 34–42.[1]

It provides a single flexible power which can be used to disperse anti-social individuals and thus provide immediate short-term respite to a community.[2] The power is intended to allow a problem to be dealt with instantly, allowing it to be 'nipped in the bud' before it can escalate.

The power replaced the following powers:

(a) authorisations under s 30(2) of the Anti-Social Behaviour Act 2003 (ASBA 2003); and

(b) directions under s 27 of the Violent Crime Reduction Act 2006 (VCRA 2006).

The repealed dispersal powers under the ASBA 2003 could only be used: (i) within a 'dispersal zone' which was designated following a time-consuming consultation with the local authority; and (ii) for groups of two or more people.[3] The VCRA 2006 power was limited to 'alcohol-related' crime and disorder.[4]

In the White Paper the Government recognised the limitations on the police's ability to use the old powers to disperse people, in particular the need to pre-arrange the area in which the powers could be used.[5] As such with the new dispersal power there is no longer a need for a 'dispersal zone' to be in place in advance. The advantage is clear: the power can be used more readily by the police and it is possible for people to be dispersed from an area where there is no habitual problem with anti-social behaviour.

During the Parliamentary debates concern was expressed about the ease with which the proposed power could be authorised in contrast to the old powers, and about the need for 'proper and effective democratic oversight' of its use.[6] To that end, attempts were made to introduce a requirement for the police to consult with the local authority before authorisations were given.

The Government refused to amend the provisions on the basis that to do so would 'undermine the flexibility and utility of the power and would reinstate precisely the difficulties that [they] were seeking to remove'.[7] However, it was recognised that there was a need for proper supervision of the new power. Accordingly in response to points made by the Home Affairs Select Committee and the Joint Committee on Human Rights, the requirement for authorisation by an officer of at least the rank of inspector was introduced as a safeguard against the improper use of the power. The requirement for pre-authorisation is in contrast to some of the old powers, for example VCRA 2006, s 27.

---

1 All statutory references are to the Anti-Social Behaviour, Crime and Policing Act 2014 unless otherwise stated.
2 Revised *Statutory Guidance for Frontline Professionals*, p 34.
3 ASBA 2003, s 30(3).
4 VCRA 2006, s 27(2)(a).
5 *Putting Victims First, More Effective Responses to Anti-Social Behaviour*, May 2012, para 3.29.
6 HoL Committee stage, 3rd sitting, 20 November 2013, Baroness Smith of Basildon, col 1018.
7 HoL Committee stage, 3rd sitting, 20 November 2013, Parliamentary Under-Secretary of State, Home Office, Lord Taylor of Holbeach, col 1021.

The Revised Guidance states that where practical the authorising police officer may wish to consult with the local authority or community representatives before making an authorisation.[8] It goes on to suggest that where consultation has not been possible, the officer may wish to notify the local authority if authorisation has been given or the power has been used. Consultation and notification are not therefore statutory requirements. However, police forces may find that consultation helps them obtain community consensus about the use of powers which might otherwise prove controversial.

The dispersal power allows the police and PCSOs[9] to require someone to leave an area (and not return). They are also given supplementary powers to require the surrender of items. For example, an officer could require someone who is riding a quad bike on a housing estate (and causing noise/disturbance) to move on and not return. Using the surrender provisions, the person could also be required to surrender the quad bike. Similarly, an individual who is using their dogs to intimidate and harass the users of a local park could be required to leave the park and not return.[10]

The Secretary of State may issue specific guidance to chief officers of police about the use of these powers by officers under their direction or control. At the time of writing no specific guidance had been issued.

The enforceability of authorisations or directions given prior to the Act coming into force is considered in more detail in 5.25 below.

B WHAT IS THE DISPERSAL POWER?

5.02 The dispersal power is created by s 35 of the Act. It allows a person to be excluded from an area in a public place[11] for a maximum of 48 hours.[12] Under the now repealed provisions of the ASBA 2003 the maximum exclusion period was 24 hours.[13]

If an authorisation has been given under s 34 and the conditions set out in s 35(2)–(3) are met, a person can be required to leave a locality (or part of a locality) and not to return to that locality (or part of the locality) for the period specified in the direction.[14] The requirement for an authorisation and the conditions to be satisfied are considered at 5.04–5.06 below.

The exclusion period cannot exceed 48 hours. The period should start during the period specified in the s 34 authorisation (the period can expire after the authorisation as long as it has started during it).[15]

---

8   Revised *Statutory Guidance for Frontline Professionals*, p 35.
9   If designated by the chief constable.
10 This example is from para 3.35 of *Putting Victims First, More Effective Responses to Anti-Social Behaviour*, May 2012.
11 s 35(10) defines a 'public place' as: '…a place to which at the material time the public or a section of the public has access, on payment or otherwise, as of right or by virtue of express or implied permission.'
12 s 35(4).
13 ASBA 2003, s 30(4)(c).
14 s 35(1).
15 s 35(4).

C WHO CAN USE THE POWER?

5.03 The power can be used by:

(a) police officers in uniform;[16] and

(b) PCSOs where they have been designated to have the powers conferred on a constable by the chief constable.

D AUTHORISATION BEFORE THE POWER CAN BE USED

5.04 The use of the powers set out in s 35 of the Act must be authorised by a police officer of at least the rank of inspector.[17]

There was some suggestion during the Parliamentary debates that the authorisation should be by a more senior officer than an inspector in view of the powerful nature of the remedy. There were also concerns expressed about the scope for a misjudgement which could cause community disruption and provoke riotous behaviour far worse than the disorder originally expected.[18] The Government's response was that the authorisation needed to be made by officers who had sufficient local knowledge and information and inspectors were thought to be the appropriate rank.[19]

When can an authorisation be given?

5.05 An authorisation can be given if the officer (of at least the rank of inspector[20]) is satisfied on reasonable grounds that the use of the powers may be necessary for the purpose of removing or reducing the likelihood of:[21]

(a) members of the public in the locality being harassed, alarmed or distressed; or

(b) the occurrence of crime or disorder in the locality.

The authorisation must identify the locality in which the power can be used during a specified period of not more than 48 hours.[22]

What must be included in an authorisation?

5.06 An authorisation must:[23]

(a) be in writing;

---

16 s 35 and s 37.
17 s 34(1).
18 HoL Committee stage, 3rd sitting, 20 November 13, Lord Harris of Haringey, col 1024.
19 HoL Committee stage, 3rd sitting, 20 November 2013, Lord Taylor of Holbeach, col 1024.
20 s 34(1).
21 s 34(2).
22 s 34(1).
23 s 34(4).

(b)   be signed by the officer giving the authorisation; and

(c)   specify the grounds upon which it is given.

Specifying the grounds upon which the authorisation is given is a mandatory requirement which requires more than repeating that the statutory test is met. The authorisation must specify the reason why the test is believed to be met: *Sierney v DPP*.[24] Police forces will need to ensure that the authorisations are recorded in a form which allows officers on the ground to readily ascertain whether an authorisation exists before deploying the dispersal power.

In a situation where the police have intelligence to suggest there will be problems in a particular area on a particular date the authorisation could be sought in advance in readiness for deploying the dispersal power. Where the use of the power has not been pre-authorised, the explanatory notes to the Act suggest that the officer on the ground will need to contact an inspector and explain the situation to him with a view to getting immediate authorisation to use the power.

Human rights

5.07   The need to seek authorisation has been included in order to ensure that the power is used proportionately and in appropriate circumstances. The Revised Guidance recognises that restricting an individual's freedom of movement is 'a serious issue' and therefore 'the power should not be invoked lightly'.[25] There are express exceptions in s 36 of the Act for those engaged in peaceful picketing or peaceful processions of which appropriate notice was given (or was not required) – see further 5.12 below.[26] The officer giving the authorisation must have particular regard to the rights of freedom of expression and freedom of assembly set out in Articles 10 and 11 of the European Convention on Human Rights.[27] These rights are considered in more detail in Chapter 2 at 2.01–2.08.

---

24   [2006] EWHC 716 (Admin), [2007] Crim LR 60. The court approved the authorisation given in *R (Parminder Singh) v Chief Constable of the West Midlands Police* [2006] EWCA Civ 1118, [2006] 1 WLR 3374. The authorisation was given under ASBA 2003, s 30(2) and was described by the court as a 'good example of the extent of the detail required by Parliament'. The authorisation was in the following terms:

'In Broad Street there is an increasing amount of anti-social behaviour and violent incidents associated with both alcohol and the volume of individuals, increasing during the run up to Christmas, condensed into a small area. This order is to allow the police to take positive action against the small minority who are intent on causing alarm, distress and harassment to the majority looking for a safe and enjoyable night out. Anti-social behaviour can be evidenced in a police document. The anti-social behaviour detailed above is a significant and persistent problem in this locality.'

25   Revised *Statutory Guidance for Frontline Professionals*, p 34.

26   There were similar exceptions in ASBA 2003, s 30(5). In *R (Parminder Singh) v Chief Constable of the West Midlands Police* [2006] EWCA Civ 1118, [2006] 1 WLR 3374, the Court of Appeal held that s 30 applied to protestors exercising their rights of freedom of expression under Article 10 of the ECHR and that an interference with a protestor's rights under Article 10 was prescribed by law and necessary in a democratic society for the prevention of disorder and crime, the protection of public safety and the protection of the rights of others and was justified under Article 10(2).

27   s 34(3).

In addition, the authorising officer may wish to consider whether there are any wider consequences of giving an authorisation. For example, could the use of the power lead to an increase in community tensions if used in a way that is seen as insensitive.

The need for the power to be used in a proportionate way is also reflected in the Revised Guidance where it suggests that the power should define a specific geographical location rather than stating 'in and around the area of...'. It goes on to state that the authorisation should not cover a larger area than is necessary. [28]

Protecting the vulnerable

5.08   The Revised Guidance contains a new section about 'protecting the vulnerable' which states:

- "• Consideration should be given to how the use of this power might impact on the most vulnerable members of society.

- • Consideration should also be given to any risks associated with displacement, including to where people may be dispersed to.

- • There is value in working in partnership to resolve ongoing problems and find long term solutions.'[29]

Readers should also note the section on youths at 5.17 below.

Transparency and scrutiny

5.09   Data on the use of the power must be published[30] in order to monitor its use and to allow the authorities to consider how problems with particular areas could be addressed on a longer-term basis. The White Paper states in terms that the publication of data is intended to act as a 'safeguard to ensure that the power is used proportionately' and to ensure that civil liberties are protected.[31] The Revised Guidance suggests that police forces may wish to put arrangements in place for recording the authorisations granted and the circumstances in which the dispersal power has been used.[32] This will enable trends and 'hotspot' areas to be identified and allow consideration to be given to longer term solutions such as Public Space Protection Orders (considered in more detail in Chapter 7).

---

28   Revised *Statutory Guidance for Frontline Professionals*, p.35.
29   Revised *Statutory Guidance for Frontline Professionals*, p 33.
30   See further 'record-keeping', 5.15 below.
31   At para 3.34.
32   Revised *Statutory Guidance for Frontline Professionals*, p 35.

E WHEN CAN THE POWER BE USED? THE TEST TO BE MET

5.10   In order to give a direction to exclude a person from an area within a public place a s 34 authorisation must exist. In addition, the following conditions must be met:[33]

- The **first condition** is that the constable has reasonable grounds to suspect that the behaviour of the person in the locality has contributed or is likely to contribute to:

  (a)   members of the public in the locality being harassed, alarmed or distressed; or

  (b)   the occurrence in the locality of crime or disorder.

- The **second condition** is that the constable considers that giving a direction to the person is necessary for the purpose of removing or reducing the likelihood of the events mentioned in (a) or (b) above.[34]

What must be included in a direction to disperse?

5.11   A direction:[35]

(a)   must be given in writing, unless that is not reasonably practicable;

(b)   must specify the area to which it relates; and

(c)   may impose requirements as to the time by which the person must leave the area and the manner in which the person must do so (including the route).

In addition, the constable must tell the person to whom the direction is given that it is an offence to fail to comply with the direction, unless there is a reasonable excuse.[36]

The police may wish to consider the use of pro-forma notebooks similar to those used for the old s 27 dispersals.[37] The Revised Guidance gives the following example of established good practice: 'in some forces, officers carry a pre-printed notepad to provide details of the direction, the consequences of a failure to comply, where to collect any confiscated items, and a map to clarify the area a person is excluded from'.[38]

Meaning of public place

5.12   The ability to direct a person to leave an area relates to a 'public place' which is defined in s 35(10) as 'a place to which at the material time the public

33   s 35(2) and (3).
34   s 35(2)(a) and (b).
35   s 35(5).
36   s 35(6).
37   VCRA 2006, s 27.
38   Revised *Statutory Guidance for Frontline Professionals*, p 36.

or a section of the public has access, on payment, or otherwise or by virtue of express or implied permission'.

Specifying the area

5.13   Section 35(5)(c) states that a direction must specify the area to which it relates. The Revised Guidance suggests that a specific geographic area should be defined as opposed to 'in and around the area of ...'.[39]

In the author's view it would be good practice to supply a map of the area. At the very least the direction should identify the area by reference to named streets or the streets on the boundary of the area.[40]

Variation or withdrawal

5.14   A constable can vary or withdraw a direction which has been given as long as this does not have the effect of extending the direction beyond 48 hours from when it was first given.[41] The Act does not impose a limit on the number of dispersals that can be given and it would therefore appear that a succession of 48 hour dispersals could be granted. Careful thought will need to be given to whether successive directions are lawful in terms of being necessary and proportionate in view of the fact that there is no power to extend beyond the original 48 hours.

If a direction is varied or withdrawn, notice of this must be given to the person to whom the direction was given, unless this is not reasonably practicable.[42] Such notice must be given in writing unless this is not reasonably practicable.[43]

F   RESTRICTIONS ON GIVING A DIRECTION

5.15   There are situations in which a direction cannot be given. These are set out in s 36 of the Act and are self-explanatory. Section 36 provides as follows (emphasis has been added):

> '(1) A constable may not give a direction under section 35 to a person who appears to the constable to be **under the age of 10**.
>
> (2) A constable may not give a direction under section 35 that prevents the person to whom it is given having access to a place where the person **lives**.
>
> (3) A constable may not give a direction under section 35 that prevents the person to whom it is given attending at a place which the person is:
>
> > (a)   required to attend for the purposes of the person's **employment, or a contract of services** to which the person is a party,

---

39   Revised *Statutory Guidance for Frontline Professionals*, p 35.
40   Revised *Statutory Guidance for Frontline Professionals*, p 35.
41   s 35(8).
42   s 35(9)(a).
43   s 35(9)(b).

(b)   required to attend by an obligation imposed by or under an enactment or by the order of a court or tribunal, or

(c)   expected to attend for the purposes of **education or training** or for the purposes of receiving **medical treatment**,

at a time when the person is required or expected (as the case may be) to attend there.

(4)   A constable may not give a direction to a person under section 35 if the person is one of a group of persons who are:

(a)   engaged in conduct that is lawful under section 220 of the Trade Union and Labour Relations (Consolidation) Act 1992 (**peaceful picketing**), or

(b)   taking part in a **public procession** of the kind mentioned in subsection (1) of section 11 of the Public Order Act 1986 in respect of which:

(i)   written notice has been given in accordance with that section, or

(ii)   written notice is not required to be given as provided by subsections (1) and (2) of that section.

G   SURRENDER OF PROPERTY

5.16   By virtue of s 37 of the Act a constable who gives a s 35 direction also has the power to direct a person to surrender any item in that person's possession or control that the constable reasonably believes has been used, or is likely to be used, in behaviour that harasses, alarms or distresses members of the public.

As with a s 35 direction, a direction under s 37 must be given in writing unless it is not reasonably practicable to do so.[44] In addition, the constable must (unless this is not reasonably practicable):

(a)   tell the person that failing without reasonable excuse to comply with the direction is an offence; and

(b)   give the person information in writing about when and how the person may recover the surrendered item.[45]

The following provisions apply where an item is surrendered:

(a)   any items surrendered to a constable must not be returned before the end of the exclusion period;[46]

---

44   s 37(2).
45   s 37(3).
46   s 37(4).

(b)   an item can be returned at the end of the period if a person asks for it to be returned (unless there is a power to retain the item under another enactment);[47]

(c)   where a person appears to be under the age of 16, the item can be retained until they are accompanied by a parent or another responsible adult;[48]

(d)   if a person has not asked for the item to be returned within 28 days beginning on the day on which the direction was given the item may be destroyed or otherwise disposed of.[49]

This is a useful supplementary power which would allow officers to seize items such as alcohol, fireworks or spray paint where these items were causing or likely to cause anti-social behaviour.

Dispersal and requiring property to be surrendered – example

The problem
Kaviraj, Yuvraj, Amaya, Arjan and their friends are riding go-peds, mo-peds, go-karts and micro scooters in a housing estate. There is a particular problem with the vehicles being used on a grassed area bordered by three streets of residential properties. The youths are also gathering in the children's play area within the grassed area where they are drinking and smoking drugs. There are four ringleaders and the presence of these youths is attracting more youths to the area. On any given night there can be 15 to 25 youths involved.

The old law
Could seek ASBOs in respect of named individuals excluding them from the grassed area, and to prevent them from riding their mechanically propelled vehicles. This would be a lengthy process and available only in respect of named individuals about whom there was evidence to support an application to the court. The ABSOs would not allow the various vehicles to be surrendered although they could include prohibitions on riding the vehicles.
    The old dispersal powers did not allow the police to require a vehicle to be surrendered.[50] The inability to require the surrender of such items meant that there was always a risk that the problem would simply move to another area.

Using the new dispersal power
Once authorisation has been obtained, a police officer (or PCSO if so designated) could require the youths to leave the area. Any youths aged under

---

47   s 37(5); this could be where it is unlawful to possess the items or where criminal offences may be charged.
48   s 37(6).
49   s 37(7).
50   Under s 12(2) of the Criminal Justice and Police Act 2001 a constable could require a person in a designated public place to surrender items reasonably believed to be alcohol or a container for alcohol.

16 could be taken home. Those involved could also be required to surrender their vehicles which would reduce the risk of the behaviour moving on elsewhere. It may be appropriate to share the information on the anti-social behaviour with Children's Services, particularly if there are safeguarding concerns.

A victim first approach

The Revised Guidance advocates a victim first approach. It advises that if the dispersal power is used in response to a complaint from a member of the public, the officer should update them about what has been done in response to their complaint to provide reassurance to the community.[51]

H YOUTHS

5.17　A direction can be given to anyone aged 10 or over.[52]

Under s 35(7), if the constable reasonably believes a person to be under the age of 16, he may remove that young person to a place where the person lives or to a place of safety but only where she/he is engaging in anti-social behaviour within the meaning of s 35(2). Police officers should have regard to all of the circumstances but in the case of a youth, the following will be particularly relevant:

- the age of the child;

- the child's conduct and his/her explanation for it;

- the time of day/night: if is it late in the night there may be more justification to remove;

- the child's presentation: consideration should be given to whether the child is in distress or otherwise vulnerable; and

- to where and to whom they might be removed or return.

The case law relating to Part 4 of the ASBA 2003 states that the power to remove a person to their place of residence carries with it a power to use reasonable force it if is necessary to do so.[53] This case law is likely to apply to the powers in the Act.

Where a person under the age of 16 is directed to surrender an item under s 37, that item may be retained until the young person is accompanied by a parent or another responsible adult.[54]

51　Revised Statutory *Guidance for Frontline Professionals, p 37.*
52　s 36(1).
53　*R (on the application of W by his parent and litigation friend PW) v Commissioner of Police for the Metropolis and another* [2006] EWCA Civ 458, [2007] QB 399.
54　s 37(6).

I RECORD-KEEPING

5.18 Section 38 imposes a requirement to keep records. A constable who gives, varies or withdraws a direction under s 35 must make a record of:

(a) the individual to whom the direction is given;

(b) the time at which the direction is given; and

(c) the terms of the direction (including, in particular, the area to which it relates and the exclusion period).

Where an item is seized under s 37 the constable giving the direction must make a record of:

(a) the individual to whom the direction is given;

(b) the time at which the direction is given; and

(c) the item to which the direction relates.

The police will need to ensure that they have a system for recording information about the dispersal notices that they have issued so that when one officer goes off duty, the next shift of officers is able to ascertain which notices were issued, to whom and how long they have left to run. See also 5.09 above on 'transparency and scrutiny'.

J OFFENCES

5.19 The Act creates two offences in relation to the dispersal powers, one relating to the s 35 direction to leave an area and a second relating to the s 37 direction to surrender property.

Section 35 direction to leave

5.20 A person who, without reasonable excuse, fails to comply with a direction given under s 35 of the Act commits an offence.[55] On summary conviction in the magistrates' court, a sentence of imprisonment not exceeding three months or a fine not exceeding level 4 on the standard scale can be imposed.[56]

Section 37 direction to surrender property

5.21 A person who, without reasonable excuse, fails to comply with a direction given under s 37 of the Act commits an offence.[57] On summary conviction in

---

55 s 39(1).
56 Currently £2,500.
57 s 39(3).

the magistrates' court, a fine not exceeding level 2 on the standard scale can be imposed.[58]

Reasonable excuse

5.22 The concept of 'reasonable excuse' did not feature in the old anti-social behaviour related dispersal[59] or in the alcohol related dispersal.[60] There are some examples of what could amount to a reasonable excuse in the context of the abatement notices served under the old rules, see 6.21 of Chapter 6 (Community Protection Notices).

Prosecutions

5.23 The Crown Prosecution Service has produced some legal guidance on dispersals which states:

'The Crown must prove all elements of the offence:

- The authorisation was in effect and was valid.

- The publicity provisions had been complied with.

- The officer was in uniform.

- The direction was given inside the relevant locality.

- The Defendant knew that he was being given a direction under the authorisation.

- The direction given was lawful.

- The Defendant failed to comply with the direction.'

Officers would be well advised to bear this list in mind when using the powers and deciding whether to refer a case for prosecution.

K   APPEALS AND CHALLENGING A DIRECTION

5.24 The Revised Guidance contains advice about how a person can challenge a direction. It suggests that if a person feels they have been given a direction

---

58   Currently £500.
59   ASBA 2003, s 32(2) provided:
(2)   A person who knowingly contravenes a direction given to him under section 30(4) commits an offence and is liable on summary conviction to—
      (a) a fine not exceeding level 4 on the standard scale, or
      (b) imprisonment for a term not exceeding 3 months,
      or to both.
60   See VCRA 2006, s 27(6).

incorrectly they should speak to the duty inspector at the local police station and that details of the ability to do this should be included on the written notice.[61]

L   EXISTING AUTHORISATIONS AND DIRECTIONS

5.25   Section 42 of the Act sets out the transitional provisions for certain orders made before 20 October 2014. The repeals or amendments introduced by the Act do not apply in relation to the authorisations and directions listed in s 42(1)–(2) or anything done in connection with them. Those authorisations and directions are:

(a)   an authorisation given under s 30(2) of the ASBA 2003; or

(b)   a direction under s 27 of the VCRA 2003 before the commencement day.

M   CONCLUSION

5.26   The dispersal power replaced provisions which were reported to be working well. Unlike the old powers, however, the new single power can be used without needing to pre-arrange the area and is not limited to alcohol-related anti-social behaviour. It can be deployed in fast-moving situations in which groups have quickly convened to cause anti-social behaviour and then moved on to another area. The power, if used proportionately, should prove to be an effective power in providing immediate respite from anti-social behaviour in a localised area.

Those deploying the dispersal power must apply the test set out in 5.10 above.[62] Reporting requirements mean that its deployment will be monitored to ensure that its repeated use is not relied upon as a long-term solution to embedded problems. The Revised Guidance recommends that police work with local councils to find a longer-term sustainable solution in areas where there are regular problems.[63]

The Act also makes provision for guidance to be issued for chief officers of police. At the time of writing no guidance had been issued.

---

61   Revised *Statutory Guidance for Frontline Professionals*, p 37.
62   The old Statutory Guidance asked practitioners to bear in mind that the powers are not intended to be used for busking or other types of street entertainment which is not causing anti-social behaviour (at p 33). That reference does not appear in the Revised Guidance. Rightly so in the author's view, not least because the test found in s 35 does not refer to the words 'anti-social behaviour'. Clearly there may be circumstances when busking or other street entertainment will meet the test for serving a CPNW or CPN.
63   Revised *Statutory Guidance for Frontline Professionals*, p 34.

CHAPTER 6

Community protection notices

Snapshot

What's out
- Litter abatement notices
- Litter clearing notices
- Street litter clearing notices
- Defacement removal notices

What's in
- Community protection notices

Key points
- Written warning required before a CPN is issued
- Ability to issue a fixed penalty notice ('FPN') on breach
- Powers to take remedial action
- Criminal offences for breach
- Powers of forfeiture and seizure
- Appeals to the magistrates' court in defined circumstances

Templates

See Appendix D for useful new precedents which were not included in the first edition of this book:

- Community Protection Warning letter

- Community Protection Notice

A INTRODUCTION: THE POWERS WHICH HAVE BEEN REPLACED

6.01   The Act replaced a number of behaviour-specific powers which dealt with individuals or businesses whose behaviour was considered to be anti-social. The Government's consultation had expressed a desire to move away from specific powers for each type of behaviour to a streamlined single power for dealing with persistent place-related behaviour.[1] The result was the community protection notice (CPN) created by Chapter 1 of Part 4 of the Act, ss 43–58.[2]

Although the title to this part of the Act only refers to CPNs, it also created a fixed penalty notice (FPN) which can be issued to anyone who is believed to have committed an offence under s 48 of the Act (failure to comply with a CPN).[3]

The use of the CPN and FPN is limited to local authorities, the police and persons designated by local authorities. As with PSPOs (covered in Chapter 7), parish councils are excluded from the definition of 'local authority'. Breach of a CPN is a criminal offence. The Government has sought to limit the availability of CPNs to experienced officers to ensure a level of control and consistency over their use.[4]

CPNs replaced the following powers:

(a)   litter abatement notices under s 92 of the Environmental Protection Act 1990 (EPA 1990);

(b)   litter clearing notices under s 92A of the EPA 1990;

(c)   street litter clearing notices under s 93 of the EPA 1990;

(d)   defacement removal notices under s 48 of the Anti-Social Behaviour Act 2003 (ASBA 2003).

The stated purpose of CPNs is to deal with particular, ongoing problems or nuisances which negatively affect the community's quality of life by targeting those responsible.[5]

---

1   *More Effective Responses to Anti-Social Behaviour*, February 2011, p 27.
2   All statutory references are to the Anti-Social Behaviour, Crime and Policing Act 2014 unless otherwise stated.
3   s 52.
4   HoL committee, 4th sitting, 25 November 2013, Parliamentary Under-Secretary of State, Home Office, Lord Taylor of Holbeach, col 1194.
5   Revised *Statutory Guidance for Frontline Professionals*, p 39.

The consultation gave examples of when the Government envisaged CPNs could be used and how this differs from the old powers:[6]

- An individual who regularly allows their dog to foul in a communal garden (this situation is not covered by old notices).

- A group regularly taking the same route home late at night whilst drunk, making noise and waking their neighbours (this is behaviour not covered by the statutory nuisance regime).

- A takeaway shop which persistently allows its customers to drop litter on the pavement outside and causes noise nuisance late at night, being required to put bins outside the shop and to ensure that customers leave quietly after 10pm (current notices can only be used to deal with one type of behaviour).

The Explanatory Notes to the Act suggest that CPNs are different from the powers they replace in the following ways:

(a) They cover a wider range of behaviour (all behaviour that is detrimental to the local community's quality of life) rather than specifically stating the behaviour covered (for example, litter or graffiti).

(b) Noise disturbance could be tackled, particularly if it is demonstrated to be occurring in conjunction with other anti-social behaviour.

(c) The notices can be issued by a wider range of agencies: the police, local authorities and private registered providers of social housing (if approved by local authorities), thereby enabling the most appropriate agency to deal with the situation.

(d) The notices can apply to businesses and individuals (which is the same as some of the notices they will replace but not all).

(e) It would be a criminal offence if a person did not comply, with a sanction of a fine (or fixed penalty notice) for non-compliance.

The enforceability of notices which were issued prior to the Act coming into force is considered in more detail at 6.28 below.

B WHAT IS A CPN?

6.02 A CPN is a notice which imposes requirements upon the individual or body to whom it is issued. The types of requirements that can be imposed are considered in more detail at 6.17 below.

---

6   *More Effective Responses to Anti-Social Behaviour*, February 2011, p 27.

C WHO CAN ISSUE A CPN OR A FPN?

Authorised persons

6.03   CPNs and FPNs can only be issued by 'authorised persons'. Section 53(1) defines authorised persons as:

(a)   a constable;

(b)   the relevant local authority;

(c)   a person designated by the relevant local authority for the purposes of this section.

Meaning of the 'relevant local authority'

6.04   The definition of a relevant local authority is found in s 53(2) and (3). For a CPN, the relevant local authority means the local authority (or, as the case may be, any of the local authorities) within whose area the conduct specified in the notice has, according to the notice, been taking place. For a FPN, the relevant local authority means the local authority (or, as the case may be, any of the local authorities) within whose area the offence in question is alleged to have taken place.

By s 57, local authority means in relation to England, a district council, a county council for an area for which there is no district council, a London borough council, the Common Council of the City of London or the Council of the Isles of Scilly. In relation to Wales, local authority means a county council or a county borough council.

Who can be designated by the relevant local authority?

6.05   Only those categories of people who have been specified in an order made by the Secretary of State can be designated persons for the purposes of s 53(1)(c).[7]

At the time of writing, the only category of person to be so designated is 'housing providers'. Housing providers are those bodies falling within the meaning of s 20 of the Act. This includes a housing trust, housing action trust and non-profit registered providers of social housing.[8]

During the Parliamentary debates, the Government made it clear that local authorities would need to use a memorandum of understanding to agree boundaries on the use of the powers if they designate them to such bodies. Local guidelines on matters such as the enforcement of notices and the recording of data about their use will also be required.[9]

---

7   s 53(4).
8   See the Anti-social Behaviour (Authorised Persons) Order 2015, SI 2015/749.
9   HoL committee, 4th sitting, 25 November 2013, Lord Taylor of Holbeach, col 1194.

Who can be designated by the police?

6.06 The Chief Constable has the power to designate Police Community Support Officers (PCSOs) to issue CPNs. PCSOs are empowered to issue FPNs without the need for designation.

D WHEN CAN A CPN BE ISSUED?

6.07 A CPN can only be issued where a written warning has been issued[10] and the appropriate individual(s) or bodies have been informed.[11]

The need for a written warning

6.08 By virtue of s 43(5) of the Act and in addition to the three-fold test set out in 6.10 below, a CPN can only be issued where the following two conditions are satisfied:

(a) the perpetrator (whether an individual or body) has been given a written warning that a CPN will be issued unless the conduct ceases to have a detrimental effect on the life of those in the locality; and

(b) where the issuing officer is satisfied that the perpetrator has had sufficient time to deal with the problem.

Informing any appropriate individual or body about the intention to issue a CPN

6.09 The requirement to inform any appropriate individuals or bodies about the intention to issue a CPN is found in s 43(6) of the Act. The individuals or bodies to be informed will need to be considered on a case-by-case basis. The examples given in the Explanatory Notes to the Act of the individuals or bodies that may be relevant are the person's landlord or the local authority. In addition, the person's parents (in the case of a young person still living with their parents), their social worker or key worker may also be appropriate persons. The Revised Guidance includes a new sentence about there being merit in involving the local council who are experienced in tackling environmental issues.[12]

---

10   s 43(5).
11   s 43(6).
12   Revised *Statutory Guidance for Frontline Professionals*, p 40.

E   THE TEST TO BE MET FOR ISSUING A CPN

6.10   An authorised person[13] may issue a CPN if satisfied on reasonable grounds that:[14]

(a)   the conduct[15] of the individual or body is having a detrimental effect on the quality of life of those in the locality; and

(b)   is of a persistent or continuing nature; and

(c)   the conduct is unreasonable.

Whether this three-fold test is met will need to be decided on a case-by-case basis. A CPN should not be issued without careful thought being given to whether the test has been met. The need to consider whether the conduct is unreasonable provides considerable room for discretion and local authorities will need to take care to avoid an over-zealous use of this power. The Revised Guidance gives an example of a case where a baby is regularly crying in the middle of the night.[16] It suggests that whilst the behaviour may be having a detrimental effect on the quality of life of those living locally and is continuing such that (a) and (b) above are satisfied, it would not be reasonable to issue a CPN as the behaviour is not unreasonable because there is nothing that can be done to control or affect the behaviour. In such a case (c) above would not be satisfied.

In some cases it will be clear that the behaviour is persistent or ongoing; an example may be a local business regularly storing rubbish on the street outside the shop. The requirement under (b) above is in the alternative, the problem can be 'persistent' *or* 'continuing'. This could allow a CPN to be served where the behaviour has been ongoing for a relatively short time but has not ceased following the written warning. This is reinforced in the Revised Guidance which gives the example of an individual storing rubbish in their garden for many months as being 'persistent'.

A CPN may be appropriate where it can be shown that the person responsible has been asked to desist from the behaviour but has chosen to ignore that advice/warning. The example given in the old Guidance was of an individual playing loud music in a park despite being given a warning to stop; this could be considered to be a 'continuing' problem even if it takes place over a few days.[17]

There is some guidance on the meaning of 'persistent' in *Ramblers Association v Coventry City Council*[18] in which it was held that the word 'persistent' used in s 129A(3)(b) of the Highways Act 1980 (which deals with gating orders) was an ordinary English word, commonly understood to mean 'continuing or recurring; prolonged', that did not require further definition. The case was cited with

---

13   See 6.05–6.06 above.
14   s 43(1).
15   'Conduct' includes a failure to act: s 57.
16   Revised *Statutory Guidance for Frontline Professionals*, p 40.
17   Further examples can be found in the Revised *Stautory Guidance for Frontline Professionals*, p 40.
18   [2008] EWHC 796 (Admin); [2009] 1 ALL ER 130.

approval by May J in *Summers v Richmond LBC*,[19] the first High Court decision relating to PSPOs.

To whom?

6.11   A CPN can be issued to an individual aged 16 or over or to a body, including a business. The rules on service are set out in Section F below (see 6.12).

Where the CPN is issued to a business, the issuing officer will need to think carefully about the person to whom the CPN is issued.

A notice to a corporate body can be issued to the secretary or clerk of that body.[20] A notice issued to a partnership may be issued to a partner or the person who controls or manages the partnership business.[21]

The Revised Guidance gives the example that in the case of a small business the recipient could be the shop owner whereas in the case of a major supermarket this may be the store manager.[22] The recipient must be someone who is able to effect a change in the behaviour.

F   SERVING A CPN[23]

Three options for service

6.12   The CPN can be personally served by handing it to the recipient. It can also be left or posted to the recipient.[24]

Where to leave or post?

6.13   Where the CPN is left or posted it must be at/to the person's 'proper address'. A person's proper address is their last known address except that:[25]

(a)   in the case of a body corporate or its secretary or clerk, it is the address of the body's registered or principal office;

(b)   in the case of a partnership or person having the control or the management of the partnership business, it is the principal office of the partnership.

For companies registered outside the United Kingdom, the CPN should be left or sent to the company's principal office within the United Kingdom.[26]

---

19   [2018] EWHC 782 (Admin), [2018] 1 WLR 4729 at [27].
20   s 55(2).
21   s 55(3).
22   Revised *Statutory Guidance for Frontline Professionals*, p 40.
23   The same rules about service apply to FPNs.
24   s 55(1).
25   s 55(4)
26   s 55(5).

If a person has an address other than their 'proper address' as an address where they (or someone on their behalf) will accept notices then this is also treated as their proper address for the service of a CPN.[27]

Conduct on or affecting premises

6.14   'Premises' includes any land.[28] Where the conduct[29] takes place on or affects premises[30] that a person owns,[31] leases, occupies, controls, operates, or maintains, the conduct is treated for the purposes of s 43 as the conduct of that person.

Section 44(1) is qualified by s 44(3) which states that an individual's conduct is not to be taken as the conduct of another person if s/he cannot reasonably be expected to control or affect it.[32]

What if the owner or occupier cannot be ascertained?

6.15   A CPN can be treated as issued if it is posted on the premises in cases where reasonable enquiries have been made to ascertain the name or proper address of the occupier (or the owner where the premises are unoccupied).[33] The time at which the CPN is treated as having been issued is the time the notice is posted on the premises.[34]

Where the owner cannot be ascertained the issuing officer will need to record the enquiries that have been made to ascertain the details for the occupier or owner. Those enquiries could include a search of the electoral roll, examining records relating to any applications for state benefits from the premises or records in respect of the payment of business rates. An Equifax or Land Registry search may also prove useful or provide lines of enquiry.

Power to enter

6.16   The issuing officer has the power to enter the premises, or indeed any other premises, to the extent reasonably necessary to enable the notice to be

27   s 55(6).
28   s 57.
29   'Conduct' includes a failure to act: s 57.
30   Conduct on or affecting premises occupied by a government department is treated for the purposes of section 43 as the conduct of the Minister in charge of that department: s 44(2).
31   s 57 provides:
      'owner', in relation to premises, means—
      (a)   a person (other than a mortgagee not in possession) entitled to dispose of the fee simple of the premises, whether in possession or in reversion;
      (b)   a person who holds or is entitled to the rents and profits of the premises under a lease that (when granted) was for a term of not less than 3 years;
32   s 44(3).
33   s 45.
34   s 45(3).

posted on the premises.[35] Officers effecting service should take care to note that the power to enter is limited to those purposes and entry beyond that necessary to post the notice on the premises could amount to a trespass.

G CONTENTS OF A CPN

Requirements

6.17   A CPN is defined in s 43(3) of the Act as a notice that imposes any of the following requirements on the individual or body issued with it:

(a)   a requirement to stop doing specified things;

(b)   a requirement to do specified things;

(c)   a requirement to take reasonable steps to achieve specified results.

This allows the issuing officer to require the anti-social behaviour to stop and to specify reasonable steps to ensure the conduct does not recur.

The requirements which are imposed must be those that are reasonable to impose in order to:[36]

(a)   prevent the detrimental effect of the conduct from continuing or recurring; or

(b)   reduce the detrimental effect of the conduct; or

(c)   reduce the risk of the continuance or recurrence of the detrimental effect.

By virtue of s 43(7) of the Act the CPN must identify the conduct which is having the effect set out in s 43(1) and explain the effect of ss 46–51 of the Act.

The issuing officer will need to impose a reasonable timeframe for compliance. Officers will need to give careful consideration to the requirements specified within a CPN and the timeframes for compliance because unreasonable requirements and/or timeframes can form the basis of an appeal to the magistrates' court.[37]

The Revised Guidance suggests that the restrictions and requirements in a CPN may be similar to those available in a Part 1 injunction (see Chapter 3) but that 'more serious conditions, such as attendance at a drug rehabilitation course, would clearly be more appropriate to a court issued order'.[38]

In *Stannard (Kieron) v CPS*[39] the High Court observed that CPNs can constitute a significant interference with an individual's freedom and that they must be:

•   clear in their terms;

•   proportionate in their effect;

•   limited in time (for the purposes legal certainty); and

---

35   s 45(2)(b).
36   s 43(4).
37   See further at 6.18 below.
38   Revised *Statutory Guidance for Frontline Professionals*, p 43.
39   [2019] EWHC 84 (Admin), at [54].

• include prohibitions and restrictions that are no more than is necessary and proportionate to address the behaviour which has led to the CPN being made.

In a postscript to the judgment, the court observed that those issuing CPNs should have a system for receiving and adjudicating requests to vary or discharge a CPN and that the CPN itself should include information on how to seek such variation/discharge.[40] This is reflected in the template CPN at Appendix D. What follows from this is that a policy or procedure for dealing with such requests will need to be formulated and applied as appropriate.

The Explanatory Notes to the Act give the example of CPN being used where a dog keeps escaping from its owner's back garden due to a broken fence. In this case the CPN could require the dog owner to repair the fence to prevent further escapes. The CPN could also require the dog owner to attend training sessions with the dog to improve the dog's behaviour if this was also an issue. The CPN would give the dog owner a timeframe to carry out the works and can state that if the work is not done, the local authority will authorise works to be done in default on a given date and at a given cost.

Further assistance can be derived from the case law relating to abatement notices served under s 80 of the EPA 1990. The settled position in the law on abatement notices is that where there is a number of methods of abating a nuisance, the recipient of the notice can simply be required to 'abate' the nuisance rather than particular requirements having to be specified by the local authority.[41] In the example of the escaping dog, the requirement could simply be to stop the dog escaping. It would then be up to the owner to mend the broken fence, or (say) put the dog on a lead or in a secure kennel from which it could not escape. If particular requirements are specified, they must be specified in sufficient detail to allow the recipient to know exactly what must be done.

Examples of how CPNs have been used
CPNs have been put to a variety of uses, some of which are set out below. This list is given for illustrative purposes and readers wishing to use the power will need to ensure the statutory test is met before issuing a CPN.

• Aggressive begging

• Anti-social behaviour towards council staff

• Feeding pigeons and seagulls

• Dog nuisance, eg fouling, noise nuisance

• Smoke and smell from bonfires

• 'County lines' drug chauffeur using hire cars to transport young people to towns and cities to sell drugs

---

40 Ibid, at [53].
41 See the Court of Appeal's decision in *Falmouth & Truro Port Health Authority Ex p. South West Water Ltd* [2001] QB 445, CA.

- On-street and garden car repairs from domestic premises
- Car cruising

H APPEALING A CPN

6.18   Section 46 of the Act makes provision for a CPN to be appealed to the magistrates' court on the following grounds:

(1)   That the conduct specified in the community protection notice:

    (a)   did not take place;

    (b)   has not had a detrimental effect on the quality of life of those in the locality;

    (c)   has not been of a persistent or continuing nature;

    (d)   is not unreasonable; or

    (e)   is conduct that the person cannot reasonably be expected to control or affect.

(2)   That any of the requirements in the notice, or any of the periods within which or times by which they are to be complied with, are unreasonable.

(3)   That there is a material defect or error in, or in connection with, the notice.

(4)   That the notice was issued to the wrong person.

Any appeal must be made within 21 days beginning on the day on which a person is issued with a CPN[42] and on appeal the magistrates' court has the power to quash the notice, modify the notice or dismiss the appeal.[43]

While an appeal is in progress, any requirement imposed in a CPN to stop doing specified things remains in effect unless the court orders otherwise. Any other requirement imposed by the CPN is of no effect. An appeal remains 'in progress' until it is finally determined or withdrawn.[44]

The case of *Stannard (Keiron) v CPS*[45] concerned an appeal of a CPN issued by the police to the defendant following a warning letter issued jointly by the police and the local authority. The warning letter had required the defendant to cease his anti-social behaviour, failing which a CPN would be issued. A CPN was served in due course; it required the defendant not to enter the town centre or to be in a group of more than three individuals including himself (amongst other things). When Stannard was prosecuted for breaching the CPN he pleaded not guilty, arguing that the police did not have the power to issue the CPN under s 43 and that he had a reasonable excuse for his failure to comply. The district judge

---

42   s 46(2).
43   s 46(4).
44   s 46(3).
45   [2019] EWHC 84 (Admin).

rejected his appeal and he appealed by way of case stated to the High Court. The High Court held:

- when dealing with the breach, the district judge did not have to satisfy herself of the reasonableness or legality of the CPN;

- that a CPN issued by the police is like a court order in the sense that it is valid until it is varied or discharged by an authorised person on review (subject to the court's oversight by way of judicial review), or on appeal; and

- that the prosecution is not under a duty to call the original evidence which led to the CPN being issued in order to satisfy the court that it had been lawfully issued.

The judgment contains a postscript to those authorised to issue CPNs reminding them they have a power not only to issue, but also to vary and discharge a CPN in appropriate circumstances. The judge said this:[46]

> 'It is not for this court to tell authorised persons how to go about their decision-making, but we would think it a minimum that such persons should operate a system for receiving and adjudicating requests for variation or discharge of CPNs; and that relevant information should briefly be given with any CPN about how to seek a variation or discharge (e.g. on a change of circumstance), in addition to information required by statute about a statutory appeal.'

The template CPN in Appendix D contains additional information to reflect the courts' observations in *Stannard*.

I   FAILURE TO COMPLY WITH A CPN

Remedial action by a local authority

6.19   Where a person issued with a CPN fails to comply with its requirements the local authority is given the power to take remedial action under s 47(2) (remedial action where the land is open to the air) and/or s 47(3) (remedial action for premises other than land open to the air).

Where land is open to the air the local authority may arrange to have the work carried out to ensure that the failure is remedied.[47] Where the land is not open to the air, the local authority is required to issue a notice under s 47(3) of the Act which specifies: (i) the work it intends to have carried out unless the default is remedied; (ii) the estimated cost of the work and which invites the defaulter to consent to the work being carried out. The work can be carried out

---

46   Ibid, at [53].
47   s 47(2).

under s 47(3) if the local authority is given the necessary consent.[48] The Act does not make provision for a route to challenge the withholding of consent. Those authorised by the local authority to carry out the work are permitted to enter the premises to the extent reasonably necessary for the purpose of carrying out the work.[49]

If remedial action is taken under s 47(2) or (3) the defaulter is liable to the local authority for the amount specified in a notice which complies with the requirements of s 47(6) of the Act (a notice which gives details of the work that was carried out and specifying the amount that is no more than the cost to the local authority of having the work carried out).

Section 47(7) makes provision for a person issued with a notice under s 47(6) of the Act to appeal to the magistrates' court within 21 days beginning with the day on which the notice was issued only on the grounds that the amount specified in the notice is excessive. The magistrates' court must confirm the amount specified or to substitute a lower amount.[50]

Section 54 of the Act deals with exemptions from liability for a local authority and persons carrying out work under ss 47(2) and 49(2)(b) of the Act.

Criminal offence

6.20   Section 48 of the Act creates an offence of failure to comply with a CPN.

An offence is not committed under s 48 if the person took all reasonable steps to comply with the notice or there is some other 'reasonable excuse' for failure to comply with it.[51]

The Act does not give any guidance on who should prosecute the breach. The author's view is that the default position, where there is a criminal offence, is for the police and CPS to be responsible for prosecuting the breach, regardless of who issued the CPN.

In the context of appeals relating to abatement notices served under s 80 of the EPA 1990 it has been held that a defendant charged with an offence of failing to comply with an abatement notice cannot ordinarily raise as a 'reasonable excuse' by way of a defence to a criminal charge a matter which he could have advanced as a ground of statutory appeal. However the rule is not absolute and there can be some special reason for not having appealed the notice.[52] An example

---

48   'Necessary consent' is defined in s.47(4) as:
    '(4) In subsection (3) "the necessary consent" means the consent of—
    (a)   the defaulter, and
    (b)   the owner of the premises on which the work is to be carried out (if that is not the defaulter).
    Paragraph (b) does not apply where the relevant authority has made reasonable efforts to contact the owner of the premises but without success.'
49   s 47(5).
50   s 47(8).
51   s 48(3).
52   *Lambert Flat Management Ltd v Lomas* [1981] 1 WLR 898, [1981] 2 ALL ER 280.

could be illness[53] or that the defendant had no knowledge of the notice at the material time.[54]

Issuing officers will need to formulate the requirements of a CPN with care and ensure that the timeframes stipulated are reasonable ones having regard to the action being required. They would also be well advised to pursue criminal charges only in those cases where they are satisfied that the CPN had come to the attention of the defendant.

Reasonable excuse for a failure to comply with a CPN

6.21   There is no comprehensive definition of what constitutes a reasonable excuse for failure to comply in the context of a breach of a CPN as the circumstances may vary and each situation will need to be considered on a case-by-case basis. There are some useful examples of the types of issues that may arise in the case law in relation to abatement notices. A lack of funds[55] and birthday celebrations in the context of offence caused by reggae music, air horns and whistles[56] have been held not to constitute a 'reasonable' excuse for failing to comply with an abatement notice. The personal circumstances of a defendant and how these impact on the ability to comply with a requirement could be relevant. For example, in the case of a single mother who had been diagnosed with HIV and who had three children, (the eldest of whom had been diagnosed with cancer and had been brought home from hospice shortly before an abatement notice was served) it was held that the circumstances are not limited to those cases where a defendant has not received an abatement notice.[57] It remains to be seen how broadly the courts will interpret s 46(2) of the Act.

Penalties on conviction – fine

6.22   An individual person guilty of an offence is liable on summary conviction to a fine not exceeding level 4 on the standard scale.[58] For a body the penalty is an unlimited fine (increased from the initial £20,000 when the Act was first introduced).

Penalty on conviction – remedial orders

6.23   The court has the power to make whatever order it considers necessary to ensure that the requirements set out in the CPN are complied with.[59] This

---

53   See further *Hope Butuyuyu v London Borough of Hammersmith and Fulham* (1997) 29 HLR 584 considered below.
54   *R (on the application of Khan) v Isleworth Crown Court* [2011] EWHC 3164, [2012] Env. LR 12.
55   *Saddleworth Urban District Council v Aggregate and Sand* (1970) 114 SJ 931.
56   *Wellingborough Borough Council v Gordon* [1993] Env LR 218.
57   *Hope Butuyuyu v London Borough of Hammersmith and Fulham* (1997) 29 HLR 584.
58   Level 4 is currently up to £2,500.
59   s 49(1).

includes an order that the defendant must carry out specified work or to allow such work to be carried out by or on behalf of the local authority.[60] This is in addition to the power given to the local authority under s 47 of the Act to take remedial action if it so chooses (which is not contingent upon a conviction for default).

If the work is to be carried out by or on behalf of the local authority, the local authority must be the one who issued the CPN, or if it did not issue the CPN, the CPN is one that could have been issued by the local authority.[61]

A crucial difference with the s 47 remedial action power is that any order that works be carried out by or on behalf of a local authority cannot authorise a person to enter the defendant's home without his consent.[62] As such any order of this nature which required work to be done at the defendant's home would be ineffective unless the defendant gave his consent (unless the work could be carried out without entering the home).

However, unlike the provisions in s 47 (where consent is needed to carry out remedial works on land which is not open to the air, as opposed to at the defendant's home) the defendant cannot escape liability for failing to comply with such an order simply because he refuses consent to enter his home.

A person in default of a CPN where the local authority then carries out work under s 49(2)(b) is liable for the amount specified in any notice given by the local authority which has set out the works carried out and the amount payable (which amount cannot be more than the cost of the works to the local authority).[63]

If the amount is considered to be excessive it can be appealed to the magistrates' court which has the power to confirm the amount or substitute a lower amount.[64] Any such appeal must be brought within 21 days beginning with the day on which the notice was issued.[65]

Forfeiture of items used in the commission of an offence

6.24   Under s 50 of the Act the magistrates' court can order a person convicted of an offence under s 48 to forfeit an item that was used in the commission of the offence to a constable or a person employed by or designated by the local authority under s 53(1)(c). This could include, for example, a music or amplification system in the case of noise nuisance.

The magistrates' court can also order that the item be destroyed or disposed of. The police or the local authority to whom the item is handed over must then make arrangements to destroy/dispose of the item in accordance with the order or in such other manner as seems appropriate to them.[66]

---

60   s 49(2).
61   s 49(3).
62   s 49(4).
63   s.49(6).
64   s 49(7)–(8).
65   s 49(7).
66   s 50(3)–(5).

Powers of seizure of items used in the commission of an offence

6.25   Under s 51 of the Act a justice of the peace can issue a warrant authorising any constable or designated person to enter premises within 14 days of the warrant being issued in order to seize an item used in the commission of an offence under s 48.

The warrant can be issued where there are reasonable grounds for believing that an offence under s 48 has been committed and that there is an item used in the commission of that offence on the premises specified in the information.[67]

J   FIXED PENALTY NOTICES

6.26   A FPN requiring the payment of a sum up to a maximum of £100[68] can be issued by an authorised person[69] where they have reason to believe an offence has been committed under s 48.

The FPN is an opportunity to discharge any liability to conviction by the payment of a specified amount to the local authority.[70]

Section 52(6) provides that a FPN must:

(a)   give reasonably detailed particulars of the circumstances alleged to constitute the offence;

(b)   state the period during which (because of subsection (5)(a)) proceedings will not be taken for the offence;[71]

(c)   specify the amount of the fixed penalty;

(d)   state the name and address of the person to whom the fixed penalty may be paid; and

(e)   specify permissible methods of payment.[72]

The FPN may specify two amounts, whereby if payment is made within a specified period (of less than 14 days) the penalty is a lower amount.[73]

---

67   s 51(1).
68   s 52(7).
69   See 6.03 above.
70   Local authority has the same meaning as in 6.04 above.
71   Section 52(5) provides:
   '(5) Where a person is issued with a notice under this section in respect of an offence—
   (a)   no proceedings may be taken for the offence before the end of the period of 14 days following the date of the notice;
   (b)   the person may not be convicted of the offence if the person pays the fixed penalty before the end of that period.'
72   Section 52(9) provides:
   '(9) Whatever other method may be specified under subsection (6)(e), payment of a fixed penalty may be made by pre-paying and posting to the person whose name is stated under subsection (6)(d), at the stated address, a letter containing the amount of the penalty (in cash or otherwise).'
73   s 52(8).

In the event of a failure to pay a FPN, a certificate which purports to be signed by the local authority's chief finance officer and states that payment has not been received or was not received by the date stipulated is evidence of the non-payment or late payment.[74] The remedy for failure to pay a FPN would be a summons by way of complaint in the magistrates' court as with other FPNs.

Using a CPN – example

The problem

Gurnam is a property developer who has purchased a house in Warren Street which requires substantial work. He intends to renovate the house and rent it out.

In order to save costs he is using the garden area at the front of his property to store the rubble and rubbish being generated by the works. He informs the neighbours that this will be a short-term solution that is cheaper than paying for several skips. He intends to arrange for the rubbish to be cleared in one go at the end of the project.

The renovations are completed and the house is rented out. In the meantime Gurnam has purchased another property and his efforts are concentrated on renovating the new house. He has not cleared the front garden at Warren Street of the rubble and rubbish which has accumulated.

The neighbours are complaining of the unsightly state of the front garden which is affecting the appearance of the whole street. They are also concerned by the constant dust and debris that keeps being spread around the street from the front garden. Gurnam has ignored the neighbours' requests to remove the rubbish. His time and money are being spent on his new project.

The solution

The council serves a written warning. The written warning informs Gurnam that the council is satisfied the accumulation of rubbish is having a detrimental impact on the quality of life of those in the locality, that it is unreasonable and of a continuing nature. The written warning states that the council will serve a CPN unless he removes the rubbish within 28 days.

Gurnam does not clear the rubbish. Before the council issues a CPN it looks at whether there are any individuals or bodies that it should inform about its intention to issue a CPN. It decides that there are no such individuals or bodies.

The CPN is issued and posted to Gurnam at the address he has given the council for the purposes of his planning and building regulation approvals.

---

74   s 52(11).

K   OVERLAP WITH STATUTORY NUISANCE

6.27   There is an overlap between a local authority's duties with regards to statutory nuisances under the EPA 1990 and its ability to issue a CPN. Section 79(1) of the EPA 1990 identifies statutory nuisances as:

> '(a) any premises in such a state as to be prejudicial to health or a nuisance;
>
> (b) smoke emitted from premises so as to be prejudicial to health or a nuisance;
>
> (c) fumes or gases emitted from premises so as to be prejudicial to health or a nuisance;
>
> (d) any dust, steam, smell or other effluvia arising on industrial, trade or business premises and being prejudicial to health or a nuisance;
>
> (e) any accumulation or deposit which is prejudicial to health or a nuisance;
>
> (f) any animal kept in such a place or manner as to be prejudicial to health or a nuisance;
>
> (fa) any insects emanating from relevant industrial, trade or business premises and being prejudicial to health or a nuisance;
>
> (fb) artificial light emitted from premises so as to be prejudicial to health or a nuisance;
>
> (g) noise emitted from premises so as to be prejudicial to health or a nuisance;
>
> (ga) noise that is prejudicial to health or a nuisance and is emitted from or caused by a vehicle, machinery or equipment in a street or in Scotland, road;
>
> (h) any other matter declared by any enactment to be a statutory nuisance;'

Clearly many of the things which meet the definition of a statutory nuisance are also capable of being conduct which is having a 'detrimental and persistent/continuing effect on the quality of life of those in the locality'.

The Revised Guidance states that the local authority will need to consider whether issuing a CPN is necessary given the powers available under the EPA 1990.[75] There is an important distinction between the powers available under the two Acts: there is a statutory *duty* to serve an abatement notice where the local authority is satisfied that a statutory nuisance exists,[76] which is in contrast to the *power* to serve a CPN.

There may be circumstances when a local authority chooses to issue a CPN despite its powers under the EPA 1990 to issue an abatement notice. Where a statutory nuisance relates to noise, the local authority has a duty to serve an abatement notice or take 'such other steps as it thinks appropriate for the

---

75   Revised *Statutory Guidance for Frontline Professionals*, p 41.

76   Save for those nuisances failing with s 79(1)(g) – noise emitted from premises so as to be prejudicial to health or a nuisance.

purpose of persuading the person to abate the nuisance or prohibit or restrict its occurrence or recurrence';[77] the local authority could decide to issue a CPN as part of these 'other steps'. However, in view of the *duty* to serve an abatement notice, the availability of CPNs should not be seen as an automatic alternative to such a notice.

In the White Paper the Government noted that even though action in respect of noise was the preserve of local authorities, the police had been called out to deal with noise 88,317 times in 2008–09.[78] Since the Act came into force, the police have had the power to serve a CPN in respect of noise. The Revised Guidance suggests that in cases where a CPN is issued, the officer will need to work with the relevant council team that deals with statutory nuisances to ensure that any restrictions or requirements in the CPN complement those that may be included in any future abatement notice.[79] Both local authorities and the police will need to ensure there are good information sharing arrangements about when CPNs have been issued, particularly in view of the local authority's statutory duty under the EPA 1990. Local authority officers should carry out a formal assessment of what the nuisance is and what enforcement action is appropriate on a case-by-case basis. Unless the nuisance is noise-related the local authority will be under a duty to serve an abatement notice but also has an additional tool in its armoury.

L EXISTING NOTICES

6.28   Section 58 of the Act sets out the transitional provisions for certain notices served before the commencement day. The repeals or amendments introduced by the Act do not apply in relation to the notices listed in s 58(2) or anything done in connection with those notices. The notices listed in s 58(2) are:

(a)   a litter abatement notice under s 92 of the EPA 1990;

(b)   a litter clearing notice under s 92A of the EPA 1990;

(c)   a street litter control notice under s 93 of the EPA 1990;

(d)   a defacement removal notice under s 48 of the ASBA 2003.

M CONCLUSION

6.29   The CPN has introduced a method of dealing with anti-social behaviour which is not specific to the behaviour complained of. As a result it will allow more than one type of anti-social behaviour to be addressed at the same time and this is a welcome improvement on the numerous behaviour-specific powers it replaces.

CPNs do not replace the statutory duties which exist under the EPA 1990. In relation to noise, they provide an additional power but many local authorities

---

77   EPA 1990, s 80(2A)(b).
78   *More Effective Responses to Anti-Social Behaviour*, May 2012, p 27.
79   Revised *Statutory Guidance for Frontline Professionals*, p 41.

continue to use noise abatement notices. They are already very well versed in using the powers available under the EPA 1990 – as are the courts – and there is little sign that the use of those powers has been affected to any great degree.

One of the biggest changes introduced by the Act was the ability to designate social landlords to issue CPNs. The intention was for them to have a more formal role in tackling anti-social behaviour in the areas where they owned/managed housing stock. Social landlords have a wealth of experience when it comes to tackling anti-social behaviour but they do not yet have any experience of issuing notices such as the CPN. At the time of writing very few local authorities had used their ability to designate housing providers to issue CPNs.

For those local authorities who are considering designating their power to issue a CPN, detailed memorandums of understanding should be prepared and careful thought will need to be given to training those responsible for issuing CPNs to ensure they are deployed effectively and in accordance with the statutory scheme.

CHAPTER 7

Public spaces protection orders

Snapshot

What's out

- Gating orders
- Designated public places orders
- Dog control orders

What's in

- Public space protection orders ('PSPOs')

Key points

- Wider behaviour covered
- Ability to include prohibitions and requirements
- No central government reporting requirements such as those that had existed with designated public place orders
- Lighter touch consultation requirements

Resources

See Appendix C for a copy of the guidance on PSPOs published by the Local Government Association:

- Public Space Protection Orders, Guidance for council published by the Local Government Association

See Appendix B for the Anti-social Behaviour, Crime and Policing Act 2014 (Publication of Public Spaces Protection Orders) Regulations 2014, SI 2014/2591

A INTRODUCTION: THE POWERS WHICH HAVE BEEN REPLACED

7.01   As the name suggests public spaces protection orders (PSPOs) are made in respect of public spaces. They place controls on the use of a space and everyone within it. Breach of a PSPO carries criminal sanctions. A single order can cover a range of behaviours resulting in less paperwork, bureaucracy and delay.

PSPOs were created by Ch 2 of Pt 4 of the Act, ss 59–75. PSPOs replace the following powers:

(a) gating orders under Pt 8A of the Highways Act 1980;

(b) designated public place orders under s 13(2) of the Criminal Justice and Police Act 2001 (CJPA 2001); and

(c)   dog control orders under Ch 1 of Pt 6 of the Clean Neighbourhoods and Environment Act 2005 (CNEA 2005).

The enforceability of orders which were issued prior to the Act coming into force is considered in more detail at 7.37 below.

The stated purpose of PSPOs is to deal with a particular nuisance or problem in a particular area that is detrimental to the local community's quality of life.[1]

The Explanatory Notes to the Act suggest that PSPOs are different from the powers they replace in the following ways:

(a)   They can prohibit a wider range of behaviour, which makes the new order more like the 'good rule and government byelaws' made under the Local Government Act 1972, but with a fixed penalty notice available on breach (although some current byelaws do allow for fixed penalty notices to be issued).

(b)   There will be less central government oversight than with byelaws, and no central government reporting requirements as with designated public place orders. This will reduce bureaucracy.

(c)   There will be lighter touch consultation requirements to save costs (for example, there is no duty to advertise in local newspapers).

There was a considerable debate in Parliament about the wide-ranging ambit of PSPOs and a concern that innocent people would be penalised or prevented entry to places they were once able to freely access.[2] There was a desire to ensure PSPOs could not be used to interfere with legitimate activities such as peaceful protests, holding placards or handing out literature. During the debates the Government was concerned to demonstrate that there was a 'very high test'[3] to be met before a PSPO could be made and that there were sufficient safeguards within the Act and the Guidance.

In terms of safeguards, the Act makes express reference to the need to have particular regard to Article 10 (right of freedom of expression) and Article 11 (right to freedom of association and assembly).[4] Local authorities are required to publicise their intention to make a PSPO so as to allow those affected to make representations.[5] There is the ability to challenge the validity of a PSPO in the High Court.[6]

Concern about the way in which PSPOs have been used has been widespread. One of the primary motivators behind the Guidance being revised was the desire to ensure that PSPOs were being used to target specific behaviour, that they were proportionate and were being implemented following an appropriate level of scrutiny.

---

1   Revised *Statutory Guidance for Frontline Professionals*, p 47.
2   HoL Committee, 4th sitting, 25 November 2013, Lord Greaves, col 1219.
3   HoL Committee, 4th sitting, 25 November 2013, Parliamentary Under-Secretary of State, Home Office, Lord Taylor of Holbeach, col 1225.
4   Section 72 of the Anti-Social Behaviour, Crime and Policing Act 2014; all statutory references are to this Act unless otherwise stated.
5   s 72(4).
6   s 66.

Two challenges to PSPOs have been heard by the High Court to date. *Summers v Richmond Upon Thames LBC*[7] concerned the introduction of a PSPO which sought to ensure that dogs are kept under proper control and to place limits on the numbers of dogs a single person can walk. *Dulgheriu & Orthova v Ealing LBC*[8] concerned the introduction of a 'safe zone' outside an abortion clinic in West London. This case will be heard by the Court of Appeal in July 2019.

Each of the cases on PSPOs will be considered in greater detail in this chapter.

B WHAT IS A PUBLIC SPACES PROTECTION ORDER?

7.02 A PSPO is an order designed to place controls on behaviour which is having, or is likely to have, a detrimental effect on the quality of life of those using a public place. It can be used to deal with existing problems and problems that are likely to arise in the future.

It attaches to the public place as opposed to an individual and can be useful in situations where the individuals responsible for an activity cannot be readily identified.

C WHO CAN MAKE A PUBLIC SPACES PROTECTION ORDER?

7.03 Only a local authority can make a PSPO in respect of a public place within its area. Section 74(1) defines a 'local authority' for the purposes of Ch 2 of the Act.

In England this will be:

- the district council;

- the county council where there is no district council;

- London Boroughs;

- The Common Council for the City of London (in its capacity as a local authority); and

- The Isles of Scilly.

In Wales this will be:

- the county council; or

- the borough council.

Parish councils and town councils (in England) and community councils (in Wales) do not have the power to issue PSPOs.

---

7   [2018] EWHC 782 (Admin), [2018] 1 WLR 4729, May J.
8   [2018] EWHC 1667 (Admin), [2018] 4 ALL ER 881, Turner J.

Designated person or body

7.04 A designated person or body can issue a PSPO. Under s 71 of the Act the Secretary of State may by order designate a person or body (other than a local authority) that has power to make byelaws in relation to particular land and to specify the land in England to which the power relates.[9]

There are limitations on the prohibitions or requirements that can be included in a PSPO which is issued by a designated person/body compared to those which could have been included in a byelaw in respect of the restricted area. In addition, a PSPO issued by a designated person/body cannot regulate an activity which is already regulated by a PSPO made by a local authority.

If a local authority issues a PSPO in relation to a particular public space, that PSPO takes priority and the PSPO made by a designated person ceases to have effect.

D   WHEN CAN A PUBLIC SPACES PROTECTION ORDER BE ISSUED?

7.05 In order to issue a PSPO the local authority must be satisfied on reasonable grounds that two conditions are met:[10]

The **first condition** is that:

(a)   activities carried on in a public place within the authority's area have had a detrimental effect on the quality of life of those in the locality; or

(b)   it is likely that activities will be carried on in a public place within that area and that they will have such an effect.

The **second condition** is that the effect, or likely effect, of the activities:

(a)   is, or is likely to be, of a persistent or continuing nature;

(b)   is, or is likely to be, such as to make the activities unreasonable; and

(c)   justifies the restrictions imposed by the notice.

In deciding whether to make a PSPO (or when deciding whether to extend the period for which a PSPO has effect or to vary or discharge a PSPO) the local authority must:

(a)   have particular regard to the rights of freedom of expression and freedom of assembly set out in Articles 10 and 11 of the European Convention on Human Rights;[11]

(b)   carry out the necessary consultation;[12]

9   See Anti-social Behaviour (Designation of the City of London Corporation) Order 2015, SI 2015/858.
10   s 59(2) and (3).
11   s 72(1).
12   s 72(3).

(c)   carry out the necessary notification;[13] and

(d)   carry out the necessary publicity.[14]

Items (a)–(d) are considered in greater detail below.

E   MEANING OF 'DETRIMENTAL EFFECT'

7.06   The Act does not define 'detrimental effect'; however, both *Summers*[15] and *Dulgheriu*[16] confirm that local authorities have a wide discretion to determine which activities had or were likely to have a 'detrimental effect' on the quality of life of those in the locality. In *Summers*, May J said:[17]

- the Act envisages the use of PSPOs to curb activities that not everyone would view as detrimentally affecting their quality of life;

- the absence of a definition points strongly towards local authorities being given a wide discretion to decide what behaviours are troublesome and require to be addressed within their area;

- deciding whether, and if so what, controls on certain behaviours are needed is the 'very essence of local politics'

In *Dulgheriu*,[18] Turner J said that the fact that Parliament chose not to define what may amount to detrimental effect should not be treated by the courts as an invitation to fill the vacuum with a definition of their own.

The judge also said that local authorities can and should consider the impact of the behaviour on vulnerable people, despite the fact that they may be less resilient and more easily upset than a 'reasonably' or 'ordinarily' robust person. This means that there is a broad discretion to regulate activities which have the requisite detrimental effect and this could include activities which would not normally be classed as 'anti-social behaviour' in the traditional sense. The focus should be on the statutory test, namely whether the activities are having a detrimental effect on the quality of life of those in the locality.

F   MEANING OF 'LOCALITY'

7.07   The activities must have a detrimental effect on the quality of life of those in the 'locality'. In *Dulgheriu* an argument that a narrow interpretation should be adopted, such as to exclude one-off or occasional visitors, was rejected.

---

13   Ibid.
14   Ibid.
15   *Summers v Richmond Upon Thames LBC* [2018] EWHC 782 (Admin), [2018] WLR 4729, May J.
16   *Dulgheriu & Orthova v Ealing LBC* [2018] EWHC 1667 (Admin), Turner J.
17   At [25].
18   [2018] EWHC 1667 (Admin).

Turner J observed that a narrow approach would serve to tie local authorities' hands when seeking to prohibit detrimental activities in public areas mainly populated by visitors, for example in the vicinity of tourist attractions. PSPOs can be made to cover one-off or infrequent visitors to a locality as well as those who are frequent visitors, or working or living within it. The Court of Appeal is expected to provide further guidance on the interpretation of locality in the appeal in the case of *Dulgheriu*, which is listed for hearing in July 2019.

G MEANING OF 'PERSISTENT OR CONTINUING'

7.08 The use of the words 'persistent or continuing' excludes one-off activities, or those which might occur more than once, but rarely.[19]

In the analogous statutory context of gating orders, which were used to close footpaths so as to prevent persistent commission of anti-social behaviour (under Part 8A of the Highways Act 1980), a court has held that 'persistent' was an ordinary English word commonly understood to mean 'continuing or recurring, prolonged'.[20]

H ARTICLE 10 (FREEDOM OF EXPRESSION) AND ARTICLE 11 (FREEDOM OF ASSOCIATION/ASSEMBLY) OF THE EUROPEAN CONVENTION ON HUMAN RIGHTS

7.09 PSPOs are a powerful remedy because they affect the behaviour of *every* person within a specified area rather than being targeted at individuals. For this reason local authorities will need to take care to ensure that they balance the need to tackle activities having a detrimental effect against the desire and entitlement of the public to use a public space.

In deciding whether to make a PSPO, what a PSPO should include, whether to extend a PSPO (and if so for how long) or whether a PSPO should be varied or discharged, the local authority is required to have 'particular regard' to the rights of freedom of expression and freedom of association/assembly set out in Articles 10 and 11 of the European Convention on Human Rights.[21] Local authorities as public authorities are required to act in a way which is compatible with Convention Rights in any event (see further the discussion in Chapter 2). Whether the need to have 'particular regard' to Article 10 gives these rights an elevated status in relation to PSPOs is as yet untested.

The full text of Articles 10 and 11 of the European Convention on Human Rights is set out in Chapter 2. Chapter 2 also deals with some of the principles that apply when looking at human rights considerations.

Local authorities will need to give careful thought to the way in which the prohibitions and requirements within a PSPO are framed to ensure that they do

---

19   See *Summers*, at [21].
20   *Ramblers Association v Coventry City Council* [2009] PTSR 715, at [21].
21   s 72(1).

not unnecessarily interfere with what would otherwise be legitimate and lawful activity.

Although the Act does not expressly prohibit PSPOs being used to interfere with picketing and processions in the way that it does with the dispersal powers,[22] local authorities should be mindful that PSPOs are aimed at *persistent* or *continuing* behaviour which is having a *detrimental* effect on the quality of life of the people in their communities; it is unlikely that picketing or processions will ever meet the test.

Even when the test for making a PSPO is met, local authorities should consider other and less restrictive ways of addressing the particular problem. This is for the obvious reason that access to public spaces should only be restricted or prevented where it is necessary. This does not mean that the least restrictive approach must be adopted but that options which are less restrictive ought to be considered. In *Lough and Others v First Secretary of State*[23] the Court of Appeal was asked to consider whether the grant of planning permission was, inter alia, a breach of Article 8 (right to respect for private and family life) and the right to peaceful enjoyment of possessions under Article 1 of the First Protocol.[24] The Court found that there had been no breach of Article 8(1) and gave some guidance on the application of Article 8(2). Pill LJ said that 'when balances are struck, the competing interests of the individual, other individuals and the community as a whole must be considered'.[25] An effective PSPO may remedy the detriment caused by the activity, but it may cause other detriment to members of the public in the limitation upon their use of public space. Local authorities will need to strike the appropriate balance between all of the competing interests.

I   PUBLIC SECTOR EQUALITY DUTY

7.10   In *Summers*[26], May J confirmed that an argument that the Public Sector Equality Duty (PSED) duty has been breached could be considered by the High Court in an appeal of a PSPO.[27] The PSED is considered in Chapter 2. In short, public authorities, and any person who exercises public functions, must have 'due regard' to the factors set out in s 149 of the Equality Act 2010.

Local authorities are reminded of the need to carry out an equality impact assessment which takes the requirements of s 149 into account.

J   THE NECESSARY CONSULTATION

7.11   In deciding whether to make a PSPO, what a PSPO should include, whether to extend a PSPO (and if so for how long) or whether a PSPO should be

---

22   See s 36(4) (restrictions on giving a direction to disperse).
23   [2004] EWCA Civ 905, [2004] 1 WLR 2557.
24   Of the European Convention on Human Rights and Fundamental Freedoms.
25   At [43].
26   [2018] EWHC 782 (Admin), [2018] WLR 4729, May J.
27   At [88].

varied or discharged, the local authority is required to carry out the 'necessary consultation', the 'necessary notification' and the 'necessary publicity'.

The 'necessary consultation' is defined in s 72(4) of the Act as consulting with:[28]

(a)   the chief officer of police, and the local policing body, for the police area that includes the restricted area;

(b)   whatever community representatives the local authority thinks it appropriate to consult; and

(c)   the owner or occupier of land within the restricted area, if, or to the extent that it is reasonably practicable to consult with the owner.[29]

Where the local authority is the owner or occupier of land within the restricted area the consultation requirement in s 72 does not apply.[30]

If the application is being made by a designated person or body (and not the local authority), the designated person/body must consult with the local authority.[31]

The Revised Guidance suggests that local authorities should consult the county council as Highways Authority where the application is not being led by that county council.[32]

In terms of community representatives, these could be the residents' association, regular users of an area affected by the proposed PSPO (extension or variation/discharge), and those involved in specific activities such as busking or street entertainment.[33]

The consultation requirements are intended to be focused at local level and will allow local authorities to make decisions which are appropriate and relevant to their areas without the need to seek approval from central Government. The intention is to allow local authorities a greater discretion than that available when making byelaws which need to be authorised by the Secretary of State. There is a textbox on the duty to consult in Chapter 3.

K   THE NECESSARY NOTIFICATION

7.12   The 'necessary notification' must be carried out in the circumstances listed in 7.11 above and is defined in s 72(4) of the Act as notifying:

(a)   the parish council or community council (if any) for the area that includes the restricted area;

(b)   in the case of a PSPO made or to be made by a district council in England, the county council (if any) for the area that includes the restricted area.

---

28   s 72(4).
29   s 72(5)(b).
30   s 72(5)(a).
31   s 72(6).
32   Revised *Statutory Guidance for Frontline Professionals*, p 49.
33   Revised *Statutory Guidance for Frontline Professionals*, p 49.

L   THE NECESSARY PUBLICITY

7.13   The 'necessary publicity' must be carried out in the circumstances listed in 7.11 above and is defined in s 72(4) of the Act as:

(a)   in the case of a proposed order or variation, publishing the text of it;

(b)   in the case of a proposed extension or discharge, publicising the proposal.

The publicity is to be carried out in accordance with the Anti-social Behaviour, Crime and Policing Act 2014 (Publication of Public Spaces Protection Orders) Regulations 2014.[34] These provide that where a PSPO has been made, varied or extended, the local authority must publish the text of the PSPO on its website. It must also ensure that notices are placed on or adjacent to the land to which the notices relate. The notices must be such as the local authority considers sufficient to draw the attention of any member of the public to the fact that the order is proposed, or, has been made, extended or varied and the effect of that order being made, varied or extended.[35]

Where a PSPO has been discharged, the local authority must publish a notice on its website identifying the order which has been discharged and the date on which it ceases to have effect. It must also ensure that notices are placed on or adjacent to the land to which the notices relates. Those notices must be such as it considers sufficient to draw the attention of any member of the public to the fact that a PSPO has been discharged and the date on which it ceases to have effect.[36]

M   CONTENTS OF A PSPO

Required content

7.14   A PSPO must:[37]

(a)   identify the activities referred to in s 59(2) (those activities which caused the order to be served);

(b)   explain the potential sanctions if the PSPO is breached (the effect of s 63 where it applies (consumption of alcohol in breach of a prohibition in an order) and s 67 (that it is an offence to fail to comply with an order); and

(c)   specify the period for which the order has effect.

---

34   SI 2014/2591.
35   Anti-social Behaviour, Crime and Policing Act 2014 (Publication of Public Spaces Protection Orders) Regulations 2014, SI 2014/2591, reg 2.
36   Anti-social Behaviour, Crime and Policing Act 2014 (Publication of Public Spaces Protection Orders) Regulations 2014, SI 2014/2591, reg 3.
37   s 59(7).

Duration and extension

7.15   A PSPO can have effect for a period of not more than three years[38] unless extended under s 60(2) of the Act.

A PSPO can be extended by the local authority that made the order if is satisfied on reasonable grounds that it is necessary to extend the order to prevent:

(a)   occurrence or recurrence after that time of the activities identified in the order; or

(b)   an increase in the frequency or seriousness of those activities after that time.[39]

A PSPO can be extended more than once[40] but any extension cannot be for more than three years and the extended order must be published in accordance with regulations made by the Secretary of State.[41]

There was some concern that the time limit could impose an unnecessary administrative burden upon local authorities who would have to renew the PSPOs every three years and that no additional funding had been provided for this purpose. The Government considered that a period of up to three years achieves proportionate balance between the needs of users and the need to protect the community.[42]

Prohibitions and requirements

7.16   Section 59(4) of the Act allows a PSPO to include prohibitions on specified things being done within a restricted area[43] and requirements that certain things be done by persons carrying on specified activities in that area or both.

Section 59(5) of the Act provides that the only prohibitions or requirements that may be imposed are ones that are reasonable to impose for the specified objectives which are:

(a)   to prevent the detrimental effect referred to in s 59(2) from continuing, occurring or recurring; or

(b)   to reduce that detrimental effect or to reduce the risk of its continuance, occurrence or recurrence.

The provisions allow for a great deal of flexibility in the prohibitions and/or requirements that are included in a PSPO.

---

38   s 60(1).
39   s 60(2).
40   s 60(4)
41   s 60(3)(b); Anti-social Behaviour, Crime and Policing Act 2014 (Publication of Public Spaces Protection Orders) Regulations 2014, SI 2014/2591.
42   HoL Committee, 4th sitting, 25 November 2013, Lord Ahmad of Wimbledon, col 1247.
43   A 'restricted area' is the public place in which the activities specified in s 59(2) are taking place.

In addition, the prohibitions or requirements may be framed:

(a)   so as to apply to all persons, or only to persons in specified categories, or to all persons except those in specified categories;

(b)   so as to apply at all times, or only at specified times, or at all times except those specified;

(c)   so as to apply in all circumstances, or only in specified circumstances, or in all circumstances except those specified.[44]

An example could be restrictions on dog walking at certain times of day or a restriction on the types (or numbers) of dog that may be walked in a particular area.

Unlike many of the old powers which were specific to certain types of behaviour, PSPOs are not constrained in this way and can apply to any activities that meet the conditions found in s 59(2) and (3) of the Act (detrimental effect and persistent/continuing).

N   VARIATION AND DISCHARGE

7.17   Section 61 makes provision for PSPOs to be varied and/or discharged.

Discharge

7.18   A PSPO can be discharged by the local authority that made it.[45] If an order is discharged, notification of the discharge needs to be given in accordance with any regulations made by the Secretary of State.[46] The discharge of the order must be published in accordance with the regulations made by the Secretary of State.[47] These are the Anti-social Behaviour, Crime and Policing Act 2014 (Publication of Public Spaces Protection Orders) Regulations.[48]

Variation

7.19   A PSPO can be varied by the local authority which made the order and it can have the effect of:

(a)   increasing the restricted area;

(b)   reducing the restricted area;

(c)   altering a prohibition or requirement;

(d)   removing a prohibition or requirement; or

---

44   s 59(6).
45   s 61(4).
46   s 61(6); Anti-social Behaviour, Crime and Policing Act 2014 (Publication of Public Spaces Protection Orders) Regulations 2014, SI 2014/2591, reg 3.
47   s 61(6).
48   SI 2014/2591.

(e)   adding a prohibition or requirement.[49]

If the area to which the PSPO applies is to be increased, this can only be done where the conditions in s 59(2) and (3) are met (the activities having, or likely to have, a detrimental impact on the quality of life of those living locally and those activities being persistent or continuing, unreasonable and the imposition of restrictions being justified).[50]

Additional prohibitions and/or requirements can only be imposed if they meet the conditions set out in s 59(5) (see 7.16 above).[51]

The varied order must be published in accordance with regulations made by the Secretary of State.[52] These are the Anti-social Behaviour, Crime and Policing Act 2014 (Publication of Public Spaces Protection Orders) Regulations 2014.[53]

O   ALCOHOL

7.20   PSPOs can include a prohibition on consuming alcohol. However, there are certain situations set out in s 62 of the Act when a prohibition on consuming alcohol cannot be imposed. These are:

(a)   premises (other than council-operated licensed premises) authorised by a premises licence to be used for the supply of alcohol;

(b)   premises authorised by a club premises certificate to be used by the club for the supply of alcohol;

(c)   a place within the curtilage of premises within para (a) or (b);

(d)   premises which by virtue of Pt 5 of the Licensing Act 2003 may at the relevant time be used for the supply of alcohol or which, by virtue of that Part, could have been so used within the 30 minutes before that time;

(e)   a place where facilities or activities relating to the sale or consumption of alcohol are at the relevant time permitted by virtue of a permission granted under s 115E of the Highways Act 1980 (highway-related uses).

A prohibition in a PSPO on consuming alcohol does not apply to council-operated licensed premises:[54]

(a)   when the premises are being used for the supply of alcohol; or

(b)   within 30 minutes after the end of a period during which the premises have been used for the supply of alcohol.

For the purposes of this section:[55]

49   s 61(1).
50   s 61(2).
51   s 61(3).
52   s 61(5).
53   SI 2014/2591.
54   s 62(2).
55   s 62(3).

'a "club premises certificate" has the meaning given by section 60 of the Licensing Act 2003[56]

a "premises licence" has the meaning given by section 11 of the Licensing Act 2003[57]

the "supply of alcohol" has the meaning given by section 14 of the Licensing Act 2003[58]'

By virtue of s 62(4) of the Act, premises are 'council-operated licensed premises' if they are used for the supply of alcohol and this is authorised by a premises licence and the licence is held by:

(a)   the local authority in whose area the premises[59] is situated;[60] or

(b)   another person but the premises are occupied or managed by or on behalf of a local authority.[61]

A person commits an offence if they fail to comply with a request not to consume alcohol or a request made pursuant to s 63(2)(a) to surrender anything in his/her possession which is reasonably believed to be alcohol or a container for alcohol.[62]

The request (not to consume or to surrender an item) may be made by a constable or an authorised person[63] and can be made where s/he believes a person is, has, or intends to consume alcohol in breach of a prohibition within a PSPO.[64]

---

56   Section 60 of the Licensing Act 2003 provides:
   '60 Club premises certificate
   (1)   In this Act "club premises certificate" means a certificate granted under this Part—
      (a)   in respect of premises occupied by, and habitually used for the purposes of, a club,
      (b)   by the relevant licensing authority, and
      (c)   certifying the matters specified in subsection (2).
   (2)   Those matters are—
      (a)   that the premises may be used by the club for one or more qualifying club activities specified in the certificate, and
      (b)   that the club is a qualifying club in relation to each of those activities (see section 61).'
57   Section 11 of the Licensing Act 2003 provides:
   'In this Act "premises licence" means a licence granted under this Part, in respect of any premises, which authorises the premises to be used for one or more licensable activities.'
58   Section 14 of the Licensing Act 2003 provides:
   'For the purposes of this Part the "supply of alcohol" means—
   (a)   the sale by retail of alcohol, or
   (b)   the supply of alcohol by or on behalf of a club to, or to the order of, a member of the club.'
59   Or part of the premises.
60   s 62(4)(a).
61   s 62(4)(b).
62   s 63(6).
63   s 63(2). Section 63(1) provides:
   'In this section "authorised person" means a person authorised for the purposes of this section by the local authority that made the public spaces protection order (or authorised by virtue of section 69(1)).'
64   s 63(1).

Failure to show evidence of authorisation

7.21   A request (not to consume alcohol or surrender an item) made by an authorised person[65] will not be valid if when asked for evidence of his/her authorisation, the authorised person fails to show such evidence.[66]

P   LAND REQUIRING SPECIAL CONSIDERATION

7.22   The Revised Guidance sets out special considerations which apply when a PSPO is going to include registered common land, a registered town or village green or open access land.[67]

Q   RESTRICTIONS ON PUBLIC RIGHTS OF WAY

7.23   During the Parliamentary debates it was made clear that the Government's intention was that a decision to restrict activity on, or access to public rights of way should not be taken lightly. The needs of the community will need to be weighed against the need to deal with activities having a detrimental effect and the Act contains additional requirements where public rights of way are affected.

Notification and considering representations

7.24   A PSPO can have the effect of restricting public rights over a highway.[68] A PSPO that has this effect cannot be made without considering:[69]

(a)   the likely effect of making the order on the occupiers of premises adjoining or adjacent to the highway;

(b)   the likely effect of making the order on other persons in the locality; and

(c)   in a case where the highway constitutes a through route, the availability of a reasonably convenient alternative route.

---

65   s 63(2).
66   s 63(4).
67   Revised *Statutory Guidance for Frontline Professionals*, p 50.
68   By virtue of s 64(10) 'highway' has the meaning given by s 328 of the Highways Act 1980 which provides:
       '328.— Meaning of "highway"
       (1)   In this Act, except where the context otherwise requires, "highway" means the whole or a part of a highway other than a ferry or waterway.
       (2)   Where a highway passes over a bridge or through a tunnel, that bridge or tunnel is to be taken for the purposes of this Act to be a part of the highway.
       (3)   In this Act, "highway maintainable at the public expense" and any other expression defined by reference to a highway is to be construed in accordance with the foregoing provisions of this section.'
69   s 64(1).

Before making a PSPO that restricts public rights over a highway the local authority is required to notify persons who will potentially be affected by the proposed order.[70] It must inform those persons of how they can see a copy of the proposed order and the period by which any representations on the order must be made.[71] The local authority is required to consider any representations made.[72]

'Persons affected' are defined in s 64(2) as 'occupiers of premises adjacent to or adjoining the highway and any other persons who are likely to be affected by the proposed order'.

If the PSPO will restrict a public right of way over a highway that is within the area of another local authority it must consult that other authority if it thinks it appropriate to do so.[73]

Dwellings

7.25   A PSPO cannot have the effect of restricting a public right of way over a highway that is the only or principal means of access to a dwelling.[74]

'Dwelling' is defined as 'a building or part of a building occupied, or intended to be occupied, as a separate dwelling'.[75]

Businesses and recreational activities

7.26   A PSPO cannot have the effect of restricting a public right of way over a highway where this is the only or principal means of accessing premises used for business or recreational activities during the periods when the premises are normally used for those purposes.[76]

Power to install, operate and maintain barriers

7.27   If a PSPO has the effect of restricting a public right of way, a local authority has the power to install, operate and maintain barriers to enforce that restriction.[77]

Categories of highway over which a public right of way may not be restricted

7.28   Section 65 of the Act lists categories of highway over which public rights of way may not be restricted by a PSPO, as follows:

---

70   s 64(2)(a).
71   s 64(2)(b)–(c).
72   s 64(2)(d).
73   s 64(3).
74   s 64(5).
75   s 64(10).
76   s 64(6).
77   s 64(7) and (8).

(a)   a special road;[78]

(b)   a trunk road;[79]

(c)   a classified[80] or principal[81] road;

(d)   a strategic road;[82]

(e)   a highway[83] in England of a description prescribed by regulations made by the Secretary of State;

---

78   As defined in s 329(1) of the Highways Act 1980.
79   Ibid.
80   Ibid.
81   As defined in s 12 of the Highways Act 1980 (also see s 13 of that Act):
   '**12.— General provision as to principal and classified roads**
   (1)   Subject to subsection (3) below, all such highways or proposed highways as immediately before the commencement of this Act—
      (a)   were principal roads for the purposes of any enactment or instrument which refers to roads or highways classified by the Minister as principal roads, either by virtue of having been so classified under section 27(2) of the Local Government Act 1966 (which is replaced by subsection (3) below), or by virtue of being treated as such in accordance with section 40(1) of the Local Government Act 1974,
      (b)   were (whether or not they also fall within paragraph (a) above) classified roads for the purposes of any enactment or instrument which refers to roads classified by the Minister (but does not specifically refer to their classification as principal roads), either by virtue of having been so classified under section 27(2) of the said Act of 1966, or by virtue of being treated as such in accordance with section 40(1) of the said Act of 1974, or
      (c)   were classified roads for the purposes of any enactment or instrument by virtue of being treated as such in accordance with section 27(4) of the said Act of 1966,
      continue to be, and to be known as, principal roads or, as the case may be, classified roads (or both principal roads and classified roads of a category other than principal roads, in the case of highways falling within both paragraph (a) and paragraph (b) above) for the purposes specified in subsection (2) below.
   (2)   So far as a highway that continues to be a principal or classified road in accordance with subsection (1) above was, immediately before the commencement of this Act, a classified road for the purposes of any enactment repealed and replaced by this Act, it is a classified road for the purposes of the corresponding provision of this Act; and so far as any such highway was immediately before the commencement of this Act a principal or classified road for the purposes of any other enactment, or any instrument, it so continues for the purposes of that enactment or instrument.
   …'
82   As defined in s 60(4) of the Traffic Management Act 2004:
   '(b)   "strategic road" means a road which is for the time being a strategic road by virtue of an order under subsection (1) or section 61(1);'
83   As defined in s.328 of the Highways Act 1980:
   '**328.— Meaning of "highway"**
   (1)   In this Act, except where the context otherwise requires, "highway" means the whole or a part of a highway other than a ferry or waterway.
   (2)   Where a highway passes over a bridge or through a tunnel, that bridge or tunnel is to be taken for the purposes of this Act to be a part of the highway.
   (3)   In this Act, "highway maintainable at the public expense" and any other expression defined by reference to a highway is to be construed in accordance with the foregoing provisions of this section.'

(f)   a highway[84] in Wales of a description prescribed by regulations made by the Welsh Ministers.

R   CHALLENGES TO PSPOS

The basis of a challenge

7.29   Section 66(2) of the Act identifies the grounds upon which an application to challenge a PSPO can be made:

(a)   that the local authority did not have power to make the order or variation, or to include particular prohibitions or requirements imposed by the order (or by the order as varied);

(b)   that a requirement under Ch 2 of Pt 4 of the Act was not complied with in relation to the order or variation.

In addition, a challenge may be made under s 67(3) as a defence to a charge that a PSPO has been breached (on the basis that the local authority did not have the power to include a particular prohibition or requirement in a PSPO).

Where and by when?

7.30   A challenge to a PSPO can only be made under s 66 or s 67(3).[85]

A challenge to the validity or variation of a PSPO is made to the High Court[86] and must be made within six weeks beginning on the date when the PSPO is made or varied.[87]

The High Court has the power to suspend the operation of some or all of the prohibitions or requirements imposed by the PSPO (or the variation of the PSPO) until the final determination of the proceedings.[88]

At the final determination of any challenge to the validity of a PSPO the High Court has the power to quash some or all of the prohibitions or requirements in the PSPO (or the variation of the PSPO) if it is satisfied that:[89]

(a)   the local authority did not have power to make the order or variation, or to include particular prohibitions or requirements imposed by the order (or by the order as varied); or

(b)   the interests of the applicant have been substantially prejudiced by a failure to comply with a requirement under Ch 2 of Pt 4 of the Act.

---

84   Ibid.
85   Section 67(3) provides that a person does not commit an offence of failing to comply with a PSPO where the local authority did not have the power to include a particular prohibition or requirement within the PSPO.
86   s 66(1).
87   s 66(3).
88   s 66(4).
89   s 66(5).

A PSPO, or any of the prohibitions or requirements imposed by it can be suspended (under s 66(4)) or quashed (under s 66(5)) generally or so far as necessary for the protection of the interests of the applicant.[90]

Interested persons

7.31   The challenge can be made by an 'interested person' defined in s 66(1) as 'an individual who lives in the restricted area or who regularly works in or visits that area'.[91] During the Parliamentary debates there was an attempt to allow national and regional organisations who represent people who use rights of way, walk on public access land or people who visit town and village greens to be included within the definition of 'interested persons'. This would have included, inter alia, the Ramblers Association, the British Mountaineering Council, the Open Spaces Society and others. However, the Act was not so amended on the basis that the purpose of this provision of the Act was to empower local people who are individually affected by the use of a PSPO.[92]

S   BREACH AND FIXED PENALTY NOTICES

7.32   If a person does anything that is lawfully[93] prohibited by a PSPO, or fails to do something lawfully[94] required by a PSPO, he commits an offence unless he has a reasonable excuse.[95]

On summary conviction the magistrates' court can impose a fine not exceeding level 3[96] on the standard scale.

FPNs

7.33   Section 68 of the Act deals with fixed penalty notices (FPNs). A FPN is defined in s 68(2) of the Act as a 'notice offering the person to whom it is issued the opportunity of discharging any liability to conviction for the offence by payment of a fixed penalty' to the local authority that made the PSPO.[97]

---

90   s 66(6).
91   In *Dulgheriu & Orthova v Ealing LBC* [2018] EWHC 1667 (Admin) it was held that this term is narrower than the words 'those in the locality' who must be detrimentally affected by the behaviour: at [38]–[43].
92   HoL Committee, 4th sitting, 25 November 2013, Lord Taylor of Holbeach, col 1276. Although it is interesting to to note that Lord Ahmad of Wimbledon commented that interest groups and other such bodies would still be able to challenge the PSPO by way of judicial review (HoL, Report stage, 1st sitting, 8 January 2014, col 1613). His observation does not sit well with the language of s 66(7)
93   s 67(3).
94   Ibid.
95   s 67(1).
96   Currently £1,000.
97   s 68(2).

FPNs can be issued by a constable or an authorised person where they have reason to believe an offence has been committed under s 63 or 67.

Where a FPN is issued, no proceedings can be taken before a period of 14 days following the date of the notice[98] or where the person issued with the notice pays the fixed penalty before the end of the 14 days.[99]

Contents of a FPN

7.34   Section 68(5) provides that a FPN must:

(a)   give reasonably detailed particulars of the circumstances alleged to constitute the offence;

(b)   state the period during which (because of subs (4)(a)) proceedings will not be taken for the offence;

(c)   specify the amount of the fixed penalty (which cannot exceed £100[100]);

(d)   state the name and address of the person to whom the fixed penalty may be paid; and

(e)   specify permissible methods of payment.[101]

Amount due

7.35   As set out above the FPN cannot specify a fixed penalty of more than £100. A FPN may specify two amounts, whereby the penalty is the lower amount if payment is made within a specified period of less than 14 days.[102]

In the event of a failure to pay a FPN, a certificate which purports to be signed by the local authority's chief finance officer and states that payment has not been received or was not received by the date stipulated is evidence of the non-payment or late payment.[103]

---

98   s 68(4)(a).
99   s 68(4)(b).
100 s 68(6).
101 s 68(8) and (9) provide:
  '(8) Whatever other method may be specified under subsection (5)(e), payment of a fixed penalty may be made by pre-paying and posting to the person whose name is stated under subsection (5)(d), at the stated address, a letter containing the amount of the penalty (in cash or otherwise).
  (9) Where a letter is sent as mentioned in subsection (8), payment is regarded as having been made at the time at which that letter would be delivered in the ordinary course of post.'
102 s 68(7).
103 s 68(10); s 68(11) defines 'chief finance officer' as the person with responsibility for the authority's financial affairs.

T POWERS OF POLICE COMMUNITY SUPPORT OFFICERS

7.36   Police Community Support Officers (PCSOs) have the following powers with regards to PSPOs where they have been designated to have the powers conferred on a constable by the chief constable:

(a)   to require a person not to consume alcohol or to require a person to surrender alcohol or anything believed to be alcohol under s 63(2) of the Act;

(b)   to dispose of anything surrendered to them under s 63(2)(b); and

(c)   to issue FPNs under s 68 in respect of a failure to comply with a PSPO.

U EXISTING ORDERS

7.37   Section 75 of the Act sets out the transitional provisions for certain orders made before the commencement day. The repeals or amendments introduced by the Act do not apply in relation to the orders listed in s 75(2) or anything done in connection with those orders. The orders listed in s 75(2) are:

(a)   a gating order under Pt 8A of the HA 1980;

(b)   an order under s 13(2) of the CJPA 2001 (power of local authority to designate public place for restrictions on alcohol consumption);

(c)   a dog control order under Ch 1 of Pt 6 of the CNEA 2005.

  If an existing order is still in force as at 20 October 2017 it will be treated as if the provisions of the existing order were provisions of a PSPO made under the Act.[104]

Using a PSPO – example

The behaviour in Woofwoof Park

Woofwoof Park is a local park owned by and within the jurisdiction of the Craven District Council. The Council has received numerous complaints about problems in the park, which include:

● dog walkers with too many dogs such that they are unable to keep them all under control;

● dogs not being kept on a lead;

● dogs being allowed to foul and the faeces not being removed;

● problems with people drinking alcohol;

● people acting in an abusive manner towards park wardens and members of the public; and

---

104   s 75(3).

- alleyways in the park being used for dealing or taking drugs.

The old law
Under the old law the following orders would have been required to deal with this behaviour:

- a dog control order;[105]

- a designated public place order to deal with the consumption of alcohol;[106]

- individual ASBOs in respect of those engaging in anti-social behaviour.

Each of these powers had its own statutory regime enabling the orders to be put into place and different ways in which they were enforced.

Using a PSPO
The Council is considering using a PSPO to deal with all of the problems in Woofwoof Park. The PSPO could include *prohibitions* on:

- walking more than four dogs at a time;

- drinking alcohol;

- engaging in anti-social behaviour; and

- using drugs;

and requirements that:

- a person must pick up after their dog; and

- must keep their dog on a lead.

The PSPO has a single method of enforcing breaches even when more than one type of behaviour is involved.

Consultation
Before making the PSPO the Council consulted with the chief officer of the Craven District Police, the Woofwoof Park Walking Club, the Friends of Woofwoof Park (a local community group) and the owner of the café within the park grounds.

Publicity
The Council published the proposed text of the PSPO and placed a notice on its website. It also placed notices on the information boards within the park.

Notification
The Council notified the County Council. There were no relevant Parish or Community Councils to be notified.

---

105 Under Ch 1 of Pt 6 of the Clean Neighbourhoods and Environment Act 2005.
106 Under s 13(2) of the CJPA 2001.

Publicity after the PSPO is made
A notice was put on the Council's website with full details of the requirements and prohibitions in the PSPO, the date on which the PSPO would take effect and the period over which it would run. The Council also published a map to show the area covered by the PSPO. Notices were placed at the each of the points of entry to the park and on the information boards within the park.

Variation
The park wardens report that the dog owners/walkers are allowing their dogs to foul outside the gates of the park in areas not covered by the PSPO. The Council wishes to vary the PSPO to cover a bigger area and conducts the necessary consultation, notification and publicity. The PSPO is varied to include the streets surrounding the park. The varied PSPO is published in the same way as above.

V CONCLUSION

7.38   The continued enforceability of existing orders means that there could be a number of orders in place in respect of the same area, each with its own enforcement regime. Local authorities should undertake a review of any existing orders with a view to deciding whether to make a single PSPO which covers all of the issues and which has a single method of enforcement.

Possible targets for behaviour which is 'detrimental to the quality of life in a locality' include rough sleepers, aggressive begging, buskers,[107] spitting[108]

---

107 Birmingham City Council has sent a letter, signed by Simon Cooper, Environmental Health to all of its buskers suggesting further restrictions/bans on busking in the city centre. For those considered using PSPOs for placing controls on busking, the following extract from the Parliamentary debates (21 January 2014, HoL, Lord Taylor of Holbeach, col 570), should be noted:

'My Lords, the new anti-social behaviour powers are designed to protect the activities of the law-abiding majority. The Government are certainly not seeking to restrict reasonable behaviour and activity, and we do not believe that these powers do. Live music and street entertainment play an important role in community life and can generate a positive atmosphere that is enjoyed by all. As a result, these reforms are completely consistent with our policies on busking and live music ... I can certainly give my noble friend the assurance that the guidance will achieve what he and the Government wish to see from it. I do not think that there is a difference across government on this issue. We believe that the tests and safeguards set out in the new anti-social behaviour powers will ensure that they will be used only where reasonable. Where behaviour is having a positive effect on a community, and I see busking as having that effect, it would not meet the tests for the new powers. Instead, the powers are directed against the anti-social minority who give street performers a bad name; I might illustrate them as being aggressive beggars and drunken louts.'

108 See explanatory notes to the Act, para 173. Enfield Council passed a bye law banning spitting in December 2013; in future a PSPO could be used instead.

and charity collectors or 'chuggers'.[109] Whether PSPOs can be used for this type of conduct will depend on whether the test is fulfilled by the particular circumstances in each area.

The long-stop date for the enforceability of existing orders is 20 October 2020. After this date the old orders will no longer be capable of being enforced. Local authorities who have not yet replaced their gating orders, dog control orders, or designated public place orders would be well advised to review whether there are continuing (or anticipated) activities that are having a detrimental effect on the quality of life of those in their area and consider the need for a PSPO.

---

109 The Head of Environmental Services at Rugby Borough Council gave a presentation to its Crime and Disorder Committee on 28 November 2013, in which he gave an example of PSPOs being used to control the areas and times within which charity collectors may operate.

CHAPTER 8

Closure orders

Snapshot

What's out

Specific closure powers relating to:

- drugs
- persistent disorder or nuisance
- noisy premises
- licensed premises

What's in

- a single closure power for ANY type of premises, residential, commercial, licensed, owner-occupied

Key points

- Two stage process; service of a closure notice followed by an application to the magistrates' court for a closure order

- Both closure notices and closure orders can be flexible about who's excluded, when and in what circumstances

- Maximum three months extendable for a further three months, six months overall

- Access to secure against entry and to conduct essential maintenance or repairs is allowed

Templates

See Appendix D for useful precedents which have been updated since the first edition of this book:

- Application for a closure order
- Closure notice
- Closure order

A INTRODUCTION: THE POWERS WHICH HAVE BEEN REPLACED

8.01 Chapter 3 of Pt 4 of the Act creates a single power to close premises associated with nuisance or disorder. The relevant sections are ss 76–93.[1]

The closure orders replace the following powers:

(a) drugs closure orders under s 2 of the Anti-Social Behaviour Act 2003 (ASBA 2003);

(b) closure of premises associated with persistent disorder or nuisance under s 11B of the ASBA 2003;

(c) noisy premises closure orders under s 40 of the ASBA 2003;

(d) powers relating to licenced premises under s 161 and s 165(2)(b)–(d) of the Licensing Act 2003 (LA 2003).

The stated purpose of the closure power is to create a fast, flexible power that can be used to protect victims and communities from premises which are causing nuisance or disorder.[2]

---

1   All statutory references are to the Anti-Social Behaviour, Crime and Policing Act 2014 unless otherwise stated.

2   Revised *Statutory Guidance for Frontline Professionals*, p 58.

The single closure power could be used to deal with a myriad of problems including:

(a) **Drugs**. Premises in which drugs are being used or from which drugs are being supplied which are often the source of complaints of nuisance due to the high frequency of visitors during the day and night, the noise associated with those visitors, the presence of drugs paraphernalia or blood staining in communal areas and visitors congregating in the communal areas.

(b) **Lifestyle choices** which cause nuisance to neighbouring residents. This could include:

   (i) an alcoholic who has little or no appreciation of how her verbal abuse, swearing, frequent domestic disputes (both inside the premises and in the communal areas or public places nearby) is impacting on the neighbours;

   (ii) the playing of loud amplified music at unacceptable times of the day and/or night; and

   (iii) carrying out repeated and persistent DIY type activities at inappropriate times.

(c) **Noise and/or disturbance** from commercial premises such as pop-up Shisha Bars, raves, other venues where there is a high volume of visitors or the consumption of alcohol and/or drugs which in turn lead to unacceptable behaviour.

The major difference between the new power and the old is that there is no longer a need to prove anti-social behaviour within a 'relevant period'.[3] However, even though no time limit applies to the new power there ought be a nexus between the behaviour and timing of the application.

The enforceability of closure orders which were obtained prior to the Act coming into force are considered in more detail in 8.40 below.

B   WHEN CAN A CLOSURE ORDER BE OBTAINED?

8.02   An applicant for a closure order must serve a closure notice before making an application to the magistrates' court for a closure order. There are specific requirements to consult and inform which are set out in 8.05–8.06 below.

---

3   This requirement existed for drugs and closures for persistent disorder or nuisance where the relevant period was three months prior to the application being made: ASBA 2003, Pt 1 (drugs related closures): the applicant had to show behaviour within the 'relevant period', see s 1 and s 1(10). See also ASBA 2003, Pt 1A (closures related to persistent disorder or nuisance), ss 11A(1)(a) and 11A(11).

C WHICH TYPES OF PREMISES CAN BE CLOSED USING A CLOSURE ORDER?

8.03   The power to close premises is tenure neutral. This means that both residential and commercial premises can be closed in whole or in part. This includes owner-occupied premises as well as rented premises.

The power can also be used to close licensed premises. If a closure order is made in respect of premises which have a premises licence, the court must notify the relevant licensing authority.[4]

D WHO CAN ISSUE A CLOSURE NOTICE AND APPLY FOR A CLOSURE ORDER?

8.04   Only the police or the local authority can issue a closure notice and seek a closure order from the magistrates' court.[5]

Meaning of 'local authority'

8.05   A 'local authority' is defined in s 92(1) of the Act as a:

- district council;

- a county council for an area for which there is no district council;

- a London borough council;

- the Common Council of the City of London or the Council of the Isles of Scilly (in England); and

- a county council or a county borough council (in Wales).

E CONSULTING AND INFORMING

The requirement to consult

8.06   Before issuing a closure notice the applicant (whether the police or the local authority) must ensure that it consults any body or individual it thinks is appropriate.[6] The mandatory requirement for the police to consult the local authority (and vice versa) has gone but in reality these bodies are likely to be aware of (and probably involved in) applications made by each other. It is difficult to envisage a situation in which they would not consult each other.

---

4   s 80(9).
5   s 76(1).
6   s 76(7).

Possible consultees include:

- the housing provider/landlord;

- the community mental health team; and

- social services.

The requirement to inform

8.07   In addition to the requirement to consult,[7] before a closure notice is issued, the police or local authority must have made reasonable efforts to *inform*:

- people who live on the premises (this includes those that are not habitually resident); and

- any person who has control or responsibility for the premises; or

- who has an interest in them

that the notice is going to be issued.[8]

There is a difference between the duty to inform and the duty to consult which is considered in more detail in the textbox in Chapter 3.

F   THE CLOSURE NOTICE

When can a closure notice be issued?

8.08   Section 76(1) of the Act provides that a police officer of at least the rank of inspector or a local authority may issue a closure notice if satisfied on reasonable grounds that:

(a)   the use of particular premises has resulted, or (if the notice is not issued) is likely soon to result, in nuisance to members of the public; or

(b)   there has been, or (if the notice is not issued) is likely soon to be, disorder near those premises associated with the use of those premises;

and that the notice is necessary to prevent the nuisance or disorder from continuing, recurring or occurring.

There is no longer a need to prove that the behaviour set out above has taken place within a 'relevant period'.[9]

---

7   Found in s 76(7).
8   s 76(6).
9   ASBA 2003, Pt 1 (drugs related closures): the applicant had to show behaviour within the 'relevant period' which was the three months prior to the application being made: see s 1 and s 1(10). See also ASBA 2003, Pt 1A (closures related to persistent disorder or nuisance): see ss 11A(1)(a) and 11A(11).

What is the effect of a closure notice?

8.09   The closure notice has the effect of prohibiting access to the premises for the period of time specified in the notice. Unlike the old legislation, there is a considerable degree of flexibility in the way in which the prohibition on access can take effect because the Act allows the closure notice to include exceptions to the blanket prohibition on access that used to exist.

Section 76(3) of the Act allows a closure notice to prohibit access to all persons or a class of persons, at all times or at those times specified, or in all circumstances or in specified circumstances.

There is an important exception in that the owner of the premises and any person who is habitually resident at the premises will continue to have access for the duration of the closure notice and cannot be excluded until a closure order has been made by the court.[10] The fact that they are entitled to continued access must be specified in the closure notice.

The Explanatory Notes to the Act suggest by way of example that the closure notice could be used in anticipation of a party publicised through social media[11] where the family who live there would not be prohibited access (and any additional family members could also be exempted where this was appropriate).

Applicants will need to consider whether people may require access to secure the premises against entry. For example, there may be an agent or another individual managing the premises on behalf of the owner and provision may need to be made to allow them to have access.

How long does a closure notice last?

8.10   The default position is that a closure notice lasts for up to 24 hours and prohibits access to the premises for the period specified in the notice. The 24-hour period can be extended to a maximum of 48 hours if certain conditions are satisfied. The following conditions apply for issuing the longer 48-hour notice[12] or extending a 24-hour notice:[13]

(a)   in the case of a notice issued by a police officer, the notice is authorised by an officer of at least the rank of superintendent; or

(b)   in the case of a notice issued by a local authority, the notice is signed by the chief executive officer of the authority or a person designated by him or her for the purposes of s 77(1).[14]

A 24-hour closure notice is extended by serving an 'extension notice' which is defined in s 77(5) as a notice which identifies the closure notice to which it relates and specifies the period of the extension.

---

10   s 76(4).
11   Such as Facebook, Twitter etc.
12   s 77(1).
13   s 77(4).
14   s 77(2).

Cancellation or variation of a notice

8.11　A closure notice can be cancelled or varied as regards the whole or part of the premises in accordance with s 78 of the Act.

Authorisations and delegations for serving a closure notice

8.12　Police forces will need to ensure that there is an internal process for an inspector to issue a closure notice lasting up to 24 hours[15] and that an officer of at least the rank of superintendent has issued a notice lasting up to 48 hours.[16]

Where the closure notice is issued by the local authority the provisions do not specify the level of employee that can issue the closure notice lasting up to 24 hours.[17] For closure notices lasting up to 48 hours the notice must be signed by the chief executive officer of the local authority or a person designated by him or her for the purposes of s 77(2)(b) of the Act. Local authorities will need to ensure that the appropriate authorisations and delegations are in place.

G　CONTENTS OF A CLOSURE NOTICE

8.13　Section 76(5) sets out information which a closure notice must include. A sample closure notice can be found at Appendix D. A closure notice must:

(a)　identify the premises;

(b)　explain the effect of the notice;

(c)　state that failure to comply with the notice is an offence;

(d)　state that an application will be made under s 80 for a closure order;

(e)　specify when and where the application will be heard;

(f)　explain the effect of a closure order;

(g)　give information about the names of, and means of contacting, persons and organisations in the area that provide advice about housing and legal matters.

In addition, the closure notice should state that the owner and those habitually resident are entitled to have continued access to the premises. The closure notice can also specify other exceptions to the prohibition on access (see 8.08 above).

15　s 76(1).
16　s 77(2)(a).
17　Section 76(1) is silent on this issue.

H SERVICE OF A NOTICE

8.14 Section 79 deals with the service of:

- closure notices;

- extension notices (under s 77(5));

- cancellation notices (under s 78(2)); and

- variation notices (under s 78(3)).

The following paragraphs apply to all of the notices listed above unless otherwise stated.

Who should serve the notice?

8.15 Section 79(1) provides that a notice must be served by a constable where the application is being led by the police and by a representative of the local authority where it is the local authority's application for closure.

The method of service for a notice

8.16 Sections 79(2) and (3) contain detailed rules about the service of a notice. The purpose behind the rules is to ensure that appropriate efforts are made to notify the owner of the premises, those habitually resident and any regular visitors of the fact that a notice has been issued and that an application for a closure order is to be made.

In summary, the rules require that the notice is fixed to at least one prominent place on the premises, to each normal means of access and to any outbuilding that appears to be used with or as part of the premises. A copy of the notice must also be given to anyone who lives on the premises, the person who has control/responsibility for the premises and any person who has an interest in the premises (generally this will be the owner).

Notice must also be given to people residing in other parts of the building or structure in which the premises is situated, and if their access will be impeded, a copy of the notice must also be served on them.[18]

In *R (on the application of Qin and others) v The Commissioner of Police for the Metropolis and Hammersmith Magistrates' Court*[19] it was held that 'substantial compliance' with the rules on service was sufficient. The facts of *Qin* were that the police had applied to close six massage parlours across London's West End and Chinatown which were believed to be operating as brothels. The magistrates' court declined to make the closure orders which the police had asked for. In addition, the court refused Qin's application for compensation out of central funds under s 90. The police conceded that they

---

18   s 79(3).
19   [2017] EWHC 2750.

had failed to inform all of the relevant parties that the closure notices were going to be issued and relied on the confidentiality of their operation, the suspected role of some of the interested parties in an organised criminal network and the nature of the offences being investigated. Qin argued that the closure notices were invalid and that this was relevant for the magistrates to investigate before making a closure order. On the issue of whether the relevant persons had been informed of the intention to serve a closure notice, the High Court held that there had been substantial compliance with the rules relating to the service of closure notices: all of the affected persons had notice of the closure order application and could make representations. No substantial prejudice had resulted. Therefore, the facts giving rise to the validity issue had not been relevant to the costs determination.

Forcing entry to serve the notice

8.17 Whether the notice is served by a local authority representative or a constable, both are given the power to use reasonable force to enter the premises for the purposes of fixing a notice to at least one prominent place on the premises.[20] Those serving notices should note that the power to use reasonable force is limited to the circumstances prescribed. Reasonable force could not be used (for example) to serve a copy of the notice on someone residing at the premises.

I   THE CLOSURE ORDER

Applying to the magistrates' court

8.18   The application for the closure order is made to the magistrates' court unless the closure notice has been cancelled by notice under s 78.[21] A closure order can last for a maximum of three months[22] and an application can be made to extend the closure order for a further three months.[23] The total period available is therefore six months.[24] Extensions of closure orders are considered at 8.28 below.

The application must be made by a constable, if the closure notice was issued by a police officer, and by the authority that issued the closure notice if the notice was issued by a local authority.[25] This section makes clear that it is not possible to switch from the notice being served by the police and the order being sought by the local authority (or vice versa).

---

20   s 79(4) and (5).
21   s 80(1).
22   s 80(6).
23   s 82(7).
24   s 82(8)
25   s 80(2).

The application must be heard by the magistrates' court not later than 48 hours after the service of the closure notice[26] and, in calculating when the period of 48 hours ends, Christmas day is to be disregarded.[27]

Even when a 24-hour closure notice is served, the application for a closure order has to be made not later than 48 hours after it was served.[28] It is not clear why applicants would serve a 24-hour notice which might expire before the application is heard by the court. It is likely that most of the notices will last for the longer period of 48 hours provided the relevant tests are met, in view of the logistics involved in serving the notice and making an application to the court within the prescribed timeframe. A sample application and closure order can be found in Appendix D.

The test to be met in the magistrates' court

8.19   Section 80(5) states that a magistrates' court may make a closure order if it is satisfied:

(a)   that a person has engaged, or (if the order is not made) is likely to engage, in **disorderly, offensive** or **criminal behaviour** on the premises; or

(b)   that the use of the premises has resulted, or (if the order is not made) is likely to result, in **serious nuisance** to members of the public; or

(c)   that there has been, or (if the order is not made) is likely to be, **disorder** near those premises associated with the use of those premises,

and that the order is **necessary** to prevent the behaviour, nuisance or disorder from continuing, recurring or occurring.

The magistrates' court has the power to:

•   make the closure order;

•   make a temporary order (see 8.23 below);

•   or dismiss the application.

The test has been adopted from the old provisions relating to drugs closures ('disorder or serious nuisance'[29]) and has been lowered from the need to show 'significant and persistent disorder' or 'persistent serious nuisance' which had been required by some of the previous provisions.[30]

Meaning of serious nuisance, disorder or offensive behaviour

8.20   The guidance on closure orders relating to anti-social behaviour contained a helpful list of the types of behaviour that may constitute 'significant

26   s 80(3).
27   s 80(4).
28   s 80(3).
29   ASBA 2003, s 2(3)(b).
30   ASBA 2003, Pt 1A.

and persistent nuisance or persistent serious nuisance' to members of the public.[31] It is to be noted that the test for the new closure power has changed (to require disorderly, offensive or criminal behaviour, or serious nuisance or disorder) but the list is still of some relevance. That list provided as follows:

- intimidating and threatening behaviour towards residents;

- a significant increase in crime in the immediate area surrounding the premises;

- the discharge of a firearm in, or adjacent to, the premises;

- significant problems with prostitution or sexual acts being committed in the vicinity of the premises;

- violent offences and crime being committed on or in the vicinity of the premises;

- serious disorder associated with alcohol abuse, for example in and around drinking dens;

- high numbers of people entering and leaving the premises at all times of the day or night and the resultant disruption they cause to residents; and

- noise (constant/intrusive) – excessive noise at all hours associated with visitors to the property.

'Necessary to prevent ...'

8.21   The magistrates' court is required to undertake a balancing exercise to determine whether a closure order is 'necessary'. In making that decision the court will have regard to any steps that have been taken to deal with the problem behaviour between the closure notice being served and the hearing. The limited timeframe dictates there will be little opportunity to take such steps but there may be instances where the person causing the problem has moved or is subject to another court order which prevents them from presenting an ongoing problem, for example if they have been sectioned or imprisoned.

Article 8 (right to respect for private and family life) considerations will be engaged where the closure relates to someone's home and the court will be mindful of the interference with a respondent's right to respect for their home and private life when deciding whether closure is necessary and proportionate. Applicants should provide evidence of any other steps that have been taken to try and resolve the problems to demonstrate why closure is a necessary and proportionate remedy. Applicants would also be well advised to produce evidence[32] of those steps which have been *considered* but not actually taken and to spell out the reasons why they were not utilised.

---

31 ASBA 2003, Part 1A *Notes of Guidance, Closure Orders: Premises Associated with Persistent Disorder or Nuisance*, November 2008.
32 File notes, letters of inquiry and any replies.

Meaning of 'premises'

8.22 'Premises' are defined in s 92 as 'including any land or other place (whether enclosed or not) and any outbuildings that are, or are used as, part of the premises'.

The ability to seek a closure order applies to:

- residential premises;

- commercial premises;

- rented premises;

- owner-occupied premises;

- licensed premises;

- open spaces such as parks.

The effect of a closure order and access to the premises

8.23 Section 80(7) of the Act allows a closure order to prohibit access by all persons, or by all persons except those specified,[33] or by all persons except those of a specified description, at all times or those times specified,[34] in all circumstances, or those circumstances specified.[35] For example, the closure order could make provision for the respondent to have access for a limited time in order to collect his belongings. The absence of such flexibility under the old rules could cause problems.

A closure *notice* cannot have the effect of excluding a person who is habitually resident or an owner but a closure *order* can have this effect.

These provisions allow a flexibility that was absent from the old closure powers and this is to be welcomed.

Temporary orders

8.24 Section 81(2) of the Act enables the court to make a temporary order which continues in force for a further specified period of not more than 48 hours. A temporary order may be appropriate in cases where the applicant seeks to prohibit access in respect of a specific event or around a specific date.

Defended applications and adjournments

8.25 The application for the closure order may be resisted by the defendant. This could be on a number of grounds such as the desire to seek legal advice, a

---

33   s 80(7)(a).
34   s 80(7)(b).
35   s 80(7)(c).

desire to take effective steps to deal with the problem in an alternative way (steps which could not have been taken before because the owner only became aware of the problem on receipt of the closure notice) or a desire to gather evidence which contradicts the evidence in support of the application.

Section 81(3) of the Act gives the court the power to adjourn the hearing on an application for a closure order for not more than 14 days. The power can be used in order to enable the occupier of the premises, the person with control of or responsibility for the premises or any other person with an interest in the premises to show why a closure order should not be made.

If the court adjourns a hearing under s 81(3) of the Act it may order that the closure notice remains in force until the end of the period of the adjournment.[36] The effect of the court making such an order is that the person habitually resident and the owner will still be able to have access to the premises (as well as any other persons permitted access under the original closure notice).

Although the provisions are clear in stating that the adjournment cannot be for a period of more than 14 days there are circumstances in which the court can adjourn the hearing for a longer period of time. This power to adjourn beyond 14 days is found in s 54 of the Magistrates Courts Act 1980 which provides as follows:

'**Adjournment and stays**

(1) A magistrates' court may at any time, whether before or after beginning to hear a complaint, adjourn the hearing, and may do so, notwithstanding anything in this Act, when composed of a single justice.

(2) The court may when adjourning either fix the time and place at which the hearing is to be resumed or, unless it remands the defendant under section 55 below, leave the time and place to be determined later by the court; but the hearing shall not be resumed at that time and place unless the court is satisfied that the parties have had adequate notice thereof.'

In the cases of *Commissioner of Police of the Metropolis v Hooper*[37] and *Turner v Highbury Corner Magistrates Court & Commissioner of Police of the Metropolis*,[38] the High Court held that the general power to adjourn cases contained in s 54 could be used to adjourn applications for closure orders (under the old rules) beyond the 14 days stipulated by the Anti-Social Behaviour Act 2003 if the court was satisfied that such an adjournment was in the interests of justice. The same principles would apply in relation to applications for closures under the Act.

A common reason for seeking an adjournment is a respondent's desire to seek legal advice. The inevitable consequence of the statutory provisions is that a respondent is afforded a very limited period of time in which to seek advice. In the majority of cases, the court should be pressed to deal with the application for

36   s 81(4).
37   [2005] EWHC 340 (Admin), [2005] 1 WLR 1995.
38   [2005] EWHC 2568 (Admin), [2005] 1 WLR 220.

closure at the first hearing on the basis that Parliament's intention was for closure applications to be dealt with swiftly and the circumstances are urgent. The court may be more willing to entertain an application for an adjournment where the closure relates to residential premises and the respondent's Article 8 right (right to respect for private and family life) is engaged. However, given the nature of these provisions, applications should not be routinely adjourned.

No power to vary

8.26 Applicants should be mindful of the fact that the Act does not give the court the power to vary a closure order once it has been made. This means that if the magistrates' court makes a partial closure order, but it is then discovered that the anti-social behaviour continues, there is no power to vary the existing order; a new order would need to be sought.

Vulnerable respondents

8.27 In deciding whether to adjourn, the court will need to weigh the respective interests of the persons or community affected by the anti-social behaviour and the need to provide them with some respite from the behaviour, against the need to ensure the respondent has a fair hearing.

Applicants will need to consider the situation of a respondent who has mental health difficulties or is otherwise vulnerable. Equality Act 2010 considerations may be engaged if the respondent has a disability within the meaning of that Act. Such a respondent may wish to secure the attendance of their key worker or support worker at an adjourned hearing (in addition to seeking legal advice). The courts are likely to look more favourably on applications to adjourn in these circumstances. Further information on the Equality Act 2010 can be found in Chapter 2.

J   AFTER THE CLOSURE ORDER HAS BEEN MADE

Entry after the closure order has been made

8.28 Section 85(1) of the Act makes provision for 'authorised persons' to:

- enter the premises;[39]

- do anything necessary to secure the premises against entry;[40] and

- carry out essential maintenance or repairs.[41]

---

39   s 85(1)(a).
40   s 85(1)(b).
41   s 85(5).

For the purposes of s 85 'authorised persons' are defined as a constable or a person authorised by the chief officer of police for the area in which the premises are situated where the application is made by a constable and a person authorised by the local authority where the application is made by a local authority. A person acting under s 85(1) (entry of premises in respect of which a closure order is in force or anything necessary to secure the premises against entry) may use reasonable force.[42]

These provisions are in addition to the ability to seek an order which closes the premises to all people or a class of persons, at all times or those times specified and in all circumstances or those circumstances specified.

Extending a closure order

8.29   Section 82 of the Act allows the applicant who applied for the original closure order to make an application to extend a closure order. There is no limit on the number of extension applications that can be made but the overall period of a closure order may not be extended beyond six months.[43]

The consultation requirements for an extension are more prescriptive compared with the consultation required for the original order. Where an extension is being applied for, the applicant is required to consult the 'appropriate consultee' about the intention to make an extension application. The 'appropriate consultee' is defined in s 82(4) of the Act as the local authority, in the case of an application by a police officer[44] or the chief officer of police for the area in which the premises are situated, in the case of an application by a local authority.[45]

The application to extend can be made only where the applicant is satisfied on reasonable grounds that the extension is necessary to prevent the occurrence, recurrence or continuance of:

(a)   disorderly, offensive or criminal behaviour on the premises;

(b)   serious nuisance to members of the public resulting from the use of the premises, or;

(c)   disorder near the premises associated with the use of the premises.[46]

Where an extension application is made, the justice of the peace may issue a summons directed to any person on whom the closure notice was served or any other person who appears to have an interest in the premises (but on whom the closure notice was not served).[47] That summons must be served on the person to whom it is directed.[48]

---

42   s 85(3).
43   s 82(8).
44   s 82(4)(a).
45   s 82(4)(b).
46   s 82(3).
47   s 82(5).
48   s 82(6).

Where the closure order prohibits or restricts access to other premises

8.30   If the effect of the closure order is to prohibit or restrict access to another part of a building or structure that is not subject to the closure order,[49] the owner or occupier may make an application for an order under s 87 of the Act. If such an application is made the appropriate court[50] has the power to make whatever order it thinks appropriate in relation to access.[51]

Notifying the licensing authority

8.31   The court is required to notify the relevant licensing authority if a closure order is made in respect of premises where a premises licence is in force.[52] The requirement to carry out a review of the premises licence remains.[53]

Discharge

8.32   Section 83 of the Act makes provision for the discharge of a closure order on the application of: (i) a constable (where the closure order was made on the application of a constable); and (ii) the authority that applied for the closure order (where the order was made on the application of a local authority).[54] A person on whom the closure notice was served under s 79 and anyone else who has an interest in the premises but on whom the closure notice was not served can also apply to discharge a closure order.[55]

The magistrates' court may not make an order discharging the closure order unless they are satisfied that the order is no longer necessary to prevent the occurrence, recurrence or continuance of disorderly, offensive or criminal behaviour on the premises, serious nuisance to members of the public resulting from the use of the premises, or disorder near the premises associated with the use of the premises.

---

49   s 87(1).
50   s 87(2) defines an appropriate court as:
    '(2) The appropriate court is—
    (a)   the magistrates' court, in the case of an order under section 80, 81 or 82;
    (b)   the Crown Court, in the case of an order under section 84.'
51   s 87(4).
52   s 80(9).
53   Under LA 2003, s 167 this section has been amended to reflect that fact that the closure order will be made under the Anti-Social Behaviour, Crime and Policing Act 2014.
54   s 83(2)(a) and (b).
55   s 83(2)(c) and (d).

Using a closure order – the cuckooed tenant

The problem

Mohinder is a tenant of Rainbow House, a housing association property. He is a vulnerable man with limited mobility and a history of mental health problems. Neighbours have been complaining of the numerous comings and goings to the property at all hours of the day and night. There is a regular stream of visitors who stay for a few minutes and then leave. There are often needles and other drugs paraphernalia found in the communal areas of the block and the neighbours have not seen Mohinder in a long while. Residents are disturbed by the large number of visitors, by the fact that they often ring the buzzers of other properties asking to be let into the block and by the number of visitors that hang around the communal areas and the block more generally.

After several attempts to contact the tenant the housing association learns that Mohinder has been staying with a friend as he is fearful for his safety if he were to attempt to use his own property. He tells his housing officer that his flat has been taken over by a group of men who are using and selling drugs. He wants to go back into occupation but does not feel able to ask them to leave.

The solution

The housing association informs the police and the council. Between them the council agrees that it would take the lead in seeking a closure order. The council consults with the police as required by s 76(7). It seeks disclosure from the police and collates the available evidence into a court bundle which is served at the same time as the closure notice.

At court the council asks for, and successfully obtains, a partial closure order which provides that anyone who is found in the flat who is not the named tenant, or an employee, agent or contractor of the housing association/council is committing a criminal offence.

The housing association arranges for Mohinder's flat to be cleared and supports him in moving back home. He is able to use the closure order to refuse access to unwanted visitors and feels able to call the police if people do not listen to him.

K   APPEALS

What can be appealed?

8.33   A closure notice cannot be appealed and an individual seeking to challenge the issue of a closure notice on public law grounds must do so by way of judicial review and cannot resist the making of a closure order on that basis:

R (on the application of Byrne) v Commissioner of Police of the Metropolis[56]. This was also confirmed in a case under the new rules. In *R (on the application of Qin and others) v The Commissioner of Police for the Metropolis and Hammersmith Magistrates' Court*[57] it was held that 'substantial compliance' with the rules on service was sufficient in that case. Any shortcomings in the notice will not affect the court's jurisdiction to hear the application for a closure order.[58]

A closure order can be appealed. An appeal against the decision to make or extend a closure order lies to the Crown Court[59] and must be made within 21 days[60] of the decision to which it relates. On appeal the Crown Court may make whatever order it thinks appropriate.[61] The court must notify the relevant licensing authority where it makes a closure order in relation to premises in respect of which a premises licence is in force.[62]

Who can appeal?

8.34 The following persons or bodies can appeal:

(a) the person on whom a closure notice was served under s 79;[63]

(b) anyone else who had an interest in the premises but on whom a closure notice was not served;[64]

(c) a constable (appealing a decision not to make or extend a closure order or a decision not to continue a closure notice under s 81);[65] and

(d) a local authority (appealing the same decisions set out at (c) above).[66]

L OTHER ISSUES

Exemption from liability

8.35 Section 89 of the Act deals with exempting the police and local authorities from liability for damages in proceedings for judicial review or the torts of negligence or misfeasance in public office which arises out of anything done in the exercise or purported exercise of a power under Ch 3 of Pt 4 of the Act.

---

56 [2010] EWHC 3656 (Admin).
57 [2017] EWHC 2750.
58 *R (on the application of Errington) v Metropolitan Police Authority* [2006] EWHC 1155 (Admin), (2007) 171 JP 89.
59 s 84(4).
60 s 84(5).
61 s 84(6).
62 s 84(7).
63 s 84(1)(a).
64 s 84(1)(b).
65 s 84(2).
66 s 84(3).

Reimbursement of costs incurred by the police or local authority for the purpose of clearing, securing or maintaining the premises

8.36   This relates to the costs incurred in clearing, securing or maintaining premises in respect of which a closure order is in force, not the legal costs.[67]

An applicant may apply to the court for an order under s 88 of the Act for reimbursement of such costs (in full or in part) from the owner or occupier of the premises who has been served[68] with the application.[69] Any application may not be heard unless it is made before the end of three months starting on the day on which the closure order ceases to have effect.[70]

Legal costs

8.37   The 2014 Act does not make any express provision for costs. However, the magistrates' court has a broad discretion as to costs found in s 64 of the Magistrates' Courts Act 1980. In *R (on the application of Qin and others) v The Commissioner of Police for the Metropolis and Hammersmith Magistrates' Court*[71] there was an unsuccessful application by the police to close several massage parlours in Soho, London which were believed to be offering more than simple massage services. The High Court observed that the question of costs in the context of public authorities was considered in the case of *Bradford Metropolitan District Council v Booth*[72] and could be summarised in three propositions:[73]

'(1) S.64(1) confers a discretion upon a magistrates' court to make costs as it thinks just and reasonable. That provision applies both to the quantum the costs (if any) to be paid, but also as to the party (if any) which should pay them.

(2) What the court will think just and reasonable depends on all the relevant facts and circumstances of the case before the court. The court may think it just and reasonable that costs should follow the event, but need not think so in all cases covered by the subsection.

(3) Where a complainant has successfully challenged before justices an administrative decision made by a police or regulatory authority acting honestly, reasonably, fully and on grounds that reasonably appear to be sound, in exercise of its public duty, the court should consider, in addition to any other relevant factor circumstances, both (i) the financial prejudice to the particular complainant in the particular circumstances if an order for costs is not made in his favour; and (ii) the need to

---

67   s 88(1).
68   s 88(4), the application for costs must also be served on the police if the application is made by the local authority and vice versa.
69   s 88(2).
70   s 88(3).
71   [2017] EWHC 2750.
72   [2001] LLR 578.
73   At [24]–[26].

encourage public authorities to make and stand by honest, reasonable and apparently sound administrative decisions made in the public interest without fear of exposure to undue financial prejudice if the decision is successfully challenged.'

The case re-affirms the principle that the regulatory activities of public bodies should not be subject to a 'chilling effect' by the risk of facing costs applications.[74] Where a closure order application is unsuccessful, the starting point and default position should be that no order is made; however, the conduct of the public authority may justify an award.[75]

Compensation

8.38   The appropriate court[76] has the power to make an award of compensation out of central funds if the applicant for compensation has incurred a financial loss in consequence of a closure notice or a closure order where it is satisfied:[77]

(a)   that the applicant is not associated with the use of the premises, or the behaviour on the premises, on the basis of which the closure notice was issued or the closure order made;

(b)   if the applicant is the owner or occupier of the premises, that the applicant took reasonable steps to prevent that use or behaviour;

(c)   that the applicant has incurred financial loss in consequence of the notice or order; and

(d)   that having regard to all the circumstances it is appropriate to order payment of compensation in respect of that loss.

Section 90(3) of the Act sets out the timeframe within which an application must be made.[78]

The High Court in *Qin* held that the principles set out above at 8.36 do not apply in relation to the award of compensation under s 90.

---

74   The position was also confirmed in *Beard v Devon and Cornwall Constabulary* [2017] 5 WLUK 338.
75   *R (Perinpanathan) v City of Westminster* [2010] EWCA Civ 40.
76   s 90(2) provides:
       '(2) The appropriate court is—
       (a)   the magistrates' court that considered the application for a closure order (except where paragraph (b) applies);
       (b)   the Crown Court, in the case of a closure order that was made or extended by an order of that Court on an appeal under section 84.'
77   s 90(5).
78   s 90(3) provides:
       '(3) An application under this section may not be heard unless it is made before the end of the period of 3 months starting with whichever of the following is applicable—
       (a)   the day on which the closure notice was cancelled under section 78;
       (b)   the day on which a closure order was refused;
       (c)   the day on which the closure order ceased to have effect.'

M BREACH

8.39 It is an offence for a person without reasonable excuse to remain on or to enter premises in contravention of a closure notice[79] or a closure order.[80]

It is also an offence to obstruct a person acting under s 79 of the Act (service of notices) or s 85(1) (entry by an authorised person).[81]

A person found guilty of an offence is liable on summary conviction to imprisonment for up to three months or a fine or both if the contravention relates to a closure notice (or obstruction) and imprisonment not exceeding 51 weeks or a fine or both if the contravention relates to a closure order.[82]

N EXISTING CLOSURE ORDERS

8.40 Section 93 of the Act sets out the transitional provisions for existing orders. The repeals or amendments introduced by the Act do not apply in relation to the orders listed in s 93(3) or anything done in connection with those orders. Existing orders remain in force and can be extended under the old rules. The orders listed in s 93(3) are:

(a)   an order made under ASBA 2003, s 2;

(b)   an order made under ASBA 2003, s 11B;

(c)   an order made under ASBA 2003, s 40;

(d)   an order made under LA 2003, s 161;

(e)   an order made under LA 2003, s 165(2)(b), (c) or (d).

O CONCLUSION

8.41 The closure power consolidates the old powers relating to licensed and non-licensed premises. The power can be used in a variety of situations for both commercial and residential premises.

There is no longer a need to show anti-social behaviour *and* significant and persistent disorder or persistent serious nuisance to members of the public.[83] Applicants should be careful to ensure that the evidence in support of the application is directed at the test that needs to be met in the magistrates' court. For closures where the old anti-social behaviour related powers[84] would have been used it should now be easier to obtain a closure order by virtue of the reduced threshold under the Act.

---

79   s 86(1).
80   s 86(2).
81   s 86(3).
82   s 86(4) and (5).
83   As there was under ASBA 2003, s 11B(4).
84   ASBA 2003, Pt 1A.

CHAPTER 9

Mandatory powers of possession

Snapshot

What's in

- Mandatory grounds for possession
- Only to be used in the most serious cases of anti-social behaviour
- Purpose: to expedite relief for victims of serious anti-social behaviour
- 1 of 5 conditions must be established, these are set out in the text box at 9.04 below
- Procedure for secure tenants = Notice + Right of Review
- Procedure for assured tenants = Notice + Review IF provided by landlord
- If 1 of the conditions is met, the court MUST grant the order where the correct procedure has been followed
- The court is not required to consider reasonableness

- The court has no power to postpone possession for more than 14 days (up to 6 weeks in cases of exceptional hardship)
- Amplification of existing Grounds 2 (secure tenancies) and 14 (assured tenancies), to include nuisance to landlords anywhere
- New 'riot' ground for possession

Templates

See Appendix D for useful precedents which have been updated since the first edition of this book:

- Suggested Notice of Seeking Possession for secure tenancies
- Prescribed Notice of Seeking Possession for assured tenancies
- Suggested application form for a review of the decision to rely on mandatory grounds

---

A   INTRODUCTION

9.01   Part 5 of the Act provides:[1]

(a)   mandatory grounds of possession for secure and assured tenancies where anti-social behaviour or criminality has been proved in another court;

(b)   an extension of the existing discretionary 'nuisance' grounds for possession for secure and assured tenancies to anti-social behaviour which is directed towards the landlord; and

(c)   a further discretionary ground for possession based upon offences connected with riot, committed anywhere in the United Kingdom.

The majority of this chapter is dedicated to the changes introduced by the Act. Section B summarises the existing powers available to landlords who seek to take action in respect of a person's tenancy where there is anti-social behaviour. Those powers continue to be available and are now supplemented by the powers set out above.

B   WHAT OTHER GROUNDS ARE AVAILABLE?

9.02   Before the Act came into force, social landlords could rely (as they still can) upon the following provisions where their tenants had engaged in anti-social behaviour:[2]

---

1   All statutory references are to the Anti-Social Behaviour, Crime and Policing Act 2014 unless otherwise stated.
2   This chapter does not deal with Rent Act tenants which are governed by a different regime: see *Megarry on the Rent Acts.*

(a) **Discretionary grounds for seeking possession** of a secure[3] or assured tenancy:

    (i) Where there is a **breach of the terms and conditions of tenancy**. Ground 1 of Sch 2 to the Housing Act 1985 (HA 1985) and Ground 12 of Sch 2 to the Housing Act 1988 (HA 1988). These grounds are unaffected by the Act.

    (ii) Where there is conduct causing or likely to cause a **nuisance or annoyance** to a person residing, visiting or otherwise engaging in a lawful activity in the locality, or who has been **convicted of using the dwelling-house or allowing it to be used for immoral or illegal purposes**, or an indictable offence committed in, or in the locality of, the dwelling-house (Ground 2 of Sch 2 to the HA 1985 and Ground 14 of Sch 2 to the HA 1988). These grounds are extended by the Act to include conduct committed anywhere which affects the landlord or a person employed in connection with the exercise of the landlord's housing management functions.[4]

(b) A claim for a **demotion order** under HA 1985, s 82A or HA 1988, s 6A removing secure or assured status for a period of 12 months.

(c) Possession proceedings for **termination** of a demoted tenancy, starter tenancy, non-secure or introductory tenancy.

Under (a) above, the grounds are 'discretionary'. This means that, in addition to satisfying itself that the facts constituting the ground are established, the court must also be satisfied that it is reasonable to make a possession order. If these two criteria are met, the court retains a discretion as to whether to suspend or postpone the date for possession. Where a court makes a suspended or postponed possession order the tenant is allowed to remain in the property, usually subject to compliance with specified conditions. The test for suspension or postponement of a possession order is whether or not there is a sound basis for hope that the tenant will comply with the relevant terms of their tenancy, or conditions proposed to be attached to a suspended order. There should be cogent evidence for the hope of change, which is not merely credible but also persuasive: *City West Housing Trust v Massey.*[5] There is no temporal limit on the court's power to suspend or postpone an order for possession where it has been made on a discretionary ground.[6] The court also has the power to discharge or rescind a possession order if the tenant has complied with any conditions attached to an order for possession which has been postponed.[7]

---

3   In this chapter, references to secure tenancies include secure tenancies in both their periodic and flexible form unless the context establishes otherwise.

4   The new discretionary grounds for possession are found in the HA 1985, Sch 2, Ground 2(aa) and the HA 1988, Sch 2, Ground 14(aa) and are considered in greater details at 9.44 below.

5   [2016] EWCA Civ 704, [2016] HLR 31. See also *Manchester City Council v Higgins* [2005] EWCA Civ 1423, [2006] HLR 14.

6   HA 1985, s 85(2).

7   HA 1985, s 85(4) and HA 1988, s 9(2).

In the event that the tenant does not comply with the terms of a suspended or postponed order, landlords must now apply for the court's permission to enforce the order before obtaining and executing a warrant of possession. See Civil Procedure Rules (CPR), r 83.2(3)(e) and *Cardiff City Council v Lee*.[8]

Under (b) above, a demotion order can be made where the court is satisfied that there is anti-social behaviour and that it is reasonable to make a demotion order.[9]

Under (c) above, subject to any public law or human rights defences, an outright possession order should be granted by the court provided the procedural requirements have been complied with.[10] The court does not have any discretion to postpone the date of possession for more than 14 days after the date on which the order is made, unless it appears that exceptional hardship would be caused by requiring possession by that date. In that case, the absolute maximum postponement is six weeks.[11]

For secure and assured tenants, the new mandatory ground removes the consideration of reasonableness and the court's power to postpone the date for possession any later than six weeks from the order.[12]

C WHICH LANDLORDS CAN RELY UPON THE MANDATORY GROUNDS?

9.03   The mandatory grounds can be relied upon by the landlords of:

(i)   secure tenants;

(ii)   assured tenants; and

(iii)   assured shorthold tenants.

It is rare for private[13] landlords of assured shorthold tenancies to seek to rely on the mandatory ground in circumstances where 'no fault' s 21 notices provide the more direct route to possession.[14] However this basis of possession is not available during the first six months of any assured shorthold tenancy,[15] or during the currency of any other fixed term assured shorthold tenancy.[16] In these circumstances, the new mandatory ground introduced by the Act may prove useful.

---

8   [2016] EWCA Civ 1034, [2016] HLR 45. The relevant procedure is set out at CPR, r 83.2(4)–(7B). Applicants should use court form N325A.
9   HA 1985, s 82A(4) and HA 1988, s 64(4).
10   In relation to introductory tenancies this includes provision for a review.
11   Housing Act 1980 (HA 1980), s 89(1).
12   In *Hounslow LBC v Powell* [2011] UKSC 8, the Supreme Court declined to make a declaration of incompatibility in respect of HA 1980, s 89 on the basis that there was no good reason to believe its application was incompatible with Article 8 of the European Convention on Human Rights (ECHR).
13   'Private' landlords includes housing associations.
14   Served under HA 1988.
15   HA 1988, ss 21(4B) and 21(4D), as inserted by the Deregulation Act 2015.
16   HA 1988, s 21(1).

The stated purpose of the mandatory ground of possession is to expedite the eviction of the most anti-social tenants in order to bring faster relief for victims. The ground is intended to avoid the delay and disruption of a fully contested trial, because it applies only where another court has already made findings of fact regarding the tenant's behaviour. The Revised Guidance states that the new mandatory ground is only intended for the most serious cases of anti-social behaviour and that landlords should ensure that the ground is used selectively.[17]

D THE MANDATORY GROUNDS

9.04   The mandatory grounds inserted into HA 1985 (s 84A) and HA 1988 (Ground 7A, Pt 1 of Sch 2) are identical.[18]

Where the new grounds are relied upon the court *must* grant possession provided the landlord has followed the correct procedure which comprises: (i) the service of notice; (ii) the holding of a review (if requested);[19] and (iii) where at least one of the five conditions set out below is met.

The five conditions

(1)   Conviction of a serious offence.

(2)   Proven breach of a civil injunction made under s 1 of the Act.

(3)   Conviction for breach of a criminal behaviour order ('CBO').

(4)   The property has been subject to a closure order lasting more than 48 hours.

(5)   Conviction for breach of an abatement notice or court order requiring the abatement of a statutory nuisance.

Who must be convicted or proved to be in breach?
In respect of condition 1, 2, 3 and 5 the person who must be convicted for the serious offence or proven to have breached an order is the tenant or a person residing in or visiting the dwelling-house.

None of the conditions will be met if there is a pending appeal against the relevant conviction, finding or order.[20]

---

17   Revised *Statutory Guidance for Frontline Professionals*, p 63.
18   For secure tenancies, the ground does not appear in the second Schedule to the Act along with the other grounds of possession (all of which are discretionary), but in Part IV itself.
19   A review must be offered in the case of a secure tenancy; the Revised Guidance states that the Home Office expects housing associations to offer a similar non-statutory review.
20   HA 1985, s 84A(8); HA 1988, Sch 2, Ground 7A.

Condition 1: serious offence

9.05 The tenant, a member of the tenant's household, or a person visiting the property has been convicted of a serious offence.[21]

Points to note for Condition 1:

9.06

- The serious offence must have been committed:[22]

  (i) on or after 20 October 2014; and

  (ii) wholly or partly in the dwelling house or in its *'locality'*; or

  (iii) elsewhere against a person with a right (of whatever description) to reside in, or occupy housing accommodation in the locality of, the dwelling-house; or

  (iv) elsewhere against the landlord of the dwelling-house, or a person employed (whether or not by the landlord) in connection with the exercise of the landlord's housing management functions, and directly or indirectly related to or affected by those functions.

- Serious offences for this purpose include, for example, violent and sexual offences and those relating to offensive weapons, drugs and damage to property.[23] However, an offence is not a serious offence for this purpose if it is triable only summarily by virtue of s 22 of the Magistrates' Courts Act 1980 (namely an either-way offence where the value involved is small such as criminal damage where the value of the damage is under £5,000). A list of the relevant offences is found in Sch 2A to the HA 1985.

- The HA 1985 and HA 1988 do not define 'locality' for the purposes of the mandatory ground. Rather, it has been held (in cases predating the Act) that it is a question of fact for the judge in each case whether the place in which the conduct occurred was or was not within the 'locality': see *Manchester City Council v Lawler*.[24] It has also been held that there must be a link between the behaviour which constituted nuisance and the area in which the tenants live: thus, the housing estate in which perpetrators of anti-social behaviour live is part of their 'locality'.[25] It is suggested that local shops, schools or public transport facilities often frequented by residents of an estate or block may, depending on the circumstances, also qualify as the 'locality'.

---

21 HA 1985, s 84A(3); HA 1988, Sch 2, Ground 7A.
22 HA 1985, s 84A(3)(b); HA 1988, Sch 2, Ground 7A.
23 HA 1985, s 84A(9) and Sch 2A; HA 1988, Sch 2, Ground 7A. Ground 7A adopts the 'serious offences' listed within Sch 2A of the HA 1985.
24 (1999) 31 HLR 119.
25 *Northampton Borough Council v Lovatt* (1998) 30 HLR 875.

Condition 2: breach of civil injunction

9.07   The tenant, a member of the tenant's household, or a person visiting the property has been found by a court to have breached an injunction made under s 1 of the Act.[26]

Points to note for Condition 2:

9.08

- The provision relied upon must not be a provision *requiring* a person to participate in a particular activity.[27]

- The breach must have occurred in, or in the locality of, the dwelling-house,[28] or, in the event the breach occurred elsewhere, the provision breached must have been a provision intended to prevent either:

    (i)   conduct that is capable of causing nuisance or annoyance to a person with a right (of whatever description) to reside in, or occupy housing accommodation in the locality of, the dwelling-house, or

    (ii)   conduct that is capable of causing nuisance or annoyance to the landlord of the dwelling-house, or a person employed (whether or not by the landlord) in connection with the exercise of the landlord's housing management functions, and that is directly or indirectly related to or affects those functions.[29]

- This condition is only met where there is a proven breach of an injunction made under s 1 of the Act; it appears that it does not apply where there is a proven breach of an undertaking. Applicants will need to be mindful of this when deciding whether to agree to an undertaking to compromise an injunction application. Whilst there are clear advantages in agreeing an undertaking instead of pursuing an injunction (in terms of avoiding the need to have witnesses cross examined in order to prove the breaches, saving costs and time) a proven breach of an undertaking does not appear to be sufficient to satisfy this condition.

- Breaches of a civil injunction will be proven for the purposes of this condition if the county court makes findings of breach in the context of an application for committal or, where a power of arrest was included within the injunction, following arrest and production in court. For the purposes of this condition, there is no requirement that the defendant must have

---

26   HA 1985, s 84A(4); HA 1988, Sch 2, Ground 7A. Civil injunctions are discussed in detail in Chapter 3. In practice, civil injunctions and Condition 2 will only concern behaviour which has taken place since 23 September 2014: s 21(7) of the Act.

27   HA 1985, s 84A(4); HA 1988, Sch 2, Ground 7A.

28   HA 1985, s 84A(4)(a); HA 1988, Sch 2, Ground 7A. See comments at 9.06 above as to the meaning of 'locality'.

29   HA 1985, s 84A(4)(b); HA 1988, Sch 2, Ground 7A.

received any particular sentence, or indeed any sentence at all, for the breach. Proceedings for committal are considered at 3.44–3.54.

Condition 3: breach of a criminal behaviour order

9.09   The tenant, a member of the tenant's household, or a person visiting the property has been convicted for breaching a CBO.[30]

Points to note for Condition 3:

9.10

- The breach must have occurred in, or in the locality of, the dwelling-house,[31] or in the event the breach occurred elsewhere, the provision breached must have been a provision intended to prevent either:

    (i)   conduct that is capable of causing nuisance or annoyance to a person with a right (of whatever description) to reside in, or occupy housing accommodation in the locality of, the dwelling-house; or

    (ii)   conduct that is capable of causing nuisance or annoyance to the landlord of the dwelling-house, or a person employed (whether or not by the landlord) in connection with the exercise of the landlord's housing management functions, and that is directly or indirectly related to or affects those functions.[32]

Condition 4: the making of a closure order

9.11   The property (a) has been subject to a closure order under s 80 of the Act, and (b) access to the dwelling has been prohibited (under the closure order or under a closure notice served under s 76) for more than 48 hours.[33]

Points to note for Condition 4:

9.12   The time limit for the service of a notice under this condition is more limited than for the other conditions: three months from the day on which the closure order is made.[34]

It appears from the wording of the Act that this condition is satisfied whether the magistrates' court have made a 'full' closure order, which prohibits anyone from

---

30   HA 1985, s 84A(5); HA 1988, Sch 2, Ground 7A. CBOs are discussed in detail in Chapter 4.
31   HA 1985, s 84A(5)(a); HA 1988, Sch 2, Ground 7A.
32   HA 1985, s 84A(5)(b); HA 1988, Sch 2, Ground 7A.
33   HA 1985, s 84A(6); HA 1988, Sch 2, Ground 7A. Closure orders are discussed in detail in Chapter 8.
34   HA 1985, s 83ZA(7)(a) and (b).

entering the premises, or a 'partial' closure order, which prohibits anyone from entering *except* certain specified persons. 'Partial' closure orders are sometimes made so as to prohibit all visitors from entering a premises whilst permitting the tenant or other habitual residents to continuing living there. However, as yet there is no authority on this point from the higher courts.

Condition 5: breach of noise abatement notice or order

9.13　　The tenant, a member of the tenant's household, or a person visiting the property has been convicted for breaching a noise abatement notice[35] or order.[36]

Points to note for Condition 5:

9.14

- The offences relate to breach of abatement notices or orders under s 80(4) and s 82(8) respectively of the Environmental Protection Act 1990, and in either case the relevant nuisance must be a statutory noise nuisance: s 79(1)(g) of the 1990 Act.

E PROCEDURE: THE NOTICE IN SECURE TENANCIES

Form

9.15　　Section 83ZA of the HA 1985 prescribes the notice requirements for the use of the mandatory ground of possession against secure tenants.

Unlike notices of seeking possession served under s 83 of the HA 1985, there is no prescribed form for use by landlords when relying on the mandatory ground. Specimen forms for use for secure tenants are provided in the appendices at Appendix D.

The court has no discretion to dispense with the requirement to serve such a notice on the basis it is just and equitable to do so, as it does under HA 1985, s 83(1) in relation to claims for possession relying on the discretionary grounds of possession.[37]

A notice may survive technical drafting errors. However, the consequence of a successful argument that the notice of seeking possession on a mandatory ground is inadequate in a material particular, ie a failure to give adequate reasons, is likely

---

35　The power to serve an abatement notice is considered in Chapter 6.
36　HA 1985, s 84A(7); HA 1988, Sch 2, Ground 7A.
37　HA 1985, s 83ZA(2).

to lead to the dismissal of the proceedings given the absence of any discretion to dispense with service.[38] Care should therefore be taken over the drafting.

For this reason, many landlords choose to issue notices and commence proceedings for possession which rely upon both the mandatory and discretionary grounds of possession. This approach preserves the landlord's right to continue the proceedings in reliance on the discretionary grounds, in the event of there being any fatal defect within the mandatory ground procedure. See further 9.31 below.

Basic requirements

9.16   By HA 1985, s 83ZA(3), the notice must:

(a)   state that the court will be asked to make an order under s 84A for the possession of the dwelling-house;

(b)   set out the reasons for the landlord's decision to apply for the order (including the condition or conditions in s 84A on which the landlord proposes to rely); and

(c)   inform the tenant of any right that the tenant may have under s 85ZA to request a review of the landlord's decision and of the time within which the request must be made.

Reasons

9.17   It is to be noted that the requirement under s 83ZA(3)(b) of the HA 1985 is to give *reasons* for the landlord's decision to seek possession, in addition to identifying the condition on which the landlord proposes to rely. This is in contrast to the more limited requirement to specify the ground relied upon and give particulars of that ground under s 83(2) of the HA 1985 for existing discretionary grounds of possession.

---

38   See *Torridge DC v Jones* (1986) 18 HLR 107, CA in which the tenant's application for the claim to be struck out was successful in the Court of Appeal because the notice failed to give any particulars of the alleged rent arrears.
In relation to the HA 1988, Sch 2, Ground 8, the Court of Appeal has held that a notice which does not accurately recite the wording of a ground may nevertheless be valid if the words used convey the substance of the ground so that the tenant knows what he has to do to avoid losing his home: *Mountain v Hastings* (1993) 25 HLR 427, CA, though in that case the notice was deficient: 'It is difficult to think of any good reason why a person given the task of settling a form of notice should choose to use words differently from those in which the Crown has stated in the Schedule', per Ralph Gibson LJ at 434.
Similarly, in *Islington LBC v Dyer* [2017] PTSR 731, [2017] HLR 20, a case concerning an introductory tenancy, the Court of Appeal held that where there is no prescribed form of notice the correct approach is to ask whether, viewed objectively, the notice gave the tenant notice of the intended proceedings in compliance with the section and contained all the information prescribed by the relevant statutory provision.
In *Masih v Yousaf* [2014] EWCA Civ 234, [2014] HLR 27, the Court of Appeal declined to adopt a stricter approach to the construction of a notice relying upon mandatory grounds on the basis that the requirement under the HA 1988, s 8(2) that the notice specify the ground and the particulars applied to all of the grounds, rather than only the mandatory grounds.

When a statute requires a public body to give reasons for a decision, the reasons given should be proper, adequate and intelligible.[39] The extent of the requirement to give reasons in this specific context is as yet untested in the courts, but exhaustive narrative reference to every consideration is unlikely to be necessary. The tenant should, however, be in a position to understand the main reasons why possession has been sought, to decide whether to seek a statutory review and to be able to formulate relevant representations on such a review.[40]

It may also be prudent, even if not always necessary at the initial decision stage, to give consideration to the applicability of the Equality Act 2010 in the event that the tenant has a disability within the meaning of s 6 of the 2010 Act. For more information on the Equality Act 2010, see Chapter 2.

Some examples of how each condition could be relied upon and the possible reasons for seeking possession are given below. There is a fuller worked example in 9.45 below.

Condition 1: *conviction for a serious offence*
Possession is sought under condition 1 of s 84A of the HA 1985/Ground 7A of Sch 2 to the HA 1988.

On 12 January 2018 you were found guilty of dealing Class A drugs at Harrow Crown Court and sentenced to six months imprisonment.

The offence was committed in the dwelling house.

Reasons for seeking possession:
The landlord takes very seriously any conviction for dealing in class A drugs given the negative impact it has on housing estates and local communities and its links with other criminal activity. Prior to your conviction the landlord received several complaints from your neighbours about nuisance and annoyance caused by persons attending your home at anti-social hours and who were suspected of participating in drug consumption because of the presence of drugs paraphernalia in the communal area outside your property. The landlord seeks possession in the interests of effective housing management.

---

39 Per Megaw J in *Re Poyser Mills' Arbitration* [1964] 2 QB 467, [1963] 2 WLR 1309, approved by Lord Scarman in *Westminster City Council v Great Portland Estates Plc* [1984] 3 WLR 1035, [1985] AC 661, at 673.

40 See further, on the duty to give reasons, for example, *R v Westminster CC, ex p Ermakov* [1996] 2 All ER 302, at 309f: the reason why an obligation to give reasons was imposed was 'so that the persons affected by the decision may know why they have won or lost and, in particular be able to judge whether the decision is valid and therefore unchallengeable, or invalid and therefore open to challenge'. See also *R v Brent London Borough Council ex parte Baruwa* (1997) 29 HLR 915, at 929: Schiemann LJ describing in the context of a homelessness decision the requirement 'to give reasons which are proper, adequate and intelligible and enable the person affected to know why they have won or lost', but recognising that the law gives decision makers 'a certain latitude in how they express themselves and will recognise that not all those taking decisions find it easy in the time available to express themselves with judicial exactitude'.

Condition 2: *Proven breach of an injunction made under s 1 of the Act*
Possession is sought under condition 2, s 84A of the HA 1985/Ground 7A of Sch 2 to the HA 1988.

At a trial on 3 June 2018 at the Lambeth County Court, HHJ Cox found that you had breached the terms of an injunction made under s 1 of the Anti-Social Behaviour, Crime and Policing Act 2014.

That injunction was made on 10 March 2018 and was in the following terms [*insert details*].

On 15 April committal proceedings were issued alleging several breaches of the injunction order. At the trial on 3 June 2018 HHJ Cox found the following breach(es) proved [*insert details*]. All the breaches occurred in or in the locality of your property at [*insert address*].

Reasons for seeking possession:
The landlord has received complaints about your anti-social behaviour for a long time. Prior to seeking the injunction the landlord sought to resolve the problems by writing to you and meeting with you. You have been reminded about the importance of complying with the terms and conditions of your tenancy on numerous occasions. You breached an Acceptable Behaviour Contract which you signed on 13 December 2016. You have now breached the injunction order made by the court by continuing to engage in anti-social behaviour. The landlord seeks possession in the interests of protecting your neighbours from further anti-social acts.

Condition 3: *Conviction for breach of a CBO*
Possession is sought under condition 3 of s 84A of the HA 1985/Ground 7A of Sch 2 to the HA 1988.

On 20 January 2018 you were found guilty at Isleworth Crown Court of breaching a criminal behaviour order made on 8 October 2017. You were sentenced to four months imprisonment.

The behaviour which gave rise to the conviction took place at the housing office situated at [*insert details*].

Reasons for seeking possession:
Your behaviour was directed at the landlord's officers who were working at the housing office. This is not the first time you have been abusive towards your housing officer or other employees of the landlord. On this occasion the breach of the CBO involved you assaulting the receptionist at the housing office in the presence of members of the public who were in the waiting area. The receptionist sustained injuries which required medical attention.

The landlord seeks possession in the interests of protecting its employees and members of the public from further anti-social conduct by you.

Condition 4: *Property subject to a closure order lasting more than 48 hours*
Possession is sought under condition 4 of s 84A of the HA 1985/Ground 7A of Sch 2 to the HA 1988.

On 15 December 2018 the Croydon Magistrates' Court made a closure order in respect of your property at [*insert details*]. The duration of the closure order was three months.

Reasons for seeking possession:
Prior to the closure order being made the landlord had received numerous complaints from neighbouring residents. The complaints were of large numbers of people gathering at your property and in the landing area outside your flat during the day and night, the disturbance caused by the behaviour of your visitors (in the form of shouting, arguing, verbal abuse), the litter left behind (in the form of empty bottles, syringes and food wrappers).

The landlord seeks possession in the interests of ensuring that its residents are able to have quiet enjoyment of their homes and in the interests of effective housing management.

Condition 5: *Conviction for breach of an abatement notices or court order requiring the abatement of a statutory nuisance*
Possession is sought under condition 5 of s 84A of the HA 1985/Ground 7A of Sch 2 to the HA 1988.

On 24 March 2018 you were convicted under s 80(4) of the Environmental Protection Act 1990 for breach of an abatement notice at the Brentford magistrates' court.

The abatement notice was served on 13 January 2018 because of a statutory noise nuisance emanating from your property at [*insert address*].

Reasons for seeking possession:
The abatement notice required you to stop the noise nuisance. The landlord received several complaints about the continued playing of loud amplified music after the abatement notice was served. That music causes a disturbance to neighbouring residents. On 5 February 2018 the noise was witnessed by the Council's Environmental Protection Officers who prosecuted you for a breach of the abatement notice. The nuisance has continued and the landlord has no confidence that you will control it.

The landlord seeks possession in the interests of protecting the well-being of the other residents in the locality and in the interests of effective housing management.

Time limit for requesting a review

9.18 The time limit for requesting a review is before the end of the period of seven days beginning with the day on which the notice is served.[41]

In *Harris v Hounslow*[42] the Court of Appeal held that there was no express power within the Act to extend either the time within which a request for a review must be made, or the time within which the review had to be completed. Moreover, local authorities are generally under no duty to consider requests for extensions of time, to conduct reviews out of time, or to consider serving a fresh notice in order to 'restart the clock' on a request for a review hearing. The deadlines in respect of review are therefore strict ones, and it would appear irrelevant that the tenant may have missed the deadline to request a review through no fault of their own, eg if away from home at the time the notice was served. However, as the general principles of public law decision-making continue to apply, local authorities should consider any evidence of personal or mitigating circumstances provided by the defendant up until the date of hearing, in order to keep the proportionality of their decision to seek eviction under review.

The decision in *Harris* also means that the notification given to the tenant of the relevant time periods is of the utmost importance. It is suggested that, in order to validly notify the tenant that they have seven days in which to request a review, the notice does not need to identify a specific deadline date. That approach would mean that the true deadline depends on the date of service of the letter, which might be deferred or delayed after drafting, thus invalidating the notice. Rather, it is suggested that the notice may replicate the language of s 83ZA(3)(c) as follows: 'The time limit for requesting a review is before the end of the period of seven days beginning with the day on which the notice is served upon you'.

Condition-specific requirements

9.19 If relying on conditions 1, 3 and 5, the notice must also state the conviction on which the landlord proposes to rely.[43]

If relying on condition 2, the notice must also state the finding on which the landlord proposes to rely.[44]

If relying on condition 4, the notice must also state the closure order concerned.[45]

Legal advice

9.20 In all cases, the notice must inform the tenant that, if they need help or advice about the notice and what to do about it, they should take it immediately to a Citizens' Advice Bureau, a housing aid centre, a law centre or a solicitor.[46]

---

41 HA 1985, s 85ZA(2).
42 [2018] PTSR 1349, [2017] HLR 46.
43 HA 1985, s 83ZA(5).
44 HA 1985, s 83ZA(6)(a).
45 HA 1985, s 83ZA(7)(a).
46 HA 1985, s 83ZA(8).

Earliest date for proceedings

9.21   The notice must also specify the date after which proceedings for the possession of the dwelling-house may be begun, which in respect of a secure (or assured) periodic tenancy must not be earlier than the date on which the tenancy could be brought to an end by notice to quit given by the landlord on the same day as the notice under the section.[47] This imports the minimum notice required by the common law. The notice must expire either at the end of a period of the tenancy or on the first day of any period: *Crate v Miller*.[48] In the case of premises let as a dwelling, the Protection from Eviction Act 1977, s 5 provides for a minimum period of notice of four weeks. That period can include the day of service or of expiry: *Schnabel v Allard*.[49] In the ordinary case of a weekly secure (or assured) periodic tenancy, the period will be no earlier than 28 days from the next date which marks the end of a period of the tenancy, eg if rent is due on a Monday, the Sunday prior. A savings clause which provides 'or at the end of the period of the tenancy expiring next four weeks after the service of this notice upon you' complies with both requirements of a four-week minimum period and that the notice must end on the last day of a period of the tenancy: *Hussain v Bradford Community Housing Ltd*.[50]

In the case of a secure tenancy for a term certain (for example a fixed term flexible tenancy), the period is one month after the date of the service of the notice.[51] The one-month notice period is also effective in respect of any periodic tenancy arising by virtue of s 86 of the HA 1985 after the expiry of a term certain.[52]

Additional grounds under HA 1985, Sch 2

9.22   By s 83ZA(4) of the HA 1985, where possession is also sought on one or more of the discretionary grounds set out in Sch 2, the notice must also:

(a)   specify the ground on which the court will be asked to make the order; and

(b)   give particulars of that ground.

The extent of information required for the discretionary ground is consistent with the pre-existing provisions in HA 1985, s 83.

Service of notice

9.23   If the tenancy agreement expressly incorporates the Law of Property Act 1925, s 196, service may be effected by delivery to the premises in accordance

---

47   HA 1985, s 83ZA(10).
48   [1947] KB 946.
49   [1967] 1 QB 627, CA.
50   [2009] EWCA Civ 763, [2010] HLR 16. See also *Taylor v Spencer* [2013] EWCA Civ 1600, [2014] HLR 9.
51   HA 1985, s 83ZA(10)(b).
52   HA 1985, s 83ZA(11).

with the terms of that provision. Whether or not provision for postal delivery to the address is part of the secure tenancy agreement, in order to avoid subsequent argument about the date upon which the notice was served, landlords should if practicable effect hand delivery to the address and attempt personal service on the tenant. All forms of service should always be validated by a contemporaneous and dated certificate of service.

Time limits for service of notice

9.24   Where a landlord seeks to rely upon condition 1, 3 or 5, the notice must be served upon the tenant within the following time limits:

(i)   the period of 12 months beginning with the day of the conviction; or

(ii)   if there is an appeal against the conviction, the period of 12 months beginning with the day on which the appeal is finally determined, abandoned or withdrawn.[53]

Where a landlord proposes to rely upon condition 2, the notice must be served upon the tenant within the following time limits:

(i)   the period of 12 months beginning with the day on which the court has made the finding; or

(ii)   if there is an appeal against the finding, the period of 12 months beginning with the day on which the appeal is finally determined, abandoned or withdrawn.[54]

Where a landlord proposes to rely upon condition 4 the notice must be served on the tenant within:

(i)   the period of three months beginning with the day on which the closure order was made; or

(ii)   if there is an appeal against the making of the order, the period of three months beginning with the day on which the appeal is finally determined, abandoned or withdrawn.[55]

Notice expiry

9.25   The notice ceases to be in force 12 months after the date after which the possession proceedings may be begun.[56]

---

53   HA 1985, s 83ZA(5)(b).
54   HA 1985, s 85ZA(6); HA 1988, s 8(4E).
55   HA 1985, s 83ZA(7); HA 1988, s 8(4F).
56   HA 1985, s 84ZA(9)(b).

F PROCEDURE: THE NOTICE IN ASSURED TENANCIES

Form and particulars

9.26   Section 8 of the HA 1988 is amended to make provision for notice relying on Ground 7A against assured tenants.

Unlike Notices of Seeking Possession relying on the mandatory ground for possession under s 83ZA of the HA 1985 in respect of secure tenancies, landlords of assured tenants are required to use the existing form already prescribed for use under s 8(3) of the HA 1988. The form of the notice required in England is Form 3 in the Schedule to the Assured Tenancies and Agricultural Occupancies (Forms) (England) Regulations 2015, or a form substantially to the same effect.[57]

The court has no discretion to dispense with the requirement of such a notice on the basis it is just and equitable to do so, as it does under s 8(1)(b) of the HA 1988 in relation to claims for possession relying on other of the existing grounds of possession.[58] Unless therefore, notwithstanding a deficiency, the form remains substantially to the same effect as the prescribed form, the notice will be a nullity and the claim dismissed.[59]

The required information

9.27   The suggested notice in Appendix D makes provision for the required information in relation to statements of the landlord's intention and the earliest and latest dates on which proceedings may be commenced against an assured tenant.[60]

By HA 1988, s 8(3A), the earliest date on which proceedings for the possession of the dwelling-house of an assured tenancy may be begun must not be earlier than the date on which the tenancy could be brought to an end by notice to quit given by the landlord on the same day as the notice under the section. See further 9.21 above.

If in addition to Ground 7A, any other ground for possession in Sch 2 is relied upon, the earliest date remains as prescribed by s 8(3A) in relation to the mandatory ground of possession (see above at 9.21), and not the earlier date of service of the notice which would otherwise apply to a notice relying on Ground 14.[61]

---

57   See the Asssured Tenancies and Agricultural Occupancies (Forms) (England) Regulations 2015, SI 2015/620, reg 3(c) and Form 3 in the Schedule. In Wales, the Assured Tenancies and Agricultural Occupancies (Forms) Regulations 1997, SI 1997/194 remains in force.
58   HA 1988, s 8(5), which now applies to Ground 7A (mandatory ground for anti-social behaviour), Ground 7B (immigration disqualification – the so-called 'right to rent'), and Ground 8 (mandatory rent arrears possession).
59   See *Torridge DC v Jones* (1986) 18 HLR 107, CA, *Mountain v Hastings* (1993) 25 HLR 427, CA, *Islington LBC v Dyer* [2017] HLR 20 and fn 38 above.
60   HA 1988, s 8(3).
61   HA 1988, s 8(3A), (4), (4A).

Time limits for service of notice

9.28   The time limits for the service of the notice of seeking possession are the same as those for secure tenancies and are set out at 9.24 above: see HA 1988, ss 8(4C)–(4F).

G STATUTORY REVIEW FOR SECURE TENANCIES

9.29   Secure tenants of local housing authorities and housing action trusts have a right to request a review of the decision to seek possession under s 84A of the HA 1985. There is no statutory right of review for assured tenants. However, the Revised Guidance states that the Home Office expects Housing Associations to offer a similar non-statutory review procedure (giving the example of the practice of some social housing providers in relation to starter tenancies).[62]

The regulations made under the Act are the Absolute Ground for Possession for Anti-Social Behaviour (Review Procedure) (England) Regulations 2014[63] ('Review Regulations 2014') which came into force on 20 October 2014 under the power conferred by s 85ZA(7) of the HA 1985.

There are strict time limits for the request for and conduct of a review. For time limits for the request for a review, see 9.30 below. The deadline for carrying out and notifying the tenant of a decision on review is before the day specified in the Notice under s 83ZA as the earliest date on which possession proceedings may commence; see 9.21 above.

The provisions are broadly similar to those already in force for the conduct of a review of a decision to seek possession of dwelling-houses let under an introductory tenancy under the Housing Act 1996 (HA 1996), s 129. Those provisions were upheld as compliant with the tenant's right to a fair trial under Article 6 ECHR: *R (McLellan) v Bracknell Forest Borough Council*.[64] These provisions are likely to provide assistance to the courts in considering the statutory provisions for review in the context of mandatory grounds. The regulations on introductory tenancies and mandatory grounds reviews are

62   Revised *Statutory Guidance for Frontline Professionals*, p 66.
63   SI 2014/2554. In Wales, the Secure Tenancies (Absolute Ground for Possession for Anti-social Behaviour) (Review Procedure) (Wales) Regulations 2014, SI 2014/3278 are in force under s 83ZA(8) of the HA 1985.
64   [2001] EWCA Civ 1510, [2002] QB 1129. The decision of the Court of Appeal on this point was not disturbed by the subsequent Supreme Court decision in *Hounslow LBC v Powell* [2011] UKSC 8, which served to enhance the protection afforded to any introductory tenant by permitting an introductory tenant to raise a proportionality defence based on Article 8 in the county court, rather than by way of judicial review.

also drafted in similar terms to the provisions for review of the period of a flexible tenancy.[65]

Request for review

9.30   The request for a review must be made in writing before the end of the period of seven days beginning with the day on which the notice is served.[66]

The seven-day deadline is strict and a local authority has no power to extend the deadline or to carry out a review out of time: see *Harris v Hounslow*[67] and the discussion at 9.18 above.

By reg 2 of the Review Regulations 2014, an application for a review must include the following information:

(a)   the applicant's name and address;

(b)   a description of the original decision in respect of which the review is sought including the date on which the decision was made;

(c)   a statement of the grounds on which the review is sought;

(d)   a statement as to whether or not the applicant requires the review to be conducted by way of an oral hearing; and

(e)   a statement as to whether or not the applicant agrees to receive communications relating to the review by email, and if the former, the email address to which such communications should be sent.

There is no prescribed form for a request for a review, but a draft form which makes provision for the material particulars set out in reg 2 of the Review Regulations 2014 can be found in Appendix D.

Timing of the review

9.31   The review must be carried out and the tenant notified before the day specified in the notice.[68] In most cases therefore (where the term of the tenancy is weekly periodic), this will be a maximum period of between four and five weeks.

---

65   Flexible Tenancies (Review Procedures) Regulations 2012, SI 2012/695. In addition, the Housing and Planning Act 2016 includes provisions which will phase out lifetime ('old-style') secure tenancies in England and replace them with fixed term secure tenancies. At the time of publication these provisions had not yet been brought into force and the Government has indicated that it does not intend to implement them 'at this time'. However in the event these provisions are enacted, further regulations will be required to implement tenants' rights to review the decision to renew fixed term tenancies and the length of such tenancies. It is likely that these review procedures would also be drafted in similar terms: see Housing and Planning Act 2016, s 118 and Sch 7.

66   HA 1985, s 85ZA(2).

67   [2018] PTSR 1349, [2017] HLR 46.

68   HA 1985, s 85ZA(6).

The Act does not provide for any extension of the time limit for conducting the review, nor does it specify the consequence of a failure to conduct a review within the maximum prescribed period. The Court of Appeal made clear in *Harris v Hounslow*[69] that where the failure to conduct a review within the deadline is because the tenant has failed to request a review within seven days, no sanction is imposed and the local authority remains entitled to possession. That is because the local authority has neither power nor discretion to carry out the review out of time.

The position is less clear where a tenant has validly requested a review within seven days, but the landlord has nonetheless failed to carry out the review and/ or notify the tenant of the outcome before the day specified in the notice. This scenario has not yet come before the higher courts in relation to the mandatory grounds for possession.

However guidance may be taken from the context of introductory tenancies, where similar issues were considered in *R (on the application of McDonagh) v Salisbury DC.*[70] There, Jackson J held that the conduct of a review beyond the specified date did not render the notice or the claim for possession invalid because:

(1) HA 1996 did not specify any consequence for non-compliance with the time limit;

(2) in *McDonagh*, no party had argued an earlier out-of-time review was invalid; and

(3) the process would otherwise be prolonged and repetitive.

McDonagh was further considered by Mr Justice Sullivan in *R (on the application of Chelfat) v Tower Hamlets LBC,*[71] who held that the failure to hold a review within the time limit prescribed by s 129 of the HA 1996 was not fatal to those proceedings because the parties had expressly agreed that a review could occur after the proceedings had commenced. Moreover, as s 129 did not prescribe any consequences for a failure on the part of the landlord to carry out a review in time, whether the delay was fatal to the decision to commence possession proceedings would turn on the facts. Where the failure was due to a genuine oversight capable of being remedied, there would be no good reason to prevent a landlord from remedying the position by carrying out the review out of time.

The pragmatic approach advocated in *Chelfat* appears to be largely consistent with the view taken by the Court of Appeal in *Harris,* which emphasised that the purpose of the mandatory ground is to deal with the most serious cases of anti-social behaviour so as to provide swift relief to its victims.

69   [2018] PTSR 1349, [2017] HLR 46, and discussed at 9.19 and 9.31 above.
70   [2001] EWHC Admin 567, QBD.
71   [2006] EWHC 313 (Admin), [2006] ACD 61.

Communications and service

9.32 Where an application includes a statement to the effect that the applicant agrees to receive communications relating to the review by email, any notice, document or other communication sent in connection with the review by the landlord to the email address referred to in the applicant's request for a review is to be taken as having been received by the applicant on the day on which it was sent to that address.[72] Otherwise, a notice, document or other communication sent in connection with the review by the landlord is to be taken as having been received by the applicant on:

(a) the day it is given to the applicant in person;

(b) the second business day after it is sent by first class post to the address given by the applicant on their request for review; or

(c) the day it is delivered by hand to the address given by the applicant on their request for review.[73]

Oral hearing

9.33 The applicant has a right to an oral hearing. If an oral hearing is requested it must be acknowledged by a written notice stating the date, time and place of the oral hearing.[74] The date for the oral hearing must not be earlier than five days after the day on which the notice sent by the landlord has been received by the applicant.[75] The landlord may at the request of the tenant postpone the hearing if that request is made on any date before the date on which the hearing is to be held.[76]

The person conducting the hearing has the power to adjourn the hearing upon the application of the applicant.[77] The exercise of this discretion does not appear to be expressly limited to applications made other than on the date of the hearing, and may be exercised on the date of the hearing itself at the request of the applicant, or indeed at the date of the hearing in the absence of the applicant if the person conducting the hearing considers it appropriate to do so, having regard to any explanation offered for the absence.[78]

However it is suggested that the powers to postpone or adjourn the hearing should be exercised cautiously, having regard to the final date by which the review must be completed and the decision notified, and taking into account the guidance provided in *Harris* and *Chelfat*.[79]

---

72   Review Regulations 2014, reg 4.
73   Review Regulations 2014, reg 4(2).
74   Review Regulations 2014, reg 6(1).
75   Review Regulations 2014, reg 6(2).
76   Review Regulations 2014, reg 6(3).
77   Review Regulations 2014, reg 9.
78   Review Regulations 2014, reg 8.
79   See discussion in *9.32* above.

The hearing must be conducted by a person appointed by the landlord, who may be (but is not required to be) an officer or employee of the landlord.[80] That person must be of greater seniority than the person involved in the original decision and must not have been involved in the original decision.[81]

Hearings must be conducted with a minimum amount of formality and in accordance with any directions given by the person conducting it.[82] At the hearing both the applicant and the decision-maker may make relevant oral or written representations, be accompanied or represented (whether or not that person is professionally qualified), call persons to give relevant evidence, and put questions to any person who gives evidence.[83]

Written representations

9.34   Where the applicant does not require the review to be by way of oral hearing, it must proceed by written representations. The landlord must give at least five days' written notice to the applicant informing the applicant that they may make written representations before the review.[84]

Considerations on review

9.35   The review is a fresh decision. Accordingly, the person conducting the review should consider afresh the appropriateness of bringing proceedings for possession by reference to the evidence and merits, rather than considering whether the original decision maker has acted reasonably in reaching his decision; see *McDonagh*[85] for analysis of analogous provisions for review under HA 1996, s 196.

In *McDonagh*, whilst Jackson J recognised there was no statutory requirement for disclosure of the material on which the Council relied, the suggestion that it would be lawful for an authority to produce a bundle of material on the day of the review, for digestion by both the Board conducting the review and the applicant was rejected. Provision of documents the day before, however, could have sufficed. It may therefore be desirable (if practicable) to prepare an initial bundle to be sent out to the tenant with the notice giving the deadline for receipt of representations. In *Eastland Homes Partnership Ltd v Whyte*[86] it was held that fairness dictated that it was essential that the tenant knew what material the landlord was proposing to put forward in an introductory tenancy review.

Jackson J in *McDonagh* also had cause to decide whether the review should consider the state of affairs at the date of the landlord's notice under s 128

---

80   Review Regulations 2014, reg 7(1).
81   Review Regulations 2014, reg 7(2), (3).
82   Review Regulations 2014, reg 7(4).
83   Review Regulations 2014, reg 7(5), (6).
84   Review Regulations 2014, reg 5(2).
85   [2001] EWHC Admin 567, QBD.
86   [2010] EWHC 695 (QB).

of the HA 1996 or the state of affairs at the time of the review or the state of affairs at some intermediate date. He concluded that a decision whether or not to bring legal proceedings must be based upon the state of affairs at the date of that decision. If, as is anticipated by the Guidance, reliance on the mandatory ground for possession is reserved for the most serious cases, it is anticipated that landlords will act reasonably quickly to seek to evict, so the scope for material changes in circumstances should in any case be limited.

It has also been held that a review panel may also rely on reasons not contained in the notice served under s 128 of the HA 1996, provided that any prejudice to the tenant is averted by giving him an opportunity to address new allegations: *R (on the application of Laporte) v Newham LBC.*[87]

Decision and reasons

9.36 The decision must be made by the person conducting the review and the landlord must notify the tenant in writing of the decision on the review.[88] If the decision is to confirm the original decision, the landlord must still also notify the tenant of the reasons for the decision.[89] For guidance on the adequacy of reasons, see 9.17 above.

Section 85ZA refers to the decision whether to 'confirm' the original decision to seek possession. There are conflicting decisions about whether identical statutory language in HA 1996 in relation to introductory tenancies can sustain conditional review decisions under s 129 of the HA 1996, which have purported to 'confirm' decisions to seek possession but which have postponed execution of that decision pending a period of time for good behaviour or payment of rent.

In *Cardiff City Council v Stone*[90] the Court of Appeal upheld the possession order in circumstances in which the local housing authority had served the introductory tenant with a notice of possession proceedings pursuant to s 128 because of rent arrears and, on review under s 129, confirmed the decision to terminate the tenancy but suspended the action for possession on condition that rent would be paid weekly. When that condition was breached proceedings were issued without further notice.

By contrast, and whilst not deprecating the understandable policy objective of granting a further period of grace for compliance with tenancy terms, the risks of this approach were recognised by the Court of Appeal in *Camden London Borough Council v Stafford*[91] and explained by Maurice Kay LJ at [21] as follows:

'a section 128 notice is a jurisdictional document. Only a properly served notice, confirmed on a section 129 review (where sought), opens the door to possession proceedings. For this reason, it is important that, when the original decision is confirmed on review, jurisdiction should be a matter of

87 [2004] EWHC 227 (Admin), [2004] JHL D49.
88 HA 1985, s 85ZA(4).
89 HA 1985, s 85ZA(5).
90 [2003] EWCA Civ 298, [2003] HLR 678.
91 [2012] EWCA Civ 839, [2013] PTSR 195.

clarity ... Thus, complex "alternatives to possession" of an open-ended kind should not be attached to a review decision which is confirmatory in the sense of section 129(5). Whilst I see the force of the policy considerations articulated in Stone's case, it behoves local authorities to ensure that, if they wish to preserve their original decision, they express confirmation of it with clarity and without encrusting it with complex "alternatives".'

In *Forbes v Lambeth London Borough Council*[92] a s 128 notice was given to an introductory tenant because the premises were being used 'for selling of drugs and for immoral purposes'. Following a review, the local housing authority wrote a notice to the tenant titled 'Re: Decision not to terminate your introductory tenancy' and informed him his tenancy would be monitored. The local housing authority's attempt to argue that the tenant's subsequent misconduct entitled it to issue proceedings without further service of a s 128 notice failed.

Given the exceptional and serious circumstances in which the Revised Guidance advises the mandatory ground for possession should be used, it is perhaps unlikely that landlords will be willing to provide further periods of grace for tenants to demonstrate improved behaviour. In light of the conflicting decisions set out above regarding introductory tenancies under HA 1996, any decision to confirm a decision to seek possession on a mandatory ground but subject to a period of grace on condition of good conduct is likely to be vulnerable to challenge.

Defective review

9.37 If an authority fails to conduct a review which is adequate for the purposes of s 85ZA (eg by failing to consider afresh the merits of an applicant's case), they may wish to discharge their duty by conducting a further full and adequate review later on. This would be consistent with the approach advocated in *R (on the application of McDonagh) v Salisbury DC*.[93] However as *Harris v Hounslow* has ruled that local authorities have no power to conduct reviews after the deadline to do so has expired, a local authority in this position should consider serving a fresh notice in order to 'restart the clock'. Although *Harris* clarified that a local authority has no *obligation* to serve a fresh notice, it did not rule on the question of whether it has *discretion* to do so. Rather, Lewison LJ said:[94]

> 'Even if the landlord had a power (as opposed to a duty) to serve a fresh notice superseding one that had already been served, it would need to have good reason to do so, particularly in the light of the legislative purpose of bringing speedy relief to the victims of anti-social behaviour.'

It is suggested that, in cases involving serious allegations of anti-social behaviour, landlords may rely on this decision to argue that their need to provide

92   [2003] EWHC 222 (QB), [2003] HLR 702.
93   [2001] EWHC Admin 567, QBD and discussed at 9.32 above.
94   At [23].

relief to the victims of nuisance outweighs any minor or technical defects in procedure, particularly when those defects have subsequently been remedied.

However, in order to protect its right to possession any local authority in this position would be well advised to also serve notice, on a without prejudice basis, and issue proceedings which rely in the alternative upon the discretionary grounds of possession.

H PROCEDURE: CLAIM FOR POSSESSION

9.38   In the event that the decision on review is to confirm the original decision and the landlord wishes to press ahead with possession proceedings, the claim should be commenced in the ordinary way in accordance with Part 55 of the CPR.

Landlords commonly issue claims which also rely, further or in the alternative, on one or more of the discretionary grounds set out in Sch 2 to the HA 1985 or HA 1988: see 9.22 above.

I DEFENCES

9.39   Other than challenging a landlord's compliance with the procedural requirements, a tenant may raise two other types of defence to a public authority landlord who brings a claim for possession based on the mandatory ground of possession:

(a)   a public law defence; and

(b)   a proportionality defence (the availability of which is expressly recognised by s 84A(1) of the HA 1985).

Following the decision of the Court of Appeal in *R (Weaver) v London & Quadrant Housing Trust*, these defences may – though not necessarily must – also be available to tenants of housing trusts, housing associations and registered social landlords.[95] However, they are not available to occupiers who are subject to possession proceedings by a private landlord.

---

95   In *R (on the application of Weaver) v London & Quadrant Housing Trust* [2009] EWCA Civ 587, [2010] 1 WLR 363, the Court considered whether the decision of a RSL to terminate a tenancy was an act of a public nature which could render the RSL a public authority and, therefore, amenable to judicial review. It was held that the act of terminating a tenancy of social housing was within the remit of s 6(5) of the Human Rights Act 1998 (HRA 1998) and therefore L&Q were a public authority amenable to judicial review and for the purposes of the HRA 1998.
     However, in *R (on the application of Macleod) v Peabody Trust Governors* [2016] HLR 27, the High Court held that an RSL was not amenable to judicial review in respect of a decision to refuse a tenant permission for a mutual exchange. On the specific facts of that case, it was held that the landlord was not exercising a public function when it made its decision.

Public law defences

9.40   Possession proceedings brought by a public authority may be defended by an occupier on the ground that the proceedings are an improper exercise of the authority's powers, and the occupier is not required to issue separate proceedings in the Administrative Court for judicial review: *Wandsworth LBC v Winder*;[96] *Doherty v Birmingham City Council.*[97] Following the Supreme Court decision in *Manchester City Council v Pinnock*[98] that proposition also extends to tenants of introductory and demoted tenancies, and non-secure tenants accommodated pursuant to a local authority's homelessness functions. Therefore it is, or rather remains, open to the tenant of a secure or assured tenancy to raise as a defence to a possession claim based on a mandatory ground that the public authority landlord has acted unlawfully, and that as a consequence the claim should be dismissed.

The grounds of judicial review of administrative action are traditionally classified as illegality (unlawfulness), irrationality (unreasonableness) and procedural impropriety (unfairness). In the context of reliance upon the mandatory ground of possession, some anticipated public law defences might be, for example, a breach of natural justice in a review hearing,[99] or a failure to follow policy in relation to a vulnerable tenant who had perpetrated serious anti-social behaviour.

The following examples illustrate the approach which may be taken towards public law defences to possession claims in this context:

- In *Leicester CC v Shearer*[100] a local housing authority ('the Council') had acted unlawfully in deciding to commence possession proceedings against a tenant ('S') without giving proper consideration to the option of granting her a direct let of the relevant property. S had not submitted an application for re-housing because she had been wrongly told that there was no prospect of the Council re-letting to her the property she was occupying. The Council had acted unlawfully because it had misled S into thinking that the sole purpose of requesting the application was to consider rehousing her away from the property, when in fact it was needed to consider granting her a direct let of the property in accordance with its own policy. The claim for possession was dismissed.

---

96   [1985] AC 461, HL.
97   [2008] UKHL 57, [2009] 1 AC 367, [2008] HLR 47. And see also, eg *Bristol DC v Clark* [1975] 1 WLR 1443, CA; *Cannock Chase DC v Kelly* [1978] 1 WLR 1, CA; *Barber v Croydon LBC* [2010] EWCA Civ 51, [2010] HLR 26; *Leicester CC v Shearer* [2013] EWCA Civ 1467.
98   [2010] UKSC 45, [2011] HLR 7.
99   A cautionary example of the effect of an unlawful decision to issue proceedings following a defective review hearing is *Eastland Homes Partnership Ltd v Whyte* [2010] EWHC 695 (QB). In that case the court held that the decision could not be retrospectively validated and the claim was dismissed. However for unlawful acts capable of future validation, see *Barnsley MBC v Norton* [2011] EWCA Civ 834, [2012] PTSR 56.
100   [2013] EWCA Civ 1467.

- In *McGlynn v Welwyn Hatfield*[101] a summary possession order against a local authority tenant was set aside because the local authority had indicated in a letter to its non-secure tenant ('M') that it would not seek a possession order unless it was satisfied that a serious breach of the tenancy agreement had occurred. In view of the lapse of time after service of the notice to quit and before the issue of possession proceedings, it was seriously arguable that a reasonable local authority would not have issued the possession proceedings unless satisfied that there had been some significant further breach by the tenant, and it had been seriously arguable that the local authority had not been satisfied that a serious breach had occurred. However the court considered the facts were such as to make this 'an unusual case'.

- In *Barber v Croydon*[102] the non-secure tenant ('B') suffered from learning difficulties and a personality disorder. B threatened, spat at and kicked a caretaker. The landlord local authority ('the Council') thereupon served a notice to quit and issued a claim for possession. In pressing ahead with possession proceedings against B after receipt of an expert report highlighting the link between B's mental health disorder and the isolated incident, the Council had reached a decision which no housing authority could reasonably have taken. Among other things, there had been a failure to consult specialist agencies and to take advice as to whether some alternative remedy such as an acceptable behaviour contract would solve the problem. The need to look at alternatives was required by the Council's own policy on vulnerable adults.

- In *Barnsley MBC v Norton*[103] the tenant ('N') occupied accommodation tied to his employment with the local authority ('the Council') at a school, which came to an end. The Council issued possession proceedings. N's child ('S') had cerebral palsy and was pregnant at the time of the proceedings. The Council had a statutory duty to pay due regard to S's disability under s 49A of the Disability Discrimination Act 1995 (DDA 1995), the predecessor to the Equality Act 2010. It had breached its duty by failing to address the public sector equality duty (under s 49A(1)(d) of the DDA 1995, now s 149 of the Equality Act 2010) before commencing the proceedings or at any stage of the proceedings. However, the Court of Appeal upheld the possession order on the basis that the judge below had been entitled to find that consideration of S's needs would not have made any difference to the decision to seek possession and that the Council's duty under DDA 1995 (and the Equality Act 2010 which had since come into force) was a continuing one, which would have to be discharged in consideration of alternative accommodation for N and his family, including within the context of the local authority's homelessness duties under Pt VII of the HA 1996.

101 [2009] EWCA Civ 285, [2010] HLR 10.
102 [2010] EWCA Civ 51, [2010] HLR 26.
103 [2011] EWCA Civ 834, [2012] PTSR 56, [2011] Eq LR 1167, [2011] HLR 46.

- *Davies v Hertfordshire CC*[104] was also a case in which the right of the tenant ('D') to occupy accommodation tied to his employment at a local authority school automatically came to an end upon the termination of his employment. D had dependent children. At trial the local authority admitted that when it brought proceedings for possession it had not considered its duties under s 11 of the Children Act 2004 (ie to safeguard and promote the welfare of children when exercising its functions). The Court of Appeal confirmed that, in principle, failure to comply with s 11 could provide a defence to possession, even where possession would otherwise be mandatory. However the possession order was upheld: even if the local authority complied with the duty, the outcome for the defendant would ultimately have been the same. This decision suggests that a public law defence will not succeed where there is no meaningful link between a public body's failings and the basis upon which possession is sought.

A public law challenge may therefore be directed at one, or a number of, decisions taken by a public authority in the sequence of decisions which comprise the possession proceedings, such as for example, the decision to issue a notice of seeking possession, the decision upon a review to confirm the possession proceedings, and a decision to press ahead with proceedings once a defence or an expert report had been received.

There is no requirement for the defendant to obtain permission (as is imposed by CPR, Part 54 in applications for judicial review) where an occupier raises a public law defence to a claim for possession.

However, it has been held that in order for a defence to a possession claim to warrant a direction for a substantive trial,[105] the court must be satisfied that the claim crosses the high threshold of being 'seriously arguable'. Case law has now established that proportionality defences (on which see further 9.41 below) will not easily meet this test.[106] Nevertheless, when defences are raised which allege discrimination under the Equality Act 2010, particularly cases involving disability, the Supreme Court has indicated that it will only be appropriate to dismiss the defence summarily in rare cases: see *Akerman-Livingstone v Aster Communities Ltd.*[107] As a result, cases raising disability discrimination as a defence are more likely to proceed to trial, even where the landlord relies upon mandatory grounds of possession.

A number of cases have held that, in taking steps to comply with the public sector equality duty (Equality Act 2010, s 149) in cases where defendants suffer from a disability, local authorities must ensure that they have applied a 'sharp focus' to key questions surrounding the disability and its impact on the defendant's behaviour and on his or her need for accommodation. Although these cases were decided in the context of homelessness decisions under Pt VII of

---

104 [2018] EWCA Civ 379, [2018] HLR 21.

105 See CPR, r 55.8(2), which provides that claims for possession should not be allocated for trial unless 'genuinely disputed on grounds which appear substantial'.

106 *Lambeth LBC v Kay* [2006] UKHL 10, [2006] 2 AC 465, HL, per Lord Hope at [110]; *Doherty v Birmingham City Council* [2009] AC 367, at [56], [123] and [157]; and *Manchester City Council v Pinnock* [2010] UKSC 45, [2011] HLR 7 per Lord Neuberger at [81].

107 [2015] UKSC 15, [2015] HLR 20, at [35]–[36]. See further discussion of this case at 2.16.

the HA 1996, they provide useful guidance which is also relevant to decision-making regarding the use of mandatory grounds for possession.[108]

Proportionality defences

9.41   In *Manchester City Council v Pinnock*,[109] the Supreme Court held that if domestic law is to be compatible with Article 8 ECHR (right to respect for family and private life), a court asked to make an order for possession of a person's home at the suit of a local authority must have the power to assess the proportionality of the order and, as part of that process, to resolve any relevant dispute of fact. The question is always whether the eviction is a proportionate means of achieving a legitimate aim.[110]

In *Hounslow LBC v Powell*[111] it was held that the decision in *Manchester City Council v Pinnock* applied to cases let on introductory tenancies and let pursuant to the HA 1996, Pt 7 functions. It was reiterated that any proportionality defence should initially be dealt with summarily and should be rejected unless it could cross the threshold of being 'seriously arguable'.[112]

The importance of a judge considering this question at an early stage was subsequently emphasised in *Corby BC v Scott; West Kent HA v Haycraft*.[113] In *Thurrock BC v West*[114] the Court of Appeal provided further guidance on the principles to be applied when considering whether a proportionality defence is seriously arguable. This guidance can be summarised as follows:

(1)   It is a defence to a claim by a local authority for possession of a defendant's home that possession is not necessary in a democratic society within Article 8(2), that is to say it would be disproportionate in all the circumstances. An order for possession in such a case would be an infringement of the defendant's right under Article 8 to respect for his or her home and so unlawful within the HRA 1998, s 6(1).

(2)   The test is whether the eviction is a proportionate means of achieving a legitimate aim.

(3)   The threshold for establishing an arguable case that a local authority is acting disproportionately and so in breach of Article 8 where repossession would otherwise be lawful is a high one, and will be met in only a small proportion of cases.

---

108 *Haque v Hackney LBC* [2017] EWCA Civ 4, [2017] HLR 14; *Lomax v Gosport BC* [2018] EWCA Civ 1846, [2018] HLR 40.
109 [2010] UKSC 45, [2011] HLR 7.
110 In answering that question, the Court of Appeal has recently held that where the tenant under an introductory tenancy breached the terms of his tenancy, but by the time of a possession hearing had complied with the terms for almost a year, the improvement in his behaviour could be taken into account when deciding whether it was disproportionate to make a possession order, see *Southend-on-Sea BC v Armour* [2014] EWCA Civ 231, [2014] HLR 23.
111 [2011] UKSC 8.
112 Per Lord Neuberger, at [33].
113 [2012] EWCA Civ 276.
114 [2012] EWCA Civ 1435, [2013] HLR 5.

(4)   The reasons why the threshold is so high lie in the public policy and public benefit inherent in the functions of the housing authority in dealing with its housing stock, a precious and limited public resource. Local authorities, like other social landlords, hold their housing stock for the benefit of the whole community and they are best equipped – certainly better equipped than the courts – to make management decisions about the way such stock should be administered.

(5)   The fact that a local authority has a legal right to possession, aside from Article 8, and is to be assumed to be acting in accordance with its duties (in the absence of cogent evidence to the contrary), will be a strong factor in support of the proportionality of making an order for possession without the need for explanation or justification by the local authority. It is always open to (though not necessary for) a local authority to adduce evidence of particularly strong or unusual reasons for wanting possession.

(6)   An Article 8 defence on the grounds of lack of proportionality must be pleaded and sufficiently particularised to show that it reaches the high threshold of being seriously arguable.

(7)   Unless there is some good reason not to do so, the court must at the earliest opportunity summarily consider whether the Article 8 defence, as pleaded, and on the assumption that the pleaded facts relied upon are correct, reaches that threshold. If the pleaded defence does not reach that threshold, it must be struck out or dismissed. The resources of the court and of the parties should not be further expended on it.

(8)   Even where an Article 8 defence is established, in a case where the defendant would otherwise have no legal right to remain in the property, the circumstances in which the defence could operate to give the defendant an unlimited and unconditional right to remain are limited. That could be the practical effect of a simple refusal of possession without any qualification. Where the defendant has never been a tenant or licensee of the local authority the circumstances in which an order would be refused must be even more limited.

These principles were more recently confirmed by the Court of Appeal in *Holley v Hillingdon LBC*,[115] which also ruled that the fact that a tenant may have lived at the property for many years would not in and of itself render an order for possession disproportionate.

The HRA 1998 is considered in Chapter 2 at 2.02–2.08.

J   THE PROCEDURE AND THE COURT'S POWERS AT THE HEARING

9.42   If an Article 8 defence is raised then unless there is some good reason not to do so, the court must at the earliest opportunity summarily consider whether the defence as pleaded, assuming that the pleaded facts relied upon are

---

115   [2016] EWCA Civ 1052, [2017] HLR 3.

correct, reaches the threshold of being seriously arguable. If it is, directions may be required for allocation and a substantive hearing (trial) at a future date.

If a public law defence is raised, consideration should also be given at the first hearing to whether it is seriously arguable and thus can be addressed at a preliminary hearing, or if directions are required for a substantive hearing at a future date.

Otherwise, if the court is satisfied that any of the five conditions in s 84A are met and that the landlord has complied with any of its obligations under s 85ZA (review of decision to seek possession) it *must* proceed to make an order for possession.[116]

Therefore, where the court is dealing with an application for a possession order under a mandatory ground for possession, the options are as follows. The court can:

(1) make an immediate order for possession or an order to take effect within up to 14 days;

(2) make an order, the operation of which is postponed up to the limit permitted by HA 1980, s 89 (ie six weeks from the date of the making of the order);

(3) make directions for a preliminary hearing to consider pleaded defences on a summary basis, or if it decides that the defences are 'seriously arguable', allocate the case and list for a trial to consider the defences; or

(4) Following a preliminary hearing or trial, refuse to make the order on the ground that it would infringe Article 8 or on the basis that the tenant has established a public law defence to the claim for possession.

K LANDLORD ANTI-SOCIAL BEHAVIOUR

9.43 Ground 2 of Sch 2 to the HA 1985 and Ground 14 of Sch 2 to the HA 1988 have been extended to include 'conduct causing or likely to cause a nuisance or annoyance to the landlord of the dwelling-house, or a person employed (whether or not by the landlord) in connection with the exercise of the landlord's housing management functions, and that is directly or indirectly related to or affects those functions'. Unlike conduct causing a nuisance to a person residing, visiting or otherwise engaging in a lawful activity in the locality, the relevant conduct against a landlord is not limited to the locality of the dwelling-house.

The full text of Grounds 2 and 14 have been in force since 13 May 2014 as follows:[117]

'The tenant or a person residing in or visiting the dwelling-house—

---

116 HA 1985, s 84A(1); HA 1988, s 7(3).
117 In relation to England only: Anti-social Behaviour, Crime and Policing Act 2014 (Commencement No. 2, Transitional and Transitory Provisions) Order 2014, SI 2014/949.

(a) has been guilty of conduct causing or likely to cause a nuisance or annoyance to a person residing, visiting or otherwise engaging in a lawful activity in the locality,

(aa) has been guilty of conduct causing or likely to cause a nuisance or annoyance to the landlord of the dwelling-house, or a person employed (whether or not by the landlord) in connection with the exercise of the landlord's housing management functions, and that is directly or indirectly related to or affects those functions, or

(b) has been convicted of—

    (i) using the dwelling-house or allowing it to be used for immoral or illegal purposes, or

    (ii) an indictable offence committed in, or in the locality of, the dwelling-house.'

L RIOT

9.44 Following widespread city centre rioting in the summer of 2011, and concerns about 'riot tourism', the then Department for Communities and Local Government formulated proposals to extend the scope of the discretionary ground for anti-social behaviour so that landlords would have powers to evict a tenant where they, or a member of their household, are convicted of involvement in riot-related offences anywhere in the UK.[118]

The new Grounds 2ZA and 14ZA were inserted into Sch 2 to the HA 1985 and HA 1988 with effect from 13 May 2014,[119] and provide as follows:

'The tenant or an adult residing in the dwelling-house has been convicted of an indictable offence which took place during, and at the scene of, a riot in the United Kingdom.

In this Ground—

"adult" means a person aged 18 or over;

"indictable offence" does not include an offence that is triable only summarily by virtue of section 22 of the Magistrates' Courts Act 1980 (either way offences where value involved is small);

"riot" is to be construed in accordance with section 1 of the Public Order Act 1986.

This Ground applies only in relation to dwelling-houses in England.'

---

118 A New Mandatory Power of Possession for Anti-Social Behaviour, August 2011, https://www. gov.uk/government/uploads/system/uploads/attachment_data/file/8460/1959275.pdf.

119 Paragraph 1 of Sch 2 to the Anti-social Behaviour, Crime and Policing Act 2014 (Commencement No 2, Transitional and Transitory Provisions) Order 2014, SI 2014/949.

This ground of possession is unlikely to be used often: the author of this book is unaware of any cases to date in which this ground has been relied upon or succeeded within a claim for possession.

M CASE STUDY

9.45

Bryan

The facts

Bryan holds a secure tenancy on a housing estate, Poplars. In early summer 2017, Bryan was subject to a prohibitory provision in a CBO, which prevents him from drinking in the Old Nick pub. The provision was originally imposed when Bryan was convicted in the local magistrates' court of the offence of affray committed when Bryan was drunk in Poplars after a drinking session at the Old Nick. The application for the CBO was made by the Crown Prosecution Service but at the request of the local authority in order to prevent Bryan from causing further nuisance and annoyance, which had become a daily occurrence over a six-month period when drunk and accompanied by friends from the pub. The Old Nick pub is not in the locality of Poplars, but on another estate in the Borough.

Breach of the CBO

Bryan has breached the CBO by drinking in the Old Nick. This came to the attention of the police when they were investigating further criminal damage caused by Bryan to the community centre on his return from the pub, inebriated. This time, the damage was serious and caused the centre to be closed whilst it was secured and repaired.

Bryan is convicted on 6 March 2018 of his breach of the CBO. The Council wish to rely on Condition 3 of the mandatory ground for possession.

Service of a notice of seeking possession under HA 1985, s 83ZA

The Council has until 5 March 2019 to serve a notice under HA 1985, s 83ZA. The decision to rely on the ground is made on 13 March 2018 by Bryan's tenancy officer in conjunction with the Tenancy Manager for the Poplar Estate. In addition to complying with all the other requirements, the notice gives the following reasons:

> 'The Council has decided to rely on the mandatory ground for possession. The community centre is a valuable local resource for the benefit of all tenants on the estate. It had to be closed for a week after the damage you caused. It cost £1,400 to repair. This is the second time you have caused criminal damage to the centre. In addition, you have caused nuisance and distress to many neighbours and residents

---

during an extended period (over 6 months) when drunk because of your aggressive and volatile behaviour, often at anti-social hours. The police have had to attend to intervene. Previous injunctions have been obtained in relation to other individuals associated with you, but you continue to bring visitors to the estate who show disregard for the property and comfort of those who live there. The CBO was sought to tackle at least part of the problem, your drinking at the Old Nick, but that has not worked. You may be vulnerable because of your drinking. The Council is not aware of any other vulnerability you have. You have been offered tenancy support but refused it. Referrals have been made to an organisation to help you with your drinking, but despite promises to do so, we have been informed you haven't attended. It is acknowledged your rent account is up to date. However, the impact on your neighbours and your environment is extremely serious and the Council has no confidence that your conduct will improve.'

The notice is served on Bryan personally by his tenancy officer on 16 March 2018. That gives Bryan until the end of 22 March 2018 to request a review. He does so by presenting his request in person in writing on 22 March 2018 at the Council offices. He says he wants an oral hearing.

The notice also informs Bryan that the earliest date proceedings can be commenced against him is 15 April 2018. Bryan has a weekly secure tenancy. Bryan's rent is due on a Monday, and his current rent period therefore ends on Sunday 18 March 2018. 28 days from Sunday is 15 April 2018, the earliest date on which possession can be sought.

The review procedure

The Council write to acknowledge his request on 23 March 2018, and invite him to attend the oral hearing on 30 March 2018, the earliest date on which the review could proceed given the five-day minimum period after the notice is received specified in the regulations. Under cover of that letter, Bryan is sent a clip of documents, including his convictions for offences on the estate, and the reports of anti-social behaviour the Council is relying on, and the warning and referral letters he has been sent.

The review hearing is conducted by the Deputy Head of Housing at the Council, whose job description has been broadened to include conducting oral hearings on review.

Bryan turns up at the review hearing. He is drunk and incomprehensible. He does not have a representative. The Deputy Head of Housing decides to adjourn the hearing for a few days and make some directions which she writes down for Bryan to read when he is sober. The hearing is to take place on 6 April 2018. Because that date is more than one day later than the oral hearing, a further written notice is sent to Bryan reminding him of the adjourned date.

Bryan arrives on 6 April 2018, sober. He does not wish to ask questions of the tenancy officer who outlines the reasons the Council has relied upon. He presents some letters from his GP which show he has compensated cirrhossis of the liver, which means he has a number of chronic symptoms affecting him every day. Bryan apologises for his conduct and promises to seek help. The Deputy Head of Housing decides to proceed on the basis that Bryan has a disability for the purposes of the Equality Act 2010, and reviews the terms of s 149 of the 2010 Act (the public sector equality duty) in addition to the Council's policy on vulnerable tenants to be satisfied that appropriate referrals have been made to support agencies in relation to Bryan's drinking.

The decision upheld on review

The Deputy Head reads all of the material, but decides to confirm the decision to seek possession, relying on the reasons set out in the notice, and making a note of the following:

> 'I am confirming the decision to seek possession on a mandatory ground. I rely on the reasons set out in the notice. I have also taken into account your expressions of contrition and your plan to seek support, but given the history of these promises, I do not have confidence that this will result in sustained changes to your anti-social conduct and relief for your neighbours. I have paid due regard to the matters set out in s.149 of the Equality Act 2010 and I recognise that a possession order will likely have a detrimental impact on you in particular as a result of your disability. However, I am satisfied that should an order be made you will be able to access appropriate health and social welfare services. A claim for possession will now be issued. I advise you to seek legal advice.'

The decision is notified to Bryan in a letter dated 9 April 2018, and personally served on him at his property on 10 April 2018.

The Council may commence possession proceedings on 16 April 2018 or any date thereafter until 15 April 2019.

N CONCLUSION

9.46   Landlords will need to ensure that they have procedures and policies in place for lawful decision making when relying upon the mandatory grounds of possession. Both the courts and defendants to claims can be expected to carefully monitor procedural compliance with the requirements of notices and review hearings under the provisions of HA 1985 and HA 1988, in addition to substantive compliance with public law principles of administrative decision making.

CHAPTER 10

Anti-social behaviour case reviews

Snapshot

What's in

- Victims given the ability to demand action, starting with a review of their case
- A narrower definition of ASB – case reviews are available where there is behaviour causing 'harassment, alarm or distress'
- Creation of a review threshold
- Co-operation and information sharing required
- An ASB case review policy and procedure required

A INTRODUCTION

10.01 The stated purpose of the White Paper was to 'put victims first' by providing 'more effective responses to anti-social behaviour'.[1] Much of this book has been concerned with the latter and the ways in which the Act seeks to make the powers more effective. This chapter looks at how the Government has put its desire to put victims first into effect.

Empowering the victims of anti-social behaviour was at the heart of the Government's consultation on reforming the anti-social behaviour powers. The

---

1   *Putting Victims First: More Effective Responses to Anti-Social Behaviour*, May 2012.

initial consultation[2] highlighted the uncertainty about who was responsible for tackling anti-social behaviour and identified that victims can find themselves being passed from one agency to another or having to repeatedly report the same problem. It found a tendency amongst some agencies to give insufficient attention to the impact of the behaviour on the victim and the wider community. All of these issues had been highlighted by the IPCC in the Pilkington case[3] but similar concerns continued to exist several years after their deaths.

Part 6 of the Act deals with local involvement and accountability.[4] Sections 104–105 and Sch 4 look at the way in which complaints of anti-social behaviour are responded to and introduce the concept of an 'ASB case review'. The intention is that victims will be able to use the ASB case review (also referred to as the Community Trigger) to demand action. That action would start with a review of the case.

Both the old and the Revised Guidance refers to an ASB case review as the 'Community Trigger' even though this phrase is not found in the Act as passed. In this chapter the process will be referred to as the ASB case review.

B   THE COMMUNITY TRIGGER TRIALS

10.02   The ability to trigger an ASB case review was trialled in four areas. The trials in Manchester, Brighton and Hove, West Lindsey and Boston (Lincolnshire) started on 1 June 2012 and the London Borough of Richmond started its trial on 17 August 2012. The areas were chosen because they were considered to represent a 'cross-section' of the country[5] and each took a different approach in their trials.

The Home Office's document, *Empowering Communities, Protecting Victims: Summary Report on the Community Trigger Trials* was published in May 2013. The report details the processes adopted by each trial area, how the trigger was used during the trials and the lessons learnt. The summary report is essential reading for readers who have not yet produced an ASB case review policy and procedure.

C   THE MEANING OF ANTI-SOCIAL BEHAVIOUR FOR THE PURPOSES OF AN ASB CASE REVIEW

10.03   For the purposes of an ASB case review, anti-social behaviour has a narrower definition than in s 2 of the Act.[6] Section 105(4) provides that anti-

---

2   *More Effective Responses to Anti-Social Behaviour*, February 2011, p 24.
3   See further Chapter 1.
4   All statutory references are to the Anti-Social Behaviour, Crime and Policing Act 2014 unless otherwise stated.
5   *Empowering Communities, Protecting Victims: Summary Report on the Community Trigger trials*, May 2013, p 4, available at https://www.gov.uk/government/uploads/system/uploads/ attachment_data/file/207468/community-trigger-trials-report-v4.pdf.
6   Section 2(1) provides:
     '(1) In this Part "anti-social behaviour" means—

social behaviour means 'behaviour causing harassment alarm or distress to members or any member of the public'. The intention is that an ASB case review will be available in the more serious cases of anti-social behaviour, lower level nuisance or annoyance will not suffice.

D WHO DOES THE ASB CASE REVIEW AFFECT?

10.04   Section 104 of the Act requires 'relevant bodies' to carry out a review of their response to a complaint of anti-social behaviour if (1) a request for a review is made and (2) if the 'review threshold'[7] is met.

'Relevant bodies' are defined in s.105(2)[8] and (3)[9] as:

(a)   the relevant district council or the unitary authority;

(b)   the chief officer of police for the police area which that local government area is within;

(c)   clinical commissioning groups in England and local health boards in Wales; and

(d)   any local providers of social housing who are among the relevant bodies by virtue of the co-option arrangements made in relation to that local government area. This includes a registered provider of social housing that grants tenancies of dwelling houses in the area or manages any house or other property in the area.[10]

The 'responsible authorities'[11] are required to make arrangements to include local providers of social housing among the relevant bodies in their area by a process of co-option.

(a)   conduct that has caused, or is likely to cause, harassment, alarm or distress to any person,
(b)   conduct capable of causing nuisance or annoyance to a person in relation to that person's occupation of residential premises, or
(c)   conduct capable of causing housing-related nuisance or annoyance to any person.'
7   See 10.05 below.
8   For England.
9   For Wales.
10   Defined in s 105(2) for England and s 105(3) for Wales.
11   Defined in Sch 4, para. 5 as:
    (a)   in relation to a local government area in England—
        (i)   the relevant district council or the unitary authority,
        (ii)   the chief officer of police for the police area which that local government area is within, and
        (iii)   each clinical commissioning group established under section 14V of the National Health Service Act 2006 whose area is wholly or partly within that local government area;
    (b)   in relation to a local government area in Wales—
        (i)   the council for the area,
        (ii)   the chief officer of police for the police area which that local government area is within, and
        (iii)   each Local Health Board whose area is wholly or partly within that local government area.

Each of the relevant bodies in a local government area is required to: (i) make arrangements for conducting ASB case reviews; and (ii) publish the procedures which will apply to the reviews.[12]

The focus of the ASB case review is to bring all of the relevant agencies together with a view to focusing on a more joined-up, problem solving approach to finding a solution.

E   THE REVIEW THRESHOLD

10.05   The review threshold operates as a filter to ensure that appropriate cases are put forward for a full ASB case review. Those cases which are old or where there is anticipated but no actual anti-social behaviour occurring, or that do meet the test of 'harassment, alarm or distress' would not normally meet the review threshold.

The relevant bodies must decide whether the review threshold has been met in accordance with their published procedures and inform the applicant of their decision.

The statutory review threshold is met by three 'qualifying complaints' (see below at 10.6).[13] The relevant bodies are able to set their own threshold for determining when an ASB case review is triggered and could decide that its review threshold is met by one or two qualifying complaints. In setting the review threshold the relevant bodies may have reference to the persistence of the anti-social behaviour, the harm or potential harm caused by the behaviour and the adequacy of the response to the behaviour.[14]

Qualifying complaints

10.06   A complaint is a 'qualifying complaint' if it is made within one month beginning on the date on which the anti-social behaviour occurred and the application for the case review is made within six months beginning on the date on which the complaint was made. Relevant bodies can specify different periods of time in their review procedures.[15]

Where a person has made two or more complaints about anti-social behaviour which meet the statutory requirements[16] the relevant body must decide which of those complaint(s) are to be treated as qualifying complaints in accordance with their review procedures.

12   s 104(2).
13   s 104(4)(b).
14   s 104(5).
15   s 104(11).
16   Set out in s 104(11).

F WHO CAN SEEK AN ASB CASE REVIEW?

10.07   An ASB case review can be requested by the victim or by someone acting on their behalf such as a friend, family member, carer, local MP or councillor as long as the victim's consent has been obtained.[17]

G FORMULATING POLICY

10.08   In making and revising ASB case review procedures, the relevant bodies in a local government area must consult the local policing body[18] and a local authority must consult such local providers of social housing as they consider appropriate.[19]

The policies can be formulated jointly with other relevant bodies in an area[20] and there may be different arrangements for different parts of an area.[21]

ASB case reviews – essential considerations

- Who the victim should contact

- How should the victim make contact (some have created an online form for review requests that all of the relevant bodies in their area have agreed to use)

- What the review threshold will be

- How the decision on whether the review threshold is met is to be made

- Whether the decision will be taken by the lead agency or collectively

- The procedure for informing all other relevant bodies

- The procedure for information sharing (some trial areas used IT systems which their partner agencies could access to log complaints and share information)

- How a decision on the review application will be made

- When and how a victim will be informed of the decision as to whether the threshold is met

- The procedures for undertaking a review if the threshold is met

- The process for informing a victim of the outcome of the case review and the proposed further action, with timescales

---

17   Revised *Statutory Guidance for Frontline Professionals*, p 4.
18   Sch 4, para 1.
19   Sch 4, para 2.
20   Sch 4, para 8.
21   Sch 4, para 9.

- Escalation/appeal if the victim is dissatisfied with a decision that the review threshold has not been met or the outcome of the review itself. This could feed into an existing complaints process.

A success story – a case study from Leeds City Council[22]

The Bishans

The Bishans is a city centre development of residential apartments. They are all privately owned with a mixture of owner occupiers and private lets to tenants.

The problem

A private company bought a number of flats in Block B of the site. The apartments were then let out on a short-term basis on sites such as booking. com and AirBnB with a minimum duration as low as one night, effectively turning the block into a hotel. The site was used by groups to stay in Leeds for social occasions, particularly on weekends. Groups such as stag and hen parties began booking several rooms to stay to enjoy the Leeds nightlife. They generated high levels of anti-social behaviour for the other residents living on the site with numerous examples of noise, litter, abusive behaviour, damage and drug use.

Research shows that this is a national problem, not just local to Leeds.

The investigation

Complaints were received by the Leeds City Council planning department and the Anti-social behaviour team in early 2017. The planning department decided that using a residential building in this way was a breach of planning control as it amounted to a change of use (by effectively using the building as a hotel). The ASB team opened a case centering on noise nuisance. A warning notice was served following an investigation and the case was referred back to the planning department.

The problems persisted and the LAST Team Leodis were asked to investigate following a tweet from a complainant to the Safer Leeds, Chief Superintendent and Chief Constable with a plea for help.

A number of meetings were held to discuss options. The planning department were looking at taking action but this could have taken 12–24 months to resolve due to the legal process. Planning notices had been served on the owners but the use of short-term lets continued. An agreement was reached for a closure order to be sought and to pause planning enforcement action. The intention was to restrict access to the site to those that were

---

22 With thanks to Harvinder Saimbhi, Head of Operational Delivery, Communities and Environment at Leeds City Council, the name of the site has been changed but the contents of the case study are accurate.

habitually resident thereby preventing the building being used for short-term lets.

Community meetings were held with residents, six of whom gave statements in support of the closure order application. Mobile phone images and video footage were used to evidence the behaviour of the guests on short-term lets. Guest feedback was downloaded from the booking sites showing that even the guests were complaining of anti-social behaviour in the block when they had stayed there. Statements were submitted from the planning department confirming the breach of planning control. Statements from the ASB team confirmed the action that had been taken to date.

The action

A closure notice was served and the case was brought before Leeds Magistrates' Court. The case was adjourned for two weeks for a full hearing. At the second hearing the owners recognised the problems and presented a plan to deal with the anti-social behaviour including measures such as additional security, concierge staff and a dedicated hotline. The Council agreed that no further action would be taken in light of the owners' assurances.

Activating the community trigger

After a lull reports of anti-social behaviour re-surfaced. The residents activated the community trigger process in response to the renewed anti-social behaviour.

The outcome

In response to the trigger application a number of multi-agency meetings were held. A planning enforcement notice was served and the Council's legal services wrote a letter to the owners of the site to confirm their intention to seek a further closure order due to the renewed anti-social behaviour. The owners responded by confirming that they would cease to use the building on a short-let basis and would revert to standard long-term tenancies.

The owners have complied with their assurances and residents report a reduction in anti-social behaviour and a return to normality.

H CO-OPERATION AND INFORMATION SHARING

10.09 The local providers of social housing are required to co-operate with the relevant bodies in their area when ASB case reviews are being undertaken.[23]

In order to do this the case review process could be on the agendas of existing multi-agency meetings or specific meetings could be convened.

The Act includes powers to request the disclosure of information for purposes connected with the carrying out of an ASB case review. If a request for disclosure is made to a person that exercises public functions, that person *must* comply

---

23 Sch 4, para 6(2).

with the request (subject to para 7(4) of Sch 4 to the Act). Those who are not exercising public functions *may* comply with the request (subject to para 7(4) of Sch 4 to the Act).

Paragraph 7(4) of Sch 4 to the Act provides that disclosure is not required or authorised where it relates to non-exempt personal data which would be a breach of any provision of the data protection legislation or which is prohibited by Parts 1 to 7 of Chapter 1 of Part 9 of the Regulation of Investigatory Powers Act 2016.

Subject to the matters set out in para 7(4) of Sch 4 of the Act, disclosure does not breach any obligation of confidence owed by the person making the disclosure or any other restriction in disclosing the information.[24]

Information sharing

Community Safety Partnerships were set up under ss 5–7 of the Crime and Disorder Act 1998 (CDA 1998). They are made up of representatives from the responsible authorities:[25]

- police

- local authorities

- fire and rescue authorities

- the probation service

- health.

The responsible authorities are required to formulate and implement strategies for: (i) the reduction of crime and disorder in the area (including anti-social and other behaviour adversely affecting the local environment); (ii) combatting the misuse of drugs, alcohol and other substances in the area, and (iii) reducing re-offending in the area.[26]

The Community Safety Partnership may include local providers of social housing and/or private landlords via co-option arrangements.

CDA 1998, s 115 allows a person to disclose information to a relevant authority, which he would not have the power to disclose but for that section, where it is necessary or expedient for the purposes of any provision of the CDA 1998. Relevant authorities are defined as:

- the police;[27]

- in England, a county council, district council, London Borough Council, parish council, or the Common Council of the City of London;[28]

---

24 Sch 4, para 7(5).
25 CDA 1998, s 5(1).
26 CDA 1998, s 6(1).
27 CDA 1998, s 115(2)(a)–(c).
28 CDA 1998, s 115(2)(d)(ii) in relation to England.

- in Wales, a county council, county borough council or a community council;[29]

- a non-profit registered provider of social housing;[30]

- a social landlord;[31]

- the probation service;[32]

- health;[33]

- fire and rescue services.[34]

Section 115 of the CDA 1998 is the principal legislative provision which allows information to be shared.

I CONCLUSION

10.10 Whether ASB case reviews are effective in tackling anti-social behaviour is dependent upon victims knowing that the process exists. The relevant agencies should take steps to ensure the process is publicised. Victims may need to be informed of or invited to request an ASB case review where they are dissatisfied with the way in which a complaint has been handled.

The relevant bodies may find that the case review is an effective way of encouraging their partner agencies to take action where previously they had been reluctant.

The ASB case reviews should lead to multi-agency accountability which cannot be achieved by using a single agency's complaints process. In the first edition of this book the author expressed the hope that if an ASB case review had been available to Ms Pilkington it may have led to a different outcome; the request for a review of the case would have required the various agencies to share information and produce a plan of action to tackle the problems being faced by the family. However, it appears that there has been very limited take up of the case review process. A study undertaken by Sheffield Hallam University and ASB Help found that the community trigger was not effective in stopping the long-term anti-social behaviour for most victims, and in some cases the anti-social behaviour became worse.[35]

---

29   In relation to Wales, CDA 1998, s 115(2)(d)(iii).
30   CDA 1998, s 115(2)(dza).
31   As defined by s.1 of the Housing Act 1996; CDA 1998, s 115(2)(da).
32   CDA 1998, s 115(2)(e)–(ec).
33   CDA 1998, s 115(2)(fa)–(fb).
34   CDA 1998, s 115(2)(h)–(j).
35   Heap, V. and Herrera, J. (2018) *Investigating the Community Trigger in Action: A Report for Safer Bristol Community Safety Partnership.* Sheffield: Helena Kennedy Centre for International Justice.

However, there are success stories such as that found in the case study provided by Leeds City Council. The case review process is capable of delivering real change for victims if it is known about, used properly and has a genuine commitment from all of the partner agencies. Work to encourage this continues and will help to ensure that it is the 'important safety net for victims' which it sets out to be.

Appendix A
Statutes

Contents	

Anti-social Behaviour, Crime and Policing Act 2014

(2014 CHAPTER 12)

PART I
INJUNCTIONS

Injunctions

1 Power to grant injunctions

(1) A court may grant an injunction under this section against a person aged 10 or over ('the respondent') if two conditions are met.

(2) The first condition is that the court is satisfied, on the balance of probabilities, that the respondent has engaged or threatens to engage in anti-social behaviour.

(3) The second condition is that the court considers it just and convenient to grant the injunction for the purpose of preventing the respondent from engaging in anti-social behaviour.

(4) An injunction under this section may for the purpose of preventing the respondent from engaging in anti-social behaviour—

(a) prohibit the respondent from doing anything described in the injunction;

(b) require the respondent to do anything described in the injunction.

(5) Prohibitions and requirements in an injunction under this section must, so far as practicable, be such as to avoid—

(a) any interference with the times, if any, at which the respondent normally works or attends school or any other educational establishment;

(b) any conflict with the requirements of any other court order or injunction to which the respondent may be subject.

(6) An injunction under this section must—

(a) specify the period for which it has effect, or

(b) state that it has effect until further order.

In the case of an injunction granted before the respondent has reached the age of 18, a period must be specified and it must be no more than 12 months.

(7) An injunction under this section may specify periods for which particular prohibitions or requirements have effect.

(8) An application for an injunction under this section must be made to—

(a) a youth court, in the case of a respondent aged under 18;

(b) the High Court or the county court, in any other case.

Paragraph (b) is subject to any rules of court made under section 18(2).

2   Meaning of 'anti-social behaviour'

(1) In this Part 'anti-social behaviour' means—

(a) conduct that has caused, or is likely to cause, harassment, alarm or distress to any person,

(b) conduct capable of causing nuisance or annoyance to a person in relation to that person's occupation of residential premises, or

(c) conduct capable of causing housing-related nuisance or annoyance to any person.

(2) Subsection (1)(b) applies only where the injunction under section 1 is applied for by—

(a) a housing provider,

(b) a local authority, or

(c) a chief officer of police.

(3) In subsection (1)(c) 'housing-related' means directly or indirectly relating to the housing management functions of—

(a) a housing provider, or

(b) a local authority.

(4) For the purposes of subsection (3) the housing management functions of a housing provider or a local authority include—

(a) functions conferred by or under an enactment;

(b) the powers and duties of the housing provider or local authority as the holder of an estate or interest in housing accommodation.

Contents of injunctions

3 Requirements included in injunctions

(1) An injunction under section 1 that includes a requirement must specify the person who is to be responsible for supervising compliance with the requirement.

The person may be an individual or an organisation.

(2) Before including a requirement, the court must receive evidence about its suitability and enforceability from—

(a) the individual to be specified under subsection (1), if an individual is to be specified;

(b) an individual representing the organisation to be specified under subsection (1), if an organisation is to be specified.

(3) Before including two or more requirements, the court must consider their compatibility with each other.

(4) It is the duty of a person specified under subsection (1)—

(a) to make any necessary arrangements in connection with the requirements for which the person has responsibility (the 'relevant requirements');

(b) to promote the respondent's compliance with the relevant requirements;

(c) if the person considers that the respondent—

    (i)   has complied with all the relevant requirements, or

    (ii)   has failed to comply with a relevant requirement,

to inform the person who applied for the injunction and the appropriate chief officer of police.

(5) In subsection (4)(c) 'the appropriate chief officer of police' means—

(a) the chief officer of police for the police area in which it appears to the person specified under subsection (1) that the respondent lives, or

(b) if it appears to that person that the respondent lives in more than one police area, whichever of the relevant chief officers of police that person thinks it most appropriate to inform.

(6) A respondent subject to a requirement included in an injunction under section 1 must—

(a) keep in touch with the person specified under subsection (1) in relation to that requirement, in accordance with any instructions given by that person from time to time;

(b) notify the person of any change of address.

These obligations have effect as requirements of the injunction.

4 Power of arrest

(1) A court granting an injunction under section 1 may attach a power of arrest to a prohibition or requirement of the injunction if the court thinks that—

(a) the anti-social behaviour in which the respondent has engaged or threatens to engage consists of or includes the use or threatened use of violence against other persons, or

(b) there is a significant risk of harm to other persons from the respondent.

'Requirement' here does not include one that has the effect of requiring the respondent to participate in particular activities.

(2) If the court attaches a power of arrest, the injunction may specify a period for which the power is to have effect which is shorter than that of the prohibition or requirement to which it relates.

Applications for injunctions

5 Applications for injunctions

(1) An injunction under section 1 may be granted only on the application of—

(a) a local authority,

(b) a housing provider,

(c) the chief officer of police for a police area,

(d) the chief constable of the British Transport Police Force,

(e) Transport for London,

(ea) Transport for Greater Manchester,

(f) the Environment Agency,

(g) the Natural Resources Body for Wales,

(h) the Secretary of State exercising security management functions, or a Special Health Authority exercising security management functions on the direction of the Secretary of State, or

(i) the Welsh Ministers exercising security management functions, or a person or body exercising security management functions on the direction of the Welsh Ministers or under arrangements made between the Welsh Ministers and that person or body.

(2) In subsection (1) 'security management functions' means—

(a) the Secretary of State's security management functions within the meaning given by section 195(3) of the National Health Service Act 2006;

(b) the functions of the Welsh Ministers corresponding to those functions.

(3) A housing provider may make an application only if the application concerns anti-social behaviour that directly or indirectly relates to or affects its housing management functions.

(4) For the purposes of subsection (3) the housing management functions of a housing provider include—

(a) functions conferred by or under an enactment;

(b) the powers and duties of the housing provider as the holder of an estate or interest in housing accommodation.

(5) The Secretary of State may by order—

(a) amend this section;

(b) amend section 20 in relation to expressions used in this section.

6 Applications without notice

(1) An application for an injunction under section 1 may be made without notice being given to the respondent.

(2) If an application is made without notice the court must either—

(a) adjourn the proceedings and grant an interim injunction (see section 7), or

(b) adjourn the proceedings without granting an interim injunction, or

(c) dismiss the application.

Interim injunctions

7 Interim injunctions

(1) This section applies where the court adjourns the hearing of an application (whether made with notice or without) for an injunction under section 1.

(2) The court may grant an injunction under that section lasting until the final hearing of the application or until further order (an 'interim injunction') if the court thinks it just to do so.

(3) An interim injunction made at a hearing of which the respondent was not given notice may not have the effect of requiring the respondent to participate in particular activities.

(4) Subject to that, the court has the same powers (including powers under section 4) whether or not the injunction is an interim injunction.

Variation and discharge

8 Variation or discharge of injunctions

(1) The court may vary or discharge an injunction under section 1 on the application of—

(a) the person who applied for the injunction, or

(b) the respondent.

(2) In subsection (1) 'the court' means—

(a) the court that granted the injunction, except where paragraph (b) applies;

(b) the county court, where the injunction was granted by a youth court but the respondent is aged 18 or over.

(3) The power to vary an injunction includes power—

(a) to include an additional prohibition or requirement in the injunction, or to extend the period for which a prohibition or requirement has effect;

(b) to attach a power of arrest, or to extend the period for which a power of arrest has effect.

(4) If an application under this section is dismissed, the party by which the dismissed application was made may make no further application under this section without—

(a) the consent of the court, or

(b) the agreement of the other party.

(5) Section 3 applies to additional requirements included under subsection (3)(a) above as it applies to requirements included in a new injunction.

Breach of injunctions

9   Arrest without warrant

(1) Where a power of arrest is attached to a provision of an injunction under section 1, a constable may arrest the respondent without warrant if he or she has reasonable cause to suspect that the respondent is in breach of the provision.

(2) A constable who arrests a person under subsection (1) must inform the person who applied for the injunction.

(3) A person arrested under subsection (1) must, within the period of 24 hours beginning with the time of the arrest, be brought before—

(a) a judge of the High Court or a judge of the county court, if the injunction was granted by the High Court;

(b) a judge of the county court, if—

(i)   the injunction was granted by the county court, or

(ii) the injunction was granted by a youth court but the respondent is aged 18 or over;

(c) a justice of the peace, if neither paragraph (a) nor paragraph (b) applies.

(4) In calculating when the period of 24 hours ends, Christmas Day, Good Friday and any Sunday are to be disregarded.

(5) The judge before whom a person is brought under subsection (3)(a) or (b) may remand the person if the matter is not disposed of straight away.

(6) The justice of the peace before whom a person is brought under subsection (3)(c) must remand the person to appear before the youth court that granted the injunction.

10 Issue of arrest warrant

(1) If the person who applied for an injunction under section 1 thinks that the respondent is in breach of any of its provisions, the person may apply for the issue of a warrant for the respondent's arrest.

(2) The application must be made to—

(a) a judge of the High Court, if the injunction was granted by the High Court;

(b) a judge of the county court, if—

   (i) the injunction was granted by the county court, or

   (ii) the injunction was granted by a youth court but the respondent is aged 18 or over;

(c) a justice of the peace, if neither paragraph (a) nor paragraph (b) applies.

(3) A judge or justice may issue a warrant under this section only if the judge or justice has reasonable grounds for believing that the respondent is in breach of a provision of the injunction.

(4) A warrant issued by a judge of the High Court must require the respondent to be brought before that court.

(5) A warrant issued by a judge of the county court must require the respondent to be brought before that court.

(6) A warrant issued by a justice of the peace must require the respondent to be brought before—

(a) the youth court that granted the injunction, if the person is aged under 18;

(b) the county court, if the person is aged 18 or over.

(7) A constable who arrests a person under a warrant issued under this section must inform the person who applied for the injunction.

(8) If the respondent is brought before a court by virtue of a warrant under this section but the matter is not disposed of straight away, the court may remand the respondent.

11 Remands

Schedule 1 (remands under sections 9 and 10) has effect.

12 Powers in respect of under-18s

Schedule 2 (breach of injunctions: powers of court in respect of under-18s) has effect.

Exclusion from home

13 Power to exclude person from home in cases of violence or risk of harm

(1) An injunction under section 1 may have the effect of excluding the respondent from the place where he or she normally lives ('the premises') only if—

(a) the respondent is aged 18 or over,

(b) the injunction is granted on the application of—

    (i)   a local authority,

    (ii)   the chief officer of police for the police area that the premises are in, or

    (iii)   if the premises are owned or managed by a housing provider, that housing provider, and

(c) the court thinks that—

    (i)   the anti-social behaviour in which the respondent has engaged or threatens to engage consists of or includes the use or threatened use of violence against other persons, or

    (ii)   there is a significant risk of harm to other persons from the respondent.

(2) For the purposes of this section a housing provider owns a place if—

(a) the housing provider is a person (other than a mortgagee not in possession) entitled to dispose of the fee simple of the place, whether in possession or in reversion, or

(b) the housing provider is a person who holds or is entitled to the rents and profits of the place under a lease that (when granted) was for a term of not less then 3 years.

Supplemental

14 Requirements to consult etc

(1) A person applying for an injunction under section 1 must before doing so—

(a) consult the local youth offending team about the application, if the respondent will be aged under 18 when the application is made;

(b) inform any other body or individual the applicant thinks appropriate of the application.

This subsection does not apply to a without-notice application.

(2) Where the court adjourns a without-notice application, before the date of the first on-notice hearing the applicant must—

(a) consult the local youth offending team about the application, if the respondent will be aged under 18 on that date;

(b) inform any other body or individual the applicant thinks appropriate of the application.

(3) A person applying for variation or discharge of an injunction under section 1 granted on that person's application must before doing so—

(a) consult the local youth offending team about the application for variation or discharge, if the respondent will be aged under 18 when that application is made;

(b) inform any other body or individual the applicant thinks appropriate of that application.

(4) In this section—

'local youth offending team' means—

(a) the youth offending team in whose area it appears to the applicant that the respondent lives, or

(b) if it appears to the applicant that the respondent lives in more than one such area, whichever one or more of the relevant youth offending teams the applicant thinks it appropriate to consult;

'on-notice hearing' means a hearing of which notice has been given to the applicant and the respondent in accordance with rules of court;

'without-notice application' means an application made without notice under section 6.

15 Appeals against decisions of youth courts

(1) An appeal lies to the Crown Court against a decision of a youth court made under this Part.

(2) On an appeal under this section the Crown Court may make—

(a) whatever orders are necessary to give effect to its determination of the appeal;

(b) whatever incidental or consequential orders appear to it to be just.

(3) An order of the Crown Court made on an appeal under this section (other than one directing that an application be re-heard by the youth court) is to be treated for the purposes of section 8 as an order of the youth court.

16 Special measures for witnesses

(1) Chapter 1 of Part 2 of the Youth Justice and Criminal Evidence Act 1999 (special measures directions in the case of vulnerable and intimidated witnesses) applies to proceedings under this Part as it applies to criminal proceedings, but with—

(a) the omission of the provisions of that Act mentioned in subsection (2) (which make provision appropriate only in the context of criminal proceedings), and

(b) any other necessary modifications.

(2) The provisions are—

(a) section 17(4) to (7);

(b) section 21(4C)(e);

(c) section 22A;

(d) section 27(10);

(e) section 32.

(3) Rules of court made under or for the purposes of Chapter 1 of Part 2 of that Act apply to proceedings under this Part—

(a) to the extent provided by rules of court, and

(b) subject to any modifications provided by rules of court.

(4) Section 47 of that Act (restrictions on reporting special measures directions etc) applies with any necessary modifications—

(a) to a direction under section 19 of that Act as applied by this section;

(b) to a direction discharging or varying such a direction.

Sections 49 and 51 of that Act (offences) apply accordingly.

17   Children and young persons: disapplication of reporting restrictions

Section 49 of the Children and Young Persons Act 1933 (restrictions on reports of proceedings in which children and young persons are concerned) does not apply to proceedings under this Part.

18   Rules of court

(1) Rules of court may provide that an appeal from a decision of the High Court, the county court or a youth court—

(a) to dismiss an application for an injunction under section 1 made without notice being given to the respondent, or

(b) to refuse to grant an interim injunction when adjourning proceedings following such an application,

may be made without notice being given to the respondent.

(2) Rules of court may provide for a youth court to give permission for an application for an injunction under section 1 against a person aged 18 or over to be made to the youth court if—

(a) an application to the youth court has been made, or is to be made, for an injunction under that section against a person aged under 18, and

(b) the youth court thinks that it would be in the interests of justice for the applications to be heard together.

(3) In relation to a respondent attaining the age of 18 after proceedings under this Part have begun, rules of court may—

(a) provide for the transfer of the proceedings from the youth court to the High Court or the county court;

(b) prescribe circumstances in which the proceedings may or must remain in the youth court.

19 Guidance

(1) The Secretary of State may issue guidance to persons entitled to apply for injunctions under section 1 (see section 5) about the exercise of their functions under this Part.

(2) The Secretary of State may revise any guidance issued under this section.

(3) The Secretary of State must arrange for any guidance issued or revised under this section to be published.

20 Interpretation etc

(1) In this Part—

'anti-social behaviour' has the meaning given by section 2;

'harm' includes serious ill-treatment or abuse, whether physical or not;

'housing accommodation' includes—

(a) flats, lodging-houses and hostels;

(b) any yard, garden, outhouses and appurtenances belonging to the accommodation or usually enjoyed with it;

(c) any common areas used in connection with the accommodation;

'housing provider' means—

(a) a housing trust, within the meaning given by section 2 of the Housing Associations Act 1985, that is a charity;

(b) a housing action trust established under section 62 of the Housing Act 1988;

(c) in relation to England, a non-profit private registered provider of social housing;

(d) in relation to Wales, a Welsh body registered as a social landlord under section 3 of the Housing Act 1996;

(e) any body (other than a local authority or a body within paragraphs (a) to (d)) that is a landlord under a secure tenancy within the meaning given by section 79 of the Housing Act 1985;

'local authority' means—

(a) in relation to England, a district council, a county council, a London borough council, the Common Council of the City of London or the Council of the Isles of Scilly;

(b) in relation to Wales, a county council or a county borough council;

'respondent' has the meaning given by section 1(1).

(2) A person's age is treated for the purposes of this Part as being that which it appears to the court to be after considering any available evidence.

21 Saving and transitional provision

(1) In this section 'existing order' means any of the following injunctions and orders—

(a) an anti-social behaviour injunction under section 153A of the Housing Act 1996;

(b) an injunction under section 153B of that Act (injunction against unlawful use of premises);

(c) an injunction in which anything is included by virtue of section 153D(3) or (4) of that Act (power to include provision banning person from premises or area, or to include power of arrest, in injunction against breach of tenancy agreement);

(d) an order under section 1 or 1B of the Crime and Disorder Act 1998 (anti-social behaviour orders etc);

(e) an individual support order under section 1AA of that Act made in connection with an order under section 1 or 1B of that Act;

(f) an intervention order under section 1G of that Act;

(g) a drinking banning order under section 3 or 4 of the Violent Crime Reduction Act 2006.

(2) The repeal or amendment by this Act of provisions about any of the existing orders specified in subsection (1)(a) to (d), (f) and (g) does not apply in relation to—

(a) an application made before the commencement day for an existing order;

(b) an existing order (whether made before or after that day) applied for before that day;

(c) anything done in connection with such an application or order.

(3) The repeal or amendment by this Act of provisions about an order specified in subsection (1)(e) does not apply in relation to—

(a) an individual support order made before the commencement day;

(b) anything done in connection with such an order.

(4) As from the commencement day there may be no variation of an existing order that extends the period of the order or of any of its provisions.

(5) At the end of the period of 5 years beginning with the commencement day—

(a) in relation to any of the existing orders specified in subsection (1) (a), (b) and (d) to (g) that is still in force, this Part has effect, with any necessary modifications (and with any modifications specified in an order under section

185(7)), as if the provisions of the order were provisions of an injunction under section 1;

(b) the provisions of this Part set out in subsection (6) apply to any injunction specified in subsection (1)(c) that is still in force as they apply to an injunction under section 1;

(c) subsections (2) to (4) cease to have effect.

(6) The provisions referred to in subsection (5)(b) are—

(a) section 1(7);

(b) sections 4(2) and 9 (if a power of arrest is attached);

(c) sections 6 to 8;

(d) section 10;

(e) section 11 and Schedule 1;

(f) section 12 and Schedule 2;

(g) section 18(1).

(7) In deciding whether to grant an injunction under section 1 a court may take account of conduct occurring up to 6 months before the commencement day.

(8) In this section 'commencement day' means the day on which this Part comes into force.

PART 2
CRIMINAL BEHAVIOUR ORDERS

Criminal behaviour orders

22 Power to make orders

(1) This section applies where a person ('the offender') is convicted of an offence.

(2) The court may make a criminal behaviour order against the offender if two conditions are met.

(3) The first condition is that the court is satisfied, beyond reasonable doubt, that the offender has engaged in behaviour that caused or was likely to cause harassment, alarm or distress to any person.

(4) The second condition is that the court considers that making the order will help in preventing the offender from engaging in such behaviour.

(5) A criminal behaviour order is an order which, for the purpose of preventing the offender from engaging in such behaviour—

(a) prohibits the offender from doing anything described in the order;

(b) requires the offender to do anything described in the order.

(6) The court may make a criminal behaviour order against the offender only if it is made in addition to—

(a) a sentence imposed in respect of the offence, or

(b) an order discharging the offender conditionally.

(7) The court may make a criminal behaviour order against the offender only on the application of the prosecution.

(8) The prosecution must find out the views of the local youth offending team before applying for a criminal behaviour order to be made if the offender will be under the age of 18 when the application is made.

(9) Prohibitions and requirements in a criminal behaviour order must, so far as practicable, be such as to avoid—

(a) any interference with the times, if any, at which the offender normally works or attends school or any other educational establishment;

(b) any conflict with the requirements of any other court order or injunction to which the offender may be subject.

(10) In this section 'local youth offending team' means—

(a) the youth offending team in whose area it appears to the prosecution that the offender lives, or

(b) if it appears to the prosecution that the offender lives in more than one such area, whichever one or more of the relevant youth offending teams the prosecution thinks appropriate.

23   Proceedings on an application for an order

(1) For the purpose of deciding whether to make a criminal behaviour order the court may consider evidence led by the prosecution and evidence led by the offender.

(2) It does not matter whether the evidence would have been admissible in the proceedings in which the offender was convicted.

(3) The court may adjourn any proceedings on an application for a criminal behaviour order even after sentencing the offender.

(4) If the offender does not appear for any adjourned proceedings the court may—

(a) further adjourn the proceedings,

(b) issue a warrant for the offender's arrest, or

(c) hear the proceedings in the offender's absence.

(5) The court may not act under paragraph (b) of subsection (4) unless it is satisfied that the offender has had adequate notice of the time and place of the adjourned proceedings.

(6) The court may not act under paragraph (c) of subsection (4) unless it is satisfied that the offender—

(a) has had adequate notice of the time and place of the adjourned proceedings, and

(b) has been informed that if the offender does not appear for those proceedings the court may hear the proceedings in his or her absence.

(7) Subsection (8) applies in relation to proceedings in which a criminal behaviour order is made against an offender who is under the age of 18.

(8) In so far as the proceedings relate to the making of the order—

(a) section 49 of the Children and Young Persons Act 1933 (restrictions on reports of proceedings in which children and young persons are concerned) does not apply in respect of the offender;

(b) section 39 of that Act (power to prohibit publication of certain matters) does so apply.

24 Requirements included in orders

(1) A criminal behaviour order that includes a requirement must specify the person who is to be responsible for supervising compliance with the requirement.

The person may be an individual or an organisation.

(2) Before including a requirement, the court must receive evidence about its suitability and enforceability from—

(a) the individual to be specified under subsection (1), if an individual is to be specified;

(b) an individual representing the organisation to be specified under subsection (1), if an organisation is to be specified.

(3) Before including two or more requirements, the court must consider their compatibility with each other.

(4) It is the duty of a person specified under subsection (1)—

(a) to make any necessary arrangements in connection with the requirements for which the person has responsibility (the 'relevant requirements');

(b) to promote the offender's compliance with the relevant requirements;

(c) if the person considers that the offender—

(i)   has complied with all the relevant requirements, or

(ii)   has failed to comply with a relevant requirement,

to inform the prosecution and the appropriate chief officer of police.

(5) In subsection (4)(c) 'the appropriate chief officer of police' means—

(a) the chief officer of police for the police area in which it appears to the person specified under subsection (1) that the offender lives, or

(b) if it appears to that person that the offender lives in more than one police area, whichever of the relevant chief officers of police that person thinks it most appropriate to inform.

(6) An offender subject to a requirement in a criminal behaviour order must—

(a) keep in touch with the person specified under subsection (1) in relation to that requirement, in accordance with any instructions given by that person from time to time;

(b) notify the person of any change of address.

These obligations have effect as requirements of the order.

25 Duration of order etc

(1) A criminal behaviour order takes effect on the day it is made, subject to subsection (2).

(2) If on the day a criminal behaviour order ('the new order') is made the offender is subject to another criminal behaviour order ('the previous order'), the new order may be made so as to take effect on the day on which the previous order ceases to have effect.

(3) A criminal behaviour order must specify the period ('the order period') for which it has effect.

(4) In the case of a criminal behaviour order made before the offender has reached the age of 18, the order period must be a fixed period of—

(a) not less than 1 year, and

(b) not more than 3 years.

(5) In the case of a criminal behaviour order made after the offender has reached the age of 18, the order period must be—

(a) a fixed period of not less than 2 years, or

(b) an indefinite period (so that the order has effect until further order).

(6) A criminal behaviour order may specify periods for which particular prohibitions or requirements have effect.

Interim orders

26 Interim orders

(1) This section applies where a court adjourns the hearing of an application for a criminal behaviour order.

(2) The court may make a criminal behaviour order that lasts until the final hearing of the application or until further order ('an interim order') if the court thinks it just to do so.

(3) Section 22(6) to (8) and section 25(3) to (5) do not apply in relation to the making of an interim order.

(4) Subject to that, the court has the same powers whether or not the criminal behaviour order is an interim order.

Variation and discharge

27 Variation or discharge of orders

(1) A criminal behaviour order may be varied or discharged by the court which made it on the application of—

(a) the offender, or

(b) the prosecution.

(2) If an application by the offender under this section is dismissed, the offender may make no further application under this section without—

(a) the consent of the court which made the order, or

(b) the agreement of the prosecution.

(3) If an application by the prosecution under this section is dismissed, the prosecution may make no further application under this section without—

(a) the consent of the court which made the order, or

(b) the agreement of the offender.

(4) The power to vary an order includes power to include an additional prohibition or requirement in the order or to extend the period for which a prohibition or requirement has effect.

(5) Section 24 applies to additional requirements included under subsection (4) as it applies to requirements included in a new order.

(6) In the case of a criminal behaviour order made by a magistrates' court, the references in this section to the court which made the order include a reference to any magistrates' court acting in the same local justice area as that court.

Review of orders (under-18s)

28 Review of orders

(1) If—

(a) a person subject to a criminal behaviour order will be under the age of 18 at the end of a review period (see subsection (2)),

(b) the term of the order runs until the end of that period or beyond, and

(c) the order is not discharged before the end of that period,

a review of the operation of the order must be carried out before the end of that period.

(2) The 'review periods' are—

(a) the period of 12 months beginning with—

(i)   the day on which the criminal behaviour order takes effect, or

(ii)   if during that period the order is varied under section 27, the day on which it is varied (or most recently varied, if the order is varied more than once);

(b) a period of 12 months beginning with—

(i)   the day after the end of the previous review period, or

(ii)   if during that period of 12 months the order is varied under section 27, the day on which it is varied (or most recently varied, if the order is varied more than once).

(3) A review under this section must include consideration of—

(a) the extent to which the offender has complied with the order;

(b) the adequacy of any support available to the offender to help him or her comply with it;

(c) any matters relevant to the question whether an application should be made for the order to be varied or discharged.

(4) Those carrying out or participating in a review under this section must have regard to any relevant guidance issued by the Secretary of State under section 32 when considering—

(a) how the review should be carried out;

(b) what particular matters the review should deal with;

(c) what action (if any) it would be appropriate to take as a result of the findings of the review.

29   Carrying out and participating in reviews

(1) A review under section 28 is to be carried out by the chief officer of police of the police force maintained for the police area in which the offender lives or appears to be living.

(2) The chief officer, in carrying out a review under section 28, must act in co-operation with the council for the local government area in which the offender lives or appears to be living; and the council must co-operate in the carrying out of the review.

(3) The chief officer may invite the participation in the review of any other person or body.

(4) In this section 'local government area' means—

(a) in relation to England, a district or London borough, the City of London, the Isle of Wight and the Isles of Scilly;

(b) in relation to Wales, a county or a county borough.

For the purposes of this section, the council for the Inner and Middle Temples is the Common Council of the City of London.

Breach of orders

30 Breach of order

(1) A person who without reasonable excuse—

(a) does anything he or she is prohibited from doing by a criminal behaviour order, or

(b) fails to do anything he or she is required to do by a criminal behaviour order,

commits an offence.

(2) A person guilty of an offence under this section is liable—

(a) on summary conviction, to imprisonment for a period not exceeding 6 months or to a fine, or to both;

(b) on conviction on indictment, to imprisonment for a period not exceeding 5 years or to a fine, or to both.

(3) If a person is convicted of an offence under this section, it is not open to the court by or before which the person is convicted to make an order under subsection (1)(b) of section 12 of the Powers of Criminal Courts (Sentencing) Act 2000 (conditional discharge).

(4) In proceedings for an offence under this section, a copy of the original criminal behaviour order, certified by the proper officer of the court which made it, is admissible as evidence of its having been made and of its contents to the same extent that oral evidence of those things is admissible in those proceedings.

(5) In relation to any proceedings for an offence under this section that are brought against a person under the age of 18—

(a) section 49 of the Children and Young Persons Act 1933 (restrictions on reports of proceedings in which children and young persons are concerned) does not apply in respect of the person;

(b) section 45 of the Youth Justice and Criminal Evidence Act 1999 (power to restrict reporting of criminal proceedings involving persons under 18) does so apply.

(6) If, in relation to any proceedings mentioned in subsection (5), the court does exercise its power to give a direction under section 45 of the Youth Justice and Criminal Evidence Act 1999, it must give its reasons for doing so.

Supplemental

31 Special measures for witnesses

(1) Chapter 1 of Part 2 of the Youth Justice and Criminal Evidence Act 1999 (special measures directions in the case of vulnerable and intimidated witnesses) applies to criminal behaviour order proceedings as it applies to criminal proceedings, but with—

(a) the omission of the provisions of that Act mentioned in subsection (2) (which make provision appropriate only in the context of criminal proceedings), and

(b) any other necessary modifications.

(2) The provisions are—

(a) section 17(4) to (7);

(b) section 21(4C)(e);

(c) section 22A;

(d) section 27(10);

(e) section 32.

(3) Rules of court made under or for the purposes of Chapter 1 of Part 2 of that Act apply to criminal behaviour order proceedings—

(a) to the extent provided by rules of court, and

(b) subject to any modifications provided by rules of court.

(4) Section 47 of that Act (restrictions on reporting special measures directions etc) applies with any necessary modifications—

(a) to a direction under section 19 of that Act as applied by this section;

(b) to a direction discharging or varying such a direction.

Sections 49 and 51 of that Act (offences) apply accordingly.

(5) In this section 'criminal behaviour order proceedings' means proceedings in a magistrates' court or the Crown Court so far as relating to the issue whether to make a criminal behaviour order.

32   Guidance

(1) The Secretary of State may issue guidance to—

(a) chief officers of police, and

(b) the councils mentioned in section 29(2),

about the exercise of their functions under this Part.

(2) The Secretary of State may revise any guidance issued under this section.

(3) The Secretary of State must arrange for any guidance issued or revised under this section to be published.

33   Saving and transitional provision

(1) The repeal or amendment by this Act of provisions about any of the orders specified in subsection (2) does not—

(a) prevent an order specified in that subsection from being made in connection with criminal proceedings begun before the commencement day;

(b) apply in relation to an order specified in that subsection which is made in connection with criminal proceedings begun before that day;

(c) apply in relation to anything done in connection with such an order.

(2) The orders are—

(a) an order under section 1C of the Crime and Disorder Act 1998 (orders on conviction in criminal proceedings);

(b) an individual support order under section 1AA of that Act made in connection with an order under section 1C of that Act;

(c) a drinking banning order under section 6 of the Violent Crime Reduction Act 2006 (orders on conviction in criminal proceedings).

(3) As from the commencement day there may be no variation of an order specified in subsection (2) that extends the period of the order or of any provision of the order.

(4) At the end of the period of 5 years beginning with the commencement day—

(a) this Part has effect in relation to any order specified in subsection (2) that is still in force as if the provisions of the order were provisions of a criminal behaviour order;

(b) subsections (1) to (3) cease to have effect.

This Part, as it applies by virtue of paragraph (a), has effect with any necessary modifications (and with any modifications specified in an order under section 185(7)).

(5) In deciding whether to make a criminal behaviour order a court may take account of conduct occurring up to 1 year before the commencement day.

(6) In this section 'commencement day' means the day on which this Part comes into force.

PART 3 DISPERSAL POWERS

34 Authorisations to use powers under section 35

(1) A police officer of at least the rank of inspector may authorise the use in a specified locality, during a specified period of not more than 48 hours, of the powers given by section 35.

'Specified' means specified in the authorisation.

(2) An officer may give such an authorisation only if satisfied on reasonable grounds that the use of those powers in the locality during that period may be necessary for the purpose of removing or reducing the likelihood of—

(a) members of the public in the locality being harassed, alarmed or distressed, or

(b) the occurrence in the locality of crime or disorder.

(3) In deciding whether to give such an authorisation an officer must have particular regard to the rights of freedom of expression and freedom of assembly set out in articles 10 and 11 of the Convention.

'Convention' has the meaning given by section 21(1) of the Human Rights Act 1998.

(4) An authorisation under this section—

(a) must be in writing,

(b) must be signed by the officer giving it, and

(c) must specify the grounds on which it is given.

35 Directions excluding a person from an area

(1) If the conditions in subsections (2) and (3) are met and an authorisation is in force under section 34, a constable in uniform may direct a person who is in a public place in the locality specified in the authorisation—

(a) to leave the locality (or part of the locality), and

(b) not to return to the locality (or part of the locality) for the period specified in the direction ('the exclusion period').

(2) The first condition is that the constable has reasonable grounds to suspect that the behaviour of the person in the locality has contributed or is likely to contribute to—

(a) members of the public in the locality being harassed, alarmed or distressed, or

(b) the occurrence in the locality of crime or disorder.

(3) The second condition is that the constable considers that giving a direction to the person is necessary for the purpose of removing or reducing the likelihood of the events mentioned in subsection (2)(a) or (b).

(4) The exclusion period may not exceed 48 hours.

The period may expire after (as long as it begins during) the period specified in the authorisation under section 34.

(5) A direction under this section—

(a) must be given in writing, unless that is not reasonably practicable;

(b) must specify the area to which it relates;

(c) may impose requirements as to the time by which the person must leave the area and the manner in which the person must do so (including the route).

(6) The constable must (unless it is not reasonably practicable) tell the person to whom the direction is given that failing without reasonable excuse to comply with the direction is an offence.

(7) If the constable reasonably believes that the person to whom the direction is given is under the age of 16, the constable may remove the person to a place where the person lives or a place of safety.

(8) Any constable may withdraw or vary a direction under this section; but a variation must not extend the duration of a direction beyond 48 hours from when it was first given.

(9) Notice of a withdrawal or variation of a direction—

(a) must be given to the person to whom the direction was given, unless that is not reasonably practicable, and

(b) if given, must be given in writing unless that is not reasonably practicable.

(10) In this section 'public place' means a place to which at the material time the public or a section of the public has access, on payment or otherwise, as of right or by virtue of express or implied permission.

(11) In this Part 'exclusion period' has the meaning given by subsection (1)(b).

36 Restrictions

(1) A constable may not give a direction under section 35 to a person who appears to the constable to be under the age of 10.

(2) A constable may not give a direction under section 35 that prevents the person to whom it is given having access to a place where the person lives.

(3) A constable may not give a direction under section 35 that prevents the person to whom it is given attending at a place which the person is—

(a) required to attend for the purposes of the person's employment, or a contract of services to which the person is a party,

(b) required to attend by an obligation imposed by or under an enactment or by the order of a court or tribunal, or

(c) expected to attend for the purposes of education or training or for the purposes of receiving medical treatment,

at a time when the person is required or expected (as the case may be) to attend there.

(4) A constable may not give a direction to a person under section 35 if the person is one of a group of persons who are—

(a) engaged in conduct that is lawful under section 220 of the Trade Union and Labour Relations (Consolidation) Act 1992 (peaceful picketing), or

(b) taking part in a public procession of the kind mentioned in subsection (1) of section 11 of the Public Order Act 1986 in respect of which—

(i) written notice has been given in accordance with that section, or

(ii) written notice is not required to be given as provided by subsections (1) and (2) of that section.

(5) In deciding whether to give a direction under section 35 a constable must have particular regard to the rights of freedom of expression and freedom of assembly set out in articles 10 and 11 of the Convention.

'Convention' has the meaning given by section 21(1) of the Human Rights Act 1998.

37 Surrender of property

(1) A constable who gives a person a direction under section 35 may also direct the person to surrender to the constable any item in the person's possession or control that the constable reasonably believes has been used or is likely to be used in behaviour that harasses, alarms or distresses members of the public.

(2) A direction under this section must be given in writing, unless that is not reasonably practicable.

(3) A constable who gives a person a direction under this section must (unless it is not reasonably practicable)—

(a) tell the person that failing without reasonable excuse to comply with the direction is an offence, and

(b) give the person information in writing about when and how the person may recover the surrendered item.

(4) The surrendered item must not be returned to the person before the end of the exclusion period.

(5) If after the end of that period the person asks for the item to be returned, it must be returned (unless there is power to retain it under another enactment).

(6) But if it appears to a constable that the person is under the age of 16 and is not accompanied by a parent or other responsible adult, the item may be retained until the person is so accompanied.

(7) If the person has not asked for the return of the item before the end of the period of 28 days beginning with the day on which the direction was given, the item may be destroyed or otherwise disposed of.

38 Record-keeping

(1) A constable who gives a direction under section 35 must make a record of—

(a) the individual to whom the direction is given,

(b) the time at which the direction is given, and

(c) the terms of the direction (including in particular the area to which it relates and the exclusion period).

(2) A constable who withdraws or varies a direction under section 35 must make a record of—

(a) the time at which the direction is withdrawn or varied,

(b) whether notice of the withdrawal or variation is given to the person to whom the direction was given and if it is, at what time, and

(c) if the direction is varied, the terms of the variation.

(3) A constable who gives a direction under section 37 must make a record of—

(a) the individual to whom the direction is given,

(b) the time at which the direction is given, and

(c) the item to which the direction relates.

39 Offences

(1) A person given a direction under section 35 who fails without reasonable excuse to comply with it commits an offence.

(2) A person guilty of an offence under subsection (1) is liable on summary conviction—

(a) to imprisonment for a period not exceeding 3 months, or

(b) to a fine not exceeding level 4 on the standard scale,

(3) A person given a direction under section 37 who fails without reasonable excuse to comply with it commits an offence.

(4) A person guilty of an offence under subsection (3) is liable on summary conviction to a fine not exceeding level 2 on the standard scale.

41 Guidance

(1) The Secretary of State may issue guidance to chief officers of police about the exercise, by officers under their direction or control, of those officers' functions under this Part.

(2) The Secretary of State may revise any guidance issued under this section.

(3) The Secretary of State must arrange for any guidance issued or revised under this section to be published.

42 Saving and transitional provision

(1) The repeal by this Act of Part 4 of the Anti-social Behaviour Act 2003, and the repeal or amendment by this Act of provisions related to that Part, do not apply in relation to—

(a) an authorisation given under section 30(2) of that Act before the commencement day, or

(b) anything done in connection with such an authorisation.

(2) The repeal by this Act of section 27 of the Violent Crime Reduction Act 2006, and the repeal or amendment by this Act of provisions related to that section, do not apply in relation to—

(a) a direction given under that section before the commencement day, or

(b) anything done in connection with such a direction.

(3) In this section 'commencement day' means the day on which this Part comes into force.

PART 4
COMMUNITY PROTECTION

Chapter I
Community protection notices

Community protection notices

43 Power to issue notices

(1) An authorised person may issue a community protection notice to an individual aged 16 or over, or a body, if satisfied on reasonable grounds that—

(a) the conduct of the individual or body is having a detrimental effect, of a persistent or continuing nature, on the quality of life of those in the locality, and

(b) the conduct is unreasonable.

(2) In subsection (1) 'authorised person' means a person on whom section 53 (or an enactment amended by that section) confers power to issue community protection notices.

(3) A community protection notice is a notice that imposes any of the following requirements on the individual or body issued with it—

(a) a requirement to stop doing specified things;

(b) a requirement to do specified things;

(c) a requirement to take reasonable steps to achieve specified results.

(4) The only requirements that may be imposed are ones that are reasonable to impose in order—

(a) to prevent the detrimental effect referred to in subsection (1) from continuing or recurring, or

(b) to reduce that detrimental effect or to reduce the risk of its continuance or recurrence.

(5) A person (A) may issue a community protection notice to an individual or body (B) only if—

(a) B has been given a written warning that the notice will be issued unless B's conduct ceases to have the detrimental effect referred to in subsection (1), and

(b) A is satisfied that, despite B having had enough time to deal with the matter, B's conduct is still having that effect.

(6) A person issuing a community protection notice must before doing so inform any body or individual the person thinks appropriate.

(7) A community protection notice must—

(a) identify the conduct referred to in subsection (1);

(b) explain the effect of sections 46 to 51.

(8) A community protection notice may specify periods within which, or times by which, requirements within subsection (3)(b) or (c) are to be complied with.

44 Occupiers of premises etc

(1) Conduct on, or affecting, premises (other than premises within subsection (2)) that a particular person—

(a) owns,

(b) leases,

(c) occupies,

(d) controls,

(e) operates, or

(f) maintains,

is treated for the purposes of section 43 as conduct of that person.

(2) Conduct on, or affecting, premises occupied for the purposes of a government department is treated for the purposes of section 43 as conduct of the Minister in charge of that department.

(3) This section does not treat an individual's conduct as that of another person if that person cannot reasonably be expected to control or affect it.

45 Occupier or owner unascertainable

(1) This section applies where—

(a) an authorised person has power to issue a community protection notice,

(b) the detrimental effect referred to in section 43(1) arises from the condition of premises or the use to which premises have been put, and

(c) the authorised person has made reasonable enquiries to find out the name or proper address of the occupier of the premises (or, if the premises are unoccupied, the owner) but without success.

(2) The authorised person may—

(a) post the community protection notice on the premises;

(b) enter the premises, or other premises, to the extent reasonably necessary for that purpose.

(3) The community protection notice is treated as having been issued to the occupier of the premises (or, if the premises are unoccupied, the owner) at the time the notice is posted.

(4) In this section 'authorised person' has the same meaning as in section 43(1).

46 Appeals against notices

(1) A person issued with a community protection notice may appeal to a magistrates' court against the notice on any of the following grounds.

1. That the conduct specified in the community protection notice—

    (a) did not take place,

    (b) has not had a detrimental effect on the quality of life of those in the locality,

    (c) has not been of a persistent or continuing nature,

    (d) is not unreasonable, or

    (e) is conduct that the person cannot reasonably be expected to control or affect.

2. That any of the requirements in the notice, or any of the periods within which or times by which they are to be complied with, are unreasonable.

3. That there is a material defect or error in, or in connection with, the notice.

4. That the notice was issued to the wrong person.

(2) An appeal must be made within the period of 21 days beginning with the day on which the person is issued with the notice.

(3) While an appeal against a community protection notice is in progress—

(a) a requirement imposed by the notice to stop doing specified things remains in effect, unless the court orders otherwise, but

(b) any other requirement imposed by the notice is of no effect.

For this purpose an appeal is 'in progress' until it is finally determined or is withdrawn.

(4) A magistrates' court hearing an appeal against a community protection notice must—

(a) quash the notice,

(b) modify the notice (for example by extending a period specified in it), or

(c) dismiss the appeal.

Failure to comply with notice

47 Remedial action by local authority

(1) Where a person issued with a community protection notice ('the defaulter') fails to comply with a requirement of the notice, the relevant local authority may take action under subsection (2) or subsection (3) (or both).

(2) The relevant local authority may have work carried out to ensure that the failure is remedied, but only on land that is open to the air.

(3) As regards premises other than land open to the air, if the relevant local authority issues the defaulter with a notice—

(a) specifying work it intends to have carried out to ensure that the failure is remedied,

(b) specifying the estimated cost of the work, and

(c) inviting the defaulter to consent to the work being carried out,

the authority may have the work carried out if the necessary consent is given.

(4) In subsection (3) 'the necessary consent' means the consent of—

(a) the defaulter, and

(b) the owner of the premises on which the work is to be carried out (if that is not the defaulter).

Paragraph (b) does not apply where the relevant authority has made reasonable efforts to contact the owner of the premises but without success.

(5) A person authorised by a local authority to carry out work under this section may enter any premises to the extent reasonably necessary for that purpose, except that a person who is only authorised to carry out work under subsection (2) may only enter land that is open to the air.

(6) If work is carried out under subsection (2) or (3) and the relevant local authority issues a notice to the defaulter—

(a) giving details of the work that was carried out, and

(b) specifying an amount that is no more than the cost to the authority of having the work carried out,

the defaulter is liable to the authority for that amount (subject to the outcome of any appeal under subsection (7)).

(7) A person issued with a notice under subsection (6) may appeal to a magistrates' court, within the period of 21 days beginning with the day on which the notice was issued, on the ground that the amount specified under subsection (6)(b) is excessive.

(8) A magistrates' court hearing an appeal under subsection (7) must—

(a) confirm the amount, or

(b) substitute a lower amount.

(9) In this section 'the relevant local authority' means—

(a) the local authority that issued the community protection notice;

(b) if the community protection notice was not issued by a local authority, the local authority (or, as the case may be, one of the local authorities) that could have issued it.

48   Offence of failing to comply with notice

(1) A person issued with a community protection notice who fails to comply with it commits an offence.

(2) A person guilty of an offence under this section is liable on summary conviction—

(a) to a fine not exceeding level 4 on the standard scale, in the case of an individual;

(b) to a fine, in the case of a body.

(3) A person does not commit an offence under this section if—

(a) the person took all reasonable steps to comply with the notice, or

(b) there is some other reasonable excuse for the failure to comply with it.

49   Remedial orders

(1) A court before which a person is convicted of an offence under section 48 in respect of a community protection notice may make whatever order the court thinks appropriate for ensuring that what the notice requires to be done is done.

(2) An order under this section may in particular require the defendant—

(a) to carry out specified work, or

(b) to allow specified work to be carried out by or on behalf of a specified local authority.

(3) To be specified under subsection (2)(b) a local authority must be—

(a) the local authority that issued the community protection notice;

(b) if the community protection notice was not issued by a local authority, the local authority (or, as the case may be, one of the local authorities) that could have issued it.

(4) A requirement imposed under subsection (2)(b) does not authorise the person carrying out the work to enter the defendant's home without the defendant's consent.

But this does not prevent a defendant who fails to give that consent from being in breach of the court's order.

(5) In subsection (4) 'the defendant's home' means the house, flat, vehicle or other accommodation where the defendant—

(a) usually lives, or

(b) is living at the time when the work is or would be carried out.

(6) If work is carried out under subsection (2)(b) and the local authority specified under that subsection issues a notice to the defaulter—

(a) giving details of the work that was carried out, and

(b) specifying an amount that is no more than the cost to the authority of having the work carried out,

the defaulter is liable to the authority for that amount (subject to the outcome of any appeal under subsection (7)).

(7) A person issued with a notice under subsection (6) may appeal to a magistrates' court, within the period of 21 days beginning with the day on which the notice was issued, on the ground that the amount specified under subsection (6)(b) is excessive.

(8) A magistrates' court hearing an appeal under subsection (7) must—

(a) confirm the amount, or

(b) substitute a lower amount.

50 Forfeiture of item used in commission of offence

(1) A court before which a person is convicted of an offence under section 48 may order the forfeiture of any item that was used in the commission of the offence.

(2) An order under this section may require a person in possession of the item to hand it over as soon as reasonably practicable—

(a) to a constable, or

(b) to a person employed by a local authority or designated by a local authority under section 53(1)(c).

(3) An order under this section may require the item—

(a) to be destroyed, or

(b) to be disposed of in whatever way the order specifies.

(4) Where an item ordered to be forfeited under this section is kept by or handed over to a constable, the police force of which the constable is a member must ensure that arrangements are made for its destruction or disposal, either—

(a) in accordance with the order, or

(b) if no arrangements are specified in the order, in whatever way seems appropriate to the police force.

(5) Where an item ordered to be forfeited under this section is kept by or handed over to a person within subsection (2)(b), the local authority by whom the person is employed or was designated must ensure that arrangements are made for its destruction or disposal, either—

(a) in accordance with the order, or

(b) if no arrangements are specified in the order, in whatever way seems appropriate to the local authority.

51 Seizure of item used in commission of offence

(1) If a justice of the peace is satisfied on information on oath that there are reasonable grounds for suspecting—

(a) that an offence under section 48 has been committed, and

(b) that there is an item used in the commission of the offence on premises specified in the information,

the justice may issue a warrant authorising any constable or designated person to enter the premises within 14 days from the date of issue of the warrant to seize the item.

(2) In this section 'designated person' means a person designated by a local authority under section 53(1)(c).

(3) A constable or designated person may use reasonable force, if necessary, in executing a warrant under this section.

(4) A constable or designated person who has seized an item under a warrant under this section—

(a) may retain the item until any relevant criminal proceedings have been finally determined, if such proceedings are started before the end of the period of 28 days following the day on which the item was seized;

(b) otherwise, must before the end of that period return the item to the person from whom it was seized.

(5) In subsection (4) 'relevant criminal proceedings' means proceedings for an offence under section 48 in the commission of which the item is alleged to have been used.

52 Fixed penalty notices

(1) An authorised person may issue a fixed penalty notice to anyone who that person has reason to believe has committed an offence under section 48.

(2) In subsection (1) 'authorised person' means a person on whom section 53 (or an enactment amended by that section) confers power to issue fixed penalty notices under this section.

(3) A fixed penalty notice is a notice offering the person to whom it is issued the opportunity of discharging any liability to conviction for the offence by payment of a fixed penalty to a local authority specified in the notice.

(4) The local authority specified under subsection (3) must be—

(a) the local authority that issued the community protection notice to which the fixed penalty notice relates;

(b) if the community protection notice was not issued by a local authority, the local authority (or, as the case may be, one of the local authorities) that could have issued it.

(5) Where a person is issued with a notice under this section in respect of an offence—

(a) no proceedings may be taken for the offence before the end of the period of 14 days following the date of the notice;

(b) the person may not be convicted of the offence if the person pays the fixed penalty before the end of that period.

(6) A fixed penalty notice must—

(a) give reasonably detailed particulars of the circumstances alleged to constitute the offence;

(b) state the period during which (because of subsection (5)(a)) proceedings will not be taken for the offence;

(c) specify the amount of the fixed penalty;

(d) state the name and address of the person to whom the fixed penalty may be paid;

(e) specify permissible methods of payment.

(7) An amount specified under subsection (6)(c) must not be more than £100.

(8) A fixed penalty notice may specify two amounts under subsection (6)(c) and specify that, if the lower of those amounts is paid within a specified period (of less than 14 days), that is the amount of the fixed penalty.

(9) Whatever other method may be specified under subsection (6)(e), payment of a fixed penalty may be made by pre-paying and posting to the person whose name is stated under subsection (6)(d), at the stated address, a letter containing the amount of the penalty (in cash or otherwise).

(10) Where a letter is sent as mentioned in subsection (9), payment is regarded as having been made at the time at which that letter would be delivered in the ordinary course of post.

(11) In any proceedings, a certificate that—

(a) purports to be signed by or on behalf of the chief finance officer of the local authority concerned, and

(b) states that payment of a fixed penalty was, or was not, received by the dated specified in the certificate,

is evidence of the facts stated.

(12) In this section 'chief finance officer', in relation to a local authority, means the person with responsibility for the authority's financial affairs.

Who may issue notices

53 Authorised persons

(1) A community protection notice or a fixed penalty notice may be issued by—

(a) a constable;

(b) the relevant local authority (see subsections (2) and (3));

(c) a person designated by the relevant local authority for the purposes of this section.

(2) For a community protection notice, 'the relevant local authority' means the local authority (or, as the case may be, any of the local authorities) within whose area the conduct specified in the notice has, according to the notice, been taking place.

(3) For a fixed penalty notice, 'the relevant local authority' means the local authority (or, as the case may be, any of the local authorities) within whose area the offence in question is alleged to have taken place.

(4) Only a person of a description specified in an order made by the Secretary of State for the purposes of subsection (1)(c) may be designated under that subsection.

Supplemental

54 Exemption from liability

(1) A local authority exercising or purporting to exercise a power under section 47(2) is not liable to an occupier or owner of land for damages or otherwise (whether at common law or otherwise) arising out of anything done or omitted to be done in the exercise or purported exercise of that power.

(2) A person carrying out work under section 47(2), or a person by or on whose behalf work is carried out under section 49(2)(b), is not liable to an occupier or owner of land for damages or otherwise (whether at common law or otherwise) arising out of anything done or omitted to be done in carrying out that work.

(3) Subsections (1) and (2) do not apply—

(a) to an act or omission shown to have been in bad faith, or

(b) to liability arising out of a failure to exercise due care and attention.

(4) Subsections (1) and (2) do not apply so as to prevent an award of damages made in respect of an act or omission on the ground that the act or omission was unlawful by virtue of section 6(1) of the Human Rights Act 1998.

(5) This section does not affect any other exemption from liability (whether at common law or otherwise).

55 Issuing of notices

(1) A notice under this Chapter may be issued to a person by—

(a) handing it to the person,

(b) leaving it at the person's proper address, or

(c) sending it by post to the person at that address.

(2) A notice under this Chapter to a body corporate may be issued to the secretary or clerk of that body.

(3) A notice under this Chapter to a partnership may be issued to a partner or a person who has the control or management of the partnership business.

(4) For the purposes of this section and of section 7 of the Interpretation Act 1978 (service of documents by post) in its application to this section, the proper address of a person is the person's last known address, except that—

(a) in the case of a body corporate or its secretary or clerk, it is the address of the body's registered or principal office;

(b) in the case of a partnership or person having the control or the management of the partnership business, it is the principal office of the partnership.

(5) For the purposes of subsection (4) the principal office of a company registered outside the United Kingdom, or of a partnership carrying on business outside the United Kingdom, is its principal office within the United Kingdom.

(6) If a person has specified an address in the United Kingdom, other than the person's proper address within the meaning of subsection (4), as the one at which the person or someone on the person's behalf will accept notices of the same description as a notice under this Chapter, that address is also treated for the purposes of this section and section 7 of the Interpretation Act 1978 as the person's proper address.

56 Guidance

(1) The Secretary of State may issue—

(a) guidance to chief officers of police about the exercise, by officers under their direction or control, of those officers' functions under this Chapter;

(b) guidance to local authorities about the exercise of their functions under this Chapter and those of persons designated under section 53(1)(c).

(2) The Secretary of State may revise any guidance issued under this section.

(3) The Secretary of State must arrange for any guidance issued or revised under this section to be published.

57 Interpretation of Chapter 1

In this Chapter—

'conduct' includes a failure to act;

'local authority' means—

    (a)   in relation to England, a district council, a county council for an area for which there is no district council, a London borough council, the Common Council of the City of London or the Council of the Isles of Scilly;

    (b)   in relation to Wales, a county council or a county borough council;

'owner', in relation to premises, means—

    (a)   a person (other than a mortgagee not in possession) entitled to dispose of the fee simple of the premises, whether in possession or in reversion;

    (b)   a person who holds or is entitled to the rents and profits of the premises under a lease that (when granted) was for a term of not less then 3 years;

'premises' includes any land.

58   Saving and transitional provision

(1) The repeal or amendment by this Act of provisions about any of the notices specified in subsection (2) does not apply in relation to—

(a) a notice specified in that subsection served before the commencement day;

(b) anything done in connection with such a notice.

(2) The notices are—

(a) a litter abatement notice under section 92 of the Environmental Protection Act 1990;

(b) a litter clearing notice under section 92A of that Act;

(c) a street litter control notice under section 93 of that Act;

(d) a defacement removal notice under section 48 of the Anti-social Behaviour Act 2003.

(3) A community protection notice that contains no requirement that could not have been contained in one of the notices specified in subsection (2) may be issued in respect of conduct before the commencement day.

(4) Subsection (3) applies only during the period of 3 months beginning with the commencement day.

(5) In this section 'commencement day' means the day on which this Chapter comes into force.

Chapter 2
Public spaces protection orders

Public spaces protection orders

59 Power to make orders

(1) A local authority may make a public spaces protection order if satisfied on reasonable grounds that two conditions are met.

(2) The first condition is that—

(a) activities carried on in a public place within the authority's area have had a detrimental effect on the quality of life of those in the locality, or

(b) it is likely that activities will be carried on in a public place within that area and that they will have such an effect.

(3) The second condition is that the effect, or likely effect, of the activities—

(a) is, or is likely to be, of a persistent or continuing nature,

(b) is, or is likely to be, such as to make the activities unreasonable, and

(c) justifies the restrictions imposed by the notice.

(4) A public spaces protection order is an order that identifies the public place referred to in subsection (2) ('the restricted area') and—

(a) prohibits specified things being done in the restricted area,

(b) requires specified things to be done by persons carrying on specified activities in that area, or

(c) does both of those things.

(5) The only prohibitions or requirements that may be imposed are ones that are reasonable to impose in order—

(a) to prevent the detrimental effect referred to in subsection (2) from continuing, occurring or recurring, or

(b) to reduce that detrimental effect or to reduce the risk of its continuance, occurrence or recurrence.

(6) A prohibition or requirement may be framed—

(a) so as to apply to all persons, or only to persons in specified categories, or to all persons except those in specified categories;

(b) so as to apply at all times, or only at specified times, or at all times except those specified;

(c) so as to apply in all circumstances, or only in specified circumstances, or in all circumstances except those specified.

(7) A public spaces protection order must—

(a) identify the activities referred to in subsection (2);

(b) explain the effect of section 63 (where it applies) and section 67;

(c) specify the period for which the order has effect.

(8) A public spaces protection order must be published in accordance with regulations made by the Secretary of State.

60 Duration of orders

(1) A public spaces protection order may not have effect for a period of more than 3 years, unless extended under this section.

(2) Before the time when a public spaces protection order is due to expire, the local authority that made the order may extend the period for which it has effect if satisfied on reasonable grounds that doing so is necessary to prevent—

(a) occurrence or recurrence after that time of the activities identified in the order, or

(b) an increase in the frequency or seriousness of those activities after that time.

(3) An extension under this section—

(a) may not be for a period of more than 3 years;

(b) must be published in accordance with regulations made by the Secretary of State.

(4) A public spaces protection order may be extended under this section more than once.

61 Variation and discharge of orders

(1) Where a public spaces protection order is in force, the local authority that made the order may vary it—

(a) by increasing or reducing the restricted area;

(b) by altering or removing a prohibition or requirement included in the order, or adding a new one.

(2) A local authority may make a variation under subsection (1)(a) that results in the order applying to an area to which it did not previously apply only if the conditions in section 59(2) and (3) are met as regards activities in that area.

(3) A local authority may make a variation under subsection (1)(b) that makes a prohibition or requirement more extensive, or adds a new one, only if the prohibitions and requirements imposed by the order as varied are ones that section 59(5) allows to be imposed.

(4) A public spaces protection order may be discharged by the local authority that made it.

(5) Where an order is varied, the order as varied must be published in accordance with regulations made by the Secretary of State.

(6) Where an order is discharged, a notice identifying the order and stating the date when it ceases to have effect must be published in accordance with regulations made by the Secretary of State.

Prohibition on consuming alcohol

62 Premises etc to which alcohol prohibition does not apply

(1) A prohibition in a public spaces protection order on consuming alcohol does not apply to—

(a) premises (other than council-operated licensed premises) authorised by a premises licence to be used for the supply of alcohol;

(b) premises authorised by a club premises certificate to be used by the club for the supply of alcohol;

(c) a place within the curtilage of premises within paragraph (a) or (b);

(d) premises which by virtue of Part 5 of the Licensing Act 2003 may at the relevant time be used for the supply of alcohol or which, by virtue of that Part, could have been so used within the 30 minutes before that time;

(e) a place where facilities or activities relating to the sale or consumption of alcohol are at the relevant time permitted by virtue of a permission granted under section 115E of the Highways Act 1980 (highway-related uses).

(2) A prohibition in a public spaces protection order on consuming alcohol does not apply to council-operated licensed premises—

(a) when the premises are being used for the supply of alcohol, or

(b) within 30 minutes after the end of a period during which the premises have been used for the supply of alcohol.

(3) In this section—

'club premises certificate' has the meaning given by section 60 of the Licensing Act 2003;

'premises licence' has the meaning given by section 11 of that Act;

'supply of alcohol' has the meaning given by section 14 of that Act.

(4) For the purposes of this section, premises are 'council-operated licensed premises' if they are authorised by a premises licence to be used for the supply of alcohol and—

(a) the licence is held by a local authority in whose area the premises (or part of the premises) are situated, or

(b) the licence is held by another person but the premises are occupied by a local authority or are managed by or on behalf of a local authority.

63 Consumption of alcohol in breach of prohibition in order

(1) This section applies where a constable or an authorised person reasonably believes that a person (P)—

(a) is or has been consuming alcohol in breach of a prohibition in a public spaces protection order, or

(b) intends to consume alcohol in circumstances in which doing so would be a breach of such a prohibition.

In this section 'authorised person' means a person authorised for the purposes of this section by the local authority that made the public spaces protection order (or authorised by virtue of section 69(1)).

(2) The constable or authorised person may require P—

(a) not to consume, in breach of the order, alcohol or anything which the constable or authorised person reasonably believes to be alcohol;

(b) to surrender anything in P's possession which is, or which the constable or authorised person reasonably believes to be, alcohol or a container for alcohol.

(3) A constable or an authorised person who imposes a requirement under subsection (2) must tell P that failing without reasonable excuse to comply with the requirement is an offence.

(4) A requirement imposed by an authorised person under subsection (2) is not valid if the person—

(a) is asked by P to show evidence of his or her authorisation, and

(b) fails to do so.

(5) A constable or an authorised person may dispose of anything surrendered under subsection (2)(b) in whatever way he or she thinks appropriate.

(6) A person who fails without reasonable excuse to comply with a requirement imposed on him or her under subsection (2) commits an offence and is liable on summary conviction to a fine not exceeding level 2 on the standard scale.

Restrictions on public rights of way

64 Orders restricting public right of way over highway

(1) A local authority may not make a public spaces protection order that restricts the public right of way over a highway without considering—

(a) the likely effect of making the order on the occupiers of premises adjoining or adjacent to the highway;

(b) the likely effect of making the order on other persons in the locality;

(c) in a case where the highway constitutes a through route, the availability of a reasonably convenient alternative route.

(2) Before making such an order a local authority must—

(a) notify potentially affected persons of the proposed order,

(b) inform those persons how they can see a copy of the proposed order,

(c) notify those persons of the period within which they may make representations about the proposed order, and

(d) consider any representations made.

In this subsection 'potentially affected persons' means occupiers of premises adjacent to or adjoining the highway, and any other persons in the locality who are likely to be affected by the proposed order.

(3) Before a local authority makes a public spaces protection order restricting the public right of way over a highway that is also within the area of another local authority, it must consult that other authority if it thinks it appropriate to do so.

(4) A public spaces protection order may not restrict the public right of way over a highway for the occupiers of premises adjoining or adjacent to the highway.

(5) A public spaces protection order may not restrict the public right of way over a highway that is the only or principal means of access to a dwelling.

(6) In relation to a highway that is the only or principal means of access to premises used for business or recreational purposes, a public spaces protection order may not restrict the public right of way over the highway during periods when the premises are normally used for those purposes.

(7) A public spaces protection order that restricts the public right of way over a highway may authorise the installation, operation and maintenance of a barrier or barriers for enforcing the restriction.

(8) A local authority may install, operate and maintain barriers authorised under subsection (7).

(9) A highway over which the public right of way is restricted by a public spaces protection order does not cease to be regarded as a highway by reason of the restriction (or by reason of any barrier authorised under subsection (7)).

(10) In this section—

'dwelling' means a building or part of a building occupied, or intended to be occupied, as a separate dwelling;

'highway' has the meaning given by section 328 of the Highways Act 1980.

65 Categories of highway over which public right of way may not be restricted

(1) A public spaces protection order may not restrict the public right of way over a highway that is—

(a) a special road;

(b) a trunk road;

(c) a classified or principal road;

(d) a strategic road;

(e) a highway in England of a description prescribed by regulations made by the Secretary of State;

(f) a highway in Wales of a description prescribed by regulations made by the Welsh Ministers.

(2) In this section—

'classified road', 'special road' and 'trunk road' have the meaning given by section 329(1) of the Highways Act 1980;

'highway' has the meaning given by section 328 of that Act;

'principal road' has the meaning given by section 12 of that Act (and see section 13 of that Act);

'strategic road' has the meaning given by section 60(4) of the Traffic Management Act 2004.

Validity of orders

66   Challenging the validity of orders

(1) An interested person may apply to the High Court to question the validity of—

(a) a public spaces protection order, or

(b) a variation of a public spaces protection order.

'Interested person' means an individual who lives in the restricted area or who regularly works in or visits that area.

(2) The grounds on which an application under this section may be made are—

(a) that the local authority did not have power to make the order or variation, or to include particular prohibitions or requirements imposed by the order (or by the order as varied);

(b) that a requirement under this Chapter was not complied with in relation to the order or variation.

(3) An application under this section must be made within the period of 6 weeks beginning with the date on which the order or variation is made.

(4) On an application under this section the High Court may by order suspend the operation of the order or variation, or any of the prohibitions or requirements imposed by the order (or by the order as varied), until the final determination of the proceedings.

(5) If on an application under this section the High Court is satisfied that—

(a) the local authority did not have power to make the order or variation, or to include particular prohibitions or requirements imposed by the order (or by the order as varied), or

(b) the interests of the applicant have been substantially prejudiced by a failure to comply with a requirement under this Chapter,

the Court may quash the order or variation, or any of the prohibitions or requirements imposed by the order (or by the order as varied).

(6) A public spaces protection order, or any of the prohibitions or requirements imposed by the order (or by the order as varied), may be suspended under subsection (4) or quashed under subsection (5)—

(a) generally, or

(b) so far as necessary for the protection of the interests of the applicant.

(7) An interested person may not challenge the validity of a public spaces protection order, or of a variation of a public spaces protection order, in any legal proceedings (either before or after it is made) except—

(a) under this section, or

(b) under subsection (3) of section 67 (where the interested person is charged with an offence under that section).

Failure to comply with orders

67 Offence of failing to comply with order

(1) It is an offence for a person without reasonable excuse—

(a) to do anything that the person is prohibited from doing by a public spaces protection order, or

(b) to fail to comply with a requirement to which the person is subject under a public spaces protection order.

(2) A person guilty of an offence under this section is liable on summary conviction to a fine not exceeding level 3 on the standard scale.

(3) A person does not commit an offence under this section by failing to comply with a prohibition or requirement that the local authority did not have power to include in the public spaces protection order.

(4) Consuming alcohol in breach of a public spaces protection order is not an offence under this section (but see section 63).

68 Fixed penalty notices

(1) A constable or an authorised person may issue a fixed penalty notice to anyone he or she has reason to believe has committed an offence under section 63 or 67 in relation to a public spaces protection order.

(2) A fixed penalty notice is a notice offering the person to whom it is issued the opportunity of discharging any liability to conviction for the offence by payment of a fixed penalty to a local authority specified in the notice.

(3) The local authority specified under subsection (2) must be the one that made the public spaces protection order.

(4) Where a person is issued with a notice under this section in respect of an offence—

(a) no proceedings may be taken for the offence before the end of the period of 14 days following the date of the notice;

(b) the person may not be convicted of the offence if the person pays the fixed penalty before the end of that period.

(5) A fixed penalty notice must—

(a) give reasonably detailed particulars of the circumstances alleged to constitute the offence;

(b) state the period during which (because of subsection (4)(a)) proceedings will not be taken for the offence;

(c) specify the amount of the fixed penalty;

(d) state the name and address of the person to whom the fixed penalty may be paid;

(e) specify permissible methods of payment.

(6) An amount specified under subsection (5)(c) must not be more than £100.

(7) A fixed penalty notice may specify two amounts under subsection (5)(c) and specify that, if the lower of those amounts is paid within a specified period (of less than 14 days), that is the amount of the fixed penalty.

(8) Whatever other method may be specified under subsection (5)(e), payment of a fixed penalty may be made by pre-paying and posting to the person whose name is stated under subsection (5)(d), at the stated address, a letter containing the amount of the penalty (in cash or otherwise).

(9) Where a letter is sent as mentioned in subsection (8), payment is regarded as having been made at the time at which that letter would be delivered in the ordinary course of post.

(10) In any proceedings, a certificate that—

(a) purports to be signed by or on behalf of the chief finance officer of the local authority concerned, and

(b) states that payment of a fixed penalty was, or was not, received by the dated specified in the certificate,

is evidence of the facts stated.

(11) In this section—

'authorised person' means a person authorised for the purposes of this section by the local authority that made the order (or authorised by virtue of section 69(2));

'chief finance officer', in relation to a local authority, means the person with responsibility for the authority's financial affairs.

Supplemental

70 Byelaws

A byelaw that prohibits, by the creation of an offence, an activity regulated by a public spaces protection order is of no effect in relation to the restricted area during the currency of the order.

71 Bodies other than local authorities with statutory functions in relation to land

(1) The Secretary of State may by order—

(a) designate a person or body (other than a local authority) that has power to make byelaws in relation to particular land, and

(b) specify land in England to which the power relates.

(2) This Chapter has effect as if—

(a) a person or body designated under subsection (1) (a 'designated person') were a local authority, and

(b) land specified under that subsection were within its area.

But references in the rest of this section to a local authority are to a local authority that is not a designated person.

(3) The only prohibitions or requirements that may be imposed in a public spaces protection order made by a designated person are ones that it has power to impose (or would, but for section 70, have power to impose) by making a byelaw in respect of the restricted area.

(4) A public spaces protection order made by a designated person may not include provision regulating, in relation to a particular public space, an activity that is already regulated in relation to that space by a public spaces protection order made by a local authority.

(5) Where a public spaces protection order made by a local authority regulates, in relation to a particular public space, an activity that a public spaces protection order made by a designated person already regulates, the order made by the designated person ceases to have that effect.

(6) If a person or body that may be designated under subsection (1)(a) gives a notice in writing under this subsection, in respect of land in relation to which it has power to make byelaws, to a local authority in whose area the land is situated—

(a) no part of the land may form, or fall within, the restricted area of any public spaces protection order made by the local authority;

(b) if any part of the land—

(i) forms the restricted area of a public spaces protection order already made by the local authority, or

(ii) falls within such an area,

the order has ceases to have effect (where sub-paragraph (i) applies), or has effect as if the restricted area did not include the land in question (where sub-paragraph (ii) applies).

72 Convention rights, consultation, publicity and notification

(1) A local authority, in deciding—

(a) whether to make a public spaces protection order (under section 59) and if so what it should include,

(b) whether to extend the period for which a public spaces protection order has effect (under section 60) and if so for how long,

(c) whether to vary a public spaces protection order (under section 61) and if so how, or

(d) whether to discharge a public spaces protection order (under section 61),

must have particular regard to the rights of freedom of expression and freedom of assembly set out in articles 10 and 11 of the Convention.

(2) In subsection (1) 'Convention' has the meaning given by section 21(1) of the Human Rights Act 1998.

(3) A local authority must carry out the necessary consultation and the necessary publicity, and the necessary notification (if any), before—

(a) making a public spaces protection order,

(b) extending the period for which a public spaces protection order has effect, or

(c) varying or discharging a public spaces protection order.

(4) In subsection (3)—

'the necessary consultation' means consulting with—

(a) the chief officer of police, and the local policing body, for the police area that includes the restricted area;

(b) whatever community representatives the local authority thinks it appropriate to consult;

(c) the owner or occupier of land within the restricted area;

'the necessary publicity' means—

(a) in the case of a proposed order or variation, publishing the text of it;

(b) in the case of a proposed extension or discharge, publicising the proposal;

'the necessary notification' means notifying the following authorities of the proposed order, extension, variation or discharge—

    (a)   the parish council or community council (if any) for the area that includes the restricted area;

    (b)   in the case of a public spaces protection order made or to be made by a district council in England, the county council (if any) for the area that includes the restricted area.

(5) The requirement to consult with the owner or occupier of land within the restricted area—

(a) does not apply to land that is owned and occupied by the local authority;

(b) applies only if, or to the extent that, it is reasonably practicable to consult the owner or occupier of the land.

(6) In the case of a person or body designated under section 71, the necessary consultation also includes consultation with the local authority which (ignoring subsection (2) of that section) is the authority for the area that includes the restricted area.

(7) In relation to a variation of a public spaces protection order that would increase the restricted area, the restricted area for the purposes of this section is the increased area.

73 Guidance

(1) The Secretary of State may issue—

(a) guidance to local authorities about the exercise of their functions under this Chapter and those of persons authorised by local authorities under section 63 or 68;

(b) guidance to chief officers of police about the exercise, by officers under their direction or control, of those officers' functions under this Part.

(2) The Secretary of State may revise any guidance issued under this section.

(3) The Secretary of State must arrange for any guidance issued or revised under this section to be published.

74 Interpretation of Chapter 2

(1) In this Chapter—

'alcohol' has the meaning given by section 191 of the Licensing Act 2003;

'community representative', in relation to a public spaces protection order that a local authority proposes to make or has made, means any individual or body appearing to the authority to represent the views of people who live in, work in or visit the restricted area;

'local authority' means—

(a)   in relation to England, a district council, a county council for an area for which there is no district council, a London borough council, the Common Council of the City of London (in its capacity as a local authority) or the Council of the Isles of Scilly;

(b)   in relation to Wales, a county council or a county borough council;

'public place' means any place to which the public or any section of the public has access, on payment or otherwise, as of right or by virtue of express or implied permission;

'restricted area' has the meaning given by section 59(4).

(2) For the purposes of this Chapter, a public spaces protection order 'regulates' an activity if the activity is—

(a) prohibited by virtue of section 59(4)(a), or

(b) subjected to requirements by virtue of section 59(4)(b),

whether or not for all persons and at all times.

75   Saving and transitional provision

(1) The repeal or amendment by this Act of provisions about any of the orders specified in subsection (2) does not apply in relation to—

(a) an order specified in that subsection made before the commencement day;

(b) anything done in connection with such an order.

(2) The orders are—

(a) a gating order under Part 8A of the Highways Act 1980;

(b) an order under section 13(2) of the Criminal Justice and Police Act 2001 (power of local authority to designate public place for restrictions on alcohol consumption);

(c) a dog control order under Chapter 1 of Part 6 of the Clean Neighbourhoods and Environment Act 2005.

(3) At the end of the period of 3 years beginning with the commencement day—

(a) this Chapter has effect in relation to any order specified in subsection (2) that is still in force as if the provisions of the order were provisions of a public spaces protection order;

(b) subsection (1) ceases to have effect.

This Part, as it applies by virtue of paragraph (a), has effect with any necessary modifications (and with any modifications specified in an order under section 185(7)).

(4) In this section 'commencement day' means the day on which this Chapter comes into force.

Chapter 3
Closure of premises associated with nuisance or disorder etc

Closure notices

76 Power to issue closure notices

(1) A police officer of at least the rank of inspector, or the local authority, may issue a closure notice if satisfied on reasonable grounds—

(a) that the use of particular premises has resulted, or (if the notice is not issued) is likely soon to result, in nuisance to members of the public, or

(b) that there has been, or (if the notice is not issued) is likely soon to be, disorder near those premises associated with the use of those premises,

and that the notice is necessary to prevent the nuisance or disorder from continuing, recurring or occurring.

(2) A closure notice is a notice prohibiting access to the premises for a period specified in the notice.

For the maximum period, see section 77.

(3) A closure notice may prohibit access—

(a) by all persons except those specified, or by all persons except those of a specified description;

(b) at all times, or at all times except those specified;

(c) in all circumstances, or in all circumstances except those specified.

(4) A closure notice may not prohibit access by—

(a) people who habitually live on the premises, or

(b) the owner of the premises,

and accordingly they must be specified under subsection (3)(a).

(5) A closure notice must—

(a) identify the premises;

(b) explain the effect of the notice;

(c) state that failure to comply with the notice is an offence;

(d) state that an application will be made under section 80 for a closure order;

(e) specify when and where the application will be heard;

(f) explain the effect of a closure order;

(g) give information about the names of, and means of contacting, persons and organisations in the area that provide advice about housing and legal matters.

(6) A closure notice may be issued only if reasonable efforts have been made to inform—

(a) people who live on the premises (whether habitually or not), and

(b) any person who has control of or responsibility for the premises or who has an interest in them,

that the notice is going to be issued.

(7) Before issuing a closure notice the police officer or local authority must ensure that any body or individual the officer or authority thinks appropriate has been consulted.

(8) The Secretary of State may by regulations specify premises or descriptions of premises in relation to which a closure notice may not be issued.

77 Duration of closure notices

(1) The maximum period that may be specified in a closure notice is 24 hours unless subsection (2) applies.

(2) The maximum period is 48 hours—

(a) if, in the case of a notice issued by a police officer, the officer is of at least the rank of superintendent, or

(b) if, in the case of a notice issued by a local authority, the notice is signed by the chief executive officer of the authority or a person designated by him or her for the purposes of this subsection.

(3) In calculating when the period of 48 hours ends, Christmas Day is to be disregarded.

(4) The period specified in a closure notice to which subsection (2) does not apply may be extended by up to 24 hours—

(a) if, in the case of a notice issued by a police officer, an extension notice is issued by an officer of at least the rank of superintendent, or

(b) if, in the case of a notice issued by a local authority, the authority issues an extension notice signed by the chief executive officer of the authority or a person designated by the chief executive officer for the purposes of this subsection.

(5) An extension notice is a notice which—

(a) identifies the closure notice to which it relates, and

(b) specifies the period of the extension.

(6) In this section 'chief executive officer', in relation to a local authority, means the head of the paid service of the authority designated under section 4 of the Local Government and Housing Act 1989.

78 Cancellation or variation of closure notices

(1) This section applies where a closure notice is in force and the relevant officer or authority is no longer satisfied as mentioned in section 76(1), either—

(a) as regards the premises as a whole, or

(b) as regards a particular part of the premises.

(2) In a case within subsection (1)(a) the relevant officer or authority must issue a cancellation notice.

A cancellation notice is a notice cancelling the closure notice.

(3) In a case within subsection (1)(b) the relevant officer or authority must issue a variation notice.

A variation notice is a notice varying the closure notice so that it does not apply to the part of the premises referred to in subsection (1)(b).

(4) A cancellation notice or a variation notice that relates to a closure notice which was—

(a) issued by a local authority, and

(b) signed as mentioned in section 77(2)(b),

must be signed by the person who signed the closure notice (or, if that person is not available, by another person who could have signed as mentioned in section 77(2)(b)).

(5) A cancellation notice or a variation notice that relates to a closure notice which was—

(a) issued by a local authority, and

(b) extended under section 77(4)(b),

must be signed by the person who signed the extension notice (or, if that person is not available, by another person who could have signed the extension notice).

(6) In this section 'the relevant officer or authority' means—

(a) in the case of a closure notice issued by a police officer and not extended under section 77(4)(a), that officer (or, if that officer is not available, another officer of the same or higher rank);

(b) in the case of a closure notice issued by a police officer and extended under section 77(4)(a), the officer who issued the extension notice (or, if that officer is not available, another officer of the same or higher rank);

(c) in the case of a closure notice issued by a local authority, that authority.

79 Service of notices

(1) A closure notice, an extension notice, a cancellation notice or a variation notice must be served by—

(a) a constable, in the case of a notice issued by a police officer;

(b) a representative of the authority that issued the notice, in the case of a notice issued by a local authority.

(2) The constable or local authority representative must if possible—

(a) fix a copy of the notice to at least one prominent place on the premises,

(b) fix a copy of the notice to each normal means of access to the premises,

(c) fix a copy of the notice to any outbuildings that appear to the constable or representative to be used with or as part of the premises,

(d) give a copy of the notice to at least one person who appears to the constable or representative to have control of or responsibility for the premises, and

(e) give a copy of the notice to the people who live on the premises and to any person who does not live there but was informed (under section 76(6)) that the notice was going to be issued.

(3) If the constable or local authority representative reasonably believes, at the time of serving the notice, that there are persons occupying another part of the building or other structure in which the premises are situated whose access to that part will be impeded if a closure order is made under section 80, the constable or representative must also if possible serve the notice on those persons.

(4) The constable or local authority representative may enter any premises, using reasonable force if necessary, for the purposes of complying with subsection (2) (a).

(5) In this section 'representative', in relation to a local authority, means—

(a) an employee of the authority, or

(b) a person, or employee or a person, acting on behalf of the authority.

Closure orders

80   Power of court to make closure orders

(1) Whenever a closure notice is issued an application must be made to a magistrates' court for a closure order (unless the notice has been cancelled under section 78).

(2) An application for a closure order must be made—

(a) by a constable, if the closure notice was issued by a police officer;

(b) by the authority that issued the closure notice, if the notice was issued by a local authority.

(3) The application must be heard by the magistrates' court not later than 48 hours after service of the closure notice.

(4) In calculating when the period of 48 hours ends, Christmas Day is to be disregarded.

(5) The court may make a closure order if it is satisfied—

(a) that a person has engaged, or (if the order is not made) is likely to engage, in disorderly, offensive or criminal behaviour on the premises, or

(b) that the use of the premises has resulted, or (if the order is not made) is likely to result, in serious nuisance to members of the public, or

(c) that there has been, or (if the order is not made) is likely to be, disorder near those premises associated with the use of those premises,

and that the order is necessary to prevent the behaviour, nuisance or disorder from continuing, recurring or occurring.

(6) A closure order is an order prohibiting access to the premises for a period specified in the order.

The period may not exceed 3 months.

(7) A closure order may prohibit access—

(a) by all persons, or by all persons except those specified, or by all persons except those of a specified description;

(b) at all times, or at all times except those specified;

(c) in all circumstances, or in all circumstances except those specified.

(8) A closure order—

(a) may be made in respect of the whole or any part of the premises;

(b) may include provision about access to a part of the building or structure of which the premises form part.

(9) The court must notify the relevant licensing authority if it makes a closure order in relation to premises in respect of which a premises licence is in force.

81 Temporary orders

(1) This section applies where an application has been made to a magistrates' court under section 80 for a closure order.

(2) If the court does not make a closure order it may nevertheless order that the closure notice continues in force for a specified further period of not more than 48 hours, if satisfied—

(a) that the use of particular premises has resulted, or (if the notice is not continued) is likely soon to result, in nuisance to members of the public, or

(b) that there has been, or (if the notice is not continued) is likely soon to be, disorder near those premises associated with the use of those premises,

and that the continuation of the notice is necessary to prevent the nuisance or disorder from continuing, recurring or occurring.

(3) The court may adjourn the hearing of the application for a period of not more than 14 days to enable—

(a) the occupier of the premises,

(b) the person with control of or responsibility for the premises, or

(c) any other person with an interest in the premises,

to show why a closure order should not be made.

(4) If the court adjourns the hearing under subsection (3) it may order that the closure notice continues in force until the end of the period of the adjournment.

82   Extension of closure orders

(1) At any time before the expiry of a closure order, an application may be made to a justice of the peace, by complaint, for an extension (or further extension) of the period for which the order is in force.

(2) Those entitled to make an application under this section are—

(a) where the closure order was made on the application of a constable, a police officer of at least the rank of inspector;

(b) where the closure order was made on the application of a local authority, that authority.

(3) A police officer or local authority may make an application under this section only if satisfied on reasonable grounds that it is necessary for the period of the order to be extended to prevent the occurrence, recurrence or continuance of—

(a) disorderly, offensive or criminal behaviour on the premises,

(b) serious nuisance to members of the public resulting from the use of the premises, or

(c) disorder near the premises associated with the use of the premises,

and also satisfied that the appropriate consultee has been consulted about the intention to make the application.

(4) In subsection (3) 'the appropriate consultee' means—

(a) the local authority, in the case of an application by a police officer;

(b) the chief officer of police for the area in which the premises are situated, in the case of an application by a local authority.

(5) Where an application is made under this section, the justice of the peace may issue a summons directed to—

(a) any person on whom the closure notice was served under section 79, or

(b) any other person who appears to the justice to have an interest in the premises but on whom the closure notice was not served,

requiring the person to appear before the magistrates' court to respond to the application.

(6) If a summons is issued under subsection (5), a notice stating the date, time and place of the hearing of the application must be served on the persons to whom the summons is directed.

(7) If the magistrates' court is satisfied as mentioned in subsection (3)(a), (b) or (c), it may make an order extending (or further extending) the period of the closure order by a period not exceeding 3 months.

(8) The period of a closure order may not be extended so that the order lasts for more than 6 months.

83 Discharge of closure orders

(1) At any time before the expiry of a closure order, an application may be made to a justice of the peace, by complaint, for the order to be discharged.

(2) Those entitled to make an application under this section are—

(a) a constable, where the closure order was made on the application of a constable;

(b) the authority that applied for the closure order, where the order was made on the application of a local authority;

(c) a person on whom the closure notice was served under section 79;

(d) anyone else who has an interest in the premises but on whom the closure notice was not served.

(3) Where a person other than a constable makes an application under this section for the discharge of an order that was made on the application of a constable, the justice may issue a summons directed to a constable considered appropriate by the justice requiring him or her to appear before the magistrates' court to respond to the application.

(4) If a summons is issued under subsection (3), a notice stating the date, time and place of the hearing of the application must be served on—

(a) the constable to whom the summons is directed;

(b) the persons mentioned in subsection (2)(c) and (d) (other than the complainant).

(5) Where—

(a) the order in question was made on the application of a local authority, and

(b) a person other than that authority makes an application under this section for the discharge of the order,

the justice may issue a summons directed to that authority requiring it to appear before the magistrates' court to respond to the application.

(6) If a summons is issued under subsection (5), a notice stating the date, time and place of the hearing of the application must be served on—

(a) the authority mentioned in that subsection;

(b) the persons mentioned in subsection (2)(c) and (d) (other than the complainant).

(7) The magistrates' court may not make an order discharging the closure order unless satisfied that the closure order is no longer necessary to prevent the occurrence, recurrence or continuance of—

(a) disorderly, offensive or criminal behaviour on the premises,

(b) serious nuisance to members of the public resulting from the use of the premises, or

(c) disorder near the premises associated with the use of the premises.

Appeals

84 Appeals

(1) An appeal against a decision to make or extend a closure order may be made by—

(a) a person on whom the closure notice was served under section 79;

(b) anyone else who has an interest in the premises but on whom the closure notice was not served.

(2) A constable may appeal against—

(a) a decision not to make a closure order applied for by a constable;

(b) a decision not to extend a closure order made on the application of a constable;

(c) a decision (under section 81) not to order the continuation in force of a closure notice issued by a constable.

(3) A local authority may appeal against—

(a) a decision not to make a closure order applied for by that authority;

(b) a decision not to extend a closure order made on the application of that authority;

(c) a decision (under section 81) not to order the continuation in force of a closure notice issued by that authority.

(4) An appeal under this section is to the Crown Court.

(5) An appeal under this section must be made within the period of 21 days beginning with the date of the decision to which it relates.

(6) On an appeal under this section the Crown Court may make whatever order it thinks appropriate.

(7) The Crown Court must notify the relevant licensing authority if it makes a closure order in relation to premises in respect of which a premises licence is in force.

Enforcement

85 Enforcement of closure orders

(1) An authorised person may—

(a) enter premises in respect of which a closure order is in force;

(b) do anything necessary to secure the premises against entry.

(2) In this section 'authorised person'—

(a) in relation to a closure order made on the application of a constable, means a constable or a person authorised by the chief officer of police for the area in which the premises are situated;

(b) in relation to a closure order made on the application of a local authority, means a person authorised by that authority.

(3) A person acting under subsection (1) may use reasonable force.

(4) A person seeking to enter premises under subsection (1) must, if required to do so by or on behalf of the owner, occupier or other person in charge of the premises, produce evidence of his or her identity and authority before entering the premises.

(5) An authorised person may also enter premises in respect of which a closure order is in force to carry out essential maintenance or repairs to the premises.

86 Offences

(1) A person who without reasonable excuse remains on or enters premises in contravention of a closure notice (including a notice continued in force under section 81) commits an offence.

(2) A person who without reasonable excuse remains on or enters premises in contravention of a closure order commits an offence.

(3) A person who without reasonable excuse obstructs a person acting under section 79 or 85(1) commits an offence.

(4) A person guilty of an offence under subsection (1) or (3) is liable on summary conviction—

(a) to imprisonment for a period not exceeding 3 months, or

(b) to a fine,

or to both.

(5) A person guilty of an offence under subsection (2) is liable on summary conviction—

(a) to imprisonment for a period not exceeding 51 weeks, or

(b) to a fine,

or to both.

(6) In relation to an offence committed before the commencement of section 281(5) of the Criminal Justice Act 2003, the reference in subsection (5)(a) to 51 weeks is to be read as a reference to 6 months.

Supplemental

87 Access to other premises

(1) Where—

(a) access to premises is prohibited or restricted by, or as a result of, an order under section 80, 81, 82 or 84,

(b) those premises are part of a building or structure, and

(c) there is another part of that building or structure that is not subject to the prohibition or restriction,

an occupier or owner of that other part may apply to the appropriate court for an order under this section.

(2) The appropriate court is—

(a) the magistrates' court, in the case of an order under section 80, 81 or 82;

(b) the Crown Court, in the case of an order under section 84.

(3) Notice of an application under this section must be given to—

(a) whatever constable the court thinks appropriate;

(b) the local authority;

(c) a person on whom the closure notice was served under section 79;

(d) anyone else who has an interest in the premises but on whom the closure notice was not served.

(4) On an application under this section the court may make whatever order it thinks appropriate in relation to access to any part of the building or structure mentioned in subsection (1).

It does not matter whether provision has been made under section 80(8)(b).

88 Reimbursement of costs

(1) A local policing body or a local authority that incurs expenditure for the purpose of clearing, securing or maintaining premises in respect of which a closure order is in force may apply to the court that made the order for an order under this section.

(2) On an application under this section the court may make whatever order it thinks appropriate for the reimbursement (in full or in part) by the owner or occupier of the premises of the expenditure mentioned in subsection (1).

(3) An application for an order under this section may not be heard unless it is made before the end of the period of 3 months starting with the day on which the closure order ceases to have effect.

(4) An order under this section may be made only against a person who has been served with the application for the order.

(5) An application under this section must also be served on—

(a) the local policing body for the area in which the premises are situated, if the application is made by a local authority;

(b) the local authority, if the application is made by a local policing body.

89 Exemption from liability

(1) A police officer, or the chief officer of police under whose direction or control he or she acts, is not liable for damages in proceedings for—

(a) judicial review, or

(b) the tort of negligence or misfeasance in public office,

arising out of anything done or omitted to be done by the police officer in the exercise or purported exercise of a power under this Chapter.

(2) A local authority is not liable for damages in proceedings for—

(a) judicial review, or

(b) the tort of negligence or misfeasance in public office,

arising out of anything done or omitted to be done by the authority in the exercise or purported exercise of a power under this Chapter.

(3) Subsections (1) and (2) do not apply to an act or omission shown to have been in bad faith.

(4) Subsections (1) and (2) do not apply so as to prevent an award of damages made in respect of an act or omission on the ground that the act or omission was unlawful by virtue of section 6(1) of the Human Rights Act 1998.

(5) This section does not affect any other exemption from liability (whether at common law or otherwise).

90 Compensation

(1) A person who claims to have incurred financial loss in consequence of a closure notice or a closure order may apply to the appropriate court for compensation.

(2) The appropriate court is—

(a) the magistrates' court that considered the application for a closure order (except where paragraph (b) applies);

(b) the Crown Court, in the case of a closure order that was made or extended by an order of that Court on an appeal under section 84.

(3) An application under this section may not be heard unless it is made before the end of the period of 3 months starting with whichever of the following is applicable—

(a) the day on which the closure notice was cancelled under section 78;

(b) the day on which a closure order was refused;

(c) the day on which the closure order ceased to have effect.

(4) For the purposes of subsection (3)(b) the day on which a closure order was refused is—

(a) the day on which the magistrates' court decided not to make a closure order (except where paragraph (b) applies);

(b) the day on which the Crown Court dismissed an appeal against a decision not to make a closure order.

(5) On an application under this section the court may order the payment of compensation out of central funds if it is satisfied—

(a) that the applicant is not associated with the use of the premises, or the behaviour on the premises, on the basis of which the closure notice was issued or the closure order made,

(b) if the applicant is the owner or occupier of the premises, that the applicant took reasonable steps to prevent that use or behaviour,

(c) that the applicant has incurred financial loss in consequence of the notice or order, and

(d) that having regard to all the circumstances it is appropriate to order payment of compensation in respect of that loss.

(6) In this section 'central funds' has the same meaning as in enactments providing for the payment of costs.

91 Guidance

(1) The Secretary of State may issue—

(a) guidance to chief officers of police about the exercise, by officers under their direction or control, of those officers' functions under this Chapter;

(b) guidance to local authorities about the exercise of their functions under this Chapter and those of their representatives (within the meaning of section 79).

(2) The Secretary of State may revise any guidance issued under this section.

(3) The Secretary of State must arrange for any guidance issued or revised under this section to be published.

92 Interpretation of Chapter 3

(1) In this Chapter—

'cancellation notice' has the meaning given by section 78(2);

'criminal behaviour' means behaviour that constitutes a criminal offence;

'extension notice' has the meaning given by section 77(5);

'local authority' means—

(a) in relation to England, a district council, a county council for an area for which there is no district council, a London borough council, the Common Council of the City of London or the Council of the Isles of Scilly;

(b) in relation to Wales, a county council or a county borough council;

'offensive behaviour' means behaviour by a person that causes or is likely to cause harassment, alarm or distress to one or more other persons not of the same household as that person;

'owner', in relation to premises, means—

(a) a person (other than a mortgagee not in possession) entitled to dispose of the fee simple of the premises, whether in possession or in reversion;

(b) a person who holds or is entitled to the rents and profits of the premises under a lease that (when granted) was for a term of not less then 3 years;

'premises' includes—

(a) any land or other place (whether enclosed or not);

(b) any outbuildings that are, or are used as, part of premises;

'premises licence' has the meaning given by section 11 of the Licensing Act 2003;

'relevant licensing authority' has the meaning given by section 12 of that Act;

'variation notice' has the meaning given by section 78(3).

(2) A reference in this Chapter to 'the local authority', in relation to any premises or a notice or order relating to any premises, is a reference to the local authority (or, as the case may be, any of the local authorities) within whose area the premises are situated.

(3) A reference in this Chapter to 'the premises', in relation to a closure notice or a closure order, is a reference to the premises to which the notice or order relates.

93 Saving and transitional provision

(1) The repeal or amendment by this Act of provisions about any of the notices specified in subsection (2) or orders specified in subsection (3) does not apply in relation to—

(a) any such notice issued or order made before the commencement day;

(b) anything done in connection with any such notice or order.

(2) The notices are—

(a) a notice issued under section 1 of the Anti-social Behaviour Act 2003;

(b) a notice issued under section 11A of that Act.

(3) The orders are—

(a) an order made under section 2 of the Anti-social Behaviour Act 2003;

(b) an order made under section 11B of that Act;

(c) an order made under section 40 of that Act;

(d) an order made under section 161 of the Licensing Act 2003;

(e) an order made under section 165(2)(b), (c) or (d) of that Act.

(4) A person deciding whether to issue a closure notice may take into account things that—

(a) happened before the commencement day, and

(b) would have given rise to the power to issue one of the notices specified in subsection (2) or to make an order specified in subsection (3)(c) or (d).

(5) A court deciding whether to make a closure order may take into account things that—

(a) happened before the commencement day, and

(b) would have given rise to the power to make an order specified in subsection (3) (a), (b) or (e).

(6) Subsections (4) and (5) apply only during the period of 3 months beginning with the commencement day.

(7) In this section 'commencement day' means the day on which this Chapter comes into force.

PART 6
LOCAL INVOLVEMENT AND ACCOUNTABILITY

Community remedies

101 The community remedy document

(1) Each local policing body must prepare a community remedy document for its area, and may revise it at any time.

(2) A community remedy document is a list of actions any of which might, in the opinion of the local policing body, be appropriate in a particular case to be carried out by a person who—

(a) has engaged in anti-social behaviour or has committed an offence, and

(b) is to be dealt with for that behaviour or offence without court proceedings.

(3) For the purposes of subsection (2), an action is appropriate to be carried out by a person only if it has one or more of the following objects—

(a) assisting in the person's rehabilitation;

(b) ensuring that the person makes reparation for the behaviour or offence in question;

(c) punishing the person.

(4) In preparing or revising the community remedy document for its area a local policing body must—

(a) have regard to the need to promote public confidence in the out-of-court disposal process;

(b) have regard to any guidance issued by the Secretary of State about how local policing bodies are to discharge their functions under this section;

(c) carry out the necessary consultation and take account of all views expressed by those consulted.

(5) In subsection (4)(c) 'the necessary consultation' means—

(a) consultation with the chief officer of police for the area,

(b) consultation with the local authority for any part of the area,

(c) consultation with whatever community representatives the local policing body thinks it appropriate to consult, and

(d) whatever other public consultation the local policing body thinks appropriate.

(6) A local policing body must agree the community remedy document for its area, and any revised document, with the chief officer of police for the area.

(7) Once the community remedy document, or a revised document, has been agreed with the chief officer of police, the local policing body must publish it in whatever way it thinks appropriate.

(8) The Secretary of State must publish any guidance issued under subsection (4)(b).

(9) In this section—

'anti-social behaviour' has the meaning given by section 2 (ignoring subsection (2) of that section);

'community representative', in relation to a police area, means any individual or body appearing to the local policing body to represent the views of people who live in, work in or visit the area;

'local authority' means—

(a) in relation to England, a district council, a county council for an area for which there is no district council, a London borough council, the Common Council of the City of London or the Council of the Isles of Scilly;

(b) in relation to Wales, a county council or a county borough council;

'out-of-court disposal process' means the process by which a person is dealt with under section 102 or by means of a conditional caution or youth conditional caution.

102 Anti-social behaviour etc: out-of-court disposals

(1) This section applies where—

(a) a person (P) within subsection (2) has evidence that an individual (A) has engaged in anti-social behaviour or committed an offence,

(b) A admits to P that he or she has done so,

(c) P thinks that the evidence is enough for taking proceedings against A for an injunction under section 1, or taking other court proceedings, but decides that it would be appropriate for A to carry out action of some sort instead, and

(d) if the evidence is that A has committed an offence, P does not think that it would be more appropriate for A to be given a caution or a fixed penalty notice.

(2) The persons within this subsection are—

(a) a constable;

(b) an investigating officer;

(c) a person authorised by a relevant prosecutor for the purposes of section 22 of the Criminal Justice Act 2003 (conditional cautions) or section 66A of the Crime and Disorder Act 1998 (youth conditional cautions).

(3) Before deciding what action to invite A to carry out, P must make reasonable efforts to obtain the views of the victim (if any) of the anti-social behaviour or the offence, and in particular the victim's views as to whether A should carry out any of the actions listed in the community remedy document.

(4) If the victim expresses the view that A should carry out a particular action listed in the community remedy document, P must invite A to carry out that action unless it seems to P that it would be inappropriate to do so.

(5) Where—

(a) there is more than one victim and they express different views, or

(b) for any other reason subsection (4) does not apply,

P must nevertheless take account of any views expressed by the victim (or victims) in deciding what action to invite A to carry out.

(6) In this section—

'action' includes the making of a payment to the victim (but does not include the payment of a fixed penalty);

'anti-social behaviour' has the meaning given by section 2 (ignoring subsection (2) of that section);

'community remedy document' means the community remedy document (as revised from time to time) published under section 101 for the police area in which A's anti-social behaviour or offence took place;

'caution'—

(a) in the case of a person aged 18 or over, includes a conditional caution within the meaning of Part 3 of the Criminal Justice Act 2003;

(b) in the case of a person under that age, means a youth caution or youth conditional caution within the meaning of Chapter 1 of Part 4 of the Crime and Disorder Act 1998;

'investigating officer' and 'relevant prosecutor' have the same meaning as in Part 3 of the Criminal Justice Act 2003 (see section 27 of that Act);

'victim' means the particular person who seems to P to have been affected, or principally affected, by A's anti-social behaviour or offence.

Response to complaints about anti-social behaviour

104 Review of response to complaints

(1) In a case where a person has made a complaint about anti-social behaviour in a particular local government area, the relevant bodies in that area must carry out a review of the response to that behaviour (an 'ASB case review)' if—

(a) that person, or any other person, makes an application for such a review, and

(b) the relevant bodies decide that the threshold for a review is met.

(2) The relevant bodies in each local government area must—

(a) make arrangements about the carrying out of ASB case reviews by those bodies ('review procedures'), and

(b) ensure that the current review procedures are published.

(3) The review procedures must include provision about the making of applications for ASB case reviews; and, in particular, must—

(a) specify the point of contact for making applications, and

(b) ensure that applications made to that point of contact are passed on to all the relevant bodies in the local government area.

(4) In a situation where—

(a) an application for an ASB case review is made, and

(b) at least three (or, if a different number is specified in the review procedures, at least that number of) qualifying complaints have been made about the anti-social behaviour to which the application relates,

the relevant bodies must decide that the threshold for a review is met.

(5) In any other situation where an application for an ASB case review is made, the question whether the threshold for a review is met must be decided by the relevant bodies in accordance with the review procedures; and the procedures may, in particular, include provision for this purpose which is framed by reference to any of these matters—

(a) the persistence of the anti-social behaviour about which the original complaint was made;

(b) the harm caused, or the potential for harm to be caused, by that behaviour;

(c) the adequacy of the response to that behaviour.

(6) After the relevant bodies have decided whether or not the threshold for a review is met, they must inform the applicant of their decision.

(7) The relevant bodies who carry out an ASB case review may make recommendations to a person who exercises public functions (including recommendations to a relevant body) in respect of any matters arising from the review; and the person must have regard to the recommendations in exercising public functions.

(8) The relevant bodies who carry out an ASB case review must inform the applicant of—

(a) the outcome of the review, and

(b) any recommendations made in accordance with subsection (7).

(9) As soon as practicable after the end of a reporting period, the relevant bodies in a local government area must publish information about the following matters which relates to that period—

(a) the number of applications for ASB case reviews made to those bodies;

(b) the number of times those bodies decided that the threshold for a review was not met;

(c) the number of ASB case reviews those bodies have carried out;

(d) the number of ASB case reviews carried out by those bodies that have resulted in recommendations being made.

(10) The question whether a complaint made about anti-social behaviour is a 'qualifying complaint' for the purposes of subsection (4) is to be determined in accordance with subsections (11) and (12).

(11) A complaint about anti-social behaviour is a qualifying complaint if—

(a) the complaint is made within the period of one month (or, if a different period is specified in the review procedures, that period) beginning with the date on which the behaviour is alleged to have occurred; and

(b) the application for the ASB case review is made within the period of six months (or, if a different period is specified in the review procedures, that period) beginning with the date on which the complaint is made.

(12) But where a person makes two or more complaints about anti-social behaviour which meet the requirements in subsection (11), the question of which complaint is, or which complaints are, qualifying complaints is to be decided by the relevant bodies in accordance with the review procedures.

The procedures may, in particular, include provision for this purpose which is framed by reference to whether different complaints relate to different aspects of particular anti-social behaviour (including different incidents comprised in particular anti-social behaviour).

(13) Schedule 4 (ASB case reviews: supplementary provision) has effect.

105 ASB case reviews: interpretation

(1) This section applies for the purposes of section 104, this section and Schedule 4.

(2) In relation to England—

'local government area' means an area for which there is—

    (a)   a relevant district council, or

    (b)   a unitary authority;

'relevant district council' means the council of a district so far as it is not a unitary authority;

'unitary authority' means—

    (a)   the council of a county so far as it is the council for an area for which there are no district councils,

    (b)   the council of any district comprised in an area for which there is no county council,

    (c)   a London borough council,

    (d)   the Common Council of the City of London in its capacity as a local authority, or

    (e)   the Council of the Isles of Scilly;

and, in relation to a local government area in England—

'local provider of social housing' means a private registered provider of social housing that—

    (a)   grants tenancies of dwelling-houses in that area, or

    (b)   manages any house or other property in that area;

'relevant bodies' means—

    (a)   the relevant district council or the unitary authority,

    (b)   the chief officer of police for the police area which that local government area is within,

(c)   each clinical commissioning group established under section 14V of the National Health Service Act 2006 whose area is wholly or partly within that local government area, and

(d)   any local providers of social housing who are among the relevant bodies by virtue of the co-option arrangements made in relation to that local government area.

(3) In relation to Wales—

'local government area' means—

(a)   a county, or

(b)   a county borough;

and, in relation to a local government area in Wales—

'local provider of social housing' means a body registered as a social landlord under section 3 of the Housing Act 1996 that—

(a)   grants tenancies of dwelling-houses in that area, or

(b)   manages any house or other property in that area;

'relevant bodies' means—

(a)   the council for the area,

(b)   the chief officer of police for the police area which that local government area is within,

(c)   each Local Health Board whose area is wholly or partly within that local government area, and

(d)   any local providers of social housing who are among the relevant bodies by virtue of the co-option arrangements made in relation to that local government area.

(4) These expressions have the meanings given—

'anti-social behaviour' means behaviour causing harassment, alarm or distress to members or any member of the public;

'applicant' means a person who makes an application for an ASB case review;

'ASB case review' has the meaning given in section 104(1);

'dwelling-house' has the same meaning as in the Housing Act 1985;

'co-option arrangements' has the meaning given in paragraph 5 of Schedule 4;

'reporting period', in relation to the publication of information by the relevant bodies in a local government area, means a period, not exceeding 12 months, determined by those bodies.

Schedule 4
ASB case reviews: supplementary provision

PART 1
MAKING AND REVISING REVIEW PROCEDURES ETC

1   Consultation: local policing bodies

(1) In making and revising the review procedures, the relevant bodies in a local government area must consult the local policing body for the relevant police area.

(2) The 'relevant police area' is the police area which consists of, or includes, the local government area.

2   Consultation: local providers of social housing

In making and revising the review procedures, the relevant bodies in a local government area must consult such local providers of social housing as they consider appropriate.

3   Dissatisfaction with ASB case reviews

The review procedures must include provision about what is to happen where an applicant is dissatisfied with the way in which the relevant bodies have—

(a) dealt with an application for an ASB case review, or

(b) carried out an ASB case review.

4   Assessment and revision of review procedures

The review procedures must include provision about—

(a) the assessment of the effectiveness of those procedures, and

(b) the revision of those procedures.

PART 2
INCLUSION OF LOCAL PROVIDERS OF SOCIAL HOUSING AMONG RELEVANT BODIES

5   Co-option arrangements

(1) The responsible authorities in a local government area must make arrangements ('co-option arrangements') for the inclusion of local providers of social housing among the relevant bodies in that area.

(2) In this paragraph 'responsible authorities' means—

(a) in relation to a local government area in England—

    (i)   the relevant district council or the unitary authority,

    (ii) the chief officer of police for the police area which that local government area is within, and

    (iii) each clinical commissioning group established under section 14V of the National Health Service Act 2006 whose area is wholly or partly within that local government area;

(b) in relation to a local government area in Wales—

    (i)   the council for the area,

    (ii) the chief officer of police for the police area which that local government area is within, and

    (iii) each Local Health Board whose area is wholly or partly within that local government area.

PART 3
ASB CASE REVIEWS

6   Consultation and co-operation: local providers of social housing

(1) The relevant bodies in a local government area must consult such local providers of social housing as they consider appropriate in carrying out ASB case reviews.

(2) The local providers of social housing must co-operate with the relevant bodies in the local government area in any matters specified by the relevant bodies that concern ASB case reviews.

7   Information

(1) The relevant bodies in a local government area may request any person to disclose information for a purpose connected with the carrying out of an ASB case review.

(2) If such a request is made to a person that exercises public functions, and that person possesses the requested information in connection with the exercise of such functions, the person must (subject to sub-paragraph (4)) comply with the request.

(3) If such a request is made to a person who is not required by sub-paragraph (2) to disclose the requested information, the person may (subject to sub-paragraph (4)) comply with the request.

(4) This paragraph does not require or authorise—

(a) a disclosure, in contravention of any provisions of the data protection legislation, of personal data which is not exempt from those provisions, or

(b) a disclosure which is prohibited by any of Parts 1 to 7 or Chapter 1 of Part 9 of the Investigatory Powers Act 2016.

(5) Subject to that, a disclosure under this paragraph does not breach—

(a) any obligation of confidence owed by the person making the disclosure, or

(b) any other restriction on the disclosure of information (however imposed).

(6) In this paragraph, 'the data protection legislation' has the same meaning as in the Data Protection Act 2018 (see section 3 of that Act).

PART 4
GENERAL

8   Joint review procedures or co-option arrangements

(1) The relevant bodies in two or more local government areas—

(a) may jointly make review procedures applicable to those areas;

(b) must secure that such jointly-made review procedures are in place if co-option arrangements applicable to those areas have been jointly made under sub-paragraph (2).

(2) The responsible authorities in two or more local government areas—

(a) may jointly make co-option arrangements applicable to those areas;

(b) must secure that such jointly-made co-option arrangements are in place if review procedures applicable to those areas have been jointly made under sub-paragraph (1).

(3) In a case where review procedures or co-option arrangements are made jointly in accordance with this paragraph, a reference to any of the following in section 104, section 105 or this Schedule is to be read accordingly—

(a) the relevant bodies (in the case of review procedures) or the responsible authorities (in the case of co-option arrangements);

(b) the local government area or the relevant police area (in either case).

9   Different review procedures or co-option arrangements for different parts of an area etc

(1) Review procedures may make different provision in relation to different parts of a local government area.

(2) Review procedures or co-option arrangements made jointly in accordance with paragraph 8 may make different provision in relation to—

(a) different local government areas to which the procedures or arrangements are applicable, or

(b) different parts of such areas.

Housing Act 1980

(1980 CHAPTER 51)

PART IV
JURISDICTION AND PROCEDURE

89 Restriction on discretion of court in making orders for possession of land.

(1) Where a court makes an order for the possession of any land in a case not falling within the exceptions mentioned in subsection (2) below, the giving up of possession shall not be postponed (whether by the order or any variation, suspension or stay of execution) to a date later than fourteen days after the making of the order, unless it appears to the court that exceptional hardship would be caused by requiring possession to be given up by that date; and shall not in any event be postponed to a date later than six weeks after the making of the order.

(2) The restrictions in subsection (1) above do not apply if—

(a) the order is made in an action by a mortgagee for possession; or

(b) the order is made in an action for forfeiture of a lease; or

(c) the court had power to make the order only if it considered it reasonable to make it; or

(d) the order relates to a dwelling-house which is the subject of a restricted contract (within the meaning of section 19 of the 1977 Act); or

(e) the order is made in proceedings brought as mentioned in section 88(1) above.

Housing Act 1985

(1985 CHAPTER 68)

PART IV
SECURE TENANCIES AND RIGHTS OF SECURE TENANTS

Security of tenure

83ZA Notice requirements in relation to proceedings for possession on absolute ground for anti-social behaviour

(1) This section applies in relation to proceedings for possession of a dwelling-house under section 84A (absolute ground for possession for anti-social

behaviour), including proceedings where possession is also sought on one or more of the grounds set out in Schedule 2.

(2) The court must not entertain the proceedings unless the landlord has served on the tenant a notice under this section.

(3) The notice must—

(a) state that the court will be asked to make an order under section 84A for the possession of the dwelling-house,

(b) set out the reasons for the landlord's decision to apply for the order (including the condition or conditions in section 84A on which the landlord proposes to rely), and

(c) inform the tenant of any right that the tenant may have under section 85ZA to request a review of the landlord's decision and of the time within which the request must be made.

(4) In a case where possession is also sought on one or more of the grounds set out in Schedule 2, the notice must also—

(a) specify the ground on which the court will be asked to make the order, and

(b) give particulars of that ground.

(5) A notice which states that the landlord proposes to rely upon condition 1, 3 or 5 in section 84A—

(a) must also state the conviction on which the landlord proposes to rely, and

(b) must be served on the tenant within—

(i) the period of 12 months beginning with the day of the conviction, or

(ii) if there is an appeal against the conviction, the period of 12 months beginning with the day on which the appeal is finally determined or abandoned.

(6) A notice which states that the landlord proposes to rely upon condition 2 in section 84A—

(a) must also state the finding on which the landlord proposes to rely, and

(b) must be served on the tenant within—

(i) the period of 12 months beginning with the day on which the court has made the finding, or

(ii) if there is an appeal against the finding, the period of 12 months beginning with the day on which the appeal is finally determined, abandoned or withdrawn.

(7) A notice which states that the landlord proposes to rely upon condition 4 in section 84A—

(a) must also state the closure order concerned, and

(b) must be served on the tenant within—

    (i)   the period of 3 months beginning with the day on which the closure order was made, or

    (ii)   if there is an appeal against the making of the order, the period of 3 months beginning with the day on which the appeal is finally determined, abandoned or withdrawn.

(8) A notice under this section must also inform the tenant that, if the tenant needs help or advice about the notice and what to do about it, the tenant should take it immediately to a Citizens' Advice Bureau, a housing aid centre, a law centre or a solicitor.

(9) The notice—

(a) must also specify the date after which proceedings for the possession of the dwelling-house may be begun, and

(b) ceases to be in force 12 months after the date so specified.

(10) The date specified in accordance with subsection (9)(a) must not be earlier than—

(a) in the case of a periodic tenancy, the date on which the tenancy could, apart from this Part, be brought to an end by notice to quit given by the landlord on the same day as the notice under this section;

(b) in the case of a secure tenancy for a term certain, one month after the date of the service of the notice.

(11) Where a notice under this section is served with respect to a secure tenancy for a term certain, it has effect also with respect to any periodic tenancy arising on the termination of that tenancy by virtue of section 86; and subsection (10)(a) does not apply to the notice.

84A   Absolute ground for possession for anti-social behaviour

(1) If the court is satisfied that any of the following conditions is met, it must make an order for the possession of a dwelling-house let under a secure tenancy.

This is subject to subsection (2) (and to any available defence based on the tenant's Convention rights, within the meaning of the Human Rights Act 1998).

(2) Subsection (1) applies only where the landlord has complied with any obligations it has under section 85ZA (review of decision to seek possession).

(3) Condition 1 is that—

(a) the tenant, or a person residing in or visiting the dwelling-house, has been convicted of a serious offence, and

(b) the serious offence—

    (i)   was committed (wholly or partly) in, or in the locality of, the dwelling-house,

    (ii) was committed elsewhere against a person with a right (of whatever description) to reside in, or occupy housing accommodation in the locality of, the dwelling-house, or

    (iii) was committed elsewhere against the landlord of the dwelling-house, or a person employed (whether or not by the landlord) in connection with the exercise of the landlord's housing management functions, and directly or indirectly related to or affected those functions.

(4) Condition 2 is that a court has found in relevant proceedings that the tenant, or a person residing in or visiting the dwelling-house, has breached a provision of an injunction under section 1 of the Anti-social Behaviour, Crime and Policing Act 2014, other than a provision requiring a person to participate in a particular activity, and—

(a) the breach occurred in, or in the locality of, the dwelling-house, or

(b) the breach occurred elsewhere and the provision breached was a provision intended to prevent—

    (i) conduct that is capable of causing nuisance or annoyance to a person with a right (of whatever description) to reside in, or occupy housing accommodation in the locality of, the dwelling-house, or

    (ii) conduct that is capable of causing nuisance or annoyance to the landlord of the dwelling-house, or a person employed (whether or not by the landlord) in connection with the exercise of the landlord's housing management functions, and that is directly or indirectly related to or affects those functions.

(5) Condition 3 is that the tenant, or a person residing in or visiting the dwelling-house, has been convicted of an offence under section 30 of the Anti-social Behaviour, Crime and Policing Act 2014 consisting of a breach of a provision of a criminal behaviour order prohibiting a person from doing anything described in the order, and the offence involved—

(a) a breach that occurred in, or in the locality of, the dwelling-house, or

(b) a breach that occurred elsewhere of a provision intended to prevent—

    (i) behaviour that causes or is likely to cause harassment, alarm or distress to a person with a right (of whatever description) to reside in, or occupy housing accommodation in the locality of, the dwelling-house, or

    (ii) behaviour that causes or is likely to cause harassment, alarm or distress to the landlord of the dwelling-house, or a person employed (whether or not by the landlord) in connection with the exercise of the landlord's housing management functions, and that is directly or indirectly related to or affects those functions.

(6) Condition 4 is that—

(a) the dwelling-house is or has been subject to a closure order under section 80 of the Anti-social Behaviour, Crime and Policing Act 2014, and

(b) access to the dwelling-house has been prohibited (under the closure order or under a closure notice issued under section 76 of that Act) for a continuous period of more than 48 hours.

(7) Condition 5 is that—

(a) the tenant, or a person residing in or visiting the dwelling-house, has been convicted of an offence under—

(i) section 80(4) of the Environmental Protection Act 1990 (breach of abatement notice in relation to statutory nuisance), or

(ii) section 82(8) of that Act (breach of court order to abate statutory nuisance etc.), and

(b) the nuisance concerned was noise emitted from the dwelling-house which was a statutory nuisance for the purposes of Part 3 of that Act by virtue of section 79(1)(g) of that Act (noise emitted from premises so as to be prejudicial to health or a nuisance).

(8) Condition 1, 2, 3, 4 or 5 is not met if—

(a) there is an appeal against the conviction, finding or order concerned which has not been finally determined, abandoned or withdrawn, or

(b) the final determination of the appeal results in the conviction, finding or order being overturned.

(9) In this section—

'relevant proceedings' means proceedings for contempt of court or proceedings under Schedule 2 to the Anti-social Behaviour, Crime and Policing Act 2014;

'serious offence' means an offence which—

(a) was committed on or after the day on which subsection (3) comes into force,

(b) is specified, or falls within a description specified, in Schedule 2A at the time the offence was committed and at the time the court is considering the matter, and

(c) is not an offence that is triable only summarily by virtue of section 22 of the Magistrates' Courts Act 1980 (either-way offences where value involved is small).

(10) The Secretary of State may by order amend Schedule 2A as it applies in relation to dwelling-houses in England by—

(a) adding an indictable offence;

(b) removing an offence.

(11) The Welsh Ministers may by order amend Schedule 2A as it applies in relation to dwelling-houses in Wales by—

(a) adding an indictable offence;

(b) removing an offence.

(12) An order under subsection (10) or (11)—

(a) is to be made by statutory instrument;

(b) may make different provision for different purposes;

(c) may include incidental, supplementary, consequential, transitional or saving provision.

(13) A statutory instrument containing an order under subsection (10) or (11) may not be made unless a draft of the instrument has been laid before and approved by a resolution of—

(a) each House of Parliament (in the case of an order of the Secretary of State), or

(b) the National Assembly for Wales (in the case of an order of the Welsh Ministers).

85ZA   Review of decision to seek possession on absolute ground for anti-social behaviour

(1) A tenant may request a review of a landlord's decision to seek an order for possession of a dwelling-house under section 84A if the interest of the landlord belongs to—

(a) a local housing authority, or

(b) a housing action trust.

(2) Such a request must be made in writing before the end of the period of 7 days beginning with the day on which the notice under section 83ZA is served.

(3) On a request being duly made to it, the landlord must review its decision.

(4) The landlord must notify the tenant in writing of the decision on the review.

(5) If the decision is to confirm the original decision, the landlord must also notify the tenant of the reasons for the decision.

(6) The review must be carried out, and the tenant notified, before the day specified in the notice under section 83ZA as the day after which proceedings for the possession of the dwelling-house may be begun.

(7) The Secretary of State may by regulations make provision about the procedure to be followed in connection with a review under this section that relates to an order for possession of a dwelling-house in England.

(8) The Welsh Ministers may by regulations make provision about the procedure to be followed in connection with a review under this section that relates to an order for possession of a dwelling-house in Wales.

(9) Regulations under subsections (7) and (8) may, in particular, make provision—

(a) requiring the decision on review to be made by a person of appropriate seniority who was not involved in the original decision, and

(b) as to the circumstances in which the person concerned is entitled to an oral hearing, and whether and by whom the person may be represented at such a hearing.

(10) Regulations under this section—

(a) may contain transitional or saving provision;

(b) are to be made by statutory instrument which—

    (i) in the case of regulations made by the Secretary of State, is subject to annulment in pursuance of a resolution of either House of Parliament;

    (ii) in the case of regulations made by the Welsh Ministers, is subject to annulment in pursuance of a resolution of the National Assembly for Wales.

Schedule 2
Grounds for possession of dwelling-houses let under secure tenancies

PART I
GROUNDS ON WHICH COURT MAY ORDER POSSESSION IF IT CONSIDERS IT REASONABLE

(1)

Rent lawfully due from the tenant has not been paid or an obligation of the tenancy has been broken or not performed.

(2)

The tenant or a person residing in or visiting the dwelling-house—

(a) has been guilty of conduct causing or likely to cause a nuisance or annoyance to a person residing, visiting or otherwise engaging in a lawful activity in the locality,

(aa) has been guilty of conduct causing or likely to cause a nuisance or annoyance to the landlord of the dwelling-house, or a person employed (whether or not by the landlord) in connection with the exercise of the landlord's housing management functions, and that is directly or indirectly related to or affects those functions, or

(b) has been convicted of—

(i)   using the dwelling-house or allowing it to be used for immoral or illegal purposes, or

(ii)   an indictable offence committed in, or in the locality of, the dwelling-house.

(2ZA)

The tenant or an adult residing in the dwelling-house has been convicted of an indictable offence which took place during, and at the scene of, a riot in the United Kingdom.

In this Ground—

'adult' means a person aged 18 or over;

'indictable offence' does not include an offence that is triable only summarily by virtue of section 22 of the Magistrates' Courts Act 1980 (either way offences where value involved is small);

'riot' is to be construed in accordance with section 1 of the Public Order Act 1986.

This Ground applies only in relation to dwelling-houses in England.

Schedule 2A
Absolute ground for possession for anti-social behaviour: serious offences

Violent offences

1

Murder.

2

Manslaughter.

3

Kidnapping.

4

False imprisonment.

5

An offence under any of the following sections of the Offences against the Person Act 1861—

(a) section 4 (soliciting murder),

(b) section 16 (threats to kill),

(c) section 18 (wounding with intent to cause grievous bodily harm),

(d) section 20 (malicious wounding),

(e) section 21 (attempting to choke, suffocate or strangle in order to commit or assist in committing an indictable offence),

(f) section 22 (using chloroform etc. to commit or assist in the committing of any indictable offence),

(g) section 23 (maliciously administering poison etc. so as to endanger life or inflict grievous bodily harm),

(h) section 24 (maliciously administering poison etc. with intent to injure, aggrieve or annoy any other person),

(i) section 27 (abandoning or exposing children whereby life is endangered or health permanently injured),

(j) section 28 (causing bodily injury by explosives),

(k) section 29 (using explosives etc. with intent to do grievous bodily harm),

(l) section 30 (placing explosives with intent to do bodily injury),

(m) section 31 (setting spring guns etc. with intent to do grievous bodily harm),

(n) section 38 (assault with intent to resist arrest),

(o) section 47 (assault occasioning actual bodily harm).

6

An offence under any of the following sections of the Explosive Substances Act 1883—

(a) section 2 (causing explosion likely to endanger life or property),

(b) section 3 (attempt to cause explosion, or making or keeping explosive with intent to endanger life or property),

(c) section 4 (making or possession of explosive under suspicious circumstances).

7

An offence under section 1 of the Infant Life (Preservation) Act 1929 (child destruction).

8

An offence under section 1 of the Children and Young Persons Act 1933 (cruelty to children).

9

An offence under section 1 of the Infanticide Act 1938 (infanticide).

10

An offence under any of the following sections of the Public Order Act 1986—

(a) section 1 (riot),

(b) section 2 (violent disorder),

(c) section 3 (affray).

11

An offence under either of the following sections of the Protection from Harassment Act 1997—

(a) section 4 (putting people in fear of violence),

(b) section 4A (stalking involving fear of violence or serious alarm or distress).

12

An offence under any of the following provisions of the Crime and Disorder Act 1998—

(a) section 29 (racially or religiously aggravated assaults),

(b) section 31(1)(a) or (b) (racially or religiously aggravated offences under section 4 or 4A of the Public Order Act 1986),

(c) section 32 (racially or religiously aggravated harassment etc.).

13

An offence under either of the following sections of the Female Genital Mutilation Act 2003—

(a) section 1 (female genital mutilation),

(b) section 2 (assisting a girl to mutilate her own genitalia).

14

An offence under section 5 of the Domestic Violence, Crime and Victims Act 2004 (causing or allowing the death of a child or vulnerable adult).

Sexual offences

15

An offence under section 33A of the Sexual Offences Act 1956 (keeping a brothel used for prostitution).

16

An offence under section 1 of the Protection of Children Act 1978 (indecent photographs of children).

17

An offence under section 160 of the Criminal Justice Act 1988 (possession of indecent photograph of a child).

18

An indictable offence under Part 1 of the Sexual Offences Act 2003 (sexual offences).

Offensive weapons

19

An offence under either of the following sections of the Prevention of Crime Act 1953—

(a) section 1 (prohibition of the carrying of offensive weapons without lawful authority or reasonable excuse),

(b) section 1A (threatening with offensive weapon in public).

20

An offence under any of the following provisions of the Firearms Act 1968—

(a) section 16 (possession of firearm with intent to endanger life),

(b) section 16A (possession of firearm with intent to cause fear of violence),

(c) section 17(1) (use of firearm to resist arrest),

(d) section 17(2) (possession of firearm at time of committing or being arrested for offence specified in Schedule 1 to the Act of 1968),

(e) section 18 (carrying a firearm with criminal intent),

(f) section 19 (carrying a firearm in a public place),

(g) section 20 (trespassing with firearm),

(h) section 21 (possession of firearms by persons previously convicted of crime).

21

An offence under either of the following sections of the Criminal Justice Act 1988—

(a) section 139 (having article with blade or point in public place),

(b) section 139AA (threatening with article with blade or point or offensive weapon).

Offences against property

22

An offence under any of the following sections of the Theft Act 1968—

(a) section 8 (robbery or assault with intent to rob),

(b) section 9 (burglary),

(c) section 10 (aggravated burglary).

23

An offence under section 1 of the Criminal Damage Act 1971 (destroying or damaging property).

24

An offence under section 30 of the Crime and Disorder Act 1998 (racially or religiously aggravated criminal damage).

Road traffic offences

25

An offence under section 35 of the Offences against the Person Act 1861 (injuring persons by furious driving).

26

An offence under section 12A of the Theft Act 1968 (aggravated vehicle-taking involving an accident which caused the death of any person).

27

An offence under any of the following sections of the Road Traffic Act 1988—

(a) section 1 (causing death by dangerous driving),

(b) section 1A (causing serious injury by dangerous driving),

(c) section 3A (causing death by careless driving when under influence of drink or drugs).

Drug-related offences

28

An offence under any of the following provisions of the Misuse of Drugs Act 1971—

(a) section 4 (restriction of production and supply of controlled drugs),

(b) section 5(3) (possession of controlled drugs with intent to supply),

(c)   section 8(a) or (b) (occupiers etc. of premises to be punishable for permitting unlawful production or supply etc. of controlled drugs there).

29

An offence under section 6 of that Act (restrictions of cultivation of cannabis plant) where the cultivation is for profit and the whole or a substantial part of the dwelling-house concerned is used for the cultivation.

Modern slavery

29A

An offence under either of the following sections of the Modern Slavery Act 2015—

(a)   section 1 (slavery, servitude and forced or compulsory labour),

(b)   section 2 (human trafficking)."

Inchoate offences

30

(1)   An offence of attempting or conspiring the commission of an offence specified or described in this Schedule.

(2)   An offence under Part 2 of the Serious Crime Act 2007 (encouraging or assisting) where the offence (or one of the offences) which the person in question intends or believes would be committed is an offence specified or described in this Schedule.

(3)   An offence of aiding, abetting, counselling or procuring the commission of an offence specified or described in this Schedule.

Scope of offences

31

Where this Schedule refers to offences which are offences under the law of England and Wales and another country or territory, the reference is to be read as limited to the offences so far as they are offences under the law of England and Wales.

Housing Act 1988

(1988 CHAPTER 50)

PART I
RENTED ACCOMMODATION

Chapter I Assured tenancies

Security of tenure

8 Notice of proceedings for possession.

(1) The court shall not entertain proceedings for possession of a dwelling-house let on an assured tenancy unless—

(a) the landlord or, in the case of joint landlords, at least one of them has served on the tenant a notice in accordance with this section and the proceedings are begun within the time limits stated in the notice in accordance with subsections (3) to (4B) below; or

(b) the court considers it just and equitable to dispense with the requirement of such a notice.

(2) The court shall not make an order for possession on any of the grounds in Schedule 2 to this Act unless that ground and particulars of it are specified in the notice under this section; but the grounds specified in such a notice may be altered or added to with the leave of the court.

(3) A notice under this section is one in the prescribed form informing the tenant that—

(a) the landlord intends to begin proceedings for possession of the dwelling-house on one or more of the grounds specified in the notice; and

(b) those proceedings will not begin earlier than a date specified in the notice in accordance with subsections (3A) to (4B) below; and

(c) those proceedings will not begin later than twelve months from the date of service of the notice.

(3A) If a notice under this section specifies in accordance with subsection (3)(a) Ground 7A in Schedule 2 to this Act (whether with or without other grounds), the date specified in the notice as mentioned in subsection (3)(b) is not to be earlier than—

(a) in the case of a periodic tenancy, the earliest date on which, apart from section 5(1), the tenancy could be brought to an end by a notice to quit given by the landlord on the same date as the date of service of the notice under this section;

(b) in the case of a fixed term tenancy, one month after the date on which the notice was served.

(4) If a notice under this section specifies in accordance with subsection (3) (a) above Ground 14 in Schedule 2 to this Act (whether without other grounds or with any ground other than Ground 7A), the date specified in the notice as mentioned in subsection (3)(b) above shall not be earlier than the date of the service of the notice.

(4A) If a notice under this section specifies in accordance with subsection (3)(a) above, any of Grounds 1, 2, 5 to 7, 9 and 16 in Schedule 2 to this Act (whether without other grounds or with any ground other than Ground 7A or 14), the date specified in the notice as mentioned in subsection (3)(b) above shall not be earlier than—

(a) two months from the date of service of the notice; and

(b) if the tenancy is a periodic tenancy, the earliest date on which, apart from section 5(1) above, the tenancy could be brought to an end by a notice to quit given by the landlord on the same date as the date of service of the notice under this section.

(4B) In any other case, the date specified in the notice as mentioned in subsection (3)(b) above shall not be earlier than the expiry of the period of two weeks from the date of the service of the notice.

(4C) A notice under this section that specifies in accordance with subsection (3) (a) Ground 7A in Schedule 2 to this Act (whether with or without other grounds) must be served on the tenant within the time period specified in subsection (4D), (4E) or (4F).

(4D) Where the landlord proposes to rely on condition 1, 3 or 5 in Ground 7A, the notice must be served on the tenant within—

(a) the period of 12 months beginning with the day of the conviction, or

(b) if there is an appeal against the conviction, the period of 12 months beginning with the day on which the appeal is finally determined or abandoned.

(4E) Where the landlord proposes to rely on condition 2 in Ground 7A, the notice must be served on the tenant within—

(a) the period of 12 months beginning with the day on which the court has made the finding, or

(b) if there is an appeal against the finding, the period of 12 months beginning with the day on which the appeal is finally determined, abandoned or withdrawn.

(4F) Where the landlord proposes to rely on condition 4 in Ground 7A, the notice must be served on the tenant within—

(a) the period of 3 months beginning with the day on which the closure order was made, or

(b) if there is an appeal against the making of the order, the period of 3 months beginning with the day on which the appeal is finally determined, abandoned or withdrawn.

(5) The court may not exercise the power conferred by subsection (1)(b) above if the landlord seeks to recover possession on Ground 7A, 7B or 8 in Schedule 2 to this Act.

(6) Where a notice under this section—

(a) is served at a time when the dwelling-house is let on a fixed term tenancy, or

(b) is served after a fixed term tenancy has come to an end but relates (in whole or in part) to events occurring during that tenancy,

the notice shall have effect notwithstanding that the tenant becomes or has become tenant under a statutory periodic tenancy arising on the coming to an end of the fixed term tenancy.

Schedule 2
Grounds for possession of dwelling-houses let on assured tenancies

PART I
GROUNDS ON WHICH COURT MUST ORDER POSSESSION

(Ground 7A)

Any of the following conditions is met.

Condition 1 is that—

(a) the tenant, or a person residing in or visiting the dwelling-house, has been convicted of a serious offence, and

(b) the serious offence—

   (i) was committed (wholly or partly) in, or in the locality of, the dwelling-house,

   (ii) was committed elsewhere against a person with a right (of whatever description) to reside in, or occupy housing accommodation in the locality of, the dwelling-house, or

   (iii) was committed elsewhere against the landlord of the dwelling-house, or a person employed (whether or not by the landlord) in connection with the exercise of the landlord's housing management functions, and directly or indirectly related to or affected those functions.

317

Condition 2 is that a court has found in relevant proceedings that the tenant, or a person residing in or visiting the dwelling-house, has breached a provision of an injunction under section 1 of the Anti-social Behaviour, Crime and Policing Act 2014, other than a provision requiring a person to participate in a particular activity, and—

(a) the breach occurred in, or in the locality of, the dwelling-house, or

(b) the breach occurred elsewhere and the provision breached was a provision intended to prevent—

    (i) conduct that is capable of causing nuisance or annoyance to a person with a right (of whatever description) to reside in, or occupy housing accommodation in the locality of, the dwelling-house, or

    (ii) conduct that is capable of causing nuisance or annoyance to the landlord of the dwelling-house, or a person employed (whether or not by the landlord) in connection with the exercise of the landlord's housing management functions, and that is directly or indirectly related to or affects those functions.

Condition 3 is that the tenant, or a person residing in or visiting the dwelling-house, has been convicted of an offence under section 30 of the Anti-social Behaviour, Crime and Policing Act 2014 consisting of a breach of a provision of a criminal behaviour order prohibiting a person from doing anything described in the order, and the offence involved—

(a) a breach that occurred in, or in the locality of, the dwelling-house, or

(b) a breach that occurred elsewhere of a provision intended to prevent—

    (i) behaviour that causes or is likely to cause harassment, alarm or distress to a person with a right (of whatever description) to reside in, or occupy housing accommodation in the locality of, the dwelling-house, or

    (ii) behaviour that causes or is likely to cause harassment, alarm or distress to the landlord of the dwelling-house, or a person employed (whether or not by the landlord) in connection with the exercise of the landlord's housing management functions, and that is directly or indirectly related to or affects those functions.

Condition 4 is that—

(a) the dwelling-house is or has been subject to a closure order under section 80 of the Anti-social Behaviour, Crime and Policing Act 2014, and

(b) access to the dwelling-house has been prohibited (under the closure order or under a closure notice issued under section 76 of that Act) for a continuous period of more than 48 hours.

Condition 5 is that—

(a) the tenant, or a person residing in or visiting the dwelling-house, has been convicted of an offence under—

    (i)   section 80(4) of the Environmental Protection Act 1990 (breach of abatement notice in relation to statutory nuisance), or

    (ii)   section 82(8) of that Act (breach of court order to abate statutory nuisance etc.), and

(b) the nuisance concerned was noise emitted from the dwelling-house which was a statutory nuisance for the purposes of Part 3 of that Act by virtue of section 79(1)(g) of that Act (noise emitted from premises so as to be prejudicial to health or a nuisance).

Condition 1, 2, 3, 4 or 5 is not met if—

(a) there is an appeal against the conviction, finding or order concerned which has not been finally determined, abandoned or withdrawn, or

(b) the final determination of the appeal results in the conviction, finding or order being overturned.

In this ground—

'relevant proceedings' means proceedings for contempt of court or proceedings under Schedule 2 to the Anti-social Behaviour, Crime and Policing Act 2014;

'serious offence' means an offence which—

    (a)   was committed on or after the day on which this ground comes into force,

    (b)   is specified, or falls within a description specified, in Schedule 2A to the Housing Act 1985 at the time the offence was committed and at the time the court is considering the matter, and

    (c)   is not an offence that is triable only summarily by virtue of section 22 of the Magistrates' Courts Act 1980 (either-way offences where value involved is small).

PART II
GROUNDS ON WHICH COURT MAY ORDER POSSESSION

(Ground 12)

Any obligation of the tenancy (other than one related to the payment of rent) has been broken or not performed.

(Ground 14)

The tenant or a person residing in or visiting the dwelling-house—

(a) has been guilty of conduct causing or likely to cause a nuisance or annoyance to a person residing; visiting or otherwise engaging in a lawful activity in the locality, (aa) has been guilty of conduct causing or likely to cause a nuisance or annoyance to the landlord of the dwelling-house, or a person employed (whether or not by the landlord) in connection with the exercise of the landlord's housing management functions, and that is directly or indirectly related to or affects those functions, or

(b) has been convicted of—

    (i) using the dwelling-house or allowing it to be used for immoral or illegal purposes, or

    (ii) an indictable offence committed in, or in the locality of, the dwelling-house.

(Ground14ZA)

The tenant or an adult residing in the dwelling-house has been convicted of an indictable offence which took place during, and at the scene of, a riot in the United Kingdom.

In this Ground—

'adult' means a person aged 18 or over;

'indictable offence' does not include an offence that is triable only summarily by virtue of section 22 of the Magistrates' Courts Act 1980 (either way offences where value involved is small);

'riot' is to be construed in accordance with section 1 of the Public Order Act 1986.

This Ground applies only in relation to dwelling-houses in England.

Equality Act 2010

(2010 CHAPTER 15)

PART 2
EQUALITY: KEY CONCEPTS

Chapter I Protected characteristics

4   The protected characteristics

The following characteristics are protected characteristics— age;

disability;

gender reassignment;

marriage and civil partnership;

pregnancy and maternity; race;

religion or belief; sex;

sexual orientation.

6 Disability

(1) A person (P) has a disability if—

(a) P has a physical or mental impairment, and

(b) the impairment has a substantial and long-term adverse effect on P's ability to carry out normal day-to-day activities.

(2) A reference to a disabled person is a reference to a person who has a disability.

(3) In relation to the protected characteristic of disability—

(a) a reference to a person who has a particular protected characteristic is a reference to a person who has a particular disability;

(b) a reference to persons who share a protected characteristic is a reference to persons who have the same disability.

(4) This Act (except Part 12 and section 190) applies in relation to a person who has had a disability as it applies in relation to a person who has the disability; accordingly (except in that Part and that section)—

(a) a reference (however expressed) to a person who has a disability includes a reference to a person who has had the disability, and

(b) a reference (however expressed) to a person who does not have a disability includes a reference to a person who has not had the disability.

(5) A Minister of the Crown may issue guidance about matters to be taken into account in deciding any question for the purposes of subsection (1).

(6) Schedule 1 (disability: supplementary provision) has effect.

Chapter 2
Prohibited conduct

Discrimination

13 Direct discrimination

(1) A person (A) discriminates against another (B) if, because of a protected characteristic, A treats B less favourably than A treats or would treat others.

(2) If the protected characteristic is age, A does not discriminate against B if A can show A's treatment of B to be a proportionate means of achieving a legitimate aim.

(3) If the protected characteristic is disability, and B is not a disabled person, A does not discriminate against B only because A treats or would treat disabled persons more favourably than A treats B.

(4) If the protected characteristic is marriage and civil partnership, this section applies to a contravention of Part 5 (work) only if the treatment is because it is B who is married or a civil partner.

(5) If the protected characteristic is race, less favourable treatment includes segregating B from others.

(6) If the protected characteristic is sex—

(a) less favourable treatment of a woman includes less favourable treatment of her because she is breast-feeding;

(b) in a case where B is a man, no account is to be taken of special treatment afforded to a woman in connection with pregnancy or childbirth.

(7) Subsection (6)(a) does not apply for the purposes of Part 5 (work).

(8) This section is subject to sections 17(6) and 18(7).

15 Discrimination arising from disability

(1) A person (A) discriminates against a disabled person (B) if—

(a) A treats B unfavourably because of something arising in consequence of B's disability, and

(b) A cannot show that the treatment is a proportionate means of achieving a legitimate aim.

(2) Subsection (1) does not apply if A shows that A did not know, and could not reasonably have been expected to know, that B had the disability.

19 Indirect discrimination

(1) A person (A) discriminates against another (B) if A applies to B a provision, criterion or practice which is discriminatory in relation to a relevant protected characteristic of B's.

(2) For the purposes of subsection (1), a provision, criterion or practice is discriminatory in relation to a relevant protected characteristic of B's if—

(a) A applies, or would apply, it to persons with whom B does not share the characteristic,

(b) it puts, or would put, persons with whom B shares the characteristic at a particular disadvantage when compared with persons with whom B does not share it,

(c) it puts, or would put, B at that disadvantage, and

(d) A cannot show it to be a proportionate means of achieving a legitimate aim.

(3) The relevant protected characteristics are— age;

disability;

gender reassignment;

marriage and civil partnership; race;

religion or belief; sex;

sexual orientation.

Adjustments for disabled persons

20 Duty to make adjustments

(1) Where this Act imposes a duty to make reasonable adjustments on a person, this section, sections 21 and 22 and the applicable Schedule apply; and for those purposes, a person on whom the duty is imposed is referred to as A.

(2) The duty comprises the following three requirements.

(3) The first requirement is a requirement, where a provision, criterion or practice of A's puts a disabled person at a substantial disadvantage in relation to a relevant matter in comparison with persons who are not disabled, to take such steps as it is reasonable to have to take to avoid the disadvantage.

(4) The second requirement is a requirement, where a physical feature puts a disabled person at a substantial disadvantage in relation to a relevant matter in comparison with persons who are not disabled, to take such steps as it is reasonable to have to take to avoid the disadvantage.

(5) The third requirement is a requirement, where a disabled person would, but for the provision of an auxiliary aid, be put at a substantial disadvantage in relation to a relevant matter in comparison with persons who are not disabled, to take such steps as it is reasonable to have to take to provide the auxiliary aid.

(6) Where the first or third requirement relates to the provision of information, the steps which it is reasonable for A to have to take include steps for ensuring that in the circumstances concerned the information is provided in an accessible format.

(7) A person (A) who is subject to a duty to make reasonable adjustments is not (subject to express provision to the contrary) entitled to require a disabled person, in relation to whom A is required to comply with the duty, to pay to any extent A's costs of complying with the duty.

(8) A reference in section 21 or 22 or an applicable Schedule to the first, second or third requirement is to be construed in accordance with this section.

(9) In relation to the second requirement, a reference in this section or an applicable Schedule to avoiding a substantial disadvantage includes a reference to—

(a) removing the physical feature in question,

(b) altering it, or

(c) providing a reasonable means of avoiding it.

(10) A reference in this section, section 21 or 22 or an applicable Schedule (apart from paragraphs 2 to 4 of Schedule 4) to a physical feature is a reference to—

(a) a feature arising from the design or construction of a building,

(b) a feature of an approach to, exit from or access to a building,

(c) a fixture or fitting, or furniture, furnishings, materials, equipment or other chattels, in or on premises, or

(d) any other physical element or quality.

(11) A reference in this section, section 21 or 22 or an applicable Schedule to an auxiliary aid includes a reference to an auxiliary service.

(12) A reference in this section or an applicable Schedule to chattels is to be read, in relation to Scotland, as a reference to moveable property.

(13) The applicable Schedule is, in relation to the Part of this Act specified in the first column of the Table, the Schedule specified in the second column.

Part of this Act	Applicable Schedule
Part 3 (services and public functions)	Schedule 2
Part 4 (premises)	Schedule 4
Part 5 (work)	Schedule 8
Part 6 (education)	Schedule 13
Part 7 (associations)	Schedule 15
Each of the Parts mentioned above	Schedule 21

PART 4
PREMISES

Disposal and management

33 Disposals, etc.

(1) A person (A) who has the right to dispose of premises must not discriminate against another (B)—

(a) as to the terms on which A offers to dispose of the premises to B;

(b) by not disposing of the premises to B;

(c) in A's treatment of B with respect to things done in relation to persons seeking premises.

(2) Where an interest in a commonhold unit cannot be disposed of unless a particular person is a party to the disposal, that person must not discriminate against a person by not being a party to the disposal.

(3) A person who has the right to dispose of premises must not, in connection with anything done in relation to their occupation or disposal, harass—

(a) a person who occupies them;

(b) a person who applies for them.

(4) A person (A) who has the right to dispose of premises must not victimise another (B)—

(a) as to the terms on which A offers to dispose of the premises to B;

(b) by not disposing of the premises to B;

(c) in A's treatment of B with respect to things done in relation to persons seeking premises.

(5) Where an interest in a commonhold unit cannot be disposed of unless a particular person is a party to the disposal, that person must not victimise a person by not being a party to the disposal.

(6) In the application of section 26 for the purposes of subsection (3), neither of the following is a relevant protected characteristic—

(a) religion or belief;

(b) sexual orientation.

35 Management

(1) A person (A) who manages premises must not discriminate against a person (B) who occupies the premises—

(a) in the way in which A allows B, or by not allowing B, to make use of a benefit or facility;

(b) by evicting B (or taking steps for the purpose of securing B's eviction);

(c) by subjecting B to any other detriment.

(2) A person who manages premises must not, in relation to their management, harass—

(a) a person who occupies them;

(b) a person who applies for them.

(3) A person (A) who manages premises must not victimise a person (B) who occupies the premises—

(a) in the way in which A allows B, or by not allowing B, to make use of a benefit or facility;

(b) by evicting B (or taking steps for the purpose of securing B's eviction);

(c) by subjecting B to any other detriment.

(4) In the application of section 26 for the purposes of subsection (2), neither of the following is a relevant protected characteristic—

(a) religion or belief;

(b) sexual orientation.

PART I I
ADVANCEMENT OF EQUALITY

Chapter I
Public sector equality duty

149 Public sector equality duty

(1) A public authority must, in the exercise of its functions, have due regard to the need to—

(a) eliminate discrimination, harassment, victimisation and any other conduct that is prohibited by or under this Act;

(b) advance equality of opportunity between persons who share a relevant protected characteristic and persons who do not share it;

(c) foster good relations between persons who share a relevant protected characteristic and persons who do not share it.

(2) A person who is not a public authority but who exercises public functions must, in the exercise of those functions, have due regard to the matters mentioned in subsection (1).

(3) Having due regard to the need to advance equality of opportunity between persons who share a relevant protected characteristic and persons who do not share it involves having due regard, in particular, to the need to—

(a) remove or minimise disadvantages suffered by persons who share a relevant protected characteristic that are connected to that characteristic;

(b) take steps to meet the needs of persons who share a relevant protected characteristic that are different from the needs of persons who do not share it;

(c) encourage persons who share a relevant protected characteristic to participate in public life or in any other activity in which participation by such persons is disproportionately low.

(4) The steps involved in meeting the needs of disabled persons that are different from the needs of persons who are not disabled include, in particular, steps to take account of disabled persons' disabilities.

(5) Having due regard to the need to foster good relations between persons who share a relevant protected characteristic and persons who do not share it involves having due regard, in particular, to the need to—

(a) tackle prejudice, and

(b) promote understanding.

(6) Compliance with the duties in this section may involve treating some persons more favourably than others; but that is not to be taken as permitting conduct that would otherwise be prohibited by or under this Act.

(7) The relevant protected characteristics are— age;

disability;

gender reassignment;

pregnancy and maternity; race;

religion or belief; sex;

sexual orientation.

(8) A reference to conduct that is prohibited by or under this Act includes a reference to—

(a) a breach of an equality clause or rule;

(b) a breach of a non-discrimination rule.

(9) Schedule 18 (exceptions) has effect.

150 Public authorities and public functions

(1) A public authority is a person who is specified in Schedule 19.

(2) In that Schedule—

Part 1 specifies public authorities generally;

Part 2 specifies relevant Welsh authorities;

Part 3 specifies relevant Scottish authorities.

(3) A public authority specified in Schedule 19 is subject to the duty imposed by section 149(1) in relation to the exercise of all of its functions unless subsection (4) applies.

(4) A public authority specified in that Schedule in respect of certain specified functions is subject to that duty only in respect of the exercise of those functions.

(5) A public function is a function that is a function of a public nature for the purposes of the Human Rights Act 1998.

Children and Young Persons Act 1933

(1933 CHAPTER 12)

PART III
PROTECTION OF CHILDREN AND YOUNG PERSONS IN RELATION
TO CRIMINAL AND SUMMARY PROCEEDINGS

General provisions as to proceedings in court

39 Power to prohibit publication of certain matter

(1) In relation to any proceedings, other than criminal proceedings, in any court, the court may direct that the following may not be included in a publication—

(a) the name, address or school of any child or young person concerned in the proceedings, either as being the person by or against or in respect of whom the proceedings are taken, or as being a witness therein:

(aa) any particulars calculated to lead to the identification of a child or young person so concerned in the proceedings;

(b) a picture that is or includes a picture of any child or young person so concerned in the proceedings;

except in so far (if at all) as may be permitted by the direction of the court.

(2) Any person who includes matter in a publication in contravention of any such direction shall on summary conviction be liable in respect of each offence to a fine not exceeding level 5 on the standard scale.

(3) In this section—

'publication' includes any speech, writing, relevant programme or other communication in whatever form, which is addressed to the public at large or any section of the public (and for this purpose every relevant programme shall be taken to be so addressed), but does not include a document prepared for use in particular legal proceedings;

'relevant programme' means a programme included in a programme service within the meaning of the Broadcasting Act 1990.

Juvenile courts

49 Restrictions on reports of proceedings in which children or young persons are concerned.

(1) No matter relating to any child or young person concerned in proceedings to which this section applies shall while he is under the age of 18 be included in any publication if it is likely to lead members of the public to identify him as someone concerned in the proceedings.

(2) The proceedings to which this section applies are—

(a) proceedings in a youth court;

(b) proceedings on appeal from a youth court (including proceedings by way of case stated);

(c) proceedings in a magistrates' court under Schedule 2 to the Criminal Justice and Immigration Act 2008 (proceedings for breach, revocation or amendment of youth rehabilitation orders);

(d) proceedings on appeal from a magistrates' court arising out of any proceedings mentioned in paragraph (c) (including proceedings by way of case stated).

(3) In this section 'publication' includes any speech, writing, relevant programme or other communication in whatever form, which is addressed to the public at large or any section of the public (and for this purpose every relevant programme

shall be taken to be so addressed), but does not include an indictment or other document prepared for use in particular legal proceedings.

(3A) The matters relating to a person in relation to which the restrictions imposed by subsection (1) above apply (if their inclusion in any publication is likely to have the result mentioned in that subsection) include in particular—

(a) his name,

(b) his address,

(c) the identity of any school or other educational establishment attended by him,

(d) the identity of any place of work, and

(e) any still or moving picture of him.

(4) For the purposes of this section a child or young person is 'concerned' in any proceedings if he is—

(a) a person against or in respect of whom the proceedings are taken, or

(b) a person called, or proposed to be called, to give evidence in the proceedings.

(4A) If a court is satisfied that it is in the public interest to do so, it may, in relation to a child or young person who has been convicted of an offence, by order dispense to any specified extent with the restrictions imposed by subsection (1) above in relation to any proceedings before it to which this section applies by virtue of subsection (2)(a) or (b) above, being proceedings relating to—

(a) the prosecution or conviction of the offender for the offence;

(b) the manner in which he, or his parent or guardian, should be dealt with in respect of the offence;

(c) the enforcement, amendment, variation, revocation or discharge of any order made in respect of the offence;

(d) where an attendance centre order is made in respect of the offence, the enforcement of any rules made under section 222(1)(d) or (e) of the Criminal Justice Act 2003; or

(e) where a detention and training order is made, the enforcement of any requirements imposed under section 103(6)(b) of the Powers of Criminal Courts (Sentencing) Act 2000.

(4B) A court shall not exercise its power under subsection (4A) above without—

(a) affording the parties to the proceedings an opportunity to make representations; and

(b) taking into account any representations which are duly made.

(5) Subject to subsection (7) below, a court may, in relation to proceedings before it to which this section applies, by order dispense to any specified extent

with the requirements of this section in relation to a child or young person who is concerned in the proceedings if it is satisfied—

(a) that it is appropriate to do so for the purpose of avoiding injustice to the child or young person; or

(b) that, as respects a child or young person to whom this paragraph applies who is unlawfully at large, it is necessary to dispense with those requirements for the purpose of apprehending him and bringing him before a court or returning him to the place in which he was in custody.

(6) Paragraph (b) of subsection (5) above applies to any child or young person who is charged with or has been convicted of—

(a) a violent offence,

(b) a sexual offence, or

(c) an offence punishable in the case of a person aged 21 or over with imprisonment for fourteen years or more.

(7) The court shall not exercise its power under subsection (5)(b) above—

(a) except in pursuance of an application by or on behalf of the Director of Public Prosecutions; and

(b) unless notice of the application has been given by the Director of Public Prosecutions to any legal representative of the child or young person.

(8) The court's power under subsection (4A) or (5) above may be exercised by a single justice.

(9) If a publication includes any matter in contravention of subsection (1) above, the following persons shall be guilty of an offence and liable on summary conviction to a fine not exceeding level 5 on the standard scale—

(a) where the publication is a newspaper or periodical, any proprietor, any editor and any publisher of the newspaper or periodical;

(b) where the publication is a relevant programme—

   (i)   any body corporate or Scottish partnership engaged in providing the programme service in which the programme is included; and

   (ii) any person having functions in relation to the programme corresponding to those of an editor of a newspaper;

(c) in the case of any other publication, any person publishing it.

(9A)   Where a person is charged with an offence under subsection (9) above it shall be a defence to prove that at the time of the alleged offence he was not aware, and neither suspected nor had reason to suspect, that the publication included the matter in question.

(9B) If an offence under subsection (9) above committed by a body corporate is proved—

(a) to have been committed with the consent or connivance of, or

(b) to be attributable to any neglect on the part of,

an officer, the officer as well as the body corporate is guilty of the offence and liable to be proceeded against and punished accordingly.

(9C)   In subsection (9B) above 'officer' means a director, manager, secretary or other similar officer of the body, or a person purporting to act in any such capacity.

(9D)   If the affairs of a body corporate are managed by its members, "director" in subsection (9C) above means a member of that body.

(9E)   Where an offence under subsection (9) above is committed by a Scottish partnership and is proved to have been committed with the consent or connivance of a partner, he as well as the partnership shall be guilty of the offence and shall be liable to be proceeded against and punished accordingly.

(10)In any proceedings under Schedule 2 to the Criminal Justice and Immigration Act 2008 (proceedings for breach, revocation or amendment of youth rehabilitation orders) before a magistrates' court other than a youth court or on appeal from such a court it shall be the duty of the magistrates' court or the appellate court to announce in the course of the proceedings that this section applies to the proceedings; and if the court fails to do so this section shall not apply to the proceedings.

(11)In this section—

'picture' includes a likeness however produced;

'relevant programme' means a programme included in a programme service, within the meaning of the Broadcasting Act 1990;

'sexual offence' means an offence listed in Part 2 of Schedule 15 to the Criminal Justice Act 2003;

'specified' means specified in an order under this section;

'violent offence' means an offence listed in Part 1 of Schedule 15 to the Criminal Justice Act 2003;

and a person who, having been granted bail, is liable to arrest (whether with or without a warrant) shall be treated as unlawfully at large.

Appendix B
Regulations

Contents

Absolute Ground for Possession for Anti-social Behaviour (Review Procedure) (England) Regulations 2014

SI 2014/2554

1   Citation, commencement, application and interpretation

(1) These Regulations may be cited as the Absolute Ground for Possession for Anti-social Behaviour (Review Procedure) (England) Regulations 2014 and come into force on 20th October 2014.

(2) These Regulations apply in relation to dwelling-houses in England only.

(3) In these Regulations—

'the Act' means the Housing Act 1985;

'applicant' means a tenant who has requested a review;

'business day' means any day other than a Saturday, Sunday, Christmas Day, Good Friday, or a day which is a bank holiday in England under the Banking and Financial Dealings Act 1971;

'landlord' means a person to whom a request for a review is made;

'original decision' means a landlord's decision to seek an order for possession of a dwelling-house under section 84A of the Act (absolute ground for possession for anti-social behaviour);

'review' means a review under section 85ZA(1) of the Act (review of decision to seek possession on absolute ground for anti-social behaviour).

2   Application

An application for a review must include—

(a) the applicant's name and address;

(b) a description of the original decision in respect of which the review is sought including the date on which the decision was made;

(c) a statement of the grounds on which the review is sought;

(d) a statement to the effect that the applicant does, or does not, require the review to be conducted by way of an oral hearing;

(e) a statement to the effect that the applicant does, or does not, agree to receive communications relating to the review by email, and if the former, the email address to which such communications should be sent.

3   Right to a hearing

(1) Where an application includes a statement to the effect that the applicant requires the review to be conducted by way of an oral hearing, the review must be conducted in accordance with regulations 6 to 10.

(2) In any other case, the review must be conducted in accordance with regulation 5.

4   Communication

(1) Where an application includes a statement to the effect that the applicant agrees to receive communications relating to the review by email, any notice, document or other communication sent in connection with the review by the landlord to the email address referred to in regulation 2(e) is to be taken as having been received by the applicant on the day on which it was sent to that address.

(2) In any other case, a notice, document or other communication sent in connection with the review by the landlord is to be taken as having been received by the applicant on—

(a) the day it is given to the applicant in person;

(b) the second business day after it is sent by first class post to the address referred to in regulation 2(a); or

(c) the day it is delivered by hand to the address referred to in regulation 2(a).

5   Review without a hearing

(1) Where regulation 3(2) applies, the landlord must send a written notice to the applicant stating that the applicant may make written representations in support of the application before a time specified in the notice.

(2) The time specified pursuant to paragraph (1) must not be earlier than five days after the day on which the notice referred to in that paragraph is received by the applicant.

(3) In making a decision on the review the person conducting the review must take into account any representations received in accordance with this regulation.

(4) The review must be conducted by a person appointed for that purpose by the landlord, who may be an officer or employee of the landlord.

(5) A person appointed under paragraph (4) who is an officer or employee of the landlord must be a person of greater seniority than the person who made the original decision.

(6) The person referred to in paragraph (4) must not be a person who was involved in the making of the original decision.

6   Review by way of a hearing

(1) Where regulation 3(1) applies, the landlord must send a written notice to the applicant stating the date, time and place of the oral hearing.

(2) The date referred to in paragraph (1) must not be earlier than five days after the day on which the notice referred to in that paragraph is received by the applicant.

(3) If at any time before the date on which the hearing is due to take place the applicant so requests, the landlord may postpone the hearing to a later date.

7   Procedure at hearing

(1) The hearing must be conducted by a person appointed for that purpose by the landlord, who may be an officer or employee of the landlord.

(2) A person appointed under paragraph (1) who is an officer or employee of the landlord must be a person of greater seniority than the person who made the original decision.

(3) The person referred to in paragraph (1) must not be a person who was involved in the making of the original decision.

(4) The hearing must be conducted with the minimum amount of formality and in accordance with any directions given by the person conducting it.

(5) At the hearing the applicant may—

(a) make oral or written representations relevant to the decision to be made on the review;

(b) be accompanied or represented by another person appointed by the applicant for that purpose (whether that person is professionally qualified or not);

(c) call persons to give evidence on any matter relevant to the decision to be made on the review; and

(d) put questions to any person who gives evidence at the hearing.

(6) The person who made the original decision may attend the hearing and may do any of the things the applicant may do pursuant to paragraph (5).

(7) A person appointed as a representative pursuant to paragraph (5)(b) has the same rights as the applicant (or, as the case may be, the person who made the original decision) for the purposes of the conduct of the hearing.

8 Absence of applicant at hearing

If the applicant fails to attend the hearing, the person conducting it may, having regard to all the circumstances (including any explanation offered for the absence) proceed with the hearing or give such directions with a view to the further conduct of the review as that person may think appropriate.

9 Adjournment of hearing

(1) The hearing may be adjourned by the person conducting it (on the application of the applicant or otherwise).

(2) Where the hearing is adjourned for more than one day, the person conducting it must specify a date on which the hearing is to be resumed by sending a notice in writing to that effect to the applicant and any other person whose attendance is required at the resumed hearing.

10 Decision on review

Where regulation 3(1) applies, the decision on the review must be made by the person who conducted the hearing.

Secure Tenancies (Absolute Ground for Possession for Anti-social Behaviour) (Review Procedure) (Wales) Regulations 2014

SI 2014/3278

1 Title, commencement, application and interpretation

(1) The title of these Regulations is the Secure Tenancies (Absolute Ground for Possession for Anti-social Behaviour) (Review Procedure) (Wales) Regulations 2014 and they come into force on 12 January 2015.

(2) These Regulations apply in relation to dwelling-houses in Wales.

(3) In these Regulations—

'the Act' ('y Ddeddf') means the Housing Act 1985;

'applicant' ('ceisydd') means a tenant who has requested a review;

'application' ('cais') means the written request for a review;

'business day' ('diwrnod busnes') means any day other than a Saturday, Sunday, Christmas Day, Good Friday, or day which is a bank holiday in Wales under the Banking and Financial Dealings Act 1971;

'original decision' ('penderfyniad gwreiddiol') means a landlord's decision to seek an order for possession of a dwelling-house under section 84A of the Act (absolute ground for possession for anti-social behaviour);

'review' ('adolygiad') means a review under section 85ZA of the Act (review of decision to seek possession on absolute ground for anti-social behaviour).

2   Application for review

An application for a review must include—

(a) the applicant's name and address;

(b) a description of the original decision in respect of which the review is sought including the date on which the decision was made;

(c) a statement of the grounds on which the review is sought;

(d) a statement to the effect that the applicant does, or does not, require the review to be conducted by way of an oral hearing; and

(e) a statement to the effect that the applicant does, or does not, agree to receive communications relating to the review by email, and if the former, the email address to which such communications should be sent.

3   Right to a hearing

(1) Where an application includes a statement to the effect that the applicant requires the review to be conducted by way of an oral hearing, the review must be conducted in accordance with regulations 6 to 10.

(2) In any other case, the review must be conducted in accordance with regulation 5.

4   Communication

(1) Where an application includes a statement to the effect that the applicant agrees to receive communications relating to the review by email, any notice, document or other communication sent in connection with the review by the landlord to the email address referred to in regulation 2(e) is to be taken as having been received by the applicant on the day on which it was sent to that email address.

(2) In any other case, a notice, document or other communication sent in connection with the review by the landlord to the applicant is to be taken as having been received by the applicant on—

(a) the day it is given to the applicant in person;

(b) the second business day after it is sent by first class post to the address referred to in regulation 2(a); or

(c) the day it is delivered by hand to the address referred to in regulation 2(a).

5 Review without a hearing

(1) Where regulation 3(2) applies, the landlord must send a written notice to the applicant stating that the applicant may make written representations in support of the application before a time specified in the notice.

(2) The time specified pursuant to paragraph (1) must not be earlier than ten days after the day on which the notice referred to in that paragraph is received by the applicant.

(3) In making a decision on the review the person conducting the review must take into account any representations received in accordance with paragraph (1).

(4) The review must be conducted by a person appointed for that purpose by the landlord, who may be an officer or employee of the landlord.

(5) A person appointed under paragraph (4) who is an officer or an employee of the landlord must be a person of greater seniority than the person who made the original decision.

(6) The person referred to in paragraph (4) must not be a person who was involved in the making of the original decision.

6 Review by way of hearing

(1) Where regulation 3(1) applies, the landlord must send a written notice to the applicant stating the date, time and place of the oral hearing.

(2) The date referred to in paragraph (1) must not be earlier than ten days after the day on which the notice referred to in that paragraph is received by the applicant.

(3) If at any time before the date on which the hearing is due to take place the applicant so requests, the landlord may postpone the hearing to a later date.

7 Procedure at hearing

(1) The hearing must be conducted by a person appointed for that purpose by the landlord, who may be an officer or employee of the landlord.

(2) A person appointed under paragraph (1) who is an officer or employee of the landlord must be a person of greater seniority than the person who made the original decision.

(3) The person referred to in paragraph (1) must not be a person who was involved in the making of the original decision.

(4) The hearing must be conducted with the minimum amount of formality and in accordance with any directions given by the person conducting it.

(5) At the hearing the applicant may—

(a) make oral or written representations relevant to the decision to be made on the review;

(b) be accompanied or represented by another person appointed by the applicant for the purpose (whether that person is professionally qualified or not);

(c) call persons to give evidence on any matter relevant to the decision to be made on the review; and

(d) put questions to any person who gives evidence at the hearing.

(6) The person who made the original decision may attend the hearing and may do any of the things the applicant may do pursuant to paragraph (5).

(7) A person appointed as a representative pursuant to paragraph (5)(b) has the same rights as the applicant (or, as the case may be, the person who made the original decision) for the purposes of the conduct of the hearing.

8 Absence of applicant at hearing

If the applicant fails to attend the hearing, the person conducting it may, having regard to all the circumstances (including any explanation offered for the absence) proceed with the hearing or give such directions with a view to the further conduct of the review as that person may think appropriate.

9 Adjournment of hearing

(1) The hearing may be adjourned by the person conducting it (on the application of the applicant or otherwise).

(2) Where the hearing is adjourned for more than one day, the person conducting it must specify a date on which the hearing is to be resumed by sending notice in writing to that effect to the applicant and any other person whose attendance is required at the resumed hearing.

10 Decision on review

Where regulation 3(1) applies, the decision on the review must be made by the person who conducted the hearing.

Anti-social Behaviour, Crime and Policing Act 2014 (Publication of Public Spaces Protection Orders) Regulations 2014

SI 2014/2591

1 Citation and commencement

These Regulations may be cited as the Anti-social Behaviour, Crime and Policing Act 2014 (Publication of Public Spaces Protection Orders) Regulations 2014 and come into force on 20th October 2014.

2 Publication of a public spaces protection order which has been made, extended or varied

In relation to a public spaces protection order that a local authority has made, extended or varied, that local authority must—

(a) publish the order as made, extended or varied (as the case may be) on its website; and

(b) cause to be erected on or adjacent to the public place to which the order relates such notice (or notices) as it considers sufficient to draw the attention of any member of the public using that place to—

    (i) the fact that the order has been made, extended or varied (as the case may be); and

    (ii) the effect of that order being made, extended or varied (as the case may be).

3 Publication of a notice of discharge of a public spaces protection order

(1) In relation to a public spaces protection order that a local authority has discharged, that local authority must—

(a) publish a notice on its website identifying the order which has been discharged and the date on which it ceases to have effect; and

(b) cause to be erected on or adjacent to the public place to which the order relates, a notice (or notices)—

    (i) identifying the order which has been discharged; and

    (ii) the date on which it ceases to have effect.

(2) The notice (or notices) mentioned in paragraph (1)(b) must be positioned in a manner that the local authority considers sufficient to draw it to the attention of any member of the public using that place.

Magistrates' Courts (Injunctions: Anti-Social Behaviour) Rules 2015

SI 2015/423

1   Citation, commencement and interpretation

(1) These Rules may be cited as the Magistrates' Courts (Injunctions: Anti-Social Behaviour) Rules 2015.

(2) These Rules come into force on the day on which, and immediately after, section 1 of the 2014 Act comes into force.

(3) In these Rules—

(a) 'the 2014 Act' means the Anti-Social Behaviour, Crime and Policing Act 2014;

(b) a reference to a section or Schedule by number alone means the section or Schedule so numbered in the 2014 Act;

(c) 'applicant' means the person applying or who applied for the injunction, and 'respondent' means the person against whom the injunction is or was applied for;

(d) 'defaulter' has the meaning given in paragraph 2 of Schedule 2 to the 2014 Act;

(e) 'original applicant' has the meaning given in paragraph 1(2) of Schedule 2 to the 2014 Act;

(f) 'Part 1 injunction' means an injunction under Part 1 of the 2014 Act.

2   Applications to be by complaint

An application to which these rules apply must be made by way of complaint in writing.

3   Applications for injunctions

(1) An application to a youth court for a Part 1 injunction must—

(a) state the name, address and date of birth of the respondent;

(b) state the name and address of a parent or guardian of the respondent (except where the respondent is aged 18 or over, permission having been given by the court in relation to that respondent under rule 15);

(c) be supported by evidence of the matters of which the court must be satisfied for the first and second conditions under section 1 to be met;

(d) state the terms of the Part 1 injunction applied for; and

(e) in the case of an application made on notice, include a statement that the requirement for consultation in section 14(1) has been complied with.

(2) If an application without notice is made by virtue of section 6, the application must also state the reasons why it is necessary for the application to be made without notice having been given.

(3) In the case of an application made on notice, a copy of the application must be served by the applicant on—

(a) the respondent personally; and

(b) the parent or guardian mentioned in paragraph (2)(b) personally, or by posting it to or leaving it at that parent or guardian's address.

4   Interim Part 1 injunctions

An interim Part 1 injunction which is made on an application made without notice—

(a) must be served on the respondent personally as soon as practicable; and

(b) will not take effect until it has been so served.

5   Part 1 injunction containing provisions to which a power of arrest is attached

(1) In this rule, 'relevant provision' means a provision of a Part 1 injunction to which a power of arrest is attached.

(2) Where a Part 1 injunction contains one or more relevant provisions—

(a) each relevant provision must be set out in a separate paragraph of the injunction; and

(b) subject to paragraph (3), the applicant must deliver a copy of the relevant provisions to any police station for the area where the conduct occurred.

(3) Where the Part 1 injunction has been granted without notice under section 41, the applicant must not deliver a copy of the relevant provisions to any police station under paragraph (2)(b) before the injunction containing the relevant provisions has been served on the respondent.

(4) Where an order is made varying or discharging any relevant provision, the applicant must—

(a) immediately inform any police station to which a copy of the relevant provisions was delivered under paragraph (2)(b); and

(b) deliver a copy of the order to any police station so informed.

6   Application to vary or discharge a Part 1 injunction

(1) An application under section 8(1) to vary or discharge a Part 1 injunction must be made to the court which granted the injunction.

(2) Such an application must—

(a) specify—

(i)   the reason why the person applying for variation or discharge believes the court should vary or discharge the injunction; and

(ii)   if the application is to vary the injunction, the variation which is sought; and

(b) where the application is made by the person on whose application the injunction was granted, include a statement that the consultation requirement under section 14(3) has been complied with.

7   Application for warrant of arrest

(1) An application for a warrant of arrest under section 10(1) must be substantiated on oath.

(2) Such an application may be made without notice.

8   Proceedings following arrest under the 2014 Act

(1) This rule applies where a person under the age of 18 is arrested pursuant to—

(a) a power of arrest attached to a provision of a Part 1 injunction; or

(b) a warrant of arrest.

(2) A youth court before which a person is brought following such arrest may—

(a) deal with the matter; or

(b) adjourn the proceedings.

(3) If proceedings are adjourned and the arrested person is released—

(a) the matter must be dealt with (either by the same or another youth court) within 28 days of the date on which the arrested person appears in court; and

(b) the arrested person must be given not less than 2 days' notice of the hearing.

(4) An application under paragraph 1(2) of Schedule 2 may be made even if the arrested person is not dealt with within the period in paragraph (3)(a) of this rule.

9   Recognizance

Where, in accordance with paragraph 2(3)(b) of Schedule 1, the court fixes the amount of any recognizance with a view to it being taken subsequently, the recognizance may be taken by—

(a) a District Judge (Magistrates' Court);

(b) a justice of the peace;

(c) a justices' clerk; or

(d) a police officer of the rank of inspector or above, or in charge of a police station,

with the same consequences as if it had been entered into before the court.

10 Application for supervision order or detention order

An application under paragraph 1(2) of Schedule 2 must—

(a) be supported by evidence of the breach of any provisions of the injunction which is alleged; and

(b) include a statement that the consultation required by paragraph 1(3) of Schedule 2 has been undertaken.

11 Non-compliance with supervision order

An application under paragraph 12(2) of Schedule 2 must—

(a) be supported by evidence of the failure to comply with provisions of the supervision order which is alleged; and

(b) include a statement that the consultation required by paragraph 12(3) of Schedule 2 has been undertaken.

12 Application to amend or revoke a supervision order

(1) An application under paragraph 8(1) of Schedule 2 must state the new period which it is proposed to have substituted for that specified in the supervision order.

(2) An application under paragraph 9(1) of Schedule 2 must include—

(a) confirmation of the area in which the defaulter intends to reside or is now residing; and

(b) if the application is made by the original applicant, a statement that the consultation required by paragraph 9(6) of Schedule 2 has been undertaken.

(3) An application under paragraph 10(1) of Schedule 2 must include—

(a) the reasons why it is in the interests of justice for the order to be revoked or (as the case may be) amended by removing any requirement from it; and

(b) if the application is made by the original applicant, a statement that the consultation required by paragraph 10(5) of Schedule 2 has been undertaken.

13 Application to revoke a detention order

An application under paragraph 15(1) of Schedule 2 must include—

(a) the reasons why it is in the interests of justice for the order to be revoked; and

(b) if the application is made by the injunction applicant, a statement that the consultation required by paragraph 15(5) or (6) (as applicable) of Schedule 2 has been undertaken.

14 Applications for which court's consent is required

(1) Where the consent of the court is required by section 8(4), or paragraph 10(4) or 15(4) of Schedule 2, for the making of a further application, the application for consent must include—

(a) confirmation of the date on which, and the court by which, the previous application was dismissed; and

(b) a statement of the reasons why consent should be given.

(2) Such consent—

(a) may be given by a court comprising a single justice; but

(b) may not be refused without the applicant having been given an opportunity to make oral representations.

15 Application for permission for an application for a Part 1 injunction against a person aged 18 or over

(1) A youth court may, on application, give permission for an application for a Part 1 injunction against a person aged 18 or over to be made to the youth court if the conditions in section 18(2)(a) and (b) are fulfilled.

(2) The application for permission must include—

(a) in relation to the condition in section 18(2)(a), details of the application which has been made, or is to be made, for a Part 1 injunction against a person aged under 18; and

(b) in relation to the condition in section 18(2)(b), a statement of the reasons why it is in the interests of justice for the applications to be heard together.

16 Respondent attaining age of 18 after commencement of proceedings

(1) Where a respondent attains the age of 18 after the commencement of proceedings under Part 1 of the 2014 Act, the proceedings must remain in a youth court, subject to paragraphs (2) and (3).

(2) The court in which the proceedings were continuing when the respondent attained the age of 18 may, at the request of the applicant or the respondent or of its own motion—

(a) make a direction under paragraph (3); or

(b) direct that the proceedings be transferred to a youth court for the local justice area in which the respondent currently resides, in order for that court to consider whether to make a direction under paragraph (3).

(3) The court may direct that the proceedings be transferred to the High Court or county court, having had regard in particular to—

(a) the stage which the proceedings have reached;

(b) the circumstances of the applicant and the respondent; and

(c) the need to ensure fairness between the applicant and the respondent.

(4) The court may not make a direction under paragraph (3) without a hearing, on notice to both the applicant and the respondent.

(5) The applicant and the respondent must submit to the court—

(a) in writing; and

(b) no less than 7 days before the date specified for the hearing, or such other time as the court directs,

any reasons why the proceedings should either remain in a youth court or be transferred to the High Court or county court, having regard in particular the matters mentioned in paragraph (3).

Anti-social Behaviour (Authorised Persons) Order 2015

SI 2015/749

1 Citation and commencement

This Order may be cited as the Anti-social Behaviour (Authorised Persons) Order 2015 and comes into force on the day after the day on which it is made.

2 Description of specified persons

For the purposes of section 53(1)(c) of the Anti-social Behaviour, Crime and Policing Act 2014, housing providers (within the meaning of section 20 of that Act) are specified.

Appendix C
Guidance

Contents

Home Office

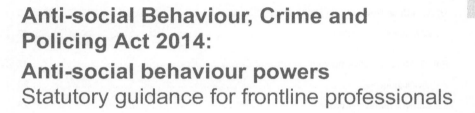

Anti-social Behaviour, Crime and Policing Act 2014:

Anti-social behaviour powers
Statutory guidance for frontline professionals

Updated December 2017

Contents

Introduction

The Home Office published statutory guidance in July 2014 to support the effective use of new powers to tackle anti-social behaviour that were introduced through the Anti-social Behaviour, Crime and Policing Act 2014. This guidance replaces that earlier guidance, updating it in the light of experience since the new powers were introduced. The changes will help to ensure that there is a greater focus on the impact of anti-social behaviour on victims and on their needs, ensuring that the relevant legal tests are met before the powers are used, underlining the importance of ensuring that the use of the powers are focused on specific behaviour that is anti-social or causing nuisance, and ensuring that the issues of local consultation, accountability and transparency are addressed. The guidance is intended to assist those frontline professionals – the police, local councils and social landlords - who are able to make use of the powers to respond to instances of anti-social behaviour in their local areas.

This updated guidance emphasises the importance of ensuring that the powers are used appropriately to provide a proportionate response to the specific behaviour that is causing harm or nuisance without impacting adversely on behaviour that is neither unlawful nor anti-social.

The powers introduced by the 2014 Act are deliberately local in nature. Those who work within and for local communities will be best placed to understand what is driving the behaviour in question, the impact that it is having, and to determine the most appropriate response.

The first part of this guidance focuses specifically on putting victims at the heart of the response to anti-social behaviour. We know that, where left unchecked, anti-social behaviour can have an overwhelming impact on its victims and in some cases, on the wider community. This is why the formal Anti-social Behaviour Case Review, commonly known as the Community Trigger, is an important safety net in ensuring that victims' voices are heard, but it is important that victims can easily access information about how to apply for a formal review and in what circumstances they can do so. The Community Remedy also gives victims a say in out-of-court punishments where the perpetrator of the anti-social behaviour is dealt with through a community resolution disposal.

The second part of the guidance focuses on the use of the powers provided by the 2014 Act. These are designed to be flexible to ensure that local agencies have the tools they need to respond to different forms of anti-social behaviour. The guidance sets out the legal tests that must be met before each of the powers can be used.

Part 1: Putting the victim first

The impact on victims and communities

The legal tests that govern the use of the anti-social behaviour powers are focused on the impact that the behaviour is having, or is likely to have, on victims and communities. When considering the response to a complaint of anti-social behaviour, agencies are encouraged to consider the effect that the behaviour in question is having on the lives of those subject to it recognising, for example, the debilitating impact that persistent or repeated anti-social behaviour can have on its victims, and the cumulative impact if that behaviour persists over a period of time.

The legislation requires the relevant local agencies to be satisfied that the specific legal tests and safeguards set out in the legislation are met before the anti-social behaviour powers are used. These tests are intended to help to ensure the appropriate and proportionate use of the powers and that they are being used to target specific problems or specific circumstances. They do allow for preventative action to be taken, for agencies to intervene early to prevent problems from escalating, and in some instances for there to be a focus on tackling the underlying causes of the anti-social behaviour.

The response to anti-social behaviour may require collaborative working between different agencies to determine the most appropriate solution. Where a report or complaint is made to one agency, that lead agency should consider the potential role of others in providing a solution if they are not themselves able to take action. This will help to ensure that reports of anti-social behaviour are not inadvertently lost between the different reporting arrangements of different agencies. It may also help to provide a mechanism for considering the potential for engaging the wider community in finding solutions to specific anti-social behaviour issues.

We recommend that, wherever possible, victims or complainants are kept informed while consideration is being given to deciding the most appropriate response, and that they are informed about the intended course of action. Local agencies also need to consider how victims are best supported.

Giving victims a say

The Anti-social Behaviour, Crime and Policing Act 2014 included two specific measures designed to give victims and communities a say in the way that complaints of anti-social behaviour are dealt with, and to help ensure that victims' voices are heard. These measures are:

- the **ASB Case Review/Community Trigger:** this gives victims of persistent anti-social behaviour the ability to demand a formal case review where the locally defined threshold is met, in order to determine whether there is further action that can be taken. The relevant bodies in the local area must agree on, and publish their Case Review/Community Trigger procedures; and

- the **Community Remedy:** this gives victims a say in the out-of-court punishment of perpetrators of anti-social behaviour when a community resolution, conditional caution or youth conditional caution is chosen as the most appropriate response.

The above measures are discussed in more detail in this part of this guidance.

1.1 The ASB Case Review (also known as the Community Trigger)

Purpose	To give victims and communities the right to request a review of their case where a local threshold is met, and to bring agencies together to take a joined up, problem-solving approach to find a solution for the victim.
Relevant bodies and responsible authorities	• Councils. • Police. • Clinical Commissioning Groups in England and Local Health Boards in Wales. • Registered providers of social housing who are co-opted into this group.
Threshold	To be defined by the local agencies, but not more than three complaints in the previous six month period. May also take account of: • the persistence of the anti-social behaviour; • the harm or potential harm caused by the anti-social behaviour; • the adequacy of response to the anti-social behaviour. The relevant bodies (listed above) must publish details of the procedure.
Details	When an ASB Case Review is requested, the relevant bodies must decide whether the threshold has been met and communicate this to the victim. **If the threshold is met:** • a case review will be undertaken by the relevant bodies. They will share information related to the case, review what action has previously been taken and decide whether additional actions are possible. The local ASB Case Review procedure should clearly state the timescales in which the review will be undertaken; • the review will see the relevant bodies adopting a problem-solving approach to ensure that all the drivers and causes of the behaviour are identified and a solution sought, whilst ensuring that the victim receives appropriate support; • the victim is informed of the outcome of the review. Where further actions are necessary an action plan will be discussed with the victim, including timescales. **If the threshold is not met:** • although the formal procedures will not be invoked, this does provide an opportunity for the relevant bodies to review the case to determine whether there is more that can be done.
Who can use the ASB Case Review procedure?	• A victim of anti-social behaviour or another person acting on behalf of the victim with his or her consent, such as a carer or family member, Member of Parliament. local councillor or other professional. • The victim may be an individual, a business or a community group.
The legislation	Sections 104 and 105 of the Anti-social Behaviour, Crime and Policing Act 2014.
Protecting the vulnerable	The ASB Case Review or Community Trigger provides an important safety net for victims of persistent anti-social behaviour and those who may be most vulnerable.

The ASB Case Review/Community Trigger

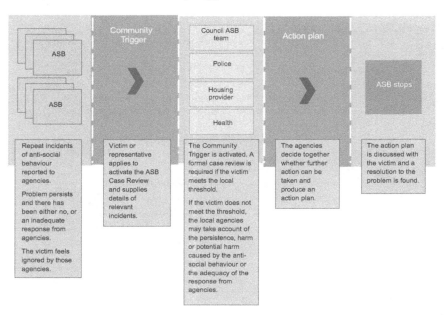

Repeat incidents of anti-social behaviour reported to agencies. Problem persists and there has been either no, or an inadequate response from agencies. The victim feels ignored by those agencies.	Victim or representative applies to activate the ASB Case Review and supplies details of relevant incidents.	The Community Trigger is activated. A formal case review is required if the victim meets the local threshold. If the victim does not meet the threshold, the local agencies may take account of the persistence, harm or potential harm caused by the anti-social behaviour or the adequacy of the response from agencies.	The agencies decide together whether further action can be taken and produce an action plan.	The action plan is discussed with the victim and a resolution to the problem is found.

Purpose

The ASB Case Review, often referred to as the 'Community Trigger', is an important statutory safety net for victims of anti-social behaviour who believe they have not had a satisfactory response to their complaints about anti-social behaviour. Where a locally determined threshold is met, victims can require the relevant bodies in the local area to undertake a formal review of the case, and those bodies have a statutory duty to undertake that review. In addition to the victim, the ASB Case Review can be activated by a person on behalf of the victim who is aware of the circumstances and acts with the victim's consent. This might include a family member, friend, carer, councillor, Member of Parliament or other professional.

Putting victims first: The 'Community Trigger' is an important safety net for victims of persistent anti-social behaviour. It provides a mechanism to ensure that their case is reviewed in order to secure a satisfactory resolution. The legislation requires the relevant local agencies to determine a local threshold for triggering the Case Review procedures. It is important that these agencies ensure that victims are aware of the procedures, the circumstances in which they can apply for a formal review, and how to do so. Consideration should also be given on how victims can best express the impact that the anti-social behaviour has had on their lives.

Who are the relevant bodies?

The relevant bodies in any area are those organisations listed below who must have an ASB Case Review/Community Trigger procedure in place and who must undertake a case review when a person asks for one and the local threshold is met. The relevant bodies are:

- the district council, unitary authority or relevant London borough council for the area;
- the police force covering the area;
- the relevant clinical commissioning group in England or local health board in Wales; and
- local providers of social housing who are co-opted into the local arrangements.

Providers of social housing as relevant bodies

The legislation allows for providers of social housing to be co-opted into local arrangements but it does not specify which housing providers should be co-opted. The recommended approach is to co-opt larger housing providers for the purposes of developing and reviewing the local procedures and setting the local threshold, with smaller providers involved where there are specific cases concerning their tenants.

For the purposes of the ASB Case Review or Community Trigger, local social housing providers include:

- in England: a private registered provider of social housing who grants tenancies of dwelling-houses in that area or who manages any house or other property in that area; and

- in Wales: a body registered as a social landlord under section 3 of the Housing Act 1996 who grants tenancies of dwelling-houses in that area or who manages any house or other property in that area.

Involving Police and Crime Commissioners

The local Police and Crime Commissioner must be consulted when the ASB Case Review/Community Trigger procedure is set up and whenever it is reviewed. In addition, the Police and Crime Commissioner can be involved directly in the procedure, for example by:

- auditing case reviews;
- providing a route for victims to query the decision on whether the threshold was met or the way in which the review was carried out; or
- monitoring use of the ASB Case Review/Community Trigger to identify any learning and best practice.

Police and Crime Commissioners also have responsibilities for the commissioning of victims services and may also want to ensure that local agencies consider how the victim is supported as part of the process.

What must the relevant bodies do?

The relevant bodies listed above must:

- set the local threshold for triggering ASB case reviews;
- establish and publish arrangements for conducting these reviews; and
- undertake a formal Case Review where an application is made and the local threshold is met.

Setting the local threshold

The relevant bodies should collectively agree an appropriate ASB Case Review/Community Trigger threshold, having regard to the nature of anti-social behaviour experienced by victims in their area and the working practices of the agencies involved.

The threshold must be no higher than three <u>qualifying complaints</u> of anti-social behaviour in a six month period.

Where a person makes an application for a case review and has made at least the set number of qualifying complaints, the threshold for a review is met and the relevant bodies must undertake the review.

What qualifies as a complaint?

For the purposes of the Case Review/Community Trigger procedures, a qualifying complaint is:

- where the anti-social behaviour was reported within one month of the alleged behaviour taking place; and
- the application to use the ASB Case Review/Community Trigger is made within six months of the report of anti- social behaviour.

It is open to the agencies involved in these reviews to set different levels to those set out above if appropriate for their area, provided that they do not lower the standard as set out here. The requirement for the anti-social behaviour to be recent is to prevent more historical incidents of anti-social behaviour being used to invoke these procedures.

The definition of anti-social behaviour in this context is behaviour causing harassment, alarm or distress to a member or members of the public. When deciding whether the threshold is met, agencies should consider the cumulative effect of the incidents and consider the harm or potential harm caused to the victim, rather than rigidly deciding whether each incident reached the level of harassment, alarm or distress.

Similarly, although housing-related anti-social behaviour has a lower test of nuisance or annoyance for an injunction under Part 1 of the 2014 Act, in such instances because of the victim's inability to separate themselves from the anti-social behaviour, the harm experienced may well result in harassment, alarm or distress for the purposes of the ASB Case Review/Community Trigger.

The ASB Case Review/Community Trigger is specifically designed to deal with anti-social behaviour. However anti- social behaviour can often be motivated by hate and the relevant bodies may wish to include reports of these incidents as part of their procedures.

Hate Crime

A hate crime is any criminal offence perceived by the victim or any other person to be motivated by hostility on the grounds of race, religion, sexual orientation, disability or transgender identity. Incidents can range from harassment, abusive language, criminal damage/damage to property, to threats and physical violence. Incidents of hate crime may manifest themselves as anti-social behaviour, but on investigation these incidents may be found to be targeted against some intrinsic part of the victim's identity (their race, religion, sexual orientation, disability or transgender identity).

There are a number of laws in place to deal with those who commit hate crimes, including public order offences and racially and religiously aggravated offences. The courts also have powers to enhance a perpetrator's sentence for any offence that is motivated by hatred or hostility towards the victim.

Action Against Hate: The UK Government's plan for tackling hate crime was published in July 2016 and brings together the work of a number of departments and agencies to prevent and tackle hate crime. While the Government plays a vital role in setting national direction, the response to hate crime will be led at the local level. An effective multi-agency response to hate crime will involve professionals, the voluntary sector and communities working together to tackle incidents early before they can escalate.

There is extensive guidance on responding to hate crime in the College of Policing Hate Crime Operational Guidance. It, and many other resources, can be viewed on the police hate crime website True Vision (www.report-it.org.uk).

Hate Crime creates fear and can have a devastating impact on individuals and communities. Individual incidents can send reverberations through communities, just as they can reinforce established patterns of prejudice and discrimination. Using Community Impact Statements to engage with communities helps criminal justice partners understand the wider impact of hate crime and can improve decision making and increase public confidence.

Setting the threshold: additional considerations

In considering whether the threshold is met, the relevant bodies should have regard to:
- the persistence of the anti-social behaviour;
- the harm or potential harm caused by the anti-social behaviour; and
- the adequacy of the response from agencies.

The harm, or the potential for harm to be caused to the victim, is an important consideration in determining whether the threshold is met because the more vulnerable will be less resilient to anti-social behaviour. People can be vulnerable for a number of reasons, and vulnerability or resilience can vary over time depending on personal circumstances and the nature of the anti-social behaviour. The relevant bodies should use their risk assessment procedures as part of the decision on whether the threshold is met. Risk assessment matrices cannot provide a definitive assessment of someone's needs, but they will assist agencies in judging an appropriate response. It may be beneficial for the relevant bodies to adopt a common risk assessment matrix, or to have an agreed matrix for the purposes of the ASB Case Review/Community Trigger.

Cases where there are repeated applications by people which, on investigation, relate to non-anti-social behaviour matters may be indicative of an underlying vulnerability or unmet need. Consequently, even where the threshold is not met, local agencies may wish to consider the possibility of hidden needs or risks which may require a response.

Behaviour which falls below the level of harassment, alarm or distress, may not meet the threshold, but when assessed on the grounds of potential harm to the victim, the impact of the behaviour may be such that the threshold is considered to be met.

Where the victim is considered to be particularly vulnerable, the relevant bodies should consider whether additional practical and emotional support can be offered to the victim.

Publishing the ASB Case Review/Community Trigger procedure

The relevant bodies must publish the ASB Case Review/Community Trigger procedure to ensure that victims are aware that they can apply to activate the procedures in appropriate circumstances.

Consideration should be given to where this information is published and how accessible the information is. For example, the title 'Community Trigger' in isolation may not be sufficient of itself to alert victims to the purpose of the procedures. More clearly linking the information to broader information about responding to anti-social behaviour, and making it clear that the procedure is about seeking a case review, is recommended.

The relevant bodies should decide an appropriate method and format for publicising the procedure, taking account of the needs of the local community. The information should be provided on the websites of all the relevant bodies, signposting the public to the lead agency's website, a point of contact and the procedures for activating the process. Consideration should be given to whether it is appropriate to translate the information into different languages.

Publishing a point of contact

The published information on the ASB Case Review/Community Trigger must include a point of contact for making an application. When publishing the point of contact it is good practice to provide a telephone number, email and postal address and a form which can be completed online.

> **Putting victims first**: Using the ASB Case Review/Community Trigger should be made as straightforward as possible for victims of anti-social behaviour.
>
> It is good practice to have a number of methods to contact an agency, recognising that some victims may feel more comfortable contacting one agency than another, or may not have access to the internet or, in the case of issues involving neighbours, may be reluctant to use the telephone for fear of being overheard. The ASB Case Review/ Community Trigger can be used by any person and agencies should consider how to make it as accessible as possible to young people, those who are vulnerable, have learning difficulties or do not speak English.

The ASB Case Review/Community Trigger procedure

The relevant bodies must work together to devise and agree the procedure for the ASB Case Review/Community Trigger. The procedure should ensure that the case review looks at what action has previously been taken in response to the victim's reports of anti-social behaviour. It must also include provision for a person to request a review of the way that their application for a case review has been dealt with, and the way in which the review was carried out.

A basic ASB Case Review/Community Trigger procedure

Each area should agree a procedure that suits the needs of victims and communities in their area. However, the basic outline of that procedure is likely to include the following steps:

- a victim of anti-social behaviour (or someone acting on their behalf) makes an application to use the ASB Case Review/Community Trigger;
- the relevant bodies decide whether the threshold is met;
- if the threshold is met, the relevant bodies share information about the case, consider whether any new relevant information needs to be obtained, review previous actions taken and propose a response. The victim is informed of the outcome, or agencies will work with the victim to devise and implement an action plan;
- if necessary, escalation and review.

When setting up the procedure the relevant bodies should consider how the ASB Case Review/Community Trigger can be built into existing processes. Many areas already have regular multi-agency meetings to discuss cases of anti-social behaviour. These may be suitable forums to undertake the case review. Alternatively, the relevant bodies may decide that it is more appropriate to have a separate forum to discuss case reviews. Where the perpetrator is under the age of 18, the youth offending team should be invited to attend the review.

Where most of the agency representatives have been involved in a particular case, consideration should be given to involving somebody independent in the review to provide an external or fresh perspective on the case and the action that has been taken.

Putting victims first: It is good practice to have somebody involved in the case review to represent the victim, such as from Victim Support or another organisation providing support for victims in the local area. Consideration should also be given to whether it is appropriate for the victim to be invited to attend the case review to help all members of the panel understand the level of harm and impact or whether, in the circumstances, there are good reasons for them not to do so. In such circumstances, it may more be appropriate to invite a representative of the victim to attend, especially where they have activated the case review on behalf of the victim.

The case review should not include a review of any decisions made by the Crown Prosecution Service (CPS). If a victim is not satisfied with a decision made by the CPS they should refer to the CPS complaints process, and the Victims' Right to Review Scheme. The latter makes it easier for victims to seek a review of a CPS decision not to bring charges against a suspect or to terminate proceedings, in relation to decisions made after 5 June 2013.

Sharing information

The effective operation of the ASB Case Review/Community Trigger requires the relevant bodies to share information for the purpose of carrying out the review. This may include details of previous complaints made by the victim, information about the effect the issue has had on others and details of what action has previously been taken. Relevant bodies should therefore have agreements in place for information sharing, risk assessments and a common understanding of the aims of the ASB Case Review/Community Trigger. Victims also need to give consent for information about them to be collected and shared between agencies.

The relevant bodies may request any person to disclose information for the purpose of the case review. If the request is made to a person who exercises public functions and they possess the information, they must disclose it. The only exception to that is where to share the information would be either:

  • in contravention of any of the provisions of the Data Protection Act 1998; or

  • prohibited by Part 1 of the Regulation of Investigatory Powers Act 2000.

Other than these two exceptions, disclosing information for the ASB Case Review/Community Trigger does not breach any obligation of confidence or any other restriction on the disclosure of information.

Sharing information: housing providers

Housing providers undertake several functions, including some that are public in nature and some that are not. If a request is made in relation to their functions that are considered to be public in nature, the information sharing duty applies. This is the case for housing providers who are co-opted into the group of relevant bodies as well as those who are not.

Sharing information

The Homes and Communities Agency's Regulatory Framework, Neighbourhood and Community Standard, requires registered housing providers to:

• co-operate with relevant partners to help improve social, environmental and economic wellbeing in areas where they own properties; and

• work in partnership with other agencies to prevent and tackle anti-social behaviour in the neighbourhoods where they own homes.

Making recommendations

The relevant bodies who undertake a case review may make recommendations to other agencies. The legislation places a duty on a person who carries out public functions to have regard to those recommendations. This means that they are not obliged to carry out the recommendations, but that they should acknowledge them and may be challenged if they choose not to carry them out without good reason.

The recommendations are likely to take the form of an action plan to resolve the anti-social behaviour. Whenever possible, the relevant bodies should involve the victim in devising the action plan to help ensure that it meets their needs. The relevant bodies will not be able to recommend the CPS to take action as it operates independently under the superintendence of the Attorney General, and must make decisions in accordance with the Code for Crown Prosecutors.

Responding to the victim

The Act places a duty on the relevant bodies to respond to the victim at particular points in the process. These include:

- the decision as to whether or not the threshold is met;
- the outcome of the review; and
- any recommendations made as an outcome of the review.

The relevant bodies should agree as part of the procedure whether one agency will communicate with all victims, or whether an appropriate agency will lead in a specific case. People who make use of the ASB Case Review/Community Trigger procedure may well feel that they have been let down by agencies in the past so it is important that they receive timely and consistent communication regarding their case.

When communicating with victims, local agencies should consider victim support issues and whether they could benefit from being signposted or referred to local victims services.

Publishing data:

The legislation states that relevant bodies must publish information covering:

- the number of applications for ASB Case Reviews received;
- the number of times the threshold for review was not met;
- the number of anti-social behaviour case reviews carried out; and
- the number of anti-social behaviour case reviews that resulted in recommendations being made.

This data can represent the whole area; it does not need to be broken down by relevant body. One relevant body can publish the information on behalf of all the relevant bodies in the area.

The data must be published at least annually, although the relevant bodies may wish to publish data more frequently, or to publish additional details. For example, the relevant bodies may publish information about which area applications came from, or the agencies that they related to, if this information is useful to communities and victims. Published information must not include details which could identify victims.

1.2   Community Remedy

Purpose	To give victims a say in the out-of-court punishment of perpetrators of less serious crime and anti-social behaviour.
The Community Remedy document	The Community Remedy document is a list of actions which may be chosen by the victim for the perpetrator to undertake in consequence of their behaviour or offending. The Act places a duty on the Police and Crime Commissioner to consult with members of the public and community representatives on what punitive, reparative or rehabilitative actions they would consider appropriate to be on the Community Remedy document.
Applicants / who can use the Community Remedy	• Police officer; • An investigating officer (which can include Police Community Support Officers for certain offences, if designated the power by their chief constable); • A person authorised by a relevant prosecutor for conditional cautions or youth conditional cautions.
Community resolutions	When dealing with anti-social behaviour or low-level offences through a community resolution the police officer may use the Community Remedy document as a means to engage the victim in having a say in the punishment of the perpetrator.
Test	• The officer must have evidence that the person has engaged in anti-social behaviour or committed an offence; • The person must admit to the behaviour or the offence (and agree to participate); • The officer must think that the evidence is enough for court proceedings including for a civil injunction, or impose a caution, but considers that a community resolution would be more appropriate.
Conditional cautions	The Community Remedy document should be considered when it is proposed that a perpetrator be given a conditional caution or youth conditional caution as a means of consulting the victim about the possible conditions to be attached to the caution.
Failure to comply	If the perpetrator fails to comply with a conditional caution or youth conditional caution they can face court action for the offence.
The legislation	Sections 101 to 103 of the Anti-social Behaviour, Crime and Policing Act 2014.

Community Remedy

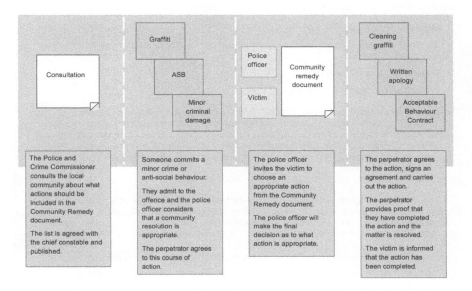

Purpose

All Police and Crime Commissioners, and the Mayor's Office for Policing and Crime in London, **must** have a Community Remedy document in place to set out how victims of less serious crime and anti-social behaviour can have a say in the punishment of perpetrators who receive an 'out of court' disposal; that is, a community resolution, conditional caution or youth conditional caution. Where a conditional caution or youth conditional caution is given, the Community Remedy provides a means of consulting the victim about possible conditions to be attached to the caution.

The Community Remedy document

The Community Remedy document is a list of actions that the victim will be invited to choose from when a community resolution is to be used. The list of actions may vary from one police force to another, based on what is available in the area and what the Police and Crime Commissioner and chief constable agree is appropriate. The Community Remedy document must be published.

361

Consultation

The Police and Crime Commissioner (and Mayor's Office for Policing and Crime in London) must consult on the actions to be included in the Community Remedy document with:

- members of the public;
- whichever community representatives the Police and Crime Commissioner considers appropriate to consult;
- the relevant local authority; and
- the chief officer of police for the area.

The public consultation may be undertaken in whatever format the Police and Crime Commissioner considers appropriate (for example, online consultation, talking to community groups or local victims groups, via local newspapers and so on) and may be undertaken as part of another consultation such as on the local Police and Crime Plan. The Community Remedy document may be revised at any time, particularly when new options are to be added.

Actions to be included in the Community Remedy document

The Police and Crime Commissioner and the chief constable will agree the actions that are listed in the Community Remedy document. These actions must be appropriate and proportionate to the types of offences for which community resolutions are used, and seek to have a positive impact on the perpetrator. Each of the actions must have:

- a punitive element, reflecting the effects on the victim and the wider community; or
- a reparative element, to provide appropriate restitution/reparation to the victim; or
- a rehabilitative element, to address the causes of the perpetrator's behaviour; or
- a combination of the above.

What could be included?

The legislation does not specify what actions should be included in the Community Remedy document. These will vary between areas, reflecting the views of local people and the availability of activities. Examples of actions that might be included are:

- mediation (for example, to resolve a neighbour dispute);
- a written or verbal apology;
- the perpetrator signing an Acceptable Behaviour Contract – where they agree not to behave anti-socially in the future – or face more formal consequences;
- take part in a restorative justice activity such as a neighbourhood justice panel;
- paying an appropriate amount for damage to be repaired or stolen property to be replaced;
- participation in structured activities that are either educational or rehabilitative, funded by the Police and Crime Commissioner as part of their efforts to reduce crime; or
- reparation to the community (for example, by doing local unpaid work for a short period).

---

14   **Anti-social behaviour powers** – Statutory guidance for frontline professionals

Community Resolutions

Community resolutions are a means of resolving less serious offences or instances of anti-social behaviour. They are used where the perpetrator has been identified and admits to the behaviour or offence in question and the police believe that there is sufficient evidence to obtain a civil injunction or other disposal, but consider that a community resolution would be a more appropriate and proportionate response.

Community resolutions can be used by:

- a police officer;

- an investigating officer (a person employed by a police force or a Police and Crime Commissioner's office or who is under the direction and control of the chief officer and has been designated as an investigating officer); and

- a police community support officer in relation to offences which their chief constable has designated them powers to deal with or more generally on the authority of a police officer of appropriate rank.

Using the community remedy document with community resolutions

When a community resolution is used, the officer must make a reasonable effort to obtain the views of the victim on whether the perpetrator should carry out any of the actions in the Community Remedy document. If the officer considers that the action chosen by the victim is appropriate, the perpetrator should be asked to carry out that action. The officer will have ultimate responsibility for ensuring that the action offered is appropriate and proportionate to the nature of the anti-social behaviour or the offence committed. Where there are multiple victims, the officer should make reasonable efforts to take the views of all victims into account.

Community resolutions are entirely voluntary. The officer should ensure that the victim understands the purpose of community resolutions and that he or she knows that they can choose not to be involved. This will help to ensure the victim has realistic expectations of what can be achieved. For example, the resolution may not be legally enforceable if the perpetrator fails to complete the agreed action.

Putting victims first: The Community Remedy gives victims more say in the out of court punishment of perpetrators. However, the victim's involvement is voluntary and the victim must not be made to feel that they should take part in a process that they are not comfortable with, that they think may put them at risk, or that they do not believe will be of benefit to them.

When using the Community Remedy the officer should consider the most appropriate way to involve the victim. If the victim is under 18 or vulnerable, they may require a family member or carer to assist their understanding of the purpose of community resolutions and choose an action from the Community Remedy document.

If the victim is not contactable, or it cannot be ascertained who the victim is, for example, if the offence is graffiti in a public place, the officer may choose an appropriate action for the perpetrator to undertake.

Appendix C   Guidance

Conditional caution and youth conditional caution

When a conditional caution or a youth conditional caution is used, the officer or authorised person must make reasonable efforts to obtain the views of the victim as to whether the perpetrator should carry out any of the actions listed in the Community Remedy document. If the officer issuing the conditional caution considers that the action chosen by the victim is appropriate, the action can form part of the conditions of the caution. The police officer or investigating officer (or prosecutor in some cases) will have ultimate responsibility for ensuring that the sanction offered to the perpetrator is appropriate and proportionate to the offence. If there are multiple victims, the officer must make reasonable efforts to take the views of all the victims into account.

Conditional cautions are available for all offences except domestic violence and hate crimes, which are excluded from the conditional caution scheme. For full details of the considerations to apply when deciding whether to use a conditional caution, see the Ministry of Justice Code of practice for adult conditional cautions:

https://www.gov.uk/government/publications/code-of-practice-for-adult-conditional-cautions

A youth conditional caution is available for any offence, except for domestic violence or hate crime. Full details can be found in the Ministry of Justice Code of practice for youth conditional cautions:

https://www.gov.uk/government/publications/code-of-practice-for-youth-conditional-cautions

Part 2: More effective powers

The powers for dealing with anti-social behaviour provided by the Anti-social Behaviour, Crime and Policing Act 2014 are deliberately flexible to allow professionals to use them to protect the public from different forms of anti-social behaviour.

Working together and sharing information

The powers allow the police, councils, social landlords and others to deal quickly with issues as they arise, with agencies working together where appropriate to ensure the best results for victims. To assist joined-up working, an effective information-sharing protocol is essential. There is already a duty on some bodies (such as the police and councils) to work together and in respect of anti-social behaviour specifically, there is a specific duty on specified bodies to work together when the ASB Case Review/Community Trigger is activated, as set out earlier in this guidance.

Vulnerability

The powers also strengthen the protection to victims and communities and provide fast and effective responses to deal with anti-social behaviour. Particular consideration should be given to the needs and circumstances of the most vulnerable when applying the powers to ensure that they are not disproportionately and unreasonably impacted upon, and local agencies must be satisfied that the behaviour meets the legal tests. Any use of these powers must be compliant with the Human Rights Act 1998, the Equality Act 2010 (in particular the public sector equality duty pursuant to section 149) along with all other relevant legislation.

Assessing the risk to victims

It is good practice for agencies to assess the risk of harm to the victim, and their potential vulnerability, when they receive a complaint about anti-social behaviour. This should be the starting point of a case-management approach to dealing with anti-social complaints. The welfare, safety and well-being of victims must be the main consideration at every stage of the process. It is therefore important to identify the effect that the reported anti-social behaviour is having on the victim, particularly if repeated incidents are having a cumulative effect on their well-being. A continuous and organised risk assessment will help to identify cases that are causing, or could result in, serious harm to the victim, either as a one-off incident or as part of a targeted and persistent campaign of anti-social behaviour against the victim.

Early and informal interventions

Early intervention, especially through informal approaches, may often be all that is necessary to stop incidents of anti-social behaviour. Such interventions can establish clear standards of behaviour and reinforce the message that anti-social behaviour is not tolerated. In many cases, awareness of the impact of the behaviour on victims, and the threat of more formal enforcement, may be sufficient to encourage an individual to change their behaviour. Frontline professionals will be best placed to decide when and how to use these approaches, but it is recommended that the use of informal methods be considered first in most cases, and particularly when dealing with young people as a means of preventing poor behaviour from escalating.

It is, however, the case that informal intervention may not be the appropriate first step in the circumstances of some cases, such as where the victim is at risk of harm, and it is right that frontline professionals make informed decisions about the approach to be taken.

Possible informal interventions include:

- **A verbal or written warning**

  In deciding whether or not to use a verbal or written warning, the police, council or housing officer should still be satisfied that there is evidence that anti-social behaviour has occurred, or is likely to occur. The warning should be specific about the behaviour in question and why it is not acceptable, the impact that this is having on the victim or community and the consequences of non-compliance.

  Where appropriate, local agencies should alert each other when a warning has been given so that it can be effectively monitored and a record should be kept so that it can be used as evidence in court proceedings later, if matters are taken to that stage.

- **A community resolution**

  Community resolutions are a means of resolving less serious offences or instances of anti-social behaviour through informal agreement between the parties involved as opposed to progression through the criminal justice process. A community resolution may be used with both youth and adult perpetrators and allows the police to deal more proportionately with less serious crime and anti-social behaviour, taking account of the needs of the victim, perpetrator and wider community.

  Community resolutions are primarily aimed at first time perpetrators where genuine remorse has been expressed, and where an out-of-court disposal is more appropriate than taking more formal action. The Community Remedy document discussed in Part 1 of this guidance must be used when dealing with anti- social behaviour or less serious offences out of court through community resolutions.

- **Mediation**

  In appropriate circumstances, mediation can be an effective way of resolving an issue by bringing all parties together. This can be effective in resolving neighbour disputes, family conflicts, lifestyle differences such as noise nuisance complaints and similar situations. However, mediation is unlikely to work if forced on those involved. All parties should be willing to come to the table and discuss their issues.

  It is not for the mediator to establish a solution to the issue as, in most cases, they will have already tried this with each party unsuccessfully. For mediation to deliver long-term solutions, those in dispute should agree a solution. The mediator should facilitate the conversation and draw up any agreement if required for all parties to sign-up to if agreement is reached.

- **Acceptable Behaviour Contracts/Agreements**

  An acceptable behaviour contract or agreement is a written agreement between a perpetrator of anti-social behaviour and the agency or agencies acting locally to prevent that behaviour. It can be an effective way of dealing with anti-social individuals, and particularly young people, to nip the problem behaviour in the bud before it escalates. They provide an opportunity to include positive requirements as well as prohibitions to help support the person tackle any underlying issues which are driving their behaviour.

The terms of an acceptable behaviour contract or agreement should be discussed with the perpetrator before they are drafted and signed to help encourage compliance. However, there is no formal sanction associated with refusing to sign, although in such circumstances, this may suggest that a Civil Injunction or a Criminal Behaviour Order might be the more appropriate approach.

Similarly, there are no formal sanctions associated with breaching an acceptable behaviour contract or agreement, and where this occurs, consideration can be given to taking further steps, such as seeking a Civil Injunction, if the circumstances warrant this. Where this is the case, the work undertaken as part of drafting the acceptable behaviour contract or agreement can form part of the evidence pack for the court.

- **Parenting contracts**

Where informal interventions are used with a young person under 18, his or her parents or guardians should be contacted in advance of the decision to take action. In many cases, they may be able to play an important part in ensuring the individual changes their behaviour. While there are formal routes such as parenting orders, at this stage it may be appropriate to include a role for the parent in any acceptable behaviour contract. However, where the behaviour of the parent or guardian is part of the issue (either because they are a bad influence or are failing to provide suitable supervision) agencies could consider a parenting contract. These are similar to an acceptable behaviour contract but are signed by the parent or guardian. They could also be considered where the child in question is under 10 and where other interventions are not appropriate for the perpetrator themselves.

- **Support and counselling**

The anti-social behaviour powers allow professionals to respond to the underlying causes of anti-social behaviour, for example through positive requirements attached to a Civil Injunction or Criminal Behaviour Order. However, providing positive support does not have to wait for formal court action, and can be given as part of any informal intervention, for example by providing support around overcoming substance misuse or alcohol dependency that may be linked to the person's anti-social behaviour.

Conclusion

In many cases, informal and early intervention can be successful in changing behaviour and protecting communities. Such interventions may be included in local plans to deal with anti-social behaviour but should not replace formal interventions where these are the most effective means of dealing with anti-social behaviour.

2.1   Civil Injunction

Purpose	To stop or prevent individuals engaging in anti-social behaviour quickly, nipping problems in the bud before they escalate.
Applicants	• Local councils; • Social landlords; • Police (including British Transport Police); • Transport for London; • Environment Agency and Natural Resources Wales; and • NHS Protect
Test	• On the balance of probabilities; • Behaviour likely to cause harassment, alarm or distress (non-housing related anti-social behaviour); or • Conduct capable of causing nuisance or annoyance (housing-related anti-social behaviour); and • Just and convenient to grant the injunction to prevent anti-social behaviour.
Details	• Issued by the county court and High Court for over 18s and the youth court for under 18s. • Injunction will include prohibitions and can also include positive requirements to get the perpetrator to address the underlying causes of their anti-social behaviour. • Agencies must consult youth offending teams in applications against under 18s.
Penalty on breach	• Breach of the injunction is not a criminal offence, but breach must be proved to the criminal standard, that is, beyond reasonable doubt. • Over 18s: civil contempt of court with unlimited fine or up to two years in prison. • Under 18s: supervision order or, as a very last resort, a civil detention order of up to three months for 14-17 year olds.
Appeals	• Over 18s to the High Court; and • Under 18s to the Crown Court.
The legislation	Sections 1 to 21 of the Anti-social Behaviour, Crime and Policing Act 2014.

Civil Injunction

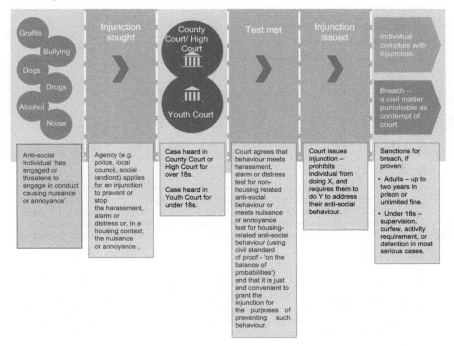

Graffiti / Bullying / Dogs / Drugs / Alcohol / Noise	Injunction sought	County Court/ High Court · Youth Court	Test met	Injunction issued	Individual complies with injunction · Breach – a civil matter punishable as contempt of court
Anti-social individual 'has engaged or threatens to engage in conduct causing nuisance or annoyance'.	Agency (e.g. police, local council, social landlord) applies for an injunction to prevent or stop the harassment, alarm or distress or, in a housing context, the nuisance or annoyance .	Case heard in County Court or High Court for over 18s. Case heard in Youth Court for under 18s.	Court agrees that behaviour meets harassment, alarm or distress test for non-housing related anti-social behaviour or meets nuisance or annoyance test for housing-related anti-social behaviour (using civil standard of proof - 'on the balance of probabilities') and that it is just and convenient to grant the injunction for the purposes of preventing such behaviour.	Court issues injunction – prohibits individual from doing X, and requires them to do Y to address their anti-social behaviour.	Sanctions for breach, if proven: · Adults – up to two years in prison or unlimited fine. · Under 18s – supervision, curfew, activity requirement, or detention in most serious cases.

Purpose

The injunction under Part 1 of the Anti-social Behaviour, Crime and Policing Act 2014 is a civil power to deal with anti-social individuals. The injunction can offer fast and effective protection for victims and communities and set a clear standard of behaviour for perpetrators, stopping the person's behaviour from escalating.

Although the injunction is a civil power, it is a formal sanction and in appropriate cases professionals will want to consider whether an informal approach might be preferable before resorting to court action, especially in the case of under 18s. However, where informal approaches have not worked or professionals decide that a formal response is needed, they are free to apply to the court for a civil injunction.

Who can apply for an injunction?

A number of agencies can apply for the injunction, which ensures that the body best placed to lead on a specific case can do so.

The agencies who can apply for an injunction are:

- a local council;
- a housing provider;
- the chief officer of police for the local area;
- the chief constable of the British Transport Police;
- Transport for London;
- the Environment Agency and Natural Resources Wales;
- NHS Protect.

The legal tests for granting an injunction

These are:

- **non-housing related**

  For anti-social behaviour in a non-housing related context the test is that the conduct concerned has caused, or is likely to cause, harassment, alarm or distress to any person. This will apply, for example, where the anti-social behaviour has occurred in a public place, such as a town or city centre, shopping mall, or local park, and where the behaviour does not affect the housing management functions of a social landlord or people in their homes.

- **housing-related**

  For anti-social behaviour in a housing context the nuisance or annoyance test will apply, that is, where the conduct is capable of causing nuisance or annoyance to a person in relation to that person's occupation of residential premises or the conduct is capable of causing housing-related nuisance or annoyance to any person. Only social landlords, local councils or the police are able to apply for an injunction under these provisions. In the case of social landlords only, "housing-related" means directly or indirectly relating to their housing management function.

  The injunction can be applied for by the police, local councils and social landlords against perpetrators in social housing, the private-rented sector and owner-occupiers. This means that it can be used against perpetrators who are not necessarily tenants of the social landlord applying for the order.

  The injunction can also be used in situations where the perpetrator has allowed another person to engage in anti-social behaviour, as opposed to actively engaging in such behaviour themselves. For example, in a case where another person, such as a visitor or lodger, is or has been behaving anti- socially, the injunction could be used against the problem visitor, lodger or owner if applicable. An agency seeking to apply for the injunction must produce evidence to the civil standard of proof, that is, 'on the balance of probabilities', and satisfy the court that it is both 'just and convenient' to grant the order.

> **Putting victims first:** In deciding whether the individual's conduct has caused or is likely to cause harassment, alarm or distress or is capable of causing nuisance or annoyance, agencies should contact all potential victims and witnesses to understand the wider harm to individuals and the community. Not only will this ensure that victims and communities feel that their problem is being taken seriously, it will also aid the evidence-gathering process for the application to the court.

22   **Anti-social behaviour powers** – Statutory guidance for frontline professionals

Details

Who can the injunction be issued against? A court may grant the injunction against anyone who is 10 years of age or over. Applications against individuals who are 18 years of age or over must be made in the county court or High Court, and applications against individuals who are under 18 must be made in the youth court.

Intergenerational or 'mixed aged' cases: Where a hearing involves more than one individual and involves both over 18s and under 18s, the applicant can apply to the youth court to have the cases heard together as joint hearings. The youth court must find that it is in the interests of justice to hear the 'mixed aged' case and, if it does so, the case can only be heard in that court – the joint hearing cannot be heard in the county court. However, subsequent hearings (breach etc.) involving individuals over 18 will take place in the county court.

Dealing with young people: Applicants must consult the local youth offending team if the application is against someone under the age of 18 and inform any other body or individual the applicant thinks appropriate, for example, a youth charity that is already working with the young person. Although the consultation requirement does not mean that the youth offending team can veto the application, it is important that applicants fully consider and take into account representations from the youth offending team as part of developing good partnership working in cases involving young people.

The youth offending team will be important in getting the young person to adhere to the conditions in the injunction and that they are understood. The conditions will be overseen by a responsible officer in the youth offending team or children and family services. The youth offending team will also work with applicants as part of a multi-agency approach to ensure that positive requirements in the injunction are tailored to the needs of the young person.

When can injunctions be used? The injunction can be used to deal with a wide range of behaviours, many of which can cause serious harm to victims and communities in both housing-related and non-housing related situations. This includes vandalism, public drunkenness, aggressive begging, irresponsible dog ownership, noisy or abusive behaviour towards neighbours, or bullying. Injunctions should not be used to stop reasonable, trivial or benign behaviour that has not caused, or is not likely to cause, anti-social behaviour to victims or communities, and potential applicants are encouraged to make reasonable and proportionate judgements about the appropriateness of the proposed response before making an application for an injunction.

The Civil Injunction can also be used to tackle gang related activity, either directly on gang members or on those being exploited by gangs in order to disrupt their operations. This can be particularly useful in cases of 'county lines' where urban gangs exploit children and vulnerable people to move drugs and money to suburban areas and market and coastal towns. In such cases, the conditions of the injunction can include prohibitions on entering certain areas or affiliating with certain individuals. They could also include positive requirements such as engaging in drug treatment if the reason they became involved with, and remain indebted to, the gang is because of a drug dependency.

Applicants should also consider consulting the relevant local authority as they may hold information which is of relevance and/or which may need to be considered as part of the application. For example, a young person may be a child in need or on a child protection plan and additional safeguarding measures may be required. The local authority may also hold information which supports the application.

What to include: The injunction will include relevant prohibitions to get individuals to stop behaving anti-socially. It can also include positive requirements to get the individual to deal with the underlying cause of their behaviour. Agencies will have the discretion to tailor the positive requirements in each case to address the respondent's individual circumstances, behaviour and needs. There may be opportunities to work with voluntary sector organisations.

Positive requirements might, for example, include the respondent:

- attending alcohol awareness classes for alcohol-related problems;

- attending dog training classes provided by animal welfare charities where the issue is to do with irresponsible dog ownership; or

- attending mediation sessions with neighbours or victims.

The prohibitions or requirements in the injunction must be reasonable and must not, so far as practicable:

- interfere with the times, if any, at which the respondent normally works or attends school or any other educational establishment; or

- conflict with the requirements of any other court order or injunction to which the respondent may be subject.

In addition, applicants should also consider the impact on any caring responsibilities the perpetrator may have and, if they have a disability, whether he or she is capable of complying with the proposed prohibitions or requirements.

A draft of the proposed terms of the injunction should include all proposed prohibitions and requirements, their duration and any powers of arrest attached. Applicants will need to be prepared for the court to examine each prohibition and requirement, and will need to be able to prove how each will help stop or prevent the respondent from engaging in or threatening to engage in anti-social behaviour in the future. It is also important that any requirement is clear about who is responsible for supervising compliance and the court must receive evidence about its suitability and enforceability. Where two or more requirements are included the court must consider their compatibility with each other.

Putting victims first: Keeping victims and communities updated on enforcement action at key points can help them to deal with the impact the behaviour is having. Victims may feel that their complaint has been ignored if they do not see changes to the behaviour. Letting victims know what is happening can make a big difference.

Duration of injunctions: Prohibitions or requirements in the injunction can be for a fixed or indefinite period for adult perpetrators. In the case of under 18s the prohibitions or requirements must have a specified time limit, with a maximum term of 12 months.

Exclusion from the home: The court may exclude a perpetrator over the age of 18 from any premises or an area specified within the terms of the injunction. This can include their home, where the court thinks that the anti-social behaviour includes the use, or threatened use, of violence against other persons, or there is a significant risk of harm. The word harm is defined in section 20 of the legislation as including "serious ill-treatment or abuse, whether physical or not" – which means that it could include emotional or psychological harm, such as harassment or racial abuse.

Social landlords will only be able to apply to the court to exclude their own tenants and visitors to properties managed by them, whilst councils and the police will be the lead agencies in applying to exclude private tenants or owner-occupiers from their homes. In cases where the police or local council is the lead agency in an application to exclude a social tenant, they should consult the landlord. If the exclusion is applied to someone in privately rented accommodation or in residential leasehold housing, the police or council should, where circumstances permit, inform and consult the landlord (generally referred to in the leasehold as the freeholder) beforehand.

We do not expect the power of exclusion to be used often and the court will pay special attention to issues of proportionality. As such, applications should only be made for exclusion in extreme cases that meet the higher threshold set out above.

Publicising an injunction issued to a young person: Making the public aware of the perpetrator and the terms of the order can be an important part of the process in dealing with anti-social behaviour and providing reassurance to victims, as well as providing the information people need to identify and report breaches. The decision to publicise the injunction will be taken by the police or council unless the court has made a section 39 order (Children and Young Persons Act 1933) prohibiting publication. When deciding whether to publicise the injunction, public authorities (including the courts) must consider that it is necessary and proportionate to interfere with the young person's right to privacy, and the likely impact on a young person's behaviour. This will need to be balanced against the need to provide re-assurance to the victims and the wider community as well as providing information so that they can report any breaches. Each case should be decided carefully on its own facts.

'Without notice' applications: Injunctions can be applied for 'without notice' being given to the perpetrator in exceptional cases to stop serious harm to victims. They should not be made routinely or in place of inadequate preparation for normal 'with notice' applications. The notification and consultation requirements that apply to 'with notice' applications do not apply to 'without notice' applications.

Interim injunctions: The court will grant an interim injunction if a 'without notice' application is successful. The court may also grant an interim injunction where a standard application is adjourned. The interim injunction can only include prohibitions, not positive requirements. When applying for an interim injunction, the applicant should ensure that the application presents the victim's case and also why the interim injunction is necessary.

Variation and discharge of injunctions: The court has the power to vary or discharge the injunction upon application by either the perpetrator or the applicant. If the applicant wishes to discharge or vary the injunction, they should notify the people and organisations they consulted as part of the initial application process. Applicants may consider applying to vary the injunction in response to changes in the respondent's behaviour. The powers of the court to vary the injunction include:

- to remove a prohibition or requirement in the injunction;
- to include a prohibition or requirement in the injunction;
- to reduce the period for which a prohibition or requirement has effect;
- to extend the period for which a prohibition or requirement has effect; or
- to attach a power of arrest, or extend the period for which a power of arrest has effect.

If the court dismisses an application to vary the injunction, the relevant party is not allowed to make a further application without the consent of the court or the agreement of the other party.

Power of arrest: The court can attach a power of arrest to any prohibition or requirement in the injunction, except a positive requirement, that is, a requirement that the respondent participates in a particular activity. The court can only attach a power of arrest if:

- the anti-social behaviour in which the respondent has engaged, or threatens to engage, consists of or includes the use, or threatened use, of violence against other persons; or

- there is a significant risk of harm to other persons from the respondent.

If the applicant believes a power of arrest is appropriate, they should present this by way of written evidence. Such evidence may indicate that the respondent poses a high level of risk to the victim or the community should any of the conditions in the injunction be breached, for example, where there is a history of violent behaviour.

Where a power of arrest is attached to a condition of the injunction, a police officer can arrest the respondent without warrant if he or she has reasonable cause to believe that a breach has occurred. The police must present the respondent to court within 24 hours of their arrest (except on Sunday, Christmas Day and Good Friday).

If the applicant thinks that the respondent has breached a term of the injunction to which a power of arrest has not been attached, they may apply to the court for an arrest warrant. The application must be made to a judge in the county court in the case of an adult and a justice of the peace in the case of respondents below the age of 18. The court may then issue a warrant for the respondent's arrest and to be brought before the court but only if it has reasonable grounds for believing the respondent has breached a provision in the injunction. The police must inform the applicant when the respondent is arrested.

Hearsay evidence: Hearsay and professional witness evidence allow for the identities of those who are unable to give evidence due to fear or intimidation, to be protected. This is especially important as cases can involve anti-social behaviour in residential areas where local people and those targeted by the behaviour may feel unable to come forward for fear of reprisals. Hearsay evidence could be provided by a police officer, healthcare official, or any other professional who has interviewed the witness directly.

Penalty on breach: Breach of the injunction is not a criminal offence. However, due to the potential severity of the penalties which the court can impose on respondents, the criminal standard of proof – 'beyond reasonable doubt' – is applied in breach proceedings.

For adults, breach is dealt with by a civil contempt of court, which is punishable by up to two years in prison and/or an unlimited fine. The imprisonment is for contempt of court, not for the conduct. For under 18s, breach proceedings are dealt with in the youth court and could result in a supervision order with a supervision, curfew or activity requirement. In the most serious cases, (that is, 'where the court determines that because of the severity or extent of the breach no other power available to it is appropriate') the court may impose a detention order on a young person for breaching the terms of the injunction, including breach of a positive requirement. For under 18s, only those between 14 and 17 years of age can be detained for breaching the injunction and they cannot be detained for longer than three months.

Remands: The court has the power to remand a perpetrator in custody or on bail after they have been arrested for suspected breach of the injunction (with or without warrant). An under 18 can only be remanded in custody on medical grounds, that is, after obtaining evidence from a registered medical practitioner the court is satisfied that the young person is suffering from a mental disorder and it would be impracticable to get a medical report for the young person if they were granted bail. The court has discretion as to whether to remand a person on bail or in custody.

Appeals: Appeals may be lodged by both the applicant and perpetrator following the grant, refusal, variation or discharge of the injunction. A decision by the county court (in the case of proceedings in respect of an adult) may be appealed to the High Court. Appeals against decisions of the youth court in under 18 cases are heard in the Crown Court.

2.2 Criminal Behaviour Order

Purpose	Issued by any criminal court against a person who has been convicted of an offence to tackle the most persistently anti-social individuals who are also engaged in criminal activity.
Applicants	The prosecution, in most cases the Crown Prosecution Service, either at its own initiative or following a request from the police or council.
Test	• That the court is satisfied beyond reasonable doubt that the offender has engaged in behaviour that has caused or is likely to cause harassment, alarm or distress to any person; and • The court considers that making the order will help prevent the offender from engaging in such behaviour.
Details	• Issued by any criminal court on conviction for any criminal offence. • The anti-social behaviour does not need to be part of the criminal offence. • Order will include prohibitions to stop the anti-social behaviour but can also include positive requirements to get the offender to address the underlying causes of their behaviour. • Agencies must find out the view of the youth offending team for applications in respect of anybody under 18.
Penalty on breach	• Breach of the order is a criminal offence and must be proved to a criminal standard of proof, that is, beyond reasonable doubt. • For over 18s on summary conviction: up to six months imprisonment or a fine or both. • For over 18s on conviction on indictment: up to five years imprisonment or a fine or both. • For under 18s: the sentencing powers in the youth court apply.
Appeal	• Appeals against orders made in the magistrates' court (which includes the youth court) lie to the Crown Court. • Appeals against orders made in the Crown Court lie to the Court of Appeal.
The legislation	Sections 22 to 33 of the Anti-social Behaviour, Crime and Policing Act 2014.

375

Criminal Behaviour Order

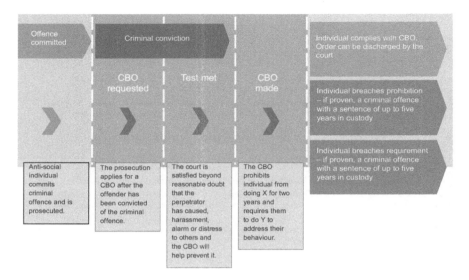

Purpose

The Criminal Behaviour Order (CBO) is available on conviction for any criminal offence in any criminal court. The court may make a CBO so long as the court imposes a sentence in respect of the offence or discharges the offender conditionally. The order is intended for tackling the most serious and persistent offenders where their behaviour has brought them before a criminal court.

Applicants: The prosecution may apply for a CBO after the offender has been convicted of a criminal offence. The prosecution can make such an application at its own initiative or following a request from a council or the police. The CBO hearing will occur after, or at the same time as, sentencing for the criminal conviction.

Good relationships between local agencies and the CPS will be important to ensure that the CBO application can be properly reviewed and notice of it served as soon as practicable, without waiting for the verdict in the criminal case. Agencies should consider setting up local information exchanges to make sure that the CBO is considered in appropriate cases where anti-social behaviour is brought before a criminal court.

The test: For a CBO to be made the court must be satisfied beyond reasonable doubt that the offender has engaged in behaviour that caused, or was likely to cause, harassment, alarm or distress to any person and that making the order will help in preventing the offender from engaging in such behaviour.

Details

When can a Criminal Behaviour Order be used? The CBO can be used to deal with a wide range of anti-social behaviours following an individual's conviction for a criminal offence; for example, threatening others in the community, persistently being drunk and aggressive in public, or to deal with anti-social behaviour associated with a more serious conviction, such as for burglary or street robbery. The CBO can also be used to address the anti-social behaviour of gang members, for example to prevent them from affiliating with certain individuals or to require them to attend a job readiness course to help them get employment.

However, an application for a CBO does not require a link between the criminal behaviour which led to the conviction and the anti-social behaviour it addresses for it to be issued by the court. Agencies must make proportionate and reasonable judgements before applying for a CBO, and conditions of an order should not be designed to stop reasonable, trivial or benign behaviour that has not caused, or is unlikely to cause, harassment, alarm or distress to victims or communities.

An application for a CBO does not require a link between the criminal behaviour which led to the conviction and the anti-social behaviour for it to be issued by the court.

Consultation: The only formal consultation requirement applies where an offender is under 18 years of age. In these cases, the prosecution must find out the views of the local youth offending team before applying for the CBO. The views of the youth offending team must be included in the file of evidence forwarded to the prosecution. In practice, the consultation with the youth offending team must be carried out by the organisation preparing the application for the CBO; that is, the council or the police.

The legislation has deliberately kept formal consultation requirements to a minimum to enable agencies to act quickly where needed to protect victims and communities. However, in most cases it is likely that the police or local council will wish to consult with other agencies. This could include local organisations that have come into contact with the individual, such as schools and colleges of further education, providers of probation services, social services, mental health services, housing providers or others. Their views should be considered before the decision is made to ask the CPS to consider applying for a CBO. This will ensure that an order is the proper course of action in each case and that the terms of the order are appropriate.

Evidence not heard in the criminal case can still be admissible at the CBO hearing, for example, evidence of other anti-social behaviour by the offender and information about why an order is appropriate in the terms asked for. Witnesses who might be reluctant to give evidence in person may have their evidence accepted as a written statement, or given by someone such as a police officer as hearsay evidence, but this will depend on the circumstances of the case.

Special measures are available in CBO proceedings for witnesses under 18 and vulnerable and intimidated adult witnesses (sections 16 and 17, Youth Justice and Criminal Evidence Act 1999). The court has to satisfy itself that the special measure, or combination of special measures, is likely to maximise the quality of the witness's evidence before granting an application for special measures.

Interim orders: In cases where an offender is convicted of an offence but the court is adjourned for sentencing, or the CBO hearing is adjourned after sentence, an interim order can be granted if the court thinks that it is just to do so. The prosecution can apply for the interim order.

Duration of a Criminal Behaviour Order: The terms of the CBO must include the duration of the order. For adults this is a minimum of two years, up to an indefinite period. For under 18s the order must be between one and three years.

Prohibitions and requirements: The CBO must clearly describe the details of what the offender is not allowed to do (prohibitions) as well as what they must do (requirements). Orders can include prohibitions or requirements or both. It is up to the court to decide which are needed to help prevent further anti-social behaviour and which measures are most appropriate and available to tackle the underlying cause of the behaviour. So far as practicable, these must not interfere with an offender's education or work commitments or conflict with any other court order or injunction that the offender is subject to. In addition practitioners should, in proposing prohibitions or requirements to the court, also consider the impact on any caring responsibilities the respondent may have and, in the event that the respondent has any disability, whether he or she is capable of complying with the proposed prohibitions or requirements.

The Crown Prosecution Service has issued a guide to assist the police and local councils in preparing CBO applications setting out the general principles to consider; for example, the prohibitions need to deal with the behaviour in question that has caused or is likely to cause harassment, alarm or distress. The order and requirements need to be proportionate and specific, and clear and easy to understand. Requirements could include:

- attendance at an anger management course where an offender finds it difficult to respond without violence;
- youth mentoring;
- a substance misuse awareness session where an offender's anti-social behaviour occurs when they have been drinking or using drugs; or
- a job readiness course to help an offender get employment and move them away from the circumstances that cause them to commit anti-social behaviour.

Before proposing any requirements evidence must be provided in support of that requirement including information about the person or organisation who will be responsible for supervising compliance and the suitability and enforceability of the requirement. For any requirements where a course is proposed, details of that course and what is involved should be provided, including frequency of appointments and the issues that the appointments will cover or address.

In addition, the responsible person or organisation must inform the police if the offender fails to comply with a requirement; must be a willing participant in the order and be prepared to assist with enforcement.

> **Putting victims first**: The potential impact on the victim or victims will be at the heart of the consideration of the terms of the CBO. Stopping the anti-social behaviour is for the benefit of the victim and thinking about how the terms of the order will impact on the victim is critical. What would they think? Would they be satisfied? It is also good practice to take the time to explain the terms of the order to the victims so that they are aware of the outcome of the court case.

Publicising a CBO issued to a young person: Making the public aware of the offender and the terms of the order can be an important part of the response to anti-social behaviour. It can provide reassurance for communities that action is being taken and it will provide the information that local people need to identify and report breaches.

The decision to publicise a CBO will be taken by the police or council unless the court has made a section 39 order (Children and Young Persons Act 1933) prohibiting publication. When deciding whether to publicise a CBO, public authorities (including the courts) must consider that it is necessary and proportionate to interfere with the young person's right to privacy, and the likely impact on a young person's behaviour. This will need to be balanced against the need to provide re-assurance to victims and the wider community as well as providing them with information so that they can report any breaches. Each case should be decided carefully on its own facts.

Applications to vary or discharge a Criminal Behaviour Order: A CBO may be varied or discharged by the court which made the original order. Either the offender or the prosecution can make an application but if this is dismissed by the court neither party can make a subsequent application without the consent of either the court or the other party. The power to vary includes extending the term of the order or including additional prohibitions or requirements. This flexibility allows for those monitoring the progress of offenders to alter the conditions of the order to suit developing or new circumstances.

Annual reviews for under 18s: Where the order is made against someone under 18 there is a requirement to conduct annual reviews. The review must include consideration of:

- the extent to which the offender has complied with the order;
- the adequacy of any support available to help them to comply with the order; and
- anything else relevant to the question of whether an application should be made to vary or discharge the order.

The police have overall responsibility for carrying out such a review, with a requirement to act in co-operation with the council. The police may invite any other person or body to participate in the review. This could include youth offending teams, educational establishments or other organisations who have been working with the young person. As a result of the review an application to vary or discharge the CBO may be made to the court.

Penalty on breach: It is a criminal offence if an offender fails to comply, without reasonable excuse, with either the requirements or prohibitions in the CBO. Failure to comply with a prohibition or requirement should be notified to the police. The court has the power to impose serious penalties on conviction, including:

- on summary conviction in the magistrates' court: a maximum of six months in prison or a fine or both;
- on conviction on indictment in the Crown Court: a maximum of five years in prison or a fine or both.

Hearings for those under 18 will take place in the youth court where the maximum sentence is a two year detention and training order.

2.3   Dispersal Power

Purpose	Requires a person committing or likely to commit anti-social behaviour, crime or disorder to leave an area for up to 48 hours.
Used by	• Police officers in uniform; and • Police Community Support Officers (if designated the power by their chief constable).
Test	• Contributing or likely to contribute to members of the public in the locality being harassed, alarmed or distressed (or the occurrence of crime and disorder); and • Direction necessary to remove or reduce the likelihood of the anti-social behaviour, crime or disorder.
Details	• Must specify the area to which it relates and can determine the time and the route to leave by. • Can confiscate any item that could be used to commit anti-social behaviour, crime or disorder. • Use in a specified locality must be authorised by a police inspector and can last for up to 48 hours. • A direction can be given to anyone who is, or appears to be, over the age of 10. • A person who is under 16 and given a direction can be taken home or to a place of safety.
Penalty on breach	• Breach is a criminal offence. • Failure to comply with a direction to leave: up to a level 4 fine and/or up to three months in prison although under 18s cannot be imprisoned. • Failure to hand over items: up to a level 2 fine.
Appeals	A person who is given a direction and feels they have been incorrectly dealt with should speak to the duty inspector at the local police station. Details should be given to the person on the written notice.
The legislation	Sections 34 to 42 of the Anti-social Behaviour, Crime and Policing Act 2014.
Protecting the vulnerable	• Consideration should be given to how the use of this power might impact on the most vulnerable members of society. • Consideration should also be given to any risks associated with displacement, including to where people may be dispersed to. • There is value in working in partnership to resolve ongoing problems and find long term solutions.

Dispersal Power

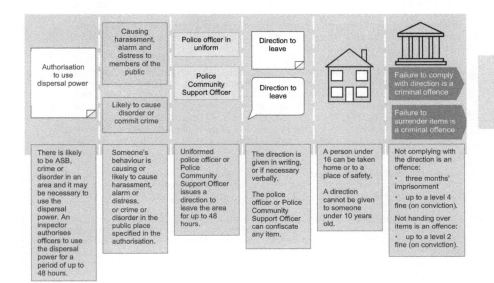

| There is likely to be ASB, crime or disorder in an area and it may be necessary to use the dispersal power. An inspector authorises officers to use the dispersal power for a period of up to 48 hours. | Someone's behaviour is causing or likely to cause harassment, alarm or crime or disorder in the public place specified in the authorisation. | Uniformed police officer or Police Community Support Officer issues a direction to leave the area for up to 48 hours. | The direction is given in writing, or if necessary verbally. The police officer or Police Community Support Officer can confiscate any item. | A person under 16 can be taken home or to a place of safety. A direction cannot be given to someone under 10 years old. | Not complying with the direction is an offence:
 • three months' imprisonment
 • up to a level 4 fine (on conviction).
 Not handing over items is an offence:
 • up to a level 2 fine (on conviction). |

Purpose

The dispersal power is a flexible power which the police can use in a range of situations to disperse anti-social individuals and provide immediate short-term respite to the local community. The power is preventative, allowing an officer to deal quickly with someone's behaviour and nip the problem in the bud before it escalates.

Restricting an individual's freedom of movement is a serious issue, and accordingly the power should not be invoked lightly. This is why the legislation requires the authorising officer to be satisfied on reasonable grounds that use of the power is necessary to remove or reduce the likelihood of people being **harassed, alarmed or distressed** or the occurrence of **crime or disorder**.

In areas where there are regular problems, it is recommended that the police work with the local council to find a sustainable long-term solution. The impact on the local community should be considered when using the dispersal power.

Who can use the power?

The dispersal power can be used by police officers in uniform. Police Community Support Officers can also use this power if designated by their chief constable.

Use of the dispersal power must be authorised by an officer of at least the rank of inspector. This helps to ensure that the power is not used to stop activities which are not causing anti-social behaviour. It may be appropriate for an officer of a more senior rank to authorise the use of the power where, for example, there is no inspector on duty who knows the specific circumstances of the area. The authorising officer can sanction use of the power in a specified locality for a period of up to 48 hours.

The inspector (or above) must record the authorisation in writing, specifying the grounds on which it is given and sign the authorisation. The decision should be based on objective grounds: this may include local knowledge of the area and information to suggest that individuals are likely to cause harassment, alarm or distress to others or engage in crime and disorder at a specific time. The authorising officer should ensure that the evidence is sufficient to justify using the power, and should take account of wider impacts, such as on community relations. The written authorisation may be admitted in evidence if the authorisation is in dispute.

Ensuring proportionality: Restricting people's freedom of movement is a serious matter and it is important that the dispersal power is used proportionately and reasonably, respecting individuals' rights of lawful freedom of expression and freedom of assembly.

The dispersal power can only be used in the specific location authorised by the inspector (or above) who should define a specific geographic location, for example by listing the streets to which it applies or the streets which form the boundary of the area, rather than stating 'in and around the area of'. The authorisation should not cover an area larger than is necessary. If the anti-social behaviour occurs outside the authorised area, the authorising officer will have to increase the area or officers will not be able to use the power.

Consultation: Wherever practicable, the authorising officer should consult the local council or community representatives before making the authorisation. This will help to understand the implications of using the power within a particular community or area and whether the community will benefit from use of the dispersal power. Working with the relevant council can also assist the police in gaining community consensus and support when it is necessary to use the dispersal power, or assist community relations where there are concerns about the use of the power in a particular area. When it has not been practical to consult the local council, the authorising officer may wish to notify the local authority of the authorisation or the use of the power.

Transparency and scrutiny: Police forces may wish to put in place appropriate arrangements for maintaining records of authorisations and use of the disposal power and the circumstances in which it is used, and to publish data on its use.   Police and Crime Commissioners have an important role in holding forces to account to ensure that officers are using the power proportionately.   Publication of data will help to highlight any 'hotspot' areas that may need a longer-term solution, such as diversionary activities for young people or security measures in pubs and clubs to prevent alcohol-related anti-social behaviour in town centres.

Details

The legal tests: Two conditions need to be met for a direction to be given:

- the officer must have reasonable grounds to suspect that the behaviour of the person has contributed, or is likely to contribute, to:
  - members of the public in the locality being harassed, alarmed or distressed; or
  - crime and disorder occurring in the locality.
- the officer considers that giving a direction to the person is necessary for the purpose of removing or reducing the likelihood of anti-social behaviour, crime or disorder.

Including behaviour that is likely to cause harassment, alarm or distress in the legal tests allows the power to be used as a preventative measure. The power is for use in public places; this includes places to which the public has access by virtue of express or implied permission such as a shopping centre.

Written notice: The direction must be given in writing, unless that is not reasonably practicable. The written notice will specify the locality to which the direction relates and for how long the person must leave the area. The officer can also impose requirements as to the time by which the person must leave the locality and the route they must take. The officer must also tell the person that failure to comply, without reasonable excuse, is an offence unless it is not reasonably practicable to do this.

The information should be provided as clearly as possible and the officer should ensure the person has understood it. If the direction is given verbally a written record of it must also be kept in order to enforce it in the event that it is breached, and for the police force to be able to monitor use of the power. The written notice may also be admitted in evidence in breach proceedings.

Many forces have already established good practice in relation to the use of dispersal powers. For instance, in some forces, officers carry a pre-printed notepad to provide details of the direction, the consequences of a failure to comply, where to collect any confiscated items, and a map to clarify the area a person is excluded from.

Dispersing young people: A police officer (or Police Community Support Officer where designated) can give a direction to anyone who is, or appears to be, over the age of 10. If the officer reasonably believes the person given the direction to be under the age of 16, the officer can take them home or to another place of safety. Under the provisions of the Children Act 2004 the police have a duty to 'safeguard and promote the welfare of children'. Police forces have safeguarding arrangements in place to ensure that children are not returned to unsafe homes or placed in potentially harmful situations.

Case law in relation to Part 4 of the Anti-social Behaviour Act 2003 states that to 'remove' a person under 16 to their place of residence carries with it a power to use reasonable force if necessary to do so: see R (on the application of W by his parent and litigation friend PW) (Claimant) v (1) Commissioner of Police for the Metropolis, (2) Richmond-upon-Thames London Borough Council (Defendants) and the Secretary of State for the Home Department (Interested Party) [2006].

Restrictions: A direction cannot be given to someone engaged in peaceful picketing that is lawful under section 220 of the Trade Union and Labour Relations (Consolidation) Act 1992 or if they are taking part in a public procession as defined in section 11 of the Public Order Act 1986.

In addition, the direction cannot restrict someone from having access to the place where they live or from attending a place where they:

- work, or are contracted to work for that period of time;

- are required to attend by a court or tribunal;

- are expected for education or training;

- are required to attend a service provision appointment or to receive medical treatment during the period of time that the direction applies.

Providing information to the public: Where use of the dispersal power has been authorised in advance, the police should consider providing information to those who may be affected.

Putting victims first: If the dispersal power is used in response to a complaint from a member of the public, the officer should update them about what has been done in response to their complaint. Keeping victims updated on enforcement action can provide reassurance to the community and result in fewer follow up calls on the issue

Surrender of property: The police officer or Police Community Support Officer can require the person given the direction to hand over items causing or likely to cause anti-social behaviour. This could be any item but typical examples are alcohol, fireworks or spray paint. The officer does not have the power to seize the item; therefore the person's consent is required to take the item. However, it is an offence for the person not to hand over the item if asked to do so.

Surrendered items will be held at the police station and can be collected after the period of the direction has expired. If the item is not collected within 28 days it can be destroyed or disposed of. If the individual is under the age of 16 they can be required to be accompanied by a parent or other responsible adult to collect the item; this will mean that the adult can be made aware of the young person's behaviour and will help encourage parental responsibility.

Recording information and publishing data: The officer giving the direction must record:

- the individual to whom the direction is given;

- the time at which the direction is given; and

- the terms of the direction (including the area to which it relates and the exclusion period).

If a direction is varied or withdrawn the officer must record the time this was done and the terms of the variation.

Penalty on breach: Failure to comply with the direction is a summary only criminal offence which will be dealt with in the magistrates' court or youth court for people under the age of 18. On conviction it carries a maximum penalty of a level 4 fine and/or three months imprisonment, although those people under the age of 18 cannot be imprisoned. Failure to surrender items is also a criminal offence with a maximum penalty of a level 2 fine.

Appeals: A person who is given a direction and feels they have been incorrectly dealt with should speak to the duty inspector at the local police station. Details should be given to the person on the written notice.

2.4 Community Protection Notice

Purpose	To stop a person aged 16 or over, business or organisation committing anti-social behaviour which spoils the community's quality of life.
Who can issue a CPN	• Council officers; • Police officers; • Police community support officers (PCSOs) if designated; and • Social landlords (if designated by the council).
Test	Behaviour has to: • have a detrimental effect on the quality of life of those in the locality; • be of a persistent or continuing nature; and • be unreasonable.
Details	• The Community Protection Notice (CPN) can deal with a range of behaviours; for instance, it can deal with noise nuisance and litter on private land. • The CPN can include requirements to ensure that problems are rectified and that steps are taken to prevent the anti-social behaviour occurring again. • A written warning must first be issued informing the perpetrator of problem behaviour, requesting them to stop, and the consequences of continuing. • A CPN can then be issued including requirement to stop things, do things or take reasonable steps to avoid further anti-social behaviour. • Can allow council to carry out works in default on behalf of a perpetrator.
Penalty on breach	• Breach is a criminal offence. • A fixed penalty notice can be issued of up to £100 if appropriate. • A fine of up to level 4 (for individuals), or £20,000 for businesses.
Appeals	• Terms of a CPN can be appealed by the perpetrator within 21 days of issue. • The cost of works undertaken on behalf of the perpetrator by the council can be challenged by the perpetrator if they think they are disproportionate.
The legislation	Sections 43 to 58 of the Anti-social Behaviour, Crime and Policing Act 2014.
Protecting the vulnerable	• Particular care should be taken to consider how use of the power might impact on more vulnerable members of society.

Community Protection Notice

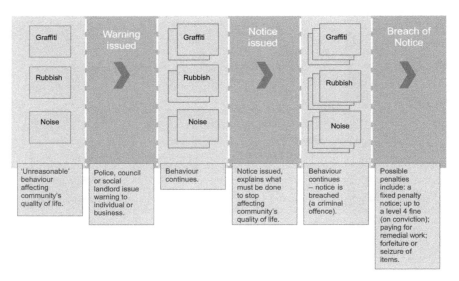

Purpose

The Community Protection Notice can be used to deal with particular, ongoing problems or nuisances which are having a detrimental effect on the community's quality of life by targeting those responsible.

Who can issue a Community Protection Notice

Local councils have traditionally taken the lead in dealing with the sort of issues that can be addressed through the use of Community Protection Notices, but the police are also able to issue these Notices, as are social landlords where they have been designated to do so by the relevant local authority, recognising their role in responding to anti-social behaviour in the dwellings they manage.

Putting victims first: To understand the impact that the behaviour is having on the quality of life of those in a locality, the agency considering the use of a Community Protection Notice should first speak to members of the community to gain a proper understanding of the harm that is being caused to individuals and the community. This will help to ensure that victims feel that the issue is being taken seriously and will also help to ensure that the decision to issue a Community Protection Notice is based on evidence of the impact that the perpetrator's behaviour is having. It will also help to ensure that officers do not use the notice to stop activities which are not causing anti-social behaviour.

386

Details

The legal tests: These focus on the impact that the behaviour is having on victims and communities. A Community Protection Notice can be issued by one of the bodies mentioned above if they are satisfied, on reasonable grounds, that the conduct of an individual, business or organisation:

- is having a detrimental effect on the quality of life of those in the locality;
- is persistent or continuing in nature; and
- is unreasonable.

Agencies should have sufficient evidence to satisfy themselves that the behaviour in question is genuinely having a detrimental effect on others' quality of life, in terms of the nuisance or harm that is being caused to others, rather than being a behaviour that others may just find annoying.

Similarly, decisions on whether behaviour is persistent or continuing in nature should be taken on a case by case basis. For example, where an individual is storing rubbish in their garden for many months, proving persistence will be relatively straightforward. However, there will be cases where behaviour is continuing over a much shorter time period and the individual has been asked to cease the behaviour but has refused to do so and persists with the behaviour.

The issuing officer must also make a judgement as to whether the behaviour in question is unreasonable. For instance, a baby crying in the middle of the night may well have a detrimental effect on immediate neighbours and is likely to be persistent in nature. However, it is unlikely to be reasonable to issue the parents with a Community Protection Notice if there is not a great deal that they can do to control or affect the behaviour.

There is significant merit in involving the local council, who will have many years of experience in tackling environmental issues, when deciding whether or not to serve a Community Protection Notice. In addition, the issuing body should be satisfied that it has sufficient evidence that the activity in question is having a detrimental effect on others' quality of life, is persistent or continuing and is unreasonable.

Who can a Community Protection Notice be issued to? A Community Protection Notice can be issued against any person aged 16 or over or to a body, including a business. Where a body is issued with a Community Protection Notice, it should be issued to the most appropriate person. In the case of a small business, it could be the shop owner whereas in the case of a major supermarket it may well be the store manager. The issuing officer will need to be satisfied that the person issued with the Community Protection Notice can be reasonably expected to control or affect the behaviour in question, taking into consideration all the available circumstances. There is also a need to have due regard to the Equality Act 2010.

The Community Protection Notice can be handed directly to the person in question or it can be posted. In circumstances where the owner or occupier cannot be determined, the issuing officer can post the Community Protection Notice on the premises and it is considered as having been served at that point. In such a scenario, the issuing officer would need to demonstrate that reasonable enquiries had been undertaken to ascertain the identity of the owner or occupier, for instance, checking with the Land Registry.

Community Protection Notices and statutory nuisance: Issuing a Community Protection Notice does not discharge the council from its duty to issue an Abatement Notice where the behaviour constitutes a statutory nuisance for the purposes of Part 3 of the Environmental Protection Act 1990. A statutory nuisance is one of the matters listed in section 79(1) of that Act which, given all the circumstances, is judged to be 'prejudicial to health or a nuisance'. For England and Wales, statutory nuisances are listed as:

- any premises in such a state to be prejudicial to health or a nuisance;
- smoke emitted from premises so as to be prejudicial to health or a nuisance;
- fumes or gases emitted from (domestic) premises so as to be prejudicial to health or a nuisance;
- any dust, steam, smell or other effluvia arising on industrial, trade or business premises and being prejudicial to health or a nuisance;
- any accumulation or deposit and being prejudicial to health or a nuisance;
- any animal kept in such a place or manner as to be prejudicial to health or a nuisance;
- any insects emanating from relevant industrial, trade or business premises and being prejudicial to health or a nuisance;
- artificial light emitted from premises so as to be prejudicial to health or a nuisance;
- noise emitted from premises so as to be prejudicial to health or a nuisance;
- noise that is prejudicial to health or a nuisance and is emitted from or caused by a vehicle, machinery or equipment in a street;
- any other matter declared by any enactment to be a statutory nuisance.

Many of these terms have special meanings, either under the 1990 Act or following decisions of the courts. In particular, 'nuisance' means something different to 'bothersome' or an 'annoyance'. The assessment of nuisance is an objective test, taking into account a range of factors and is based on what is reasonable for the 'average' person. 'Prejudicial to health' means 'injurious or likely to cause injury to health' under section 79(7) of the 1990 Act. While a Community Protection Notice can be issued for behaviour that may constitute a statutory nuisance, the interaction between the two powers should be considered. It remains a principle of law that a specific power should be used in preference to a general one.

As a Community Protection Notice can only be issued for behaviour that is persistent or continuing and unreasonable, in most cases, social landlords or the police will have sufficient time to contact the relevant council team in advance of issuing the Notice if they believe the behaviour could be a statutory nuisance. If it could be a statutory nuisance, the issuing authority should consider whether issuing a Community Protection Notice is necessary given the powers afforded to council under the 1990 Act. If they do decide to issue a Community Protection Notice in parallel, they should work with the relevant council team to ensure any restrictions or requirements complement those that may be included in any future Abatement Notice.

388

The written warning: In many cases, the behaviour in question will have been ongoing for some time. Informal interventions may well have been exhausted by the time the applicant decides to proceed with a Community Protection Notice. However, before a Notice can be issued, a written warning must be issued to the person committing anti-social behaviour.

The written warning must make clear to the individual that if they do not stop the anti-social behaviour, they could be issued with a Community Protection Notice. However, local agencies may wish to include other information in the written warning, for instance:

- outlining the specific behaviour that is considered anti-social and which is having a detrimental effect on others' quality of life, as this will ensure there is little doubt over what needs to be done to avoid the formal Notice being issued;

- outlining the time by which the behaviour is expected to have changed in order to give the alleged perpetrator a clear understanding of when the Community Protection Notice might be served;

- setting out the potential consequences of being issued with a Community Protection Notice and in particular the potential sanctions on breach, which could act as an incentive for the individual to change their behaviour before a formal Notice is issued.

How the written warning is discharged is up to each agency. In cases where a problem has been continuing for a period of time, the written warning may be included in other correspondence. However, in cases where the issue of a written warning is required more quickly, it could be a standard form of words, adaptable to any situation – for instance, a pre-agreed form of words that can be used by the officer on the spot.

Enough time should be left between the issue of a written warning and the issue of a Community Protection Notice to allow the individual or body to deal with the matter. It will be for the issuing officer to decide how long is allowed on a case by case basis. For instance, in an example where a garden is to be cleared of waste, several days or weeks may be required to enable the individual to make the necessary arrangements. However, where an individual is playing loud music in a park, as outlined above, the officer could require the behaviour to stop immediately.

> **Putting victims first**: Keeping victims and communities updated on enforcement action at important points can help them to deal with the impact of the behaviour. Victims may feel that their complaint has been ignored if they do not see immediate changes to the behaviour. However, informing them of what is happening can make a difference and result in fewer follow up calls on the issue. If a Community Protection Notice has been issued, the officer may wish to speak to those affected by the anti-social behaviour to inform them of what steps have been taken, potential timescales and possible implications for the perpetrator.

Partnership working: In many cases, the issuing agency will have already had contact with other partners in dealing with a persistent issue. For instance, in a case dealing with a build-up of litter, the council may have spoken to the local neighbourhood policing team or social landlord. However, in situations that develop more quickly, the relevant officer will have to decide whether there are other individuals or bodies that should be informed. In particular, for matters that could amount to a statutory nuisance it will often be advisable to seek the expert view of council environmental health officers before issuing a Community Protection Notice.

What to include in a Community Protection Notice A CPN can be drafted from scratch if necessary so that it is appropriate to the situation and can include any or all of the following:

- a requirement to stop doing specified things;
- a requirement to do specified things;
- a requirement to take reasonable steps to achieve specified results.

This means that not only can the relevant officer stop someone being anti-social, they can also put steps in place to ensure the behaviour does not recur.

In deciding what should be included as a requirement in a Community Protection Notice, issuing officers should consider what is reasonable to include in a notice of this type and any timescales they wish to add. The Community Protection Notice is intended to deal with short or medium-term issues. While restrictions and requirements may be similar to those in a Civil Injunction, more onerous conditions, such as attendance at a drug rehabilitation course, would clearly be more appropriate to a court issued order. The CPN could be used, for example, to require a dog owner to attend training classes or fix fencing to deal with straying incidents where this is having a detrimental effect on the community's quality of life.

Putting victims first: When the issuing officer has decided what to include as a requirement in the Community Protection Notice they should consider the desired outcome for the community. Victims will not only want the behaviour to stop, they will also want it not to occur again. Consideration should be given to whether there are requirements that could ensure the anti- social behaviour does not recur.

Penalty on breach: Failure to comply with a Community Protection Notice is an offence. Where an individual, business or organisation fails to comply with the terms of a Community Protection Notice, a number of options are available for the issuing authority and these are outlined in more detail below.

- **Fixed penalty notices**

   Depending on the behaviour in question, the issuing officer could decide that a fixed penalty notice would be the most appropriate sanction. This can be issued by a police officer, Police Community Support Officer, council officer or, if designated, a social landlord. In making the decision to issue a fixed penalty notice, the officer should be mindful that if issued, payment would discharge any liability to conviction for the offence.

Putting victims first: When deciding which sanction to choose on non-compliance with a Community Protection Notice, the issuing authority should where appropriate consider the potential wishes of the victim. While issuing a fixed penalty notice may be considered appropriate, if it does nothing to alleviate the impact on the community or leaves victims feeling ignored, this may not be the best course of action and may lead to further complaints and the requirement for more action.

   A fixed penalty notice should not be more than £100 and can specify two amounts, for instance, a lower payment if settled early, say within 14 days. In order to allow the individual time to pay, no other associated proceedings can be taken until at least 14 days after the issue. The exact wording or design of a fixed penalty notice can be determined locally to fit with local standards and protocols but must:

- give reasonably detailed particulars of the circumstances alleged to constitute the offence;

- state the period during which proceedings will not be taken for the offence;

- specify the amount or amounts payable;

- state the name and address of the person to whom the FPN should be paid; and

- specify permissible methods of payment (for example, cash, cheque, bank transfer).

- **Remedial action**

  If an individual or body fails to comply with a Community Protection Notice issued by the council, it may decide to take remedial action to address the issue. Where the Community Protection Notice has been issued by the police or a social landlord, but they believe remedial action is an appropriate sanction, they should approach the council to discuss the best way to move forward. For instance, the social landlord could undertake the work on behalf of the council.

  If it is decided that remedial action is the best way forward, the council (or the other agency in discussion with the council) should establish what works are required to put the situation right. For instance, in a situation where the complaint relates to a significant build up of rubbish in someone's front garden, remedial action could take the form of clearing the garden on the perpetrator's behalf.

  Putting victims first: Punishment of the perpetrator may not be top of the victim's priority list; they may just want to see the situation fixed. If remedial action is chosen as the most appropriate action, it may help those affected by the behaviour to know when they can expect remedial works to be undertaken

  Where this work is to be undertaken on land 'open to the air', the council or their agent (for instance, a rubbish disposal contractor) can undertake these works without the consent of the owner or occupier. Where works are required indoors the permission of the owner or occupier is required. When it has been decided what works are required, the council has to specify to the perpetrator what work it intends to carry out and the estimated cost. Once the work has been completed, the council should give the perpetrator details of the work completed and the final amount payable. In determining a 'reasonable' charge, local authorities should ensure the costs are no more than is necessary to restore the land to the standard specified in the notice. Such costs may include officer time, use of cleaning equipment (unless of a specialised nature), and administration costs relating to the clearance itself.

- **Remedial orders**

  On conviction for an offence of failing to comply with a Community Protection Notice, the prosecuting authority may ask the court to impose a remedial order and/or a forfeiture order. This could be for a number of reasons, for instance:

  - the matter may be deemed so serious that a court order is warranted;

  - works may be required to an area that requires the owner's or occupier's consent and this is not forthcoming; or

  - the issuing authority may believe that forfeiture or seizure of one or more items is required as a result of the behaviour (for instance, sound making equipment).

A remedial order may require the defendant:

- to carry out specified work (this could set out the original Community Protection Notice requirements); or

- to allow work to be carried out by, or on behalf of, a specified local authority.

Where works are required indoors, the defendant's permission is still required. But this does not prevent a defendant who fails to give that consent from being in breach of the court's order.

- **Forfeiture orders**

  Following conviction for an offence under section 48, the court may also order the forfeiture of any item that was used in the commission of the offence. This could be spray paints, sound making equipment or a poorly socialised dog where the court feels the individual is not able to manage the animal appropriately (re-homed in the case of a dog). Where items are forfeited, they can be destroyed or disposed of appropriately.

- **Seizure**

  In some circumstances, the court may issue a warrant authorising the seizure of items that have been used in the commission of the offence of failing to comply with a Community Protection Notice. In these circumstances, an enforcement officer may use reasonable force, if necessary, to seize the item or items.

  Failure to comply with any of the requirements in the court order constitutes contempt of court and could lead to a custodial sentence. If an individual is convicted of an offence under section 48, they may receive up to a level 4 fine (up to £20,000 in the case of a business or organisation).

Appeals: Anyone issued with a Community Protection Notice has the opportunity to appeal it. Appeals are heard in a magistrates' court and the Notice should provide details of the process, how an individual can appeal and the timeframe to appeal (within 21 days of the person being issued with the notice). As the legislation makes clear, an appeal can be made on the following grounds:

The test was not met if:

- **the behaviour did not take place**: in most cases, officers will have collected evidence to place beyond any reasonable doubt that the behaviour occurred. However, in cases where the officer has relied on witness statements alone, they should consider the potential for this appeal route and build their case accordingly;

- **the behaviour has not had a detrimental effect on the quality of life of those in the locality**: again, the importance of witness statements and any other evidence that the behaviour in question is having a negative impact on those nearby should be collected to ensure this defence is covered;

- **the behaviour was not persistent or continuing**: in some cases, judging persistence will be straightforward. However, in cases where a decision to issue a Community Protection Notice is taken more quickly, officers should use their professional judgement to decide whether this test is met and may need to justify this on appeal;

- **the behaviour is not unreasonable**: In many cases, individuals, businesses or organisations that are presented with evidence of the detrimental impact of their behaviour will take steps to address it. Where they do not, they may argue that what they are doing is reasonable. In deciding whether behaviour is unreasonable, officers should consider the impact the behaviour is having on the victim or victims, whether steps could be taken to alleviate this impact and whether the behaviour is necessary at all.

- **the individual cannot reasonably be expected to control or affect the behaviour**: in issuing the CPN, the officer must make a judgement based on reasonable grounds as to whether the individual, business or organisation can reasonably be expected to do something to change the behaviour. The officer should be prepared to justify this decision in court if required.

Other reasons:

- **any of the requirements are unreasonable**: requirements in a Community Protection Notice should either prevent the anti-social behaviour from continuing or recurring, or reduce the detrimental effect or reduce the risk of its continuance or recurrence. As such, it should be related to the behaviour in question;

- **there is a material defect or error with the Community Protection Notice**: this ground for appeal could be used if there was a failure to comply with a requirement in the Act, such as a failure to provide a written warning before issuing the Notice;

- **the Notice was issued to the wrong person**: this could be grounds for appeal if the Notice was posted to the wrong address or the wrong person was identified in a business or organisation.

The person issued with the Community Protection Notice must appeal within 21 days of issue. Where an appeal is made, any requirement included under section 43(3)(b) or (c), namely a requirement to do specified things or take reasonable steps to achieve specified results, is suspended until the outcome of the appeal. However, requirements stopping the individual or body from doing specified things under section 43(3)(a) continue to have effect. In addition, where remedial action is taken by a council under section 47 or 49 the individual has the opportunity to appeal on the grounds that the cost of the work being undertaken on their behalf is disproportionate.

2.5   Public Spaces Protection Order

Purpose	Designed to stop individuals or groups committing anti-social behaviour in a public space.
Who can make a PSPO	• Councils issue a Public Spaces Protection Order (PSPO) after consultation with the police, Police and Crime Commissioner and other relevant bodies.
Test	Behaviour being restricted has to: • be having, or be likely to have, a detrimental effect on the quality of life of those in the locality; • be persistent or continuing nature; and • be unreasonable.
Details	• Restrictions and requirements set by the council. • These can be blanket restrictions or requirements or can be targeted against certain behaviours by certain groups at certain times. • Can restrict access to public spaces (including certain types of highway) where that route is being used to commit anti-social behaviour. • Can be enforced by a police officer, police community support officers and council officers.
Penalty on breach	• Breach is a criminal offence. • Enforcement officers can issue a fixed penalty notice of up to £100 if appropriate. • A fine of up to level 3 on prosecution.
Appeals	• Anyone who lives in, or regularly works in or visits the area can appeal a PSPO in the High Court within six weeks of issue. • Further appeal is available each time the PSPO is varied by the council.
The legislation	Sections 59 to 75 of the Anti-social Behaviour, Crime and Policing Act 2014.
Protecting the vulnerable	• Consideration should be given to how the use of this power might impact on the most vulnerable members of society. • Consideration should also be given to any risks associated with displacement, including to where people may be dispersed to • There is value in working in partnership to resolve ongoing problems and find long term solutions.

Public Spaces Protection Order

Park	Behaviour occurs	Alcohol	Behaviour challenged	Comply	Formal sanction
Alleyway		Dogs		FPN	
Communal area		Noise		Court	
Council puts restrictions on an area where behaviour has, or is likely to have a detrimental effect on the local community.	Individual breaches conditions of an Order	Police officer, PCSO or council officer witnesses behaviour.	Individual asked to leave the area, handover alcohol, put dog on leash.	If the individual does not comply, they commit an offence	Possible sanctions include: a fixed penalty notice; up to a level 3 fine (on conviction); (or up to a level 2 fine for breach of an alcohol prohibition.

Purpose

Public Spaces Protection Orders are intended to deal with a particular nuisance or problem in a specific area that is detrimental to the local community's quality of life, by imposing conditions on the use of that area which apply to everyone. They are intended to help ensure that the law-abiding majority can use and enjoy public spaces, safe from anti-social behaviour.

Given that these orders can restrict what people can do and how they behave in public spaces, it is important that the restrictions imposed are focused on specific behaviours and are proportionate to the detrimental effect that the behaviour is causing or can cause, and are necessary to prevent it from continuing, occurring or recurring.

Who can make a PSPO?

Local councils are responsible for making Public Spaces Protection Orders: district councils should take the lead in England with county councils or unitary authorities undertaking the role where there is no district council. In London, borough councils are able to make Public Spaces Protection Orders, as is the Common Council of the City of London and the Council of the Isles of Scilly. In Wales, responsibility falls to county councils or county borough councils. Parish councils and town councils in England, and community councils in Wales are not able to make these Orders. In addition, section 71 of the Anti-social Behaviour, Crime and Policing Act 2014 allows bodies other than local authorities to make Public Spaces Protection Orders in certain circumstances by order of the Secretary of State. This power has been exercised by the Secretary of State to allow the City of London Corporation to manage a number of public spaces with the permission of, and on behalf of, local authorities.

Details

The legal tests: The legal tests focus on the impact that anti-social behaviour is having on victims and communities. A Public Spaces Protection Order can be made by the council if they are satisfied on reasonable grounds that the activity or behaviour concerned, carried out, or likely to be carried out, in a public space:

- has had, or is likely to have, a detrimental effect on the quality of life of those in the locality;
- is, or is likely to be, persistent or continuing in nature;
- is, or is likely to be, unreasonable; and
- justifies the restrictions imposed.

Putting victims first: In deciding to place restrictions on a particular public space, councils should consider the knock on effects of that decision and ensure that this is a reasonable and proportionate response to incidents of anti-social behaviour in the area. Introducing a blanket ban on a particular activity may simply displace the behaviour and create victims elsewhere.

Where can it apply? The council can make a Public Spaces Protection Order on any public space within its own area. The definition of public space is wide and includes any place to which the public or any section of the public has access, on payment or otherwise, as of right or by virtue of express or implied permission, for example a shopping centre.

Consultation and working with partners: Before making a Public Spaces Protection Order, the council must consult with the police. This should be done formally through the chief officer of police and the Police and Crime Commissioner, but details could be agreed by working level leads. This is an opportunity for the police and council to share information about the area and the problems being caused as well as discussing the practicalities of enforcement. In addition, the owner or occupier of the land should be consulted. This should include the county council (if the application for the Order is not being led by them) where they are the Highway Authority.

The council must also consult whatever community representatives they think appropriate. It is strongly recommended that the council engages in an open and public consultation to give the users of the public space the opportunity to comment on whether the proposed restriction or restrictions are appropriate, proportionate or needed at all. The council should also ensure that specific groups likely to have a particular interest are consulted, such as a local residents association, or regular users of a park or those involved in specific activities in the area, such as buskers and other street entertainers.

Openness and accountability: Before the Public Spaces Protection Order is made, the council must publish the draft order in accordance with regulations published by the Secretary of State and ensure that the draft order is available on its website.

Given that the effect of Public Spaces Protection Orders is to restrict the behaviour of everybody using the public place, the close or direct involvement of elected members will help to ensure openness and accountability. This will be achieved, for example, where the decision is put to the Cabinet or full Council.

Land requiring special consideration

Before a council makes a Public Spaces Protection Order it should consider whether the land falls into any of the following categories:

- **Registered common land**: There are around 550,000 hectares of registered common land in England and Wales. Common land is mapped as open access land under the Countryside and Rights of Way (CROW) Act 2000 with a right of public access on foot. Some commons, particularly those in urban districts, also have additional access rights and these may include rights for equestrian use.

- **Registered town or village green**: Town and village greens developed under customary law as areas of land where local people indulged in lawful sports and pastimes. These might include organised or ad-hoc games, picnics, fetes and similar activities, such as dog walking.

- **Open access land**: Open access land covers mountain, moor, heath and down and registered common land, and also some voluntarily dedicated land, for example the Forestry Commission's or Natural Resources Wales' freehold estate. Open access land provides a right of open-air recreation on foot although the landowner can voluntarily extend the right to other forms of access, such as for cycling or horse-riding.

This can be done by contacting the Commons registration authority (county council in two-tier areas; unitary authority elsewhere). If the land in question is a registered common, the council will be able to find out what common land rights exist and the access rights of any users. The Department for Environment, Food & Rural Affairs considers the model set out in 'A Common Purpose' to be good practice in consulting directly affected persons (including commoners) and the public about any type of potential change in the management of a common.

If land is a registered green, it receives considerable statutory protection under the 'Victorian Statutes'. In terms of open access land, there are various national limitations on what activities are included within the access rights. It is possible for local restrictions on CROW rights to be put in place to meet wider land use needs, and this system is normally administered by Natural England.

Where an authority is considering an order on one of these types of land, the council should consider discussing this with relevant forums and user groups (e.g. Local Access Forums, Ramblers or the British Horse Society) depending on the type of provision that is contemplated in the order. It could also be appropriate to hold a local public meeting when considering whether to make an order for an area of such land to ensure all affected persons are given the opportunity to raise concerns.

What to include in a Public Spaces Protection Order. The Order can be drafted from scratch based on the individual and specific issues being faced in a particular public space. A single Order can also include multiple restrictions and requirements. It can prohibit certain activities, such as the drinking of alcohol, as well as placing requirements on individuals carrying out certain activities, for instance making sure that people walking their dogs keep them on a lead in designated areas.

When deciding what to include, the council should consider scope. The broad aim is to keep public spaces welcoming to law abiding people and communities and not simply to restrict access. So restrictions or requirements can be targeted at specific people, designed to apply only at certain times or apply only in certain circumstances.

> **Putting victims first:** Although it may not be viable in each case, discussing potential restrictions and requirements prior to issuing an Order with those living or working nearby may help to ensure that the final Order better meets the needs of the local community and is less likely to be challenged.

In establishing which restrictions or requirements should be included, the council should be satisfied on reasonable grounds that the measures are necessary to prevent the detrimental effect on those in the locality or reduce the likelihood of the detrimental effect continuing, occurring or recurring.

As with all the anti-social behaviour powers, the council should give due regard to issues of proportionality: is the restriction proposed proportionate to the specific harm or nuisance that is being caused? Councils should ensure that the restrictions being introduced are reasonable and will prevent or reduce the detrimental effect continuing, occurring or recurring. In addition, councils should ensure that the Order is appropriately worded so that it targets the specific behaviour or activity that is causing nuisance or harm and thereby having a detrimental impact on others' quality of life. Councils should also consider whether restrictions are required all year round or whether seasonal or time limited restrictions would meet the purpose.

When the final set of measures is agreed the Order should be published in accordance with regulations made by the Secretary of State and must:

- identify the activities having the detrimental effect;
- explain the potential sanctions available on breach; and
- specify the period for which the Order has effect.

Homeless people and rough sleepers

Public Spaces Protection Orders should not be used to target people based solely on the fact that someone is homeless or rough sleeping, as this in itself is unlikely to mean that such behaviour is having an unreasonably detrimental effect on the community's quality of life which justifies the restrictions imposed. Councils may receive complaints about homeless people, but they should consider whether the use of a Public Spaces Protection Order is the appropriate response. These Orders should be used only to address any specific behaviour that is causing a detrimental effect on the community's quality of life which is within the control of the person concerned.

Councils should therefore consider carefully the nature of any potential Public Spaces Protection Order that may impact on homeless people and rough sleepers. It is recommended that any Order defines precisely the specific activity or behaviour that is having the detrimental impact on the community. Councils should also consider measures that tackle the root causes of the behaviour, such as the provision of public toilets.

The council should also consider consulting with national or local homeless charities when considering restrictions or requirements which may impact on homeless people and rough sleepers.

Controlling the presence of dogs

Under the Animal Welfare Act 2006, owners of dogs are required to provide for the welfare needs of their animals. This includes providing the necessary amount of exercise each day, which in many cases will require dogs to be let off the lead whilst still under control. Councils will be aware of the publicly accessible parks and other public places in their area which dog walkers can use to exercise their dogs without restrictions.

When deciding whether to make requirements or restrictions on dogs and their owners, local councils will need to consider whether there are suitable alternative public areas where dogs can be exercised without restrictions. Councils should consider if the proposed restrictions will displace dog walkers onto other sensitive land, such as farmland or nature conversation areas.

Councils should also consider the accessibility of these alternative sites for those with reduced mobility, including but not limited to, assistance dog users. For example, is there step free access, are there well maintained paths and what transport options are available, including in the early morning and evening.

Councils are also encouraged to publish a list of alternative sites which dog walkers can use to exercise their dogs without restrictions. Both dog walkers and non-dog walkers would then have a clear opportunity to submit their views on whether these alternatives were suitable. This should help minimise the risks of unwanted and unintended displacement effects.

Guidance published by the Department for Environment, Food and Rural Affairs on dog control states that councils must consult dog law and welfare experts e.g vets or animal welfare officers and organisations affected by restrictions before seeking to impose restrictions. Councils may also wish to consider consulting the Kennel Club. Where a Public Spaces Protection Order proposes to restrict dog walking in parks and other commonly used dog walking sites, consideration should be given to how to alert interested people to the proposed restrictions, such as posting notices of the proposed restrictions and consultation details within these spaces.

Consideration must also be given on how any dog walking restrictions being proposed would affect those who rely on assistance dogs, ensuring any prohibition or requirement is compliant with the provisions of Equality Act 2010 or considering what exemptions should apply for assistance dogs.

In relation to dogs and their owners, a Public Spaces Protection Order could, for example:

- exclude dogs from designated areas (e.g. a children's play area in a park);

- require the person in charge of the dog to pick up after it;

- require dogs to be kept on leads in a designated area;

- be framed to apply during specific times or periods (e.g. dogs excluded from a beach from 9am to 6pm, 1 May to 30 September);

- restrict the number of dogs that can be walked by one person at any one time; and

- put in place other restrictions or requirements to tackle or prevent any other activity that is considered to have a detrimental effect on the quality of life of those in the locality, or is likely to have such an effect.

Councils should also consider whether alternative options are available to deal with problems around irresponsible dog ownership or dogs being out of control. It may be that if there are local problems with specific individuals allowing their dogs to stray or run out of control for which one of the other available powers, such as the Community Protection Notice, may be more appropriate. The Department for Environment, Food and Rural Affairs has produced detailed guidance in the form of a practitioner's guide on the range of tools available to deal with irresponsible dog ownership. Targeted measures and educational days for irresponsible dog owners can bring about real improvements in the behaviour of irresponsible dog owners.

Parish and Town Councils*:*

Public Spaces Protection Orders are not available to Parish and Town Councils. Parish and Town Councils wishing to deal with dog control issues should discuss the issue with their principal authority, including whether a Public Spaces Protection Order would provide the means to address the issues being experienced by the local community. If the principal authority is satisfied that the legal tests for the use of the power are met and that it is a proportionate response to the level of harm and nuisance being caused it should consider consulting on putting in place a Public Spaces Protection Order. This ensures a single approach on dog control matters within the local community and avoids the risk of any duplication or conflicting requirements and restrictions being put in place.

Restricting alcohol: A Public Spaces Protection Order can be used to restrict the consumption of alcohol in a public space where the relevant legal tests are met. However, such an Order cannot be used to restrict the consumption of alcohol where the premises or its curtilage (a beer garden or pavement seating area) is licensed for the supply of alcohol (other than council operated licenced premises). There are also limitations where a temporary event notice has been given under Part 5 of the Licensing Act 2003, or where the sale or consumption of alcohol is permitted by virtue of permission granted under section 115E of the Highways Act 1980. This is because the licensing system already includes safeguards against premises becoming centres for anti-social behaviour. It would create confusion and duplication if Public Spaces Protection Orders were introduced here.

Groups hanging around/standing in groups/playing games

It is important that councils do not inadvertently restrict everyday sociability in public spaces. The Public Spaces Protection Order should target specifically the problem behaviour that is having a detrimental effect on the community's quality of life, rather than everyday sociability, such as standing in groups which is not in itself a problem behaviour.

Where young people are concerned, councils should think carefully about restricting activities that they are most likely to engage in. Restrictions that are too broad or general in nature may force the young people into out-of-the-way spaces and put them at risk. In such circumstances, councils should consider whether there are alternative spaces that they can use.

People living in temporary accommodation may not be able to stay in their accommodation during the day and so may find themselves spending extended times in public spaces or seeking shelter in bad weather. It is important that public spaces are available for the use and enjoyment of a broad spectrum of the public, and that people of all ages are free to gather, talk and play games.

Restricting access: In the past, Gating Orders have been used to close access to certain public rights of way where the behaviour of some has been anti-social.

A Public Spaces Protection Order can be used to restrict access to a public right of way. However, when deciding on the appropriateness of this approach, the council must consider a number of things, as set out below:

- **Can they restrict access**? A number of rights of way may not be restricted due to their strategic value.

- **What impact will the restriction have**? For instance, is it a primary means of access between two places and is there a reasonably convenient alternative route?

- **Are there any alternatives**? Previously gating was the only option, but it may be possible under a Public Spaces Protection Order to restrict the activities causing the anti-social behaviour rather than access in its totality.

There are also further consultation requirements where access is to be restricted to a public right of way. These include notifying potentially affected persons of the possible restrictions. This could include people who regularly use the right of way in their day to day travel as well as those who live nearby. Interested persons should be informed about how they can view a copy of the proposed order, and be given details of how they can make representations and by when. The council should then consider these representations.

It will be up to the council to decide how best to identify and consult with interested persons. In the past newspapers have been used, but other channels such as websites and social media may now be more effective. Where issues are more localised, councils may prefer to deal with individual households. Or, where appropriate, councils may decide to hold public meetings and discuss issues with regional or national bodies (such as the Local Access Forum) to gather views.

Duration of a Public Spaces Protection Order: The maximum duration of a Public Spaces Protection Order is three years but they can last for shorter periods of time where more appropriate. Short-term Orders could be used where it is not certain that restrictions will have the desired effect, for instance, when closing a public right of way, and in such circumstances the council might decide to make an initial Order for 12 months and then review that decision at that point.

At any point before expiry, the council can extend a Public Spaces Protection Order by up to three years if they consider it is necessary to prevent the original behaviour from occurring or recurring. They should also consult with the local police and any other community representatives they think appropriate before doing so.

Changing the terms of a Public Spaces Protection Order: A Public Spaces Protection Order can cover a number of different restrictions and requirements so there should be little need to have overlapping orders in a single public space. However, if a new issue arises in an area where an Order is already in force, the council can vary the terms of the order at any time. This can change the size of the restricted area or the specific requirements or restrictions. For instance, a Public Spaces Protection Order may exist to ensure dogs are kept on their leads in a park but, after 12 months, groups start to congregate in the park drinking alcohol which is having a detrimental effect on those living nearby. As a result, the council could vary the Order to deal with both issues. Any proposed variation to an existing Public Spaces Protection Order would require the council to undertake the necessary consultation on the proposed changes.

As well as varying the Order, a council can also seek to discharge it at any time, for instance when the issue that justified the Order has ceased or where the behaviour has stopped or the land ceases to be classified as a public space.

Penalty on breach: It is an offence for a person, without reasonable excuse, to:

- do anything that the person is prohibited from doing by a Public Spaces Protection Order (other than consume alcohol – see below); or

- fail to comply with a requirement to which the person is subject under a Public Spaces Protection Order.

A person does not commit an offence by failing to comply with a prohibition or requirement that the council did not have power to include in a Public Spaces Protection Order. A person guilty of an offence is liable on summary conviction to a fine not exceeding level 3 on the standard scale.

It is not an offence to drink alcohol in a controlled drinking zone. However, it is an offence to fail to comply with a request to cease drinking or surrender alcohol in a controlled drinking zone. This is liable on summary conviction to a fine not exceeding level 2 on the standard scale. If alcohol is confiscated, it can be disposed of by the person who confiscates it.

Depending on the behaviour in question, the enforcing officer could decide that a fixed penalty notice would be the most appropriate sanction. This can be issued by a police officer, a Police Community Support Officer, council officer or other person designated by the council. In making the decision to issue a fixed penalty notice, the officer should consider that if issued, payment would discharge any liability to conviction for the offence. However, payment is not made within the required timescale, court proceedings can be initiated (prosecution for the offence of failing to comply with the Public Spaces Protection Order).

Appeals: Any challenge to the Public Spaces Protection Order must be made in the High Court by an interested person within six weeks of it being made. An interested person is someone who lives in, regularly works in, or visits the restricted area. This means that only those who are directly affected by the restrictions have the power to challenge. This right to challenge also exists where an order is varied by a council. Additionally, as with all orders and powers, the making of a PSPO can be challenged by judicial review on public law grounds within three months of the decision or action subject to challenge.

Interested persons can challenge the validity of an Order on two grounds. They could argue that the council did not have power to make the order, or to include particular prohibitions or requirements. In addition, the interested person could argue that one of the requirements (for instance, consultation) had not been complied with.

When the application is made, the High Court can decide to suspend the operation of the Public Spaces Protection Order pending the verdict in part or in totality. The High Court has the ability to uphold the Public Spaces Protection Order, quash it, or vary it.

Enforcement: Although Public Spaces Protection Orders are made by the council in an area, enforcement is the responsibility of a wider group. Council officers are able to enforce the restrictions and requirements, as are other groups that they designate, including officers accredited under the community safety accreditation scheme. In addition, police officers and Police Community Support Officers are able to enforce Public Spaces Protection Orders.

Transition of existing orders to Public Spaces Protection Orders

Section 75 of the Anti-social Behaviour, Crime and Policing Act 2014 sets out that where a Gating Order, Dog Control Order or Designated Public Place Order is still in force three years from commencement of the Act (i.e. on 20 October 2017) the provisions of such an order will automatically be treated as if they were provisions of a Public Spaces Protection Order. The transitioned Order will then remain in force up to a maximum of three years from the point of transition i.e. 2020.

Section 75(3) of the Anti-social Behaviour, Crime and Policing Act 2014 treats transitioned orders as Public Spaces Protection Orders that have already been made. The consultation, notification and publicity requirements in section 72(3) of the Act apply before a Public Spaces Protection Order has been made; the obligation under section 59(8) of the Act to publish arises once a Public Spaces Protection Order has been made.

Councils are not required to undertake a new consultation (or associated publications, and notifications, set out in section 72(3) of the Act) where a Gating Order, Dog Control Order or Designated Public Place Order automatically transitions to a Public Spaces Protection Order after October 2017.

However, local councils should publish the Public Spaces Protection Order online when the Gating Order, Dog Control Order or Designated Public Place Order transitions in order to make the public aware of the specific provisions of the Public Spaces Protection Order.

It will be for local councils to consider what changes to signage are necessary to sufficiently draw the matters set out in Regulation 2 of the Anti-social Behaviour, Crime and Policing Act 2014 (Publication of Public Spaces Protection Orders) Regulation 2014 to members of the public's attention.

Any extension, variation or discharge of a transitioned Public Spaces Protection Order would mean that the local council would need to carry out the necessary consultation and publication as required under section 72 (3) of the Anti-social Behaviour, Crime and Policing Act 2014.

2.6   Closure Power

Purpose	To allow the police or council to close premises quickly which are being used, or likely to be used, to commit nuisance or disorder.
Applicants	• Local council. • Police.
Test	The following has occurred, or will occur, if the closure power is not used: **(a) Closure Notice (up to 48 hours):** • Nuisance to the public; or • Disorder near those premises. **(b) Closure Order (up to six months):** • Disorderly, offensive or criminal behaviour; • Serious nuisance to the public; or • Disorder near the premises.
Details	• A Closure Notice is issued out of court in the first instance. Flowing from this the Closure Order can be applied for through the courts. • **Notice**: can close premises for up to 48 hours out of court but cannot stop owner or those who habitually live there accessing the premises. • **Order**: can close premises for up to six months and can restrict all access. • Both the Notice and the Order can cover any land or any other place, whether enclosed or not including residential, business, non-business and licensed premises.
Penalty on breach	Breach is a criminal offence. • **Notice**: Up to three months in prison. • **Order**: Up to six months in prison. • **Both**: Up to an unlimited fine for residential and non-residential premises.
Who can appeal	• Any person who the Closure Notice was served on; • Any person who had not been served the Closure Notice but has an interest in the premises; • The council (where Closure Order was not made and they issued the notice); • The police (where Closure Order was not made and they issued the notice).
The legislation	Sections 76 to 93 of the Anti-social Behaviour, Crime and Policing Act 2014

404

Closure Power

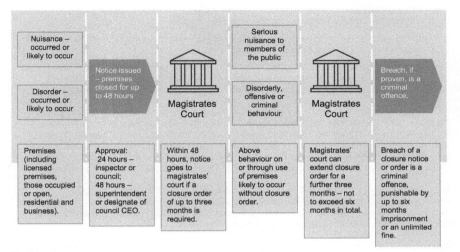

| Premises (including licensed premises, those occupied or open, residential and business). | Approval: 24 hours – inspector or council; 48 hours – superintendent or designate of council CEO. | Within 48 hours, notice goes to magistrates' court if a closure order of up to three months is required. | Above behaviour on or through use of premises likely to occur without closure order. | Magistrates' court can extend closure order for a further three months – not to exceed six months in total. | Breach of a closure notice or order is a criminal offence, punishable by up to six months imprisonment or an unlimited fine. |

Purpose

The closure power is a fast, flexible power that can be used to protect victims and communities by quickly closing premises that are causing nuisance or disorder.

Applicants

The power comes in two stages: the Closure Notice and the Closure Order which are intrinsically linked. The Closure Notice can be used by the council or the police out of court. Following the issuing of a Closure Notice, an application must be made to the magistrates' court for a Closure Order, unless the closure notice has been cancelled.

Details

The legal tests: A Closure Notice can be issued for 24 hours if the council or police officer (of at least the rank of inspector) is satisfied on reasonable grounds:

- that the use of particular premises has resulted, or (if the notice is not issued) is likely soon to result, in nuisance to members of the public; or

- that there has been, or (if the notice is not issued) is likely soon to be, disorder near those premises associated with the use of those premises, and that the notice is necessary to prevent the nuisance or disorder from continuing, recurring or occurring.

The Closure Notice can be issued in the first instance for 48 hours or extended from 24 hours up to a maximum of 48 hours by the council's chief executive officer (head of paid service) or designate thereof, or by a police superintendent.

A Closure Order can subsequently be issued if the court is satisfied:

- that a person has engaged, or (if the order is not made) is likely to engage, in disorderly, offensive or criminal behaviour on the premises; or

- that the use of the premises has resulted, or (if the order is not made) is likely to result, in serious nuisance to members of the public; or

- that there has been, or (if the order is not made) is likely to be, disorder near those premises associated with the use of those premises, and that the order is necessary to prevent the behaviour, nuisance or disorder from continuing, recurring or occurring.

A Closure Notice cannot prohibit access in respect of anyone who habitually lives on the premises. This means that the notice cannot prohibit those who routinely or regularly live at those premises. It is therefore unlikely to disallow access to, for example, students who live away from the family home for part of the year but routinely return to the family home or those who spend the majority of the week living at the pub in which they work. However, a Closure Order, granted by the court, can prohibit access to those who routinely live at the premises.

In prohibiting access through a Closure Notice it will be important to consider who is responsible for the premises and who may need access to secure the premises. This might not always be the owner, for example an individual managing premises on behalf of an owner who lives abroad may need to secure the premises on their behalf.

Approvals: The level or role of employee within the council who can issue a notice for up to 24 hours has not been specified due to the different structures in place in different areas. In considering who should be authorised as designates of the chief executive officer for the issuing of the 48 hour notice, councils will also want to consider who is delegated to issue the Closure Notice for 24 hours and consider whether the extension to 48 hours should be authorised by an officer of greater seniority, as is the case for the police. This may take into consideration the need for the power to be used quickly, its flexible nature, and equivalent requirement for a police inspector to issue a Closure Notice for 24 hours.

Notifications: With every issue of a Closure Notice, an application must be made to the magistrates' court for a Closure Order. Where the intention is to cancel the notice prior to the end of the 48 hour period because a Closure Order or a temporary order is not deemed necessary, this should be communicated to the court on application for a hearing for the Closure Order.

The police and council will want to consider when the courts will be able to hear the application for the Closure Order. The courts are required to hear the application within 48 hours of the service of the Closure Notice. This 48 hour period for the courts excludes Christmas day. To avoid undue pressure on the courts to hear applications for Closure Orders within 48 hours of serving the Closure Notice, careful thought should be given as to exactly when to serve the Closure Notice. Where possible, it is advisable to liaise with the court's listing office before serving the Closure Notice so that victims can be effectively protected at the earliest opportunity.

> **Putting victims first**: The issuing body should undertake to inform the victim of the anti-social behaviour of the Closure Notice and to inform them of the details of the Closure Order hearing where possible and appropriate.

Temporary orders: Courts can consider giving an extension of the Closure Notice if required. This can be considered as an option by the magistrates' court at the hearing for the Closure Order. The court can order a Closure Notice to stay in force for a further 48 hours if it is satisfied that this meets the test required for a Closure Notice.

A court may also order that a Closure Notice continue in force for a period of not more than 14 days in circumstances where the hearing is adjourned. A hearing can be adjourned for no more that 14 days to enable the occupier or anyone with an interest in the premises to show why a Closure Order should not be made.

Partnership working: Consultation is required as part of the Closure Notice. Before issuing a notice the police or council must ensure that they consult with anyone they think appropriate. This should include the victim, but could also include other members of the public that may be affected positively or negatively by the closure, community representatives, other organisations and bodies, the police or local council (where not the issuing organisation) or others that regularly use the premises. There may also be people who use the premises as access to other premises that are not subject to the closure notice but may be impacted on by the closure.

The method of consultation will depend on the situation and urgency. The police or council will want to consider how to keep a record of those consulted in case challenged at a later date (for instance, as part of a court case).

What to include in a Closure Notice? The Closure Notice should:

- identify the premises;
- explain the effect of the notice;
- state that failure to comply with the notice is an offence;
- state that an application will be made for a closure order;
- specify when and where the application will be heard;
- explain the effect of the closure order; and
- give information about the names of, and means of contacting, persons and organisations in the area that provide advice about housing and legal matters.

Information should be displayed clearly in simple language, avoiding the use of jargon.

Putting victims first: It is not necessary to include information about those consulted within an order so as to protect those who may have made a complaint from any retribution. However, the officer issuing the Closure Notice should keep a record of those consulted.

Access: There may be times where the closure of premises through a Closure Order has a wider impact. An item may have been left in the premises or access has become restricted to other premises. Where an item has been left on premises it is expected that the police and local council will use their discretion in either allowing access temporarily to enable the individual to retrieve their item or retrieving the item on their behalf. Where an individual accesses the premises themselves without communication to the police or council they commit an offence unless they have a reasonable excuse. It is therefore sensible for the police and council to have clear communication with individuals affected.

Where a Closure Order restricts access to other premises or part of other premises that are not subject to a Closure Order the individuals affected will be able to apply to the appropriate court to have the order considered. The court may make any order that it thinks appropriate. This may be a variation order to vary the terms of the order or it could cancel the order if considered inappropriate for it to remain in place.

Penalty on breach: An offence is committed when a person, without reasonable excuse, remains on or enters premises in contravention of a Closure Notice or a Closure Order.

Closure Notice and temporary order: Breaching a Closure Notice or temporary order is a criminal offence carrying a penalty of either imprisonment for a period of up to three months or an unlimited fine or both.

Closure Order: Breaching a Closure Order is a criminal offence carrying a penalty of either imprisonment for a period of up to six months or an unlimited fine, or both.

Obstruction: It is a criminal offence to obstruct a police officer or local council employee who is:

- serving a Closure Notice, cancellation notice or variation notice;
- entering the premises; or
- securing the premises.

This offence carries a penalty of either imprisonment for a period of up to three months or an unlimited fine, or both.

Who can appeal: A Closure Notice cannot be appealed. A Closure Order can be appealed. Appeals are to the Crown Court and must be made within 21 days beginning with the date of the decision to which the appeal relates.

An appeal against the decision to issue the order may be made by:

- a person who was served the Closure Notice; or
- anyone who has an interest in the premises upon whom the notice was not served.

Where the court decides not to issue a closure order the following may appeal:

- the police may only appeal where they issued the Closure Notice;
- the local council may only appeal where they issued the Closure Notice.

On appeal, the Crown Court may make whatever order it thinks appropriate. If the premises is licensed the court must inform the licensing authority. It should also be considered whether it is appropriate and possible to update the victim on the progress of the case.

2.7   Absolute ground for possession

Overview	The Act introduced a new absolute ground for possession of secure and assured tenancies where anti-social behaviour or criminality has already been proven by another court.
Purpose	To expedite the eviction of landlords' most anti-social tenants to bring faster relief to victims.
Applicants / Who can use the new ground	• Social landlords (local authorities and housing associations). • Private rented sector landlords.
Test	The tenant, a member of the tenant's household, or a person visiting the property has met one of the following conditions: • convicted of a serious offence (specified in Schedule 2A to the Housing Act 1985); • found by a court to have breached a civil injunction; • convicted for breaching a criminal behaviour order (CBO); • convicted for breaching a noise abatement notice; or • the tenant's property has been closed for more than 48 hours under a closure order for anti-social behaviour.
Details	• Offence/breach needs to have occurred in the locality of the property or affected a person with a right to live in the locality or affected the landlord or his or her staff/contractors; • Secure tenants of local housing authorities will have a statutory right to request a review of the landlord's decision to seek possession. Private registered providers are encouraged to adopt a similar practice.
Result of action	• If the above test is met, the court must grant a possession order (subject to any available human rights defence raised by the tenant, including proportionality) where the correct procedure has been followed.
Important changes/differences	• Unlike the discretionary grounds for possession, the landlord is not required to prove to the court that it is reasonable to grant possession. This means the court is more likely to determine cases in a single, short hearing; • This offers better protection and faster relief for victims and witnesses of anti- social behaviour, saves landlords costs, and frees up court resources and time; • It provides flexibility for landlords to obtain possession through this route for persistently anti-social tenants; • The court cannot postpone possession to a date later than 14 days after the making of the order except in exceptional circumstances, and cannot postpone for later than six weeks in any event.
The legislation	Sections 94 to 100 of the Anti-social Behaviour, Crime and Policing Act 2014

409

Absolute ground for possession

Tenant/member of their household or visitor has met one of the following conditions: 1. Convicted for serious criminal offence. 2. Found by a court to have breached a civil injunction. 3. Convicted for breach of CBO. 4. Convicted for breach of Noise Abatement Notice OR 5. Tenant's property closed under Closure Order.	Landlord considers possession on absolute ground Landlord serves Notice	Review Decision upheld	Landlord applies to court	Court Consideration	Court grants Outright Possession
Offences must have been committed in locality/affected other residents or landlord's staff anywhere.	Generally four week or one month notice period (depending on tenancy type) before landlord applies to court.	Tenant requests review of decision (statutory right of review for local authority tenants only).	Standard period between issue of the claim form and the hearing is a maximum of eight weeks	Court must grant possession subject to any available human rights defence provided set procedures have been followed	Court's discretion to suspend possession is limited to no later than 14 days or six weeks in exceptional circumstances.

Overview

Prevention and early intervention should be at the heart of all landlords' approaches to dealing with anti-social behaviour. Available evidence shows this is the case with over 82% of anti-social behaviour complaints resolved by social landlords through early intervention and informal routes without resorting to formal tools in 2015/16.

It has, however, been a source of frustration for landlords and victims that in exceptional cases where anti-social behaviour (or criminality) persists and it becomes necessary to seek possession, the processes for evicting anti-social tenants can be lengthy and expensive, prolonging the suffering of victims, witnesses and the community.

Purpose

The absolute ground for possession was introduced to speed up the possession process in cases where anti-social behaviour or criminality has been already been proven by another court. This strikes a better balance between the rights of victims and perpetrators and provides swifter relief for those victims. The absolute ground for possession is intended to be used in the most serious cases and landlords are encouraged to ensure that the ground is used selectively.

Details

Informing the tenant: Landlords should ensure that tenants are aware from the commencement of their tenancy that anti-social behaviour or criminality either by the tenant, people living with them, or their visitors could lead to a loss of their home under the absolute ground.

Applicants: The absolute ground is available for secure and assured tenancies, and can be used by both social landlords and private rented sector landlords. In practice, many private rented sector landlords continue to use the 'no fault' ground for possession, in section 21 of the Housing Act 1988, where this is available. This does not require the tenant to be in breach of any of the terms of their tenancy and, therefore, does not require the landlord to show that it is reasonable to grant possession as long as the relevant notice has been served. However, the 'no fault' ground can only be used at the end of the fixed term of the tenancy, which must be at least six months from the initial inception of the tenancy. This often limits private landlords' ability to seek possession where a tenant commits serious anti-social behaviour or criminality in the early stages of the tenancy. The absolute ground should assist private rented sector landlords to end tenancies quickly in cases of serious anti-social behaviour or criminality that occur during the fixed term of an assured short-hold tenancy.

The legal tests: The court must grant possession (subject to any available human rights defence raised by the tenant, including proportionality) provided the landlord has followed the correct procedure and at least one of the following five conditions is met:

- the tenant, a member of the tenant's household, or a person visiting the property has been convicted of a serious offence;

- the tenant, a member of the tenant's household, or a person visiting the property has been found by a court to have breached a Civil Injunction;

- the tenant, a member of the tenant's household, or a person visiting the property has been convicted for breaching a Criminal Behaviour Order;

- the tenant's property has been closed for more than 48 hours under a closure order for anti- social behaviour; or

- the tenant, a member of the tenant's household, or a person visiting the property has been convicted for breaching a noise abatement notice or order.

The offence or anti-social behaviour must have been committed in, or in the locality of, the property, affected a person with a right to live in the locality of the property or affected the landlord or the landlord's staff or contractors.

Serious offences for this purpose include, for example: violent and sexual offences and those relating to offensive weapons, drugs and damage to property. A list of the relevant offences is found in Schedule 2A to the Housing Act 1985.

The ground is available to landlords in addition to the discretionary grounds for possession set out in Schedule 2 to the Housing Act 1985 for secure tenants and Schedule 2 to the Housing Act 1988 for assured tenants. Landlords are able to choose to use the absolute ground, in addition to, or instead of the discretionary grounds for anti-social behaviour where one or more of the five conditions are met.

Partnership working: Close working relationships with the police, local councils and other local agencies are important to ensure that the landlord is always aware when one or more of the triggers for the absolute ground has occurred.

Secured and Assured Tenancies

Secure tenants are generally tenants of local councils with a very high level of security of tenure.   Apart from the absolute ground, secure tenants can only be evicted from their property on the discretionary grounds for possession in Schedule 2 to the Housing Act 1985.

Tenants of housing associations generally have **non-shorthold assured tenancies** giving them a high level of security of tenure (although not fully equivalent to that of secure tenants). They can be evicted under mandatory grounds for possession provided for in Schedule 2 to the Housing Act 1988 (for example, for rent arrears) as well as discretionary grounds for possession.

Private rented sector tenants generally have **assured shorthold tenancies** giving them limited security of tenure. They can be evicted under the grounds for possession in Schedule 2 to the Housing Act 1988 as well as the 'no fault' ground in section 21 of the Housing Act 1988. This simply requires the landlord to give the tenant the proper notice before seeking a court order (usually without a hearing).

Notice requirements: In order to seek possession under the absolute ground, landlords must serve a notice of the proceedings on the tenant, either:

- within 12 months of the relevant conviction or finding of the court being relied on (or if there is an appeal against the finding or conviction within 12 months of the appeal being finally determined, abandoned or withdrawn); or

- within three months where the tenant's property has been closed under a closure order (or if there is an appeal against the making of the closure order, within three months of the appeal being finally determined, abandoned or withdrawn).

The minimum notice period for periodic tenancies is four weeks, or the tenancy period (i.e. the rent period) if longer. In the case of a fixed term tenancy the minimum notice period is one month. The notice is valid for 12 months.

The notice must include the following information:

- the landlord's intention to seek possession under the absolute ground;

- the reasons why they are seeking possession;

- which of the five conditions for the absolute ground the landlord proposes to rely on;

- the relevant conviction, finding of the court, or closure order the landlord proposes to rely on;

- details of any right that the tenant may have to request a review of the landlord's decision to seek possession, and the time within which the request must be made;

- where and how a tenant may seek advice on the notice; and

- the date after which possession proceedings may be begun.

If the landlord wishes to seek possession on one or more of the discretionary grounds as well, he or she must also specify and give details of the relevant discretionary ground/s in the notice.

There are no prescribed forms of notice for the absolute ground for either secure or assured tenancies. In the case of secure tenancies, section 83ZA of the Housing Act 1985 (inserted by section 95 of the Anti-social Behaviour, Crime and Policing Act 2014) simply specifies that certain information must be contained in the notice.

The provisions of section 83ZA (4) also makes clear that where possession of a secure tenancy is being sought under the absolute ground as well as one of the grounds in Schedule 2 of the 1985 Act, the notice need not be served in a form prescribed by regulations as required by section 83 of the 1985 Act but should follow the requirements of section 83ZA in such circumstances.

In the case of assured tenancies, section 97 of the Anti-social Behaviour, Crime and Policing Act 2014 has amended section 8 of the 1988 Act to modify the notice requirements for possession under assured tenancies to take account of the absolute ground.

The court has no power to dispense with service of a notice for possession under the absolute ground. Therefore where a landlord decides to seek possession for anti-social behaviour on the absolute ground alongside one or more of the discretionary grounds, the court will not be able to dispense with the notice as they would have been able to do if the possession was sought solely on the discretionary ground.

The review procedure:

- Local council tenants have a statutory right to request a review of the landlord's decision to seek possession under the new absolute ground.

- The request for a review must be made in writing within seven days of the notice to seek possession being served on the tenant.

- The review must be carried out before the end of the notice.

- The landlord must communicate the outcome of the review to the tenant in writing.

- If the decision is to confirm the original decision to seek possession, the landlord must also notify the tenant of the reasons for the decision.

- If the review upholds the original decision, the landlord will proceed by applying to the court for the possession order.

- The statutory review procedure does not apply to housing associations tenants. However, we expect housing associations to offer a similar non-statutory review procedure (in the same way that they have done so for starter tenancies for example).

Putting victims first: In preparation for the court process, landlords should consider:

- reassuring victims and witnesses by letting them know what they can expect to happen in court;

- using professional witnesses where possible; and

- taking necessary practical steps with court staff to reassure and protect vulnerable victims and witnesses in court (e.g. the provision of separate waiting areas and accompanying them to and from court).

Landlords should also consider providing support/protection for victims and witnesses out of court, at home, and beyond the end of the possession proceedings when necessary.

Court hearing and defences: Tenants are entitled to a court hearing. As with other grounds of possession, tenants of public authorities or landlords carrying out a public function are able to raise any available human rights defence, including proportionality, against the possession proceedings.

The court will consider whether such a defence meets the high threshold of being 'seriously arguable' established by the Supreme Court. Subject to any available human rights defence raised by the tenant, the court must grant an order for possession where the landlord has followed the correct procedure.

Suspension of possession order: The court may not postpone the giving up of possession to a date later than 14 days after the making of the order; unless exceptional hardship would result in which case it may be postponed for up to six weeks.

Important differences

Unlike with the discretionary grounds for possession, landlords do not need to prove to the court that it is reasonable to grant possession. This means that the court will be more likely to determine cases in a single hearing, thereby expediting the process.

The absolute ground is an additional tool which provides more flexibility for landlords but is applicable only in limited circumstances – where a court has already found a tenant or member of their household guilty of anti-social behaviour or criminality in the locality of the property.

The court has no power to dispense with service of a notice for possession under the absolute ground as they can do under the discretionary ground for anti-social behaviour.

Local council tenants have a statutory right to request a review of the landlord's decision to seek possession under the absolute ground. We expect housing associations to make a similar non-statutory review procedure available to their tenants.

The court only has the discretion to suspend a possession order made under the absolute ground to a date no later than 14 days after the making of the order (unless it appears to the court that exceptional hardship would be caused, in which case it may be postponed to a date no later than six weeks after the making of the order).

Public Spaces Protection Orders

Guidance for councils

Guidance

Foreword

Local authorities understand well how anti-social behaviour can blight the lives of people in their local communities, with those affected often feeling powerless to act. Councils have a key role to play in helping make local areas safe places to live, visit and work and tackling anti-social behaviour continues to be a high priority for local authorities and their partners across the country.

Councils know the issues that affect their localities the most and are well placed to identify how best to respond. Public Spaces Protection Orders (PSPOs), introduced in 2014, sit amongst a broad range of powers and tools to help tackle anti-social behaviour locally. PSPOs are aimed at ensuring public spaces can be enjoyed free from anti-social behaviour. They are not about stopping the responsible use of the night-time economy, or preventing young people from seeing their friends – but they do provide councils with another instrument to help deal with persistent issues that are damaging their communities.

PSPOs have not been welcomed by all, attracting some criticism over their introduction, or about how particular PSPOs have been implemented. As a result, in December 2017 the Home Office updated its statutory guidance on anti-social behaviour powers, according to the Anti-Social Behaviour, Crime and Policing Act 2014. The changes are reflected in this document. In light of the updated guidance, councils may find it useful to consider the current restrictions in their local area and whether the PSPO needs to be amended at the time of its renewal. It's important to note, that when used appropriately, proportionately and with local support, PSPOs can be a positive device that help to prevent anti-social behaviour, and can provide an effective response to some of the issues local residents and businesses face on a daily basis.

This guidance aims to set out the issues to consider where local areas are contemplating introducing a PSPO, and offers practical guidance on the steps to take if councils choose to do so. It should be read in conjunction with the Home Office's statutory guidance on the Anti-social Behaviour, Crime and Policing Act 2014.

Councillor Anita Lower
Deputy Chair and Anti-social Behaviour Champion
LGA Safer and Stronger Communities Board

Public Spaces Protection Orders

Legislative background

The Anti-social Behaviour, Crime and Policing Act 2014 introduced several new tools and powers for use by councils and their partners to address anti-social behaviour (ASB) in their local areas. These tools, which replaced and streamlined a number of previous measures, were brought in as part of a Government commitment to put victims at the centre of approaches to tackling ASB, focussing on the impact behaviour can have on both communities and individuals, particularly on the most vulnerable.

PSPOs are one of the tools available under the 2014 Act. These are wide-ranging and flexible powers for local authorities, which recognise that councils are often best placed to identify the broad and cumulative impact that ASB can have. The Act gives councils the authority to draft and implement PSPOs in response to the particular issues affecting their communities, provided certain criteria and legal tests are met.

Councils can use PSPOs to prohibit specified activities, and/or require certain things to be done by people engaged in particular activities, within a defined public area. PSPOs differ from other tools introduced under the Act as they are council-led, and rather than targeting specific individuals or properties, they focus on the identified problem behaviour in a specific location.

The legislation provides for restrictions to be placed on behaviour that apply to everyone in that locality (with the possible use of exemptions). Breach of a PSPO without a reasonable excuse is an offence.

Powers to create PSPOs came into force in October 2014. As well as enabling local authorities to address a range of different issues, the Orders replace Designated Public Place Orders (DPPOs), Gating Orders and Dog Control Orders.[1] Existing DPPOs, Gating Orders and Dog Control Orders which automatically become PSPOs (as of 20 October 2017).

Overview of Public Spaces Protection Orders

The Anti-social Behaviour, Crime and Policing Act 2014 provides a broad legal framework within which PSPOs can be implemented.

Orders can be introduced in a specific public area where the local authority[2] is satisfied on reasonable grounds that certain conditions have been met. The first test concerns the nature of the anti-social behaviour, requiring that:

- activities that have taken place have had a detrimental effect on the quality of life of those in the locality, or it is likely that activities will take place and that they will have a detrimental effect
- the effect or likely effect of these activities:
  - is, or is likely to be, persistent or continuing in nature
  - is, or is likely to be, unreasonable

---

1 Replacing orders under The Criminal Justice and Police Act 2001, the Highways Act 1980 and the Clean Neighbourhoods and Environment Act 2005 respectively.

2 This covers district councils, London Boroughs, county councils in an area where there is no district council in England (along with City of London and the Council of the Isles of Scilly) and county councils or a county borough councils in Wales.

○ justifies the restrictions being imposed.

The Home Office statutory guidance re issued in December 2017 states that proposed restrictions should focus on specific behaviours and be proportionate to the detrimental effect that the behaviour is causing or can cause, and are necessary to prevent it from continuing, occurring or recurring.[3]

A single PSPO can be used to target a range of different ASB issues. Orders allow councils to introduce reasonable prohibitions and/or requirements regarding certain behaviours within the specified public area, and may also include prescribed exemptions.

As a minimum, each PSPO must set out:

• what the detrimental activities are

• what is being prohibited and/or required, including any exemptions

• the area covered

• the consequences for breach

• the period for which it has effect.

There are further specific provisions regarding some types of PSPO, which will be covered in detail below.

A PSPO can last for up to three years, after which it must be reviewed. If the review supports an extension and other requirements are satisfied, it may be extended for up to a further three years. There is no limit on the number of times an Order may be reviewed and renewed.

The legislation sets out a number of additional requirements for consultation and communication before an Order is introduced, once it is implemented and where it is extended, varied or discharged. PSPOs can be legally challenged under the 2014 Act on certain grounds.

Beyond this broad framework, detailed further below, councils can decide how best to implement PSPOs in their local areas. This guidance sets out some suggested

approaches based on good practice from around the country.

Using Public Spaces Protection Orders

Local partners have a vast range of tools and powers at their disposal to respond to concerns about anti-social behaviour in their locality, from measures aimed at tackling the causes of ASB, awareness-raising, through to enforcement.

Used proportionately and in the right circumstances, PSPOs allow local areas to counter unreasonable and persistent behaviour that affects the quality of life of its residents. They can send a clear message that certain behaviours will not be tolerated, and help reassure residents that unreasonable conduct is being addressed.

However, PSPOs will not be suitable or effective in all circumstances, and it is important to consider carefully the right approach for identifying and addressing the problem behaviour. This is especially important when the activities may also have positive benefits. Other options should actively be considered before a PSPO is pursued – and where a PSPO is used, it should be carefully framed and employed alongside other approaches as part of a broad and balanced anti-social behaviour strategy. Considering non-statutory solutions, perhaps delivered in partnership with community, civic or membership organisations may be equally valid in the right circumstances.

Choosing the right tool
Choosing the right approaches for responding to the ASB should start with identifying the specific issue or issues of concern, and considering what is likely to be the most targeted and effective response in the circumstances.

---

3   https://www.gov.uk/government/uploads/system/uploads/ attachment_data/file/670180/2017-12-13_ASB_Revised_ Statutory_Guidance_V2_0.pdf)

Some issues may be adequately addressed using other tools. For instance, awareness-raising campaigns about the impact of certain activities on others, improved community engagement, or offering support to those exhibiting certain behaviours may be enough to address the ASB identified.

In some areas, codes of practice around certain practices such as busking[4], or posters setting out 'good behaviour' associated with activities such as skateboarding, have provided effective solutions in responding to particular concerns.

Street fundraising for instance, is governed by an independently set Code of Fundraising Practice and the Institute of Fundraising provides a free service for councils to limit the location, number and frequency of fundraising visits. Around 125 councils have taken advantage of these voluntary agreements, rather than use PSPOs.

In other circumstances it may be more appropriate to use tools such as community protection notices (CPNs). CPNs are used against specific individuals responsible for causing harm, or for tackling particular problem premises, unlike PSPOs which create a broader ban covering a whole area. Similarly, in many cases existing legislation covering various forms of anti-social behaviour or public order may be adequate.

Feedback from councils suggests that effective consultation with partners, stakeholders and the wider community can help to identify the best way forward (see also support evidence and consultation, below).

"PSPOs aren't the answer for everything – you need to start by looking at what the issue really is. Often there are easier and more effective tools for dealing with the problem."

Cheshire West and Chester Council

4   See, for example, City of York Council: https://www.york.
    gov.uk/info/20081/arts_and_culture/1155/busking_in_york

Where local areas decide that introducing a PSPO may be appropriate, it should be noted that the most robust Orders directly address the detrimental behaviour, rather than activities which may not in themselves be detrimental or which target characteristics that might be shared by some of those responsible (or with the wider public). The Home Office's statutory guidance reiterates that PSPOs should be used responsibly and proportionately, only in response to issues that cause anti-social behaviour, and only where necessary to protect the public.

There are also a number of practical considerations which should be borne in mind when choosing the right tool. PSPOs can be resource-intensive to introduce and enforce and there will need to be commitment from partners to ensure it can be implemented effectively.

Councils will need to be satisfied that where they choose to pursue introducing an Order as part of their strategy, they have met the requirements of the legislation. This is covered in detail in the following sections.

Introducing a PSPO

Where councils have identified that a PSPO may be a suitable response to a particular local issue, they will then need to consider how to ensure they meet the statutory criteria. This will include determining:

- the appropriate scope of the Order
- the area covered by the restrictions
- the potential impact of the proposals
- how each of the restrictions meets the legal test.

Councils will also need to consider how best the Order should be worded and establish an evidence base to support the proposals, incorporating a consultation process. Other issues, such as the practical implications around implementation and what is possible to enforce, will also need to be borne in mind.

Early engagement with partners and stakeholders can be useful in understanding the nature of the issue, how best to respond – and, if an Order is proposed, how it might be drafted. This is likely to require involvement, and pooling of information, from a variety of sources, including councillors and officers from across council departments (including, for example, community safety, environmental health, parks, equalities, legal), police colleagues and external agencies.

It is useful for local areas to seek early contact with interest groups when scoping their proposals, to help identify how best to approach a particular issue, before the formal statutory consultation takes place. For example, a local residents' association or regular users of a park or those involved in specific activities in the area, such as buskers or other street entertainers. An effective consultation process with a range of stakeholders will also help to assess the impact of the ASB and where an appropriate balance for restrictions on behaviour should lie (see supporting evidence and consultation, below).

"Engagement with representative groups early on was really constructive – they helped advise us on other legislation we needed to be mindful of, and helped us draft something that worked."

Carmarthenshire County Council

Ongoing engagement with, and commitment from, partners will be crucial for introducing, implementing and enforcing a PSPO and ensuring there are resources available to support it.

Activity subject to an Order – overview
PSPOs can be used to restrict a broad range of activities. Under section 59 of the 2014 Act, local authorities must be satisfied on reasonable grounds that the activity subject to an Order:

• has a detrimental effect on the quality of life of those in the locality (or it is likely

that activities will take place and have such an effect)
• is (or is likely to be) persistent or continuing in nature
• is (or is likely to be) unreasonable
• justifies the restrictions being imposed.

PSPOs must set out clearly what the detrimental activities are. What may be regarded as 'anti-social' is a subjective concept, and similarly determining whether or not behaviour is detrimental and unreasonable can present some challenges and will require careful consideration.

Councils will need to assess how certain behaviours are perceived, and their impact – both on the community broadly, and on its most vulnerable individuals. Some areas have included an additional test locally that the behaviour needs to be severe enough to cause alarm, harassment or distress. Collating evidence that illustrates the detrimental impact of particular activities will be important (see supporting evidence and consultation, below).

When assessing what is 'unreasonable' activity, councils will need to balance the rights of the community to enjoy public spaces without ASB, with the civil liberties of individuals and groups who may be affected by any restrictions imposed. Further, some of those affected by possible restrictions may be vulnerable and councils need to look carefully at what impact the proposals might have on certain groups or individuals (see assessing potential impact and the Equality Act, below).

Appropriate restrictions
As set out above, the restrictions imposed by an Order must be reasonable, and either prevent or reduce the detrimental effect of the problem behaviour, or reduce the risk of that detrimental effect continuing, occurring or recurring. Ensuring that the prohibitions or requirements included in a PSPO are solid, easily understood and can withstand scrutiny is key.

Orders must state what restrictions are being imposed to either prohibit certain things, and/ or require certain things to be done by those engaged in specific activities. PSPOs are most effective and most robust to challenge where they are **tightly drafted and focus on the precise harmful behaviour identified**. Being clear on addressing the problem behaviour in an Order can help avoid the risk of unduly pursuing individuals who may not be causing any real harm.

Homeless people and rough sleepers
The Home Office guidance sets out that PSPOs should not be used to target people based solely on the fact that someone is homeless or rough sleeping, as this in itself is unlikely to mean that such behaviour is having an unreasonably detrimental effect on the community's quality of life which justifies the restrictions imposed. It suggests the council should consider whether the use of a PSPO is the appropriate response and if it will have a detrimental impact on homeless people and rough sleepers. Councils will find it useful to consult with national or local homeless charities on this issue, when councils are considering restrictions or requirements that could affect homeless people and rough sleepers.

Groups hanging around/standing in groups/playing games
It is important that any Orders put in place do not inadvertently restrict everyday sociability in public spaces. Restrictions that are too broad or general in nature may, for instance, force young people into out-of-the-way spaces and put them at risk. It is useful to consider whether there are alternative spaces that they can use. The Home Office guidance notes that people living in temporary accommodation may not be able to stay in their accommodation during the day and may find themselves spending extended time in public spaces. It's important to consider when putting in place any restrictions that public spaces are available for the use and enjoyment of a broad spectrum of the public, and that people of all ages are free to gather, talk and play games.

In the London Borough of Brent, residents and park users identified issues with public defecation, alcohol use, public disturbances and intimidation. The council introduced a PSPO targeting the cause of the ASB – groups congregating, attracted by offers of casual labour. The council was keen not to enforce against rough sleepers or job-seekers but instead outlaw the offering of employment within the area, and the running of an unlicensed transport service. The aim was to deter those seeking to exploit casual labourers and those profiting from bringing certain groups to the area.

Proposals should clearly define which specific behaviours are not permitted or are required, and any exemptions that might apply. Careful wording will help people to understand whether or not they are in breach once the Order has been implemented and give them an opportunity to modify their behaviour. It will also help to avoid any unintended consequences. Councils' legal teams should be able to advise on the precise wording to use.

Limitations
There are some limitations set out in the legislation regarding behaviours that can be restricted by PSPOs. Under the 2014 Act, local authorities must have regard to the freedoms permitted under articles 10 and 11 of the Human Rights Act 1998 when drafting, extending, varying or discharging an Order. These cover freedom of expression, and freedom of assembly and association respectively (although it is worth noting here that PSPOs might be considered appropriate for addressing aggravating behaviours such as the use of noise-enhancing equipment like amplifiers). Wherever proposals for an Order have the potential to impinge on the rights under articles 10 and 11, consideration must be given as to how to demonstrate that they satisfy the requirements of paragraph 2 in each of the articles.

Where a PSPO covers alcohol prohibition, section 62 of the 2014 Act lists a number of premises to which an Order cannot apply – such as licensed premises.

421

Further, there are some restrictions under section 63 on what action might be taken for a breach of an Order that prohibits consumption of alcohol (see enforcement and implementation, below).

Where Orders will restrict public rights of way, section 64 of the Act requires authorities to consider a number of issues, including the impact on those living nearby and the availability of alternative routes – and sets out some categories of highway where rights of way cannot be restricted. Councils may also conclude that PSPOs restricting access should only be introduced where the ASB is facilitated by the use of that right of way – otherwise it may be more appropriate to draft an Order focussed on the problem behaviour instead.

Some PSPOs have been introduced to address ASB linked with ingesting new psychoactive substances (NPS). The Psychoactive Substances Act 2016 introduces new legislation regarding the production and supply of NPS, but, unlike controlled drugs, does not criminalise the possession of substances alone.[5] Effective implementation and enforcement of PSPOs that deal with the consumption of psychoactive or intoxicating substances will require particularly careful consideration. Wording of these Orders should be precise to avoid any unintended consequences, ensuring it is clear what substances are covered or exempted.[6]

Area subject to an Order

The Act and Home Office statutory guidance set out the types of land which can be subject to a PSPO, or where additional considerations or requirements apply (eg when undertaking the consultation process). The activity restricted by an Order must be carried out in a public place, which is defined in the legislation as 'any place to which the public or any section of the public has access, on payment or otherwise, as of right or by virtue of express or implied permission'.

There may be some restrictions on the activities that can be prohibited on certain types of land (registered common land, registered town or village greens and open access land) which should also be considered. For instance, restrictions on access to registered common land may be subject to a separate consents process under The Commons Act 2006.[7] Further, for Orders that restrict public rights of way, section 65 of the 2014 Act sets out certain categories of highway to which such an Order cannot apply.

For addressing behaviour on privately-owned open spaces, other approaches may be more effective and appropriate. Private landowners are responsible for behaviours which occur upon their land and where landowners can be identified and traced, councils should work with them to address problem behaviour. Where landowners do not engage, councils may utilise other tools and powers available to them, such as Community Protection Notices or Civil Injunctions.

In Oldham, the council has successfully worked with a group of landowners and residents to enable them to find their own solutions to improve security and reduce ASB.

Determining the extent of the geographical area covered by an Order will mean identifying what is proportionate in the circumstances and restricting activities only where necessary – ie only where the legal test is met. It may be difficult to demonstrate that the statutory criteria under section 59 have been met across an entire broad geographical area; evidence about the extent of the anti-social behaviour within a locality should be used to inform appropriate boundaries (see supporting evidence and consultation, below).

---

5   Unless in a custodial institution.

6   It may be useful to refer to The Psychoactive Substances Act 2016, which includes a list of substances that might be deemed to produce a psychoactive effect when consumed but which are exempt from the scope of the 2016 Act – for instance medicinal products, nicotine or caffeine.

---

7   Further information and links to additional guidance: https://www.gov.uk/government/uploads/system/uploads/attachment_data/file/364851/Public_and_open_spaces_information_note.pdf

In some cases of course it will not be appropriate to introduce broad-scale restrictions. When drafting an Order placing restrictions on dogs for instance, it should be considered that owners have a duty under the Animal Welfare Act 2006, to provide for their animal's welfare, which includes exercising them. In determining the area covered by restrictions, councils should therefore consider how to accommodate the need for owners to exercise their animals.

The area which the PSPO will cover must be clearly defined. Mapping out areas where certain behaviours **are** permitted may also be helpful; for instance identifying specific park areas where dogs can be let off a lead without breaching the PSPO.

Controlling the presence of dogs

The Home Office guidance encourages councils to publish a list of alternative sites which dog walkers can use to exercise their dogs without restrictions. Councils should also consult dog law and welfare experts, for example, vets or animal welfare officers and organisations affected by restrictions before seeking to a PSPO. It may be useful to consult the Kennel Club on these issues.

The Department for Environment, Food and Rural Affairs has produced guidance in the form of a practitioner's guide on a range of tools available to deal with irresponsible dog ownership, for example, the use of a Community Protection Notice.

Where parish and town councils wish to deal with dog control issues, they are advised to approach the relevant authority, including whether a PSPO would provide the means to address the issues being experiencing by the local community. If the principal authority is satisfied that the legal tests for the use of the power are met and that it is a proportionate response to the level of harm and nuisance being caused it should consider consulting on putting in place a PSPO.

Practical issues, such as effective enforcement and erecting signs in (or near) an area subject to an Order – as required by the legislation – should also be borne in mind when determining how large an area the Order proposals might cover.

Displacing behaviour
Notwithstanding the requirements outlined above, when defining the area restrictions should cover, consideration should be given as to whether prohibitions in one area will displace the problem behaviour elsewhere, or into a neighbouring authority. It is worth noting here that the legislation allows for Orders to address activity that 'is likely to' occur in that public place. Local areas can therefore consider whether there are any legitimate concerns that introducing an Order in one area, and not another, could simply move issues somewhere else – and thus whether it would be appropriate to extend into a larger area or adjacent street. Councils will however need to ensure that a proportionate approach is taken overall, and that there is evidence to support using a broader approach.

Where there are concerns that activity may be displaced into other areas, authorities should contact neighbouring councils to discuss managing any unintended consequences.

Order exemptions
The legislation allows for Orders to apply only in particular circumstances and may include certain exemptions. Restricting behaviours only at certain times of day, or on a seasonal basis, can help to balance the needs of different groups and may be easier to enforce. Orders might only cover times of day when the issue is particularly acute, or when the problem behaviour will have more of an impact on others. Similarly, some types of ASB can be seasonal in their nature, for example relating to school holidays or summer weather. It may be the case that only at certain times will the behaviour be regarded as sufficiently 'detrimental' to satisfy the legislative test.

Exemptions for particular groups may be appropriate. For instance, for PSPOs controlling the use of dogs, it is likely that assistance dogs should be exempt; this will need to be explicitly stated in the wording of the Order.[8] Exemptions might also cover particular circumstances where restrictions may or may not apply. Undertaking an effective impact assessment (see assessing potential impact and the Equality Act, below) should help to identify the consequences of a proposed Order on specific groups and therefore whether certain exemptions would be appropriate.

Assessing potential impact and the Equality Act 2010

It is important for councils to consider carefully the potential impact of a PSPO on different sections of their communities. In introducing an Order, councils must take care to ensure that they comply with the requirements of the public sector equality duty under the Equality Act 2010. The Equality Act requires public authorities to have due regard to a number of equality considerations when exercising their functions. Proposals for a PSPO should therefore be reviewed to determine how they might target or impact on certain groups.

Although it is not a specific requirement of the legislation, it is recommended that areas undertake an Equality Impact Assessment (EIA) to assess whether the proposed PSPO will have disparate impact on groups with protected characteristics.[9] This process will help councils to establish any potential negative impacts and consider how to mitigate against these. This exercise will also help to ensure transparency.

Areas that have undertaken an EIA before introducing a PSPO have reported how useful this was[10], providing an opportunity to give full and separate consideration to the effect that each of the prohibitions or requirements might have on those in particular groups, and

enabling areas to consider how they could minimise any negative consequences – both in terms of the scope of the proposals and in how they might be implemented. Undertaking an EIA before introducing a PSPO can help to inform how best to balance the interests of different parts of the community, and provide evidence as to whether or not the restrictions being proposed are justified – as required by section 59 of the 2014 Act.

Duration of PSPOs

Orders can be introduced for a maximum of three years, and may be extended beyond this for further three-year period(s) where certain criteria are met (see extension, variation and discharge, below). The proposed length should reflect the need for an appropriate and proportionate response to the problem issue. Some areas have introduced shorter Orders to address very specific issues, where it is felt that a longer-term approach is unnecessary.

Supporting evidence and consultation

Local areas will, of course, need to satisfy themselves that the legislative requirements are met before an Order can be introduced, and obtaining clear evidence to support this is important. Collating information about the nature and impact of the ASB subject to the PSPO are core elements of the evidence-gathering and consultation process and will help inform the council's view as to whether the requirements under section 59 of the Act have been fulfilled.

The evidence will need to be weighed up before authorities can determine whether or not it is appropriate and proportionate to introduce a PSPO at all, and if so, whether the draft proposals are suitable. It can be used to help shape the scope of the Order, including any exemptions – such as times of day when a behaviour might be prohibited – and can also help to determine what area the Order should cover and how long it should last. The most robust Orders will be supported by a solid evidence base and rationale that sets out how

---

8   This differs from some Dog Control Orders, which automatically excluded assistance dogs from restrictions.

9   The Equality Duty covers: age, disability, gender, gender reassignment, pregnancy and maternity, race, religion or belief and sexual orientation. Marriage and civil partnership are also covered in some circumstances.

10 See example from Oxford City Council: http://mycouncil.oxford.gov.uk/ieDecisionDetails.aspx?AlId=10095

the statutory criteria for each of the proposed restrictions have been met, and demonstrates a direct link between the anti-social behaviour and the PSPO being proposed in response.

The nature of this evidence, and how it should be weighted, is largely down to councils to determine, although obtaining a range of data from different sources as part of this process will be particularly useful in informing decision-making, and may help to avoid challenge further down the line (see further evidence, below, for specific examples). The Act does however require that there is a consultation process before an Order can be made (and held again when an Order is extended, varied or discharged).

Statutory consultation – who to contact?
Before introducing, extending, varying or discharging a PSPO, there are requirements under the Act regarding consultation, publicity and notification (see also publication and communication, below).

Local authorities are obliged to consult with the local chief officer of police; the police and crime commissioner; owners or occupiers of land within the affected area where reasonably practicable, and appropriate community representatives. Any county councils (where the Order is being made by a district), parish or community councils that are in the proposed area covered by the PSPO must be notified.

There are additional requirements under the Act regarding Orders that restrict public rights of way over a highway (see below), but beyond this, and the broad requirements above, local authorities can determine for themselves what an appropriate consultation process might entail. However, this does provide an important opportunity to seek a broad range of views on the issue and can be invaluable in determining ways forward, establishing the final scope of the proposals and ascertaining their impact.

Encouraging open discussion as part of the consultation process can help to identity how best to balance the interests of different groups – both those affected by the anti-social

behaviour and those who will be restricted by the terms of an Order – and a chance to explore whether there may be any unintended consequences from the proposals; in particular, any adverse impacts on vulnerable people.

'Community representatives' are defined broadly in the Act as 'any individual or body appearing to the authority to represent the views of people who live in, work in or visit the restricted area'. This gives councils the freedom to determine who best to contact given local circumstances and the scope of the proposals. Those who will be directly affected by the Order, or groups representing their interests, should be directly approached. Further, several areas have reported that they found it useful to actively seek out stakeholders who might oppose the proposals during their consultation.

In several areas early discussions with stakeholders who might be affected by a PSPO have proven very useful. This engagement, often before a more formal consultation process, not only provides an opportunity to discuss the anti-social behaviour and its impact on others, but also gives the council an in-depth understanding of stakeholders' key concerns, and tests the impact that any restrictions on behaviour might have. This has helped scope the proposals and in some cases identified alternative ways of tackling the problem behaviour.

Identifying appropriate stakeholders to approach will obviously depend on the nature and scope of the PSPO in question. Alongside residents, users of the public space, and those likely to be directly affected by the restrictions, this might include residents' associations, local businesses, commissioned service providers, charities and relevant interest groups.

The Kennel Club (via KC Dog) has been contacted by several councils looking to introduce PSPOs affecting dogs and their owners. Where an Order will restrict access over land, utility service providers should be included within the consultation process.

Consultation approaches

Councils should use a range of means to reach out to potential respondents, some of whom may be unable to feed back in certain ways, eg online. Local demographics and the characteristics of those who may be most affected by the ASB or the Order can also help to identify the best mechanisms for ensuring a comprehensive consultation process (for instance, using social media where young people may be particularly affected). Similarly, different tools may be utilised in various ways to enrich the information gathered – for instance, a survey of park users which is repeated at various times of day to cover a range of people using the public space.

Existing meetings such as ward panels may provide opportunities to discuss the issue and encourage more formal consultation responses. Securing written statements from those particularly affected, such as landowners, can be particularly useful in building the evidence base for supporting the introduction of a PSPO.

In Cheshire West and Chester their PSPO consultation not only asked respondents whether or not they found particular activities problematic, but also whether or not that behaviour should be addressed via a PSPO. By asking open questions that allowed for free comments, it provided an opportunity for respondents to give their views on what they felt should be a proportionate response to each specific issue identified.

An effective consultation should provide an overview of what the local issues are, set out why a PSPO is being proposed, and what its impact would be. Publishing details of the extent of the problem behaviour can assist respondents to understand why a PSPO is being considered and help inform views on whether it would therefore be an appropriate response.

The consultation should also provide sufficient means for respondents to oppose the proposals and may also be used to elicit views on alternative approaches. Achieving a healthy response rate, with considered responses, will help to support the evidence base for introducing an Order and refuting challenge.

"The open consultation format was actually really useful in identifying new issues. We haven't lost anything from the process; all these things have gone into action plans to try and sort out."

Cheshire West and Chester

Examples of consultation methods from local areas include:

- online questionnaires
- postal surveys
- face-to-face interviews
- contact with residents' associations
- focus groups with stakeholders and interest groups representing those who will be affected
- discussions with service providers working directly with affected groups
- discussions at ward panel meetings
- publicity via local press or social media
- publications in libraries and other public buildings
- on-street surveys
- drop-in sessions in the area subject to the PSPO.

Surveys or questionnaires have been an integral part of councils' consultation processes for PSPOs and provide a chance to test the extent to which the proposals satisfy the statutory requirements under section 59. The questions might explore:

- what effect the activities in question have on residents, businesses and visitors – and whether this is detrimental

- how safe respondents feel and what impacts on this
- how often problem behaviours are personally encountered by individuals
- when and where problems occur
- whether the behaviour is so unreasonable that it should be banned.

Feedback from some areas suggests that seeking expert advice on drafting questions and undertaking consultations can help ensure that questions are appropriately phrased, clear and objective.

There are no statutory requirements about the length of the consultation process. However it should be ensured that its duration allows sufficient time to meaningfully engage with all those who may be impacted by the Order, taking into account for instance any holiday periods that may affect response rates – this may take several weeks or even months. Some issues may require time to fully explore and understand – councils should not be reluctant to extend the initial consultation period if it is clear that this would be beneficial in the longer-term.

Additional requirements for PSPOs restricting public rights of way

In the case of Orders restricting access over public highways (eg through the installation of gates), the Act sets out specific additional requirements for the consultation process. The council must notify those who may be potentially affected by the Order, let them know how they can see a copy of the PSPO proposals and when they need to submit any responses, and is required to consider any representations made. Councils must also consider the effect of the restrictions on occupiers of premises adjacent to or adjoining the highway, on other people in the locality and, where this is a through route, whether a reasonably convenient alternative is available. These considerations should include, for example, access for emergency services or utility companies.

Achieving support from the local community for these types of Orders is particularly

important for ensuring their success; if gates are regularly left open by residents then it is unlikely that the ASB will be addressed.

In Oldham, a two-stage process is used for consultation for PSPOs that restrict access over public highways.

After local discussions it was found that often directly-affected properties were occupied by transient residents who were less likely to respond to a consultation process. This negatively impacted upon settled residents as non-responses were not counted towards the approval rate for schemes and failure to reach the agreed approval rate resulted in proposals not being progressed any further.

Working with residents and councillors, the policy was amended and now states that if, after two contacts, there is no response from a household directly affected by the proposal, and in the absence of a clear objection, the default position becomes support for the proposed Order, thus achieving a much higher level of support for the proposals. In order to achieve a balance the approval rate required to move to the next step of broader consultation was increased to 90 per cent.

Consultation outcomes

Consultation responses will clearly require some analysis once they are collected. Councils might consider examining the demography of respondents to the consultation. This can help to gauge whether they are, for example, residents or visitors, and can be useful in determining who is likely to be impacted most by either the problem behaviour or restrictions on behaviour. This can be useful in helping to shape the final Order provisions.

"The consultation allowed us to measure the fear of crime – often things are not reported and the statistics don't show this."

Cheshire West and Chester Council

427

Councils may wish to publish the outcomes of their consultation process, and other supporting evidence, in the interests of transparency (subject to data protection requirements).

Further evidence
As noted above the 2014 Act requires local authorities to formally consult with the police and the police and crime commissioner (PCC) – and there should be further engagement with relevant lead officers from the police to help build the evidence base and identify the potential impact of an Order. Early engagement with and support from police partners is likely to be key in introducing an Order. As well as assisting with identifying the problem behaviour and therefore the scope of any responses, this can also help to draw out some of the more practical implications of introducing an Order, such as how it will be enforced – which may shape how the PSPO is drafted.

Alongside eliciting views from the police and PCC, there may be a number of additional sources of information that help to inform decision-making and support (or oppose) the introduction of an Order or specific prohibitions. These might include:

- the community safety partnership's strategic assessment
- police data on crime and anti-social behaviour incidents (including the impact of some problem behaviours, such as excessive drinking)
- hospital data on ingesting new psychoactive substances
- calls to 101
- calls to council services reporting incidents
- residents' logs and photographs of anti-social behaviour
- mapping of problem areas
- data on the effectiveness of previous Gating Orders or Dog Control Orders
- CCTV footage of incidents
- reports from council staff such as park wardens and cleaners.

Collecting data covering a prolonged period may help to satisfy the legislative requirement that the activities subject to the draft Order are persistent. Some areas have collated evidence covering a two year period in order to demonstrate this.

Political accountability, scrutiny and sign-off

Within the confines of the framework outlined above (and subject to legal challenge), councils have the freedom to determine their own procedures for introducing a PSPO, ensuring that the statutory requirements have been met and giving final approval for an Order to go ahead.

Close involvement of councillors and ensuring political buy-in throughout the implementation process are key. This provides political accountability for decisions taken – which is particularly important if the proposals may attract some opposition, and where insufficient member involvement may lead to challenge. Political support is also important to ensure that sufficient resources will be made available to implement and enforce the PSPO throughout its duration. Many areas have agreed that final approval and sign-off of PSPOs should be undertaken at cabinet/ executive or Full Council level.

In ensuring that the requirements under section 59 of the 2014 Act have been satisfied, councillors will have a significant role to play in unpicking what might be regarded as unreasonable and detrimental behaviour in the locality and what would constitute reasonable restrictions or requirements.

Discussions at senior political level by those who understand their local areas best, will help to ensure that the views of all parts of the community are reflected, and find an appropriate balance between the interests of those affected by the ASB and those likely to be affected by the proposed restrictions.

Councillors will also have an important role in examining the processes used in drafting the proposals. This will include analysing the outcomes of the consultation process and other supporting evidence offered to satisfy the statutory criteria, and determining whether, on balance this provides sufficient grounds to proceed (it should be noted here the need to ensure compliance with data protection legislation when sharing this information).

Several areas have used overview and scrutiny committees to examine draft Orders and challenge proposed ways forward. This adds a further element of democratic accountability and helps to ensure that decisions made are sound and transparent. In several cases, involvement from scrutiny committees has helped to focus the scope of Orders proposed.

Committees provide a useful mechanism to test the proposals and their potential impact, and the evidence base for introducing them; front-line councillors can provide different perspectives and may also offer suggestions for alternative approaches.

Suggested questions for overview and scrutiny committees

What evidence is there that the anti-social behaviour is or is likely to be persistent, detrimental and unreasonable?

Why is a PSPO being proposed to address this issue or issues?

Is the proposed restriction proportionate to the specific harm or nuisance that is being caused?

What alternative approaches are available and why is a PSPO appropriate in these circumstances?

Will the proposals alleviate each of the problem behaviours?

Have exemptions been considered?

What might be the unintended consequences for each aspect of the

PSPO?

What will be the impact on different groups? Has an equalities impact assessment been undertaken and what were its findings? What can be done to mitigate against any negative consequences?

How have the consultation outcomes and other evidence collated been taken into account?

How will the PSPO be enforced for each restriction/requirement? Are there sufficient resources to do this effectively?

Enforcement and implementation

Enforcement protocols

As noted earlier, issues regarding some of the more practical aspects of implementation and enforcement of PSPOs should be borne in mind from the beginning of the planning process – and may help shape the scope and wording of the Order itself. Further, effective implementation of a PSPO is likely to be part of a broader strategic approach that includes a number of different initiatives to tackle the problem issues.

Beyond this, local areas will want to develop specific protocols regarding enforcement action, before the Order is implemented. These protocols should incorporate expert input on the issues related to the ASB in question, and, recognising that there may be other options available to address a particular ASB incident, provide guidance on what might be the most appropriate legislative (or other) tool to use in different circumstances. Some areas have developed a process map to provide a step-by-step diagram to agreed enforcement procedures.

Protocols should also cover what should be done in the event of a breach. It is an offence under section 67 of the 2014 Act to breach an Order without a reasonable excuse. In the case of Orders that prohibit alcohol consumption, where it is reasonably believed that a person has been or intends to consume alcohol, it is an offence under section 63 either to fail to comply with a request not to consume or to surrender alcohol (or what is reasonably believed to be alcohol or a container for alcohol).

Procedures should therefore consider circumstances where there may be a 'reasonable excuse' for breaching the Order, for instance a medical reason for public urination (such circumstances may be covered explicitly as exemptions in the wording of the Order). Protocols also provide a further opportunity to recognise that some of those responsible for the behaviour covered in the Order may themselves be vulnerable and in need of support; they should therefore include referral pathways where there are any safeguarding concerns, and signpost to other services.

> In the London Borough of Brent enforcement of the PSPO is shared between the police and the council with joint visits from UK Border Agency and Brent's employment and skills team, who seek to offer routes into legitimate employment for jobseekers.

Who is responsible for enforcement will vary across areas. In some, enforcement will be undertaken by council officers – this may include ASB officers, housing officers, park wardens, etc – and in others this may be undertaken in partnership with police officers and/or police community support officers. Protocols may therefore require agreement regarding patrolling activity and reporting arrangements – some of which will be informed by the specific behaviour in question. Some authorities have also encouraged local people to report incidents of possible breaches, which can help shape enforcement responses going forward, particularly around timetabling patrols.

> "Local communities have helped to identify the peak periods for problems in the park – patrol times can then be planned accordingly."

Coventry City Council

As well as developing protocols, training will help delegated officers to understand how the Order should be enforced in practice. In Cheshire West and Chester, this included training from the ambulance service to reinforce that the safety of individuals was paramount and help officers understand, for instance, the possible dangers of ingesting psychoactive substances.

Some areas have used a 'soft-launch' period as the Order becomes live. This provides an opportunity to test protocols with officers before full implementation. It also gives councils the chance to raise awareness of the new pending prohibitions – and demonstrate that some behaviours have been causing concern. However areas should consider how to manage any risks if implementation is delayed.

Fixed penalty notices

As noted above, it is an offence under section 67 to breach an Order without reasonable excuse, and where Orders prohibit alcohol consumption, it is an offence under section 63 to fail to comply with a request not to consume or to surrender alcohol (or what is reasonably believed to be alcohol/a container for alcohol).

Under the Act, authorised officers have the power to issue fixed penalty notices (FPNs) to anyone they reasonably believe is in breach. Section 68 sets out a framework for issuing FPNs but councils will also have their own broader protocols around issuing fines to which they should also refer – this might cover, for instance, whether or not fines are issued to those aged under 18. Protocols should also cover when it would be appropriate to pursue an individual further where an FPN is issued but remains unpaid after the prescribed period. In addition, there will be a need to plan for practical elements before implementation, such as developing specific FPN templates for dealing with PSPO breaches.

"There was some concern that a £100 FPN might not be an adequate deterrent and that a broader financial range for FPNs, up to £400, would be preferred. However, the current arrangements do allow for a summons to court to be issued for persistent offenders where multiple FPNs have been issued."

Royal Borough of Kensington and Chelsea

It will not always be appropriate to issue FPNs. Warnings may often be sufficient, and in many areas this is the initial preferred response. In some, advice sheets are handed out in the majority of cases, informing recipients that their behaviour breaches an Order, giving them the chance to comply or providing an opportunity for them to be moved on. Councils have reported that in most cases this has been sufficient to address the behaviour and there has been no need to take further action.

Publication and communication

Using an effective communication strategy to raise awareness about a PSPO is important throughout the implementation process, and should incorporate contact with partners and stakeholders as well as members of the public. Successful communications can help with informing the appropriate scope of an Order, engaging members of the community and others during the consultation process, and ensuring effective enforcement.

The legislation also sets out a number of requirements. Draft proposals for a PSPO must be published as part of the consultation process. For new or varied Orders the text must be published; for extended or discharged Orders the proposal must be publicised.

Home Office guidance suggests the close or direct involvement of elected members will help to ensure openness and accountability. The guidance suggests this can be achieved, for example, where the decision is put to the Cabinet or full council.

The area covered by the proposals must be well defined; publishing maps of the affected area will help to clarify where behaviours are controlled. There are requirements in the legislation for notifying any parish or community councils in the affected area, and for notifying the county council where the Order is being made by a district council. There are further requirements for formal notifications regarding Orders that restrict access to public highways (see also supporting evidence and consultation, above).

Regulations set out additional requirements regarding the publication of PSPOs[11] that have been made, varied or extended, stipulating that these must be:

- published on the local authority's website
- erected on or adjacent to the place the Order relates to, and is sufficient to draw attention, setting out the effect of the Order and whether it has been made, varied or extended.

The same requirements apply where an Order has been discharged, and must also include the date at which it ceases to have effect.

Signs publishing the Order in the affected locality do not necessarily need to set out all the provisions of the Order, but rather state where this information can be found. Multiple signs are likely to be required, particularly where the Order covers a large area.

These requirements should be regarded as a minimum and a range of options should be explored; in practice it is helpful to use a variety of means to help publicise the Order to raise awareness, avoid confusion and give people the opportunity to comply.

---

11 Statutory Instruments 2014 no. 2591 The Anti-social Behaviour Crime and Policing Act 2014 (Publication of Public Spaces Protection Orders)

Effective communication helps people understand what behaviours are expected in particular areas, and reduces the need to rely on enforcement measures.

In some areas leaflets have been printed detailing the new prohibitions in different languages, for distribution by officers. Similarly the nature of the Order itself may suggest some communication channels may be more effective than others. For instance, an Order covering the ingestion of legal highs at a music festival in Chelmsford was promoted via a social media campaign to reflect the demographics of those most likely to be attending the festival and who are likely to be reached via these means.

Effective communication with residents and partners throughout can also help manage expectations about the impact of introducing an Order. Putting a PSPO in place can be a lengthy process and it is important to maintain communication about when it will come into effect and/or be enforced and if other measures are being utilised in the interim. In addition this can help residents to understand that simply having an Order in place is unlikely to resolve an issue overnight – which may be even more important where there has been media interest in the proposals.

Legal challenge

PSPOs can be challenged under the Act on the grounds that the local authority did not have the power either to make the Order or include particular prohibitions or requirements, or that proper processes had not been followed as prescribed by the legislation. Challenges must be made to the High Court within six weeks of the Order being made, and by an individual who lives in, regularly works in or visits the restricted area. The High Court can uphold, quash or vary the PSPO and may decide to suspend the operation of the PSPO pending the verdict. As with all orders and powers, the making of a PSPO can be challenged by judicial review on public law grounds within three months of the decision or action subject to challenge.

Extension, variation and discharge

A PSPO can be made for a maximum duration of up to three years, after which it may be extended if certain criteria under section 60 of the Act are met. This includes that an extension is necessary to prevent activity recurring, or there has been an increase in frequency or seriousness of the activity. Extensions can be repeated, with each lasting for a maximum of three years. Effective evaluation of Orders will be important when determining whether any extensions or variations would be appropriate.

Councils should consider carefully what length of time would be reasonable and proportionate given the nature of behaviour in question and the impact of the restrictions being posed – byelaws, which are permanent, may be more appropriate if the issue concerned is unlikely to be transient. The impact of the original Order should be evaluated before any extensions are approved – where ASB has been completely eradicated as a result of a PSPO, it is proportionate and appropriate to consider the likelihood of recurrence of problems if the Order is not extended.

Orders can also be varied under the Act, by altering the area to which it applies, or changing the requirements of the Order. The same legislative tests of detrimental impact, proportionality and reasonableness need to be satisfied, as set out earlier in this guidance. Similarly, PSPOs can be discharged before their original end date.

Where PSPOs are varied, extended or discharged, there are statutory requirements regarding publishing or publicising this and councils are required to undertake a further consultation process (see publication and communication, above). Similarly, under section 72 councils are required at all of these stages to have particular regard to articles 10 and 11 of the Human Rights Act 1998 (see limitations, above).

In light of the updated statutory guidance from the Home Office on anti-social behaviour powers, published in December 2017, councils should review their PSPOs when they are up for renewal and take into account these recent changes to the statutory guidance.

Existing Designated Public Place Orders, Gating Orders and Dog Control Orders
Any DPPOs, Gating Orders or DCOs are automatically treated as if they were provisions of a PSPO. The transitioned Order will then remain in force up to a maximum of three years (2020) from the point of transition.

There is no requirement in the legislation for councils to undertake a new consultation process where existing DPPOs, Gating Orders or DCOs automatically transition, although local areas may consider reviewing these current Orders ahead of this time to ensure their provisions meet the legal tests for PSPOs. It is recommended that councils publicise any PSPOs that replace existing DPPOs, Gating Orders or DCOs to help raise public awareness.

Local councils have the discretion to consider what changes to signage are needed to notify members of the public. Any extension, variation or discharge of a transitioned PSPO would mean the local councils should carry out the necessary consultation and publication of the proposed Order.

Evaluating impact
As noted above, evaluating the impact of a PSPO will be important when considering extending or varying an Order, however assessing the effects, and effectiveness of the Order, should form part of ongoing performance management. Several areas have introduced procedures to monitor the impact of an Order at regular intervals.

A thorough evaluation will help to determine if the PSPO has addressed each aspect of the problem behaviour, whether discharging or varying the Order would be appropriate – and why – and what any variations might look like. Crucially it will also help measure the impact on people, including identifying any unintended consequences of the provisions. It should consider whether there has been any displacement of the issue to other areas and might also look at how enforcement

protocols are being used and whether practices are appropriate and consistent.

Resources

Anti-social Behaviour, Crime and Policing Act 2014: Reform of anti-social behaviour powers – Statutory guidance for frontline professionals
Home Office, December 2017
https://www.gov.uk/government/uploads/system/uploads/attachment_data/file/670180/2017-12-13_ASB_Revised_Statutory_Guidance_V2_0.pdf

A councillors' guide to tackling new psychoactive substances
LGA 2016
http://www.local.gov.uk/councillors-guide-tackling-new-psychoactive-substances

A guide to community engagement for those contemplating management on common land
Natural England, 2012
www.historicengland.org.uk/images-books/publications/common-purpose/

Dealing with irresponsible dog ownership: Practitioner's manual
Defra, 2014
www.gov.uk/government/uploads/system/uploads/attachment_data/file/373429/dog-ownership-practitioners-manual-201411.pdf

Ending rough sleeping by 2012: A self-assessment health check
Department for Communities and Local Government, 2009
http://webarchive.nationalarchives.gov.uk/20120919132719/http:/www.communities.gov.uk/documents/housing/pdf/endroughsleeping.pdf

Reform of anti-social behaviour powers: Public and open spaces
Home Office information note,
Home Office, 2014
www.gov.uk/government/uploads/system/uploads/attachment_data/file/364851/Public_and_open_spaces_information_note.pdf

Legislation

Anti-social Behaviour, Crime and Policing Act 2014
www.legislation.gov.uk/ukpga/2014/12/part/4/chapter/2

Anti-social Behaviour, Crime and Policing Act 2014 (Publication of Public Spaces Protection Orders) Regulations 2014
http://www.legislation.gov.uk/uksi/2014/2591/contents/made

Human Rights Act 1998
www.legislation.gov.uk/ukpga/1998/42/contents

Psychoactive Substances Act 2016
www.legislation.gov.uk/ukpga/2016/2/contents

Local Government Association
Local Government House
Smith Square
London SW1P 3HZ

Telephone 020 7664 3000
Fax 020 7664 3030
Email info@local.gov.uk
www.local.gov.uk

For a copy in Braille, larger print or audio,
please contact us on 020 7664 3000.
We consider requests on an individual basis.

REF 10.21

Appendix D
Precedents

Contents

I INJUNCTION FORMS – COUNTY COURT

(a) Draft application for a civil injunction, Form N16A

Application for Injunction
(General Form)

Name of court	Claim No.
Claimant's Name and Ref.	
Defendant's Name and Ref.	
Fee Account no.	

<u>Notes on completion</u>

Tick which boxes apply and specify the legislation where appropriate

(1) Enter the full name of the person making the application

(2) Enter the full name of the person the injunction is to be directed to

(3) Set out any proposed orders requiring acts to be done. Delete if no mandatory order is sought.

(4) Set out here the proposed terms of the injunction order (if the defendant is a limited company delete the wording in brackets and insert 'whether by its servants, agents, officers or otherwise').

(5) Set out here any further terms asked for including provision for costs

(6) Enter the names of all persons who have sworn affidavits or signed statements in support of this application

(7) Enter the names and addresses of all persons upon whom it is intended to serve this application

(8) Enter the full name and address for service and delete as required

☐ By application in pending proceedings

☐ Under Statutory provision _____

☐ This application is made under Part 8 of the Civil Procedure Rules

This application raises issues under
the Human Rights Act 1998   ☐ Yes   ☐ No

The Claimant[1]

applies to the court for an injunction order in the following terms:

The Defendant[2]

must[3]

The Defendant

be forbidden (whether by himself or by instructing or encouraging or permitting any other person)[4]

And that[5]

The grounds of this application are set out in the written evidence

of[6]   sworn (signed) on

This written evidence is served with this application.

This application is to be served upon[7]

This application is filed by[8]

(the Solicitors for) the Claimant (Applicant/Petitioner)

whose address for service is

Seal

Signed   Dated

Name and address of the person application is directed to

This section to be completed by the court

To*
of

This application will be heard by the (District) Judge

at

on   the   day of   20   at   o'clock

If you do not attend at the time shown the court may make an injunction order in your absence

If you do not fully understand this application you should go to a Solicitor, Legal Advice Centre or a Citizens' Advice Bureau

The court office at

is open between 10am and 4pm Mon - Fri. When corresponding with the court, please address all forms and letters to the Court Manager and quote the claim number.

N16A General form of application for injunction (05.14)   © Crown copyright 2014

(b) Draft injunction order, Form N16(1)

Injunction Order

Name of court	
Claim No.	
Claimant	
Defendant	
Claimant's Ref.	
For completion by the court **Issued on**	

To (1)

of (2)

Seal

(1) The name of the person the order is directed to

If you do not comply with this order you may be held in contempt of court and imprisoned or fined, or your assets may be seized.

(2) The address of the person the order is directed to

On   the   of   [20   ]   the court considered an application for an injunction

(3) The terms of any injunction order are to be preceded by the words "is forbidden whether by himself or by instructing or encouraging any other person" or if the defendant is a limited company "by its servants, agents, officers or otherwise"

The Court ordered that [(1)]

(3)

[The court is satisfied that (the conduct which is prohibited by this injunction, consists of or includes the use or threatened use of violence)(there is a significant risk of harm to a person towards whom the conduct prohibited by this injunction is directed)

A power of arrest is attached to terms [   ] of this injunction whereby any constable may under the power given in [section 91 of the Anti-social Behaviour Act 2003], [section 43 of the Policing and Crime Act 2009] arrest without warrant the defendant if the constable has reasonable cause for suspecting the defendant is in breach of any of those terms of this injunction]

If you do not understand anything in this order you should go to a Solicitor, Legal Advice Centre or a Citizens' Advice Bureau

The court office at

When corresponding with the court, please address forms or letters to the Court Manager and quote the claim number.

Injunction Order - Record of Hearing   **Claim No.** ....

On ....the .... day of ....[20   ].......
Before (H   Honour) (District) Judge ....
The court was sitting at ....

The ☐ **Claimant**   **(Name)**...
was ☐   represented by Counsel
     ☐   represented by a Solicitor
     ☐   in person
The ☐ **Defendant**   **(Name)**...
was ☐   represented by Counsel
     ☐   represented by a Solicitor
     ☐   in person
     ☐   did not appear having been given notice of this hearing
     ☐   not given notice of this hearing

The court read the written evidence of

☐   the Claimant   (sworn)(signed) on ....

☐   the Defendant   (sworn)(signed) on ....

And of.. (sworn)(signed) on ....

....

The court heard spoken evidence on oath from

....

....

The Claimant gave an undertaking (through his counsel or solicitor) promising to pay any damages
ordered by the court if it later decides that the Defendant has suffered loss or damage as a result of this
order*

Delete this paragraph if the court does not require the undertaking

Signed _____   Dated_____
                          (Judges Clerk)

N16(1)   General form of injunction for interim application or originating application
          (Formal Parts - See complete N16 for wording of operative clauses)

2 INJUNCTION FORMS – YOUTH COURT

(a) Summons

SUMMONS

**ON AN APPLICATION FOR AN INJUNCTION UNDER PART 1 OF
THE
ANTI-SOCIAL BEHAVIOUR, CRIME AND POLICING ACT 2014**

IN THE [insert] YOUTH COURT

[insert address of Court]

Court code: [insert]

Date: …………………………………………..

To the Defendant: **[insert name]**

Address: **[insert address**

You are hereby summoned to appear on:

Date:…………………………………….at:………………………..

Before the [insert name] Youth Court [insert court address]

To answer an application for an injunction, which application is attached to this summons.

_____

Justice of the Peace
[by order of the clerk of the court]

NOTE: Where the court is satisfied that this summons was served on you within what appears to the court to be a reasonable time before the hearing or adjourned hearing, it may issue a warrant for your arrest or proceed in your absence.
If an injunction order is made against you and if, without reasonable excuse, you do anything which you are prohibited from doing by such an order you shall be liable to a Supervision Order or three month Detention Order. (If an adult, to imprisonment for a term not exceeding two years, or to a fine).

440

(b) Application for injunction

APPLICATION FOR A [INTERIM AND/OR FINAL] INJUNCTION

PART 1

ANTI-SOCIAL BEHAVIOUR, CRIME AND POLICING ACT 2014

IN THE [insert] YOUTH COURT

[insert address of Court]

Court code: [insert]

Date:

Defendant:

Date of Birth:

Address:

Applicant Authority:

Individuals/bodies consulted:

Individuals/bodies informed:

It is alleged that:

(a)   The Defendant [insert name] has acted in an anti-social manner, that is to say [delete as appropriate: conduct that has caused, or is likely to cause, harassment, alarm or distress to any person / conduct capable of causing nuisance or annoyance to a person in relation to that person's occupation of residential premises / conduct capable of causing housing-related nuisance or annoyance to any person], and;

EITHER:

(b)   The Court considers that it is just to make an interim injunction order.

OR

(c)   The making of a final injunction order is just and convenient for the purpose of preventing the Defendant in engaging in anti-social behaviour.

Accordingly the applicant applies for an [interim] and/or [final] injunction order containing the following prohibition(s) and requirement(s):-

Prohibitions:

[Numbered list of prohibited activities]

Requirements:

[Numbered list of required activities]

Summary of behaved complained of
[insert brief description of behaviour]

Schedule of incidents with the last six months

	Date	Description of incident	Witness	Paragraph in stmt
1.	8.1.15	The Defendant held a noisy party at her mother's Property. The party went on until 2.30am and caused nuisance and annoyance to the neighbours.	SW	Para. 6
2.	9.1.15	The Defendant and her friends caused harassment, alarm and distress by throwing a radio from the window of her mother's Property which is situated on the eighth floor of the block at Regina Road. The radio narrowly missed hitting residents and their children who were returning home from school.	SW	Para. 8
3.	25.15	The Defendant caused harassment, alarm and distress by repeatedly pressing the buzzer and kicking the door of a resident at [ ] Road with some of her friends.	JS	Para. 7
4.				
5.				

KEY:
JS: Jagjit Singh of [insert address]
SW: Saskia Williams of [insert address]

The complaint of:

Name of Applicant authority:

Address of Applicant Authority:

Reference:

Who upon oath states that the Defendant was responsible for the acts of which the particulars are given above, in respect of which this complaint is made.

Taken and sworn before me:

_____
Justice of the Peace/Justices' Clerk

(c) Draft injunction order

[INTERIM OR FINAL] INJUNCTION ORDER

PART 1

ANTI-SOCIAL BEHAVIOUR, CRIME AND POLICING ACT 2014

IN THE [insert] YOUTH COURT

[insert address of Court]

Court code: [insert]

NOTE: If you do not obey this order you will be guilty of contempt of court and you may be sent to prison (or if you are under 18, be given a supervision, curfew or activity requirement)

Date:

Defendant:

Date of Birth:

Address:

Applicant Authority:

Individuals/bodies consulted:

Individuals/bodies informed:

The Court has found on the balance of probabilities that:

    (a)   The Defendant [insert name] has acted in an anti-social manner, that is to say [delete as appropriate: conduct that has caused, or is likely to cause, harassment, alarm or distress to any person / conduct capable of causing nuisance or annoyance to a person in relation to that person's occupation of residential premises / conduct capable of causing housing-related nuisance or annoyance to any person], and;

EITHER:

    (b)   The Court considers that it is just to make an interim injunction order.

OR

(c)   The making of a final injunction order is just and convenient for the purpose of preventing the Defendant in engaging in anti-social behaviour.

It is ordered that:

[insert details of order made by the Court]

Prohibitions:

[Numbered list of prohibited activities]

Requirements:

[Numbered list of required activities]

_____
Justice of the Peace/Justices' Clerk

If you do anything which you are prohibited from doing, or fail to carry out anything you are required to do by this order, you shall be liable on conviction to a Supervision Order or a Detention Order.

If you aged 18 or over when you do anything which you are prohibited from doing, or fail to carry out anything you are required to do by this order, your actions shall be treated as a contempt of Court in the County Court. The County Court has the power to fine and/or imprison you for a breach of this order.
You may be entitled to help with your legal costs (legal aid) in the event that you breach this order and further court proceedings are taken against you.[1]

---

1   See *Brown v Haringey LBC* [2015] EWCA Civ 483, [2017] 1 WLR 542.

3 GENERAL FORM OF UNDERTAKING IN THE COUNTY COURT – FORM N117

General form of undertaking

Name of court	

Between _____ Claimant
Applicant
Petitioner

and _____ Defendant
Respondent

Claim No.	
Claimant's Ref.	
Defendant's Ref.	

This form is to be used only for an undertaking not for an injunction

(1) Name of the person giving undertaking

On the   day of   [19   ][20   ]

(1)

[appeared in person] [was represented by Solicitor / Counsel]

and gave an undertaking to the Court promising (2)

Seal

(2) Set out terms of undertaking

(3) Give the date and time or event when the undertaking will expire

(4) The judge may direct that the party who gives the undertaking shall personally sign the statement overleaf

And to be bound by these promises until (3)

The Court explained to (1)

the meaning of his undertaking and the consequences of failing to keep his promises,

And the Court accepted his undertaking (4) [and *if so ordered* directed that

(1)   should sign the statement

overleaf].

And   (enter name of Judge) **ordered** that (5)

(5) Set out any other directions given by the court

(6) Address of the person giving undertaking

Dated

To (1)
of (6)

Important Notice

- If you do not comply with your promises to the court you may be held to be in contempt of court and imprisoned or fined, or your assets may be seized.

- If you do not understand anything in this document you should go to a Solicitor, Legal Advice Centre or a Citizens' Advice Bureau

The Court Office at

is open from 10 am to 4 pm. When corresponding with the court, address all forms and letters to the Court Manager and quote the claim number.

The Court may direct that the party who gives the undertaking shall personally sign the statement below.

Statement

I understand the undertaking that I have given, and that if I break any of my promises to the Court I may be fined, my assets seized or I may sent to prison for contempt of court.

Signed

To be completed by the Court

Delivered

☐ By posting on:

☐ By hand on:

☐ Through solicitor on:

Officer:

4 NOTICE OF INTENTION TO RELY ON HEARSAY EVIDENCE

IN THE [   ] COURT   **CLAIM NO: A027J710**

B E T W E E N:

[insert details]

Claimant

and

[insert details]

Defendant

**NOTICE OF INTENTION TO RELY
ON HEARSAY EVIDENCE**

**Pursuant to:
CPR 33.2 / Crim PR 50.6 [delete as appropriate]**

Take Notice that at the trial of this claim the Claimant intends to give in evidence the following statement made by [insert full name and address] dated [insert date].

And further Take Notice that the particulars relating to the statement are as follows: the witness statement and/or its exhibits include information provided by individuals who are unwilling to be identified through fear and who are not prepared to give oral evidence in the proceedings. The way in which the information has been obtained is set out in the witness statement. The court will be invited for to give permission for the information provided by the [unidentified] individuals to be given in evidence pursuant to s.116(2)(e) of the Criminal Justice Act 2003.

Dated ……… 20…

[Signature]

[capacity of signatory e.g. Claimant's solicitor]

To the Defendant and to [insert name and address] his solicitors

5 NOTICES OF SEEKING POSSESSION ON MANDATORY GROUNDS AND OTHER GROUNDS

(a) Secure tenancies
Housing Act 1985, section 83 as amended by Housing Act 1996, section 147 and the Anti-Social Behaviour, Crime and Policing Act 2014, sections 94-95

NOTICE OF SEEKING POSSESSION

This Notice is the first step towards requiring you to give up possession of your dwelling. You should read it very carefully.

1. **To [insert name]**

   If you need advice about this Notice and what you should do about it, take it as quickly as possible to a Citizens' Advice Bureau, a Housing Aid Centre, or a Law Centre, or to a Solicitor. You may be able to receive Legal Aid but this will depend on your personal circumstances.

2. **The [insert name of landlord] intends to apply to the Court for an order requiring you to give up possession of:**

   > INSERT ADDRESS

   If you are a secure tenant under the Housing Act 1985, as amended by the Housing Act 1996 and the Anti-Social Behaviour, Crime and Policing Act 2014, you can only be required to leave your dwelling if your landlord obtains an order for possession from the Court. The order must be based on one of the Grounds which are set out in the 1985 Act.

   (see paragraphs 3 and 4 below).

   If you are willing to give up possession without a Court Order, you should notify the person who signed this Notice as soon as possible and say when you would leave.

3. **Possession will be sought on Grounds one and two of Schedule 2 to the Housing Act 1985, which read:-**

   Ground 1: Rent lawfully due from the tenant has not been paid or an obligation of the tenancy has been broken or not performed.

   Ground 2: The tenant or a person residing in or visiting the dwelling-house:

449

(a)   has been guilty of conduct causing or likely to cause a nuisance or annoyance to a person residing, visiting or otherwise engaging in a lawful activity in the locality,

(aa)   has been guilty of conduct causing or likely to cause a nuisance or annoyance to the landlord of the dwelling-house, or a person employed (whether or not by the landlord) in connection with the exercise of the landlord's housing management functions, and that is directly or indirectly related to or affects those functions, or

(b)   has been convicted of—

(i)   using the dwelling-house or allowing it to be used for immoral or illegal purposes, or

(ii)   an indictable offence committed in, or in the locality of, the dwelling-house.

Possession will also be sought under section 84A of the Housing Act 1985 as amended by the Anti-Social Behaviour, Crime and Policing Act 2014, sections 94-95 (the absolute ground for seeking possession)

Section 84A provides:

84A Absolute ground for possession for anti-social behaviour

(1)   If the court is satisfied that any of the following conditions is met, it must make an order for the possession of a dwelling-house let under a secure tenancy.

This is subject to subsection (2) (and to any available defence based on the tenant's Convention rights, within the meaning of the Human Rights Act 1998).

(2)   Subsection (1) applies only where the landlord has complied with any obligations it has under section 85ZA (review of decision to seek possession).

(3)   Condition 1 is that:

(a)   the tenant, or a person residing in or visiting the dwelling-house, has been convicted of a serious offence, and

(b)   the serious offence—

(i)   was committed (wholly or partly) in, or in the locality of, the dwelling-house,

(ii)   was committed elsewhere against a person with a right (of whatever description) to reside in, or occupy housing accommodation in the locality of, the dwelling-house, or

(iii)   was committed elsewhere against the landlord of the dwelling-house, or a person employed (whether or not by the landlord)

in connection with the exercise of the landlord's housing management functions, and directly or indirectly related to or affected those functions.

(4)   Condition 2 is that a court has found in relevant proceedings that the tenant, or a person residing in or visiting the dwelling-house, has breached a provision of an injunction under section 1 of the Anti-social Behaviour, Crime and Policing Act 2014, other than a provision requiring a person to participate in a particular activity, and—

(a)   the breach occurred in, or in the locality of, the dwelling-house, or

(b)   the breach occurred elsewhere and the provision breached was a provision intended to prevent—

(i)   conduct that is capable of causing nuisance or annoyance to a person with a right (of whatever description) to reside in, or occupy housing accommodation in the locality of, the dwelling-house, or

(ii)   conduct that is capable of causing nuisance or annoyance to the landlord of the dwelling-house, or a person employed (whether or not by the landlord) in connection with the exercise of the landlord's housing management functions, and that is directly or indirectly related to or affects those functions.

(5)   Condition 3 is that the tenant, or a person residing in or visiting the dwelling-house, has been convicted of an offence under section 30 of the Anti-social Behaviour, Crime and Policing Act 2014 consisting of a breach of a provision of a criminal behaviour order prohibiting a person from doing anything described in the order, and the offence involved—

(a)   a breach that occurred in, or in the locality of, the dwelling-house, or

(b)   a breach that occurred elsewhere of a provision intended to prevent—

(i)   behaviour that causes or is likely to cause harassment, alarm or distress to a person with a right (of whatever description) to reside in, or occupy housing accommodation in the locality of, the dwelling-house, or

(ii)   behaviour that causes or is likely to cause harassment, alarm or distress to the landlord of the dwelling-house, or a person employed (whether or not by the landlord) in connection with the exercise of the landlord's housing management functions, and that is directly or indirectly related to or affects those functions.

(6)   Condition 4 is that—

(a)   the dwelling-house is or has been subject to a closure order under section 80 of the Anti-social Behaviour, Crime and Policing Act 2014, and

451

    (b)   *access to the dwelling-house has been prohibited (under the closure order or under a closure notice issued under section 76 of that Act) for a continuous period of more than 48 hours.*

(7)   *Condition 5 is that—*

    (a)   *the tenant, or a person residing in or visiting the dwelling-house, has been convicted of an offence under—*

        (i)   *section 80(4) of the Environmental Protection Act 1990 (breach of abatement notice in relation to statutory nuisance), or*

        (ii)   *section 82(8) of that Act (breach of court order to abate statutory nuisance etc.), and*

    (b) *the nuisance concerned was noise emitted from the dwelling-house which was a statutory nuisance for the purposes of Part 3 of that Act by virtue of section 79(1)(g) of that Act (noise emitted from premises so as to be prejudicial to health or a nuisance).*

(8)   *Condition 1, 2, 3, 4 or 5 is not met if—*

    (a)   *there is an appeal against the conviction, finding or order concerned which has not been finally determined, abandoned or withdrawn, or*

    (b)   *the final determination of the appeal results in the conviction, finding or order being overturned.*

(9)   *In this section—*

"relevant proceedings" means proceedings for contempt of court or proceedings under Schedule 2 to the Anti-social Behaviour, Crime and Policing Act 2014;

"serious offence" means an offence which—

    (a)   *was committed on or after the day on which subsection (3) comes into force,*

    (b) *is specified, or falls within a description specified, in Schedule 2A at the time the offence was committed and at the time the court is considering the matter, and*

    (c)   *is not an offence that is triable only summarily by virtue of section 22 of the Magistrates' Courts Act 1980 (either-way offences where value involved is small).*

(10) *The Secretary of State may by order amend Schedule 2A as it applies in relation to dwelling-houses in England by—*

    (a)   *adding an indictable offence;*

    (b)   *removing an offence.*

*(11) The Welsh Ministers may by order amend Schedule 2A as it applies in
relation to dwelling-houses in Wales by—*

　　(a) adding an indictable offence;

　　(b) removing an offence.

(12) An order under subsection (10) or (11)—

　　(a) is to be made by statutory instrument;

　　(b) may make different provision for different purposes;

　　*(c) may include incidental, supplementary, consequential, transitional
or saving provision.*

*(13) A statutory instrument containing an order under subsection (10) or (11)
may not be made unless a draft of the instrument has been laid before and
approved by a resolution of—*

　　*(a) each House of Parliament (in the case of an order of the Secretary of
State), or*

　　*(b) the National Assembly for Wales (in the case of an order of the Welsh
Ministers).*

Whatever Grounds for possession are set out in paragraph 3 of this Notice, the
Court may allow any of the other Grounds to be added at a later stage. If this is
done, you will be told about it so you can argue at the hearing in Court about the
new Ground, as well as the Grounds set out in paragraph 3, if you want to.

4.　**Particulars of the Grounds are as follows:**

Particulars of the relevant terms and conditions of tenancy:

```
SEE SHEET ONE
```

Particulars of the why each ground is being relied upon and the reasons why
possession is sought under s.84A of the Housing Act 1985 (as amended by
the Anti-Social Behaviour Act 2014):

```
SEE SHEET TWO
```

Before the Court will grant an order on any of the Grounds 1 to 8 or 12 to 16, it
must be satisfied that it is reasonable to require you to leave. This means that, if
one of these Grounds is set out in paragraph 3 of this Notice, you will be able
to argue at the hearing in Court that it is not reasonable that you should have to
leave, even if you accept that the Ground applies.

Before the Court grants an order on any of the Grounds 9 to 16, it must be satisfied that there will be suitable alternative accommodation for you when you have to leave. This means that the Court will have to decide that, in its opinion, there will be other accommodation which is reasonably suitable for the needs of you and your family, taking into particular account various factors such as the nearness of your place of work, and the sort of housing that other people with similar needs are offered. Your new home will have to be let to you on another secure tenancy or a private tenancy under the Rent Act of a kind that will give you similar security. There is no requirement for suitable alternative accommodation where Grounds 1 to 8 apply.

If your landlord is not a local authority, and the local authority gives a certificate that it will provide you with suitable accommodation, the Court has to accept the certificate.

One of the requirements of Ground 10A is that the landlord must have approval for the redevelopment scheme from the Secretary of State (or, in the case of a housing association landlord, the Housing Corporation). The landlord must have consulted all secure tenants affected by the proposed redevelopment scheme.

---

5.   **The Court proceedings for possession will not be begun until after([2])**

....

Court proceedings cannot be begun until after this date, which cannot be earlier than the date when your tenancy or licence could have been brought to an end. This means that if you have a weekly or fortnightly tenancy, there should be at least 4 weeks between the date this Notice is given and the date in this paragraph.

After this date, Court proceedings may be begun at once or at any time during the following twelve months. Once the twelve months are up this Notice will lapse and a new Notice must be served before possession can be sought.

Court proceedings for possession of the dwelling-house can be begun immediately. The date by which the tenant is to give up possession of the dwelling-house is([3])

....

Court proceedings may be begun at once or at any time during the following twelve months. Once the twelve months are up this Notice will lapse and a new Notice must be served before possession can be sought.

---

2   Cross out this paragraph if possession is being sought on Ground 2 of Schedule 2 to the Housing Act 1985 (whether or not possession is also sought on another Ground, save for cases where possession is also sought under s.84A of the Housing Act 1985 in which case this paragraph applies)

3   Cross out this paragraph if possession not being sought on Ground 2 of Schedule 2 to the Housing Act 1985. Where Ground 2 is relied upon in addition to possession being sought under s.84A of the Housing Act 1985, this paragraph will not apply.

Possession of your dwelling-house cannot be obtained until after this date, which cannot be earlier than the date when your tenancy or licence could have been brought to an end. This means that if you have a weekly or fortnightly tenancy, there should be at least 4 weeks between the date this Notice is given and the date possession is ordered.

6.   Your Tenancy Officer is [insert name] tel: [insert]

Signed ....

On behalf of the   [insert name landlord]

Address: [   ]

Telephone: [   ]

Dated: [   ]

SHEET 1

Particulars for Ground 1

You have breached the terms and conditions of your Tenancy for the following reasons:

[INSERT DETAILS]

SCHEDULE OF BREACHES

Date(s)	Incident / Breach

Particulars for Ground 2

[INSERT or state that the matters set out under the Particulars for Ground 12 are relied upon under Ground 1]

Section 84A (absolute ground for possession)

1. The landlord relies upon the following condition(s) in s.84A of the Housing Act 1985:

2. * The landlord relies upon the following conviction(s) for the purposes of conditions 1, 3 or 5:

3. * The landlord relies upon the following finding(s) for the purposes of condition 2:

4.   * The landlord relies upon the closure order detailed below for the purposes of conditions 4:

┌─────────────────────────────────────┐
│   │
│   │
│   │
└─────────────────────────────────────┘

(* delete as appropriate)

5.   The reasons for seeking possession under s.84A of the Housing Act 1985 are:

[INSERT REASONS]

SHEET THREE

You have a right to request a review of the landlord's decision to seek an order for possession relying on s.84A of the Housing Act 1985.

This request must be made within 7 days beginning with the day on which the notice is served upon you.

If you need help or advice about this notice, and what to do about it, you should take it immediately to a Citizens Advice Bureau, a housing aid centre, a law centre or a solicitor.

[insert further details of procedure to be followed on review]

(b) Assured tenancies

FORM 3

Notice seeking possession of a property let on an Assured Tenancy or an Assured Agricultural Occupancy

Housing Act 1988 section 8 as amended by section 151 of the Housing Act 1996, section 97 of the Anti-social Behaviour, Crime and Policing Act 2014, and section 41 of the Immigration Act 2016.

- Please write clearly in black ink.

- Please cross out text marked with an asterisk (*) that does not apply.

- This form should be used where possession of accommodation let under an assured tenancy, an assured agricultural occupancy or an assured shorthold tenancy is sought on one of the grounds in Schedule 2 to the Housing Act 1988.

- Do not use this form if possession is sought on the "shorthold" ground under section 21 of the Housing Act 1988 from an assured shorthold tenant where the fixed term has come to an end or, for assured shorthold tenancies with no fixed term which started on or after 28th February 1997, after six months has elapsed. Form 6A 'Notice seeking possession of a property let on an Assured Shorthold Tenancy' is prescribed for these cases.

1   To: ....

     Name(s) of tenant(s)/licensee(s)*

2   Your landlord/licensor* intends to apply to the court for an order requiring you to give up possession of: ....

     ....

     ....

     Address of premises

3   Your landlord/licensor* intends to seek possession on ground(s) .... in Schedule 2 to the Housing Act 1988 (as amended), which read(s):

     ....

     ....

     Give the full text (as set out in the Housing Act 1988 (as amended) of each ground which is being relied on. Continue on a separate sheet if necessary.

4   Give a full explanation of why each ground is being relied on:

     ....

     ....

     Continue on a separate sheet if necessary.

Notes on the grounds for possession

- If the court is satisfied that any of grounds 1 to 8 is established, it must make an order (but see below in respect of fixed term tenancies).

- Before the court will grant an order on any of grounds 9 to 17, it must be satisfied that it is reasonable to require you to leave. This means that, if one of these grounds is set out in section 3, you will be able to suggest to the court that it is not reasonable that you should have to leave, even if you accept that the ground applies.

- The court will not make an order under grounds 1, 3 to 6[4], 9 or 16, to take effect during the fixed term of the tenancy (if there is one) and it will only make an order during the fixed term on grounds 2, 7, 7A, 8, 10 to 15 or 17 if the terms of the tenancy make provision for it to be brought to an end on any of these grounds. It may make an order for possession on ground 7B during a fixed-term of the tenancy even if the terms of the tenancy do not make provision for it to be brought to an end on this ground.

- Where the court makes an order for possession solely on ground 6 or 9, the landlord must pay your reasonable removal expenses.

5   The court proceedings will not begin until after:...

....

Give the earliest date on which court proceedings can be brought

Notes on the earliest date on which court proceedings can be brought

- Where the landlord is seeking possession on grounds 1, 2, 5 to 7, 9 or 16 (without ground 7A or 14), court proceedings cannot begin earlier than 2 months from the date this notice is served on you and not before the date on which the tenancy (had it not been assured) could have been brought to an end by a notice to quit served at the same time as this notice. This applies even if one of grounds 3, 4, 7B, 8, 10 to 13, 14ZA, 14A, 15 or 17 is also specified.

- Where the landlord is seeking possession on grounds 3, 4, 7B, 8, 10 to 13, 14ZA, 14A, 15 or 17 (without ground 7A or 14), court proceedings cannot begin earlier than 2 weeks from the date this notice is served. If one of 1, 2, 5 to 7, 9 or 16 grounds is also specified court proceedings cannot begin earlier than two months from the date this notice is served.

- Where the landlord is seeking possession on ground 7A (with or without other grounds), court proceedings cannot begin earlier than 1 month from the date this notice is served on you and not before the date on which the tenancy (had it not been assured) could have been brought to an end by a notice to quit served at the same time as this notice. A notice seeking

---

4   Amended to reflect changes shortly to be made to correct the form prescribed in the Assured Tenancies and Agricultural Occupancies (Forms) (England) Regulations 2015.

possession on ground 7A must be served on you within specified time periods which vary depending on which condition is relied upon:

- Where the landlord proposes to rely on condition 1, 3 or 5: within 12 months of the conviction (or if the conviction is appealed: within 12 months of the conclusion of the appeal);

- Where the landlord proposes to rely on condition 2: within 12 months of the court's finding that the injunction has been breached (or if the finding is appealed: within 12 months of the conclusion of the appeal);

    ○ Where the landlord proposes to rely on condition 4: within 3 months of the closure order (or if the order is appealed: within 3 months of the conclusion of the appeal).

    ○ Where the landlord is seeking possession on ground 14 (with or without other grounds other than ground 7A), court proceedings cannot begin before the date this notice is served.

- Where the landlord is seeking possession on ground 14A, court proceedings cannot begin unless the landlord has served, or has taken all reasonable steps to serve, a copy of this notice on the partner who has left the property.

- After the date shown in section 5, court proceedings may be begun at once but not later than 12 months from the date on which this notice is served. After this time the notice will lapse and a new notice must be served before possession can be sought.

6   Name and address of landlord/licensor*.

To be signed and dated by the landlord or licensor or the landlord's or licensor's agent (someone acting for the landlord or licensor). If there are joint landlords each landlord or the agent must sign unless one signs on behalf of the rest with their agreement.

Signed .... *Date* ....

....

....

....

Please specify whether: landlord / licensor / joint landlords / landlord's agent

Name(s) (Block Capitals)..

Address..

....

....

....

Telephone: Daytime .... *Evening* ....

What to do if this notice is served on you

- This notice is the first step requiring you to give up possession of your home. You should read it very carefully.

- Your landlord cannot make you leave your home without an order for possession issued by a court. By issuing this notice your landlord is informing you that he intends to seek such an order. If you are willing to give up possession without a court order, you should tell the person who signed this notice as soon as possible and say when you are prepared to leave.

- Whichever grounds are set out in section 3 of this form, the court may allow any of the other grounds to be added at a later date. If this is done, you will be told about it so you can discuss the additional grounds at the court hearing as well as the grounds set out in section 3.

- If you need advice about this notice, and what you should do about it, take it immediately to a citizens' advice bureau, a housing advice centre, a law centre or a solicitor.

6 PRO-FORMA APPLICATION FOR A REVIEW OF THE DECISION TO RELY ON MANDATORY GROUNDS

HOUSING ACT 1985
Section 85ZA
REQUEST FOR A REVIEW

This request must be made before the end of the period of 7 days beginning with the day on which you were served with notice of seeking possession under section 83ZA Housing Act 1985

You can e-mail a copy of this request to: [insert address for e-mail service] before the above period expires.

Otherwise it must be received by the Council before the above period expires. If you deliver the request by hand you should ensure you attend during the Council's open office hours and ask for a stamped notice of receipt.

I [insert name]:

request a review under section 85ZA Housing Act 1985 of my landlord's decision dated [insert date of Notice of Seeking Possession under section 83ZA if earlier than date of service of Notice of Seeking Possession]:

to seek possession of the property at [insert address property in respect of which secure tenancy is held]:

on the following grounds [explain why you wish to appeal the landlord's decision to seek possession and use an additional sheet if necessary]:

I require / I do not require the review to be conducted by way of an oral hearing [you must delete as appropriate]

I agree / do not agree to receive communications relating to this request for a review by email. (If you agree to receiving communications by email please state the email address to which communications should be sent here:...)

Signed:

Date:

7 CLOSURE OF PREMISES

(a) Application for closure order

APPLICATION FOR A PREMISES CLOSURE ORDER

SECTION 80

ANTI-SOCIAL BEHAVIOUR, CRIME AND POLICING ACT 2014

IN THE [insert] MAGISTRATES' COURT

[insert address of Court]

Court code: [insert]

Date:

Defendant:

Date of Birth:

Address:

Applicant Authority:

Relevant Authorities Consulted:

Application is made for a Closure Order in relation to the address at [insert address] (the 'Premises') on the grounds that:

(a)   that a person has engaged, or (if the order is not made) is likely to engage, in disorderly, offensive or criminal behaviour on the premises, or;

(b)   that the use of the premises has resulted, or (if the order is not made) is likely to result, in serious nuisance to members of the public, or;

(c)   that there has been, or (if the order is not made) is likely to be, disorder near those premises associated with the use of those premises,

and that the order is necessary to prevent the behaviour, nuisance or disorder from continuing, recurring or occurring.

A Closure Notice was served on the Premises on [insert date and time].

Application is made for a Closure Order for a period of [insert] months.

The circumstances giving rise to the application are set out in the witness statements of:

i.   [insert name], Anti-Social Behaviour Officer, dated [insert date];

    ii. P C [Insert name], dated [insert date];

iii.   [insert name and address], dated [insert date].

Summary of the behaviour complained of:

The allegations consist of the Defendant engaging in offensive behaviour on the Premises and of serious nuisance to members of the public. The behaviour includes verbal abuse, shouting, slamming doors, playing loud amplified music, holding late night parties and the sounds of banging, crashing and dog(s) barking. The anti-social behaviour occurs during the day but especially during the evening and night. The Defendant regularly has numerous visitors to her property who also engage in the behaviour described and whose behaviour she fails to control. This is in breach of the Defendant's tenancy agreement and in breach of the terms of a suspended order for possession made on 2.7.14.

Schedule of incidents:

	Date	Description of incident	Witness	Paragraph in stmt
1	5.1.15	Defendant verbally abused and threatened a resident who had asked her to turn her music down. The Defendant told the resident: *'Don't tell me what to do, I'll fucking smash your face in. I know where you live, I'll fucking kill you'*	JS	Para. 3 Exhibit 1
2	5.5.10	Defendant abusive towards a council employee: *'Tell fucking [name of housing officer] to take me to fucking court then, go on take me to fucking court'.*	SW	Para. 6
3	Between November 2014 and January 2015	There were numerous visitors to the Premises during the day and night, most of the visitors would only stay for a few minutes before leaving. The neighbouring residents were disturbed by the noise created by these visitors and the fact that they congregated in the communal areas of the block smoking drugs	SW JS	Para. 10 & Diaries at exhibit FS 2 Para. 15

4

5

KEY:

JR: Jagjit Singh of [insert address]

SW: Saskia Williams of [insert address]

The complaint of:

Name of Applicant authority:

Address of Applicant Authority:

Reference:

Who upon oath states that the Defendant was responsible for the acts of which the particulars are given above, in respect of which this complaint is made.

Taken and sworn before me:

_____

Justice of the Peace/Justices' Clerk

(b) Closure notice

ANTI-SOCIAL BEHAVIOUR, CRIME & POLICING ACT 2014

Part 4, Chapter 3

CLOSURE NOTICE

Re: _____

("the Premises")

Being satisfied on reasonable grounds:

- that the use of particular Premises has resulted, or (if the notice is not issued) is likely soon to result, in nuisance to members of the public, or

- that there has been, or (if the notice is not issued) is likely soon to be, disorder near those Premises associated with the use of the Premises,

and that the notice is necessary to prevent the nuisance or disorder from continuing, recurring or occurring,

and

[insert name of police force if Applicant is a local authority] OR [insert name of local authority if the Applicant is the police]being the local [authority OR police] for the area in which the Premises are situated having been consulted,

and

reasonable steps having been taken to inform people who live on the Premises (whether habitually or not) and any person who has control of or responsibility for the Premises or has an interest in them, that the notice is going to be issued,

I, [Insert name, job title and employer], for and on behalf of, the [insert name of Local Authority or police force], hereby authorise the issue of this **Closure Notice** under section 76(1) of the Anti-social Behaviour, Crime and Policing Act 2014 in respect of the Premises specified above.

Signed .... Dated..

TAKE NOTICE that

The effect of this Closure Notice is that access to these Premises by any person other than a person who habitually resides in the Premises or the owner of the Premises is hereby PROHIBITED, for a period of [insert whether 24 or 48 hours] starting at [insert time and date] and ending at [insert date and time], subject to the following exceptions:

This Closure Notice prohibits access to any person other than officers, agents, representamen, contractors acting on behalf of the [council or police – delete as appropriate]

An application for an order will be made under section 80 of the Anti-Social Behaviour, Crime and Policing Act 2014 for the closure of the Premises specified above, to [insert] Magistrates' Court on [date] at [time] when evidence for the issue of a Closure Order will be considered.

(On this date, should the court adjourn the hearing for the application of the Closure Order, the details of the court, date and time of the hearing shall be shown at the bottom of this notice.)

An order under section 80 of the Anti-social Behaviour, Crime and Policing Act 2014 would have the effect of closing the Premises to all persons for a specified period (not exceeding three months).

A person who without reasonable excuse remains in or enters premises in contravention of a closure notice or obstructs a person in the process of serving a closure notice or closing a property commits an offence under section 86 of the Anti-Social Behaviour, Crime and Policing Act 2014, liable on summary conviction to a maximum of three months' imprisonment or a fine or both.

A person who without reasonable excuse remains on or enters premises in contravention of a closure order commits an offence under section 86 of the Anti-Social Behaviour, Crime and Policing Act 2014, liable on summary conviction to imprisonment not exceeding 51 weeks or a fine or both.

Advice relating to this notice and housing and legal matters generally can be obtained from any firm of solicitors or from the Citizens' Advice Bureau [insert telephone number] or [insert name and telephone number of local advice service if applicable]

☐ With this notice is a list of additional local service providers who may be able to assist with further advice. (Check if applicable.)

The hearing for the Closure Order has now been adjourned to [insert] Magistrates' Court at .... on ....by Order of the Court

(c) Closure order

CLOSURE ORDER

SECTION 80(5)

ANTI-SOCIAL BEHAVIOUR, CRIME AND POLICING ACT 2014

IN THE [insert] MAGISTRATES' COURT

[insert address of Court]

Court code: [insert]

Date:

Defendant:

Date of Birth:

Address:

Applicant Authority:

Relevant Authorities Consulted:

The Court has found on the balance of probabilities in relation to the address at [insert address] (the 'Premises'):

(a)   that a person has engaged, or (if the order is not made) is likely to engage, in disorderly, offensive or criminal behaviour on the premises, or;

(b)   that the use of the premises has resulted, or (if the order is not made) is likely to result, in serious nuisance to members of the public, or;

(c)   that there has been, or (if the order is not made) is likely to be, disorder near those premises associated with the use of those premises,

and that the order is necessary to prevent the behaviour, nuisance or disorder from continuing, recurring or occurring.

The court orders that [insert address] be closed and no further entry will be allowed for the period of [insert] months from the date of this order. The occupier will therefore be required to find alternative accommodation.

[The Court in issuing this Closure Order prohibits <u>anyone</u> from remaining on or entering the Premises.]

[................may be admitted onto the Premises for the purpose of .... on [insert date(s)] at [insert time(s)].

[Access by ....to ....part of the Premises shall be allowed for the purpose of ....]

The Closure Order is in force for a period of 3 months from the date of this order. [_____ to _____]

A person commits an offence if they remain on or enter these Premises and can be arrested. If found guilty of an offence, they are liable to imprisonment and/ or a fine.

By order of the court

District Judge/Justice of the Peace
[By order of the clerk of the court]

8 COMMUNITY PROTECTION NOTICES

(a) Warning letter

Community Protection Warning Letter

Dear

Re: [insert description of behaviour having the detrimental effect]

The [**insert name of local authority**] is serving you with a Community Protection Warning under s.43(5)(a) of the Anti-Social Behaviour, Crime and Policing Act 2014.

The reasons for serving this warning letter are that your conduct is having a detrimental effect, of a persistent and continuing nature, on the quality of life of those in the locality and the conduct is unreasonable.

This warning requires you to comply with the following prohibitions / positive requirements / specified actions that are believed necessary to prevent the detrimental effect from continuing or recurring, to reduce the detrimental effect or to reduce the risk of its continuance. You are required to:

Action required	Date for compliance
• Stop doing the following [ ] and/or	
• To do the following [ ] and/or	
• Take the following steps to achieve the results specified [ ].	

If you fail to take the action specified in this letter the Council can serve you with a Community Protection Notice.

Failure to comply with a Community Protection Notice without reasonable excuse is a criminal offence. Failure to comply can also result in the Council taking remedial action for which you will be re-charged.

Yours etc

Service

This warning letter was served on [**insert name**] of [**insert address**] on [**insert date**]. The method of service was [ ].

(b) Community protection notice

Community Protection Notice ('CPN')

To: (name of individual or body being served)

Of: (address)

Property this notice relates to:

....

On (date) .... the local authority served you with a written warning letter regarding your conduct and requiring your compliance by ....

....

The **(name of local authority)** is serving you with a Community Protection Notice under s.43(1) of the Anti-Social Behaviour, Crime and Policing Act 2014 ('ASBCPA 2014').

The reasons for serving this CPN are that your conduct is having a detrimental effect, of a persistent and continuing nature, on the quality of life of those in the locality and the conduct is unreasonable.

The conduct is ....

This CPN requires you to comply with the following prohibitions / positive requirements / specified actions that are believed necessary to prevent the detrimental effect from continuing or recurring, to reduce the detrimental effect or to reduce the risk of its continuance. You are required to:

Action required	Date for compliance
• Stop doing the following [ ] and/or	
• To do the following [ ] and/or	
• Take the following steps to achieve the results specified [ ].	

Section 43(7) of the ASBCPA 2014 requires this CPN to explain the effect of sections 46–51. Notes on these sections can be found overleaf.

Service

This CPN was served on (name) of (address) on (date). The method of service was (handed to XX, posted through the letterbox at XX, posted to XX etc.).

Notes accompanying CPN, ASBCPA 2014, s 46–51

Section 46 – Appeals against CPNs

This section provides for a person issued with a CPN to issue an appeal within 21 days of receiving the CPN. The grounds on which an appeal can be brought are:

1.   That the conduct specified in the community protection notice—

- did not take place

- has not had a detrimental effect on the quality of life of those in the locality

- has not been of a persistent or continuing nature

- is not unreasonable, or

- is conduct that the person cannot reasonably be expected to control or affect.

2.   That any of the requirements in the notice, or any of the periods within which or times by which they are to be complied with, are unreasonable.

3.   That there is a material defect or error in, or in connection with, the notice.

4.   That the notice was issued to the wrong person.

Any appeal would be heard by the magistrates 'court which has the power to quash the notice, modify the notice (for example for extending a period specified within it), or dismiss the appeal.

Section 47 – remedial action by local authority

This section allows the local authority to take remedial action in the form of works to ensure that the failure to comply with the CPN is remedied. The order can require you to carry out works or invite you to allow specified works to be carried out by or on behalf of the local authority. The local authority can carry out works to land that is open to the air without further notice to you.

If the works relate to premises other than open to the air the local authority is required to issue the defaulter with a notice:

(a)   specifying work it intends to have carried out to ensure that the failure is remedied,

(b)   specifying the estimated cost of the work, and

(c)   inviting the defaulter to consent to the work being carried out,

Paragraph (b) does not apply where the local authority has made reasonable efforts to contact the owner of the premises without success.

The ASBCPA 2014 gives the local authority, or anyone authorised by it, the power to enter premises to carry out works. The local authority cannot enter your home without your consent.

A person issued with a notice under this section can appeal to the magistrates' court within 21 days beginning with the day on which the notice was issued. The magistrates' court has the power to confirm the amount or substitute a lower amount.

Section 48 – criminal offence for failure to comply with a CPN

This section creates a criminal offence for a failure to comply with a CPN. A person guilty of an offence is liable to a fine not exceeding level 4 on the standard scale in the case of an individual, or an unlimited fine in the case of a body.

No offence is committed where a person has taken all reasonable steps to comply with the CPN or has some other reasonable excuse for the failure to comply with it.

Section 49 – power to make a remedial order

Where a person is convicted of an offence under s 48 the court has the power to make a remedial order requiring the defendant to carry out work or to allow specified work to be carried out by or on behalf of the local authority.

A person issued with a notice under s 49(6) (a notice specifying the cost of carrying out the works for which the defaulter is liable) may appeal to the magistrates' court within 21 days beginning on the day on which the notice was issued on the ground that the amount specified under subsection (6)(b) is excessive.

Section 50 – forfeiture of item used on commission of offence

Where a person is convicted of an offence under s 48 the court has the power to order the forfeiture of any item that was used in the commission of the offence. The order may require the item to be destroyed or disposed of in whatever way the order specifies.

Section 51 – seizure of item used in commission of offence

A justice of peace may issue a warrant authorising any constable or designated person to enter premises within 14 days from the date of issue to seize any item where there are reasonable grounds for suspecting that an offence under s 48 has been committed and that there is an item used in the commission of the offence on premises specified in the information.

Any seized items can be retained until any relevant criminal proceedings have been finally determined if such proceedings are started before the end of a period of 28 days following the day on which the item was seized. Otherwise the item must be returned to the person from whom it was seized before the end of that period.

Applying to vary or discharge this CPN[5]

You can apply to vary or discharge this CPN. In order to make such an application you should [insert procedure, eg write to [name] at [address] setting out the reasons why you are asking for the CPN to be varied or discharged. We will deal with your request in accordance with our policy on applications to vary or discharge a CPN which can be found on our website at [insert website address]].

---

5   *Stannard v CPS* [2019] EWHC 84 (Admin).

Appendix E
Sample Prohibitions

Contents

The examples listed in this appendix are intended to provide a starting point for the types of terms that might be included within an injunction (see Chapter 3) or criminal behaviour order (see Chapter 4).

The suggested terms should not be treated as applicable in all cases where there is a similar pattern of behaviour. Readers will need to give careful thought to whether the terms are necessary and proportionate in view of the particular facts of their case.

In Chapter 3 at 3.17 there is a discussion of the general principles applicable to the drafting of terms. There is also a discussion of how some of the terms made in ASBOs may be relevant to injunctions under Pt 1 of the Act.

INTRODUCTORY SENTENCES

The Defendant is prohibited from:

OR

The Defendant is prohibited, whether by himself or by instructing or encouraging others, from:[1]

ANTI-SOCIAL BEHAVIOUR – GENERAL PROHIBITION

Acting or inciting others to act in an anti-social manner, that is to say, a manner that causes or is likely to cause harassment, alarm or distress to one or more persons not of the same household anywhere in [ ].[2]

ASSAULT & INTIMIDATION

Threatening any person with violence and/or being verbally abusive towards any person, anywhere in [ ].

Using abusive, offensive, threatening or intimidating language or behaviour anywhere in [ ].[3]

Causing noise nuisance by shouting or by slamming doors anywhere in [ ].

Persistently knocking on neighbours' doors and/or ringing neighbours' doorbells or intercom systems, without reasonable excuse anywhere in [ ].

Spitting, using verbal, physical or racial abuse, swearing, throwing eggs, stones, or any other items or missiles towards any person, motor vehicle or other property anywhere in [ ].

---

1   Injunctions can require a person not to encourage other people to be involved in a breach of the terms but to do so they must say this in expressly: *Circle 33 Housing Trust Ltd v Kathirkmanathan* [2009] EWCA Civ 921. The case concerned an undertaking but the principles are of equal relevance for injunctions.

2   Approved by the Court of Appeal in *R v Boness (Dean), R v Bebbington (Shaun Anthony)* [2005] EWCA Crim 2395, [2006] 1 Cr App R (S) 120; cf *Heron v Plymouth City Council* [2009] EWHC 3562 (Admin) where the court held that the condition that prevented H from causing harassment, alarm or distress to any person was too imprecise and was no more than a repetition of offences contrary to the Public Order Act 1986. Note that the defendant was already excluded from the city centre by another prohibition so query whether such a term was necessary on the facts of this case.

3   *R (on the application of Rabess) v Commissioner of Police of the Metropolis* [2007] EWHC 208 (Admin) (a case involving domestic violence).

Being in possession of a ball-bearing gun, soft air pellet gun, or any other imitation weapon in a public place anywhere in [ ].

Owning or having in your care or control a laser pointer pen or any instrument which emits a laser light beam anywhere in [ ].

Using foul or abusive language towards or gestures towards any employee of the emergency services (that is to say, Fire Brigade, Ambulance, hospital staff including security staff on NHS property) whilst they are acting in the course of their employment.

Causing harassment, alarm or distress to your tenants and/or (a) entering their rooms without consent and/or (b) cutting off their gas and electricity supply.

BEGGING

Approaching persons unknown to ask for money or alms in [ ][4]

Begging or seeking charitable donations in [ ].

Approaching any member of the public, anywhere and asking for money.

Sitting on the floor outside the shops in [ ] Road.

Attending residential properties anywhere in [ ] uninvited and asking for money.

Washing any vehicle or part of a vehicle that is not registered to you in any public place in [ ].

BURGLARY

Not to carry jewellery belonging to another person without their permission.

Not to carry any identity documents [including driver's licence, credit cards (etc.)] in someone else's name.

CLOTHING

Wearing body armour in a public place anywhere in [ ].

Wearing any article of clothing with an attached hood in any public place in the [ ] whether the hood is up or down.[5]

COMMUNICATIONS

Entering any telephone box anywhere in [ ], except to make a 999 call.

---

4   Approved in *Samuda v DPP*, also known as *Samuda v Birmingham Magistrates Court* [2008] EWHC 205 (Admin).
5   Approved in *B v Greenwich Magistrates Court* [2008] EWHC 2882.

Calling the 999 emergency telephone system for any reason other than a genuine emergency.

Making threats verbally, in writing or electronically.

CONTACT

Not to contact the complainant [who was his wife] or going within 200 metres of the house where she lives.[6]

CURFEW

Being in any place other than [ ] between the hours of [insert appropriate hours].[7]

Leaving any premises in which you are placed by social services, unless accompanied by a member of staff or a parent, or as agreed or directed by social services, or the carers of your placement anywhere in [ ].

The Defendant must:[8]

- Remain indoors between 22.00hrs and 06.00hrs each night at a probation hostel specified by the National Offender Management Service or such other address as the court shall approve.[9]

- Observe a curfew between the hours of [ ] and [ ] unless accompanied by [insert name(s) of parent or legal guardian].

DRINK

Consuming alcohol in any public place other than licensed premises anywhere in [ ].[10]

Being in possession of any opened vessel containing or purporting to contain alcoholic liquor in any public place in [ ].

Entering any on or off licensed premises within the area shown on the attached map.

Urinating in any public place anywhere in [ ].

---

6   Approved in *R v Gowan (Jason)* [2007] EWCA Crim 1360, [2008] 1 Cr App R (S) 12.
7   Approved in *Lonerghan v Lewis Crown Court and Brighton and Hove City Council* [2005] EWHC 457 (Admin).
8   As an alternative to the introductory sentences set out above.
9   Approved in *R v Starling (Michael Jonathan)* [2005] EWCA Crim 2277.
10   Approved in *R v Starling (Michael Jonathan)* [2005] EWCA Crim 2277.

EXCLUSION ZONES

Entering Birmingham City Centre.[11]

Entering the Forest Heath District Council area, save for the purpose of attending court.[12]

Entering the exclusion zone denoted in red on the attached map at any time, comprising of the Graveney Ward and Furzedown Ward and including the boundary roads, save for attendance at a police station or solicitors' offices by prior appointment.[13]

Entering the buildings or grounds of any National Health Service (NHS) or private hospital property at any time save for treatment for a medical emergency or by prior written appointment.

Entering any car park which is owned, opened or leased by Network Rail, any train operating company or London Underground Ltd whether on payment or otherwise within the counties of Hertfordshire, Bedfordshire or Buckinghamshire.[14]

Entering the area of Reading Town Centre as defined on the map overleaf unless there is a prearranged appointment with a court or probation officer.[15]

Not to attend within 100m of any McDonald's restaurant in Reading.[16]

FLY TIPPING

Carrying any form of waste material at any time without a valid waste carrier's license registered with the environmental agency anywhere in [ ].

Leaving objects in a road or on a footway that could cause obstruction to vehicles or pedestrians and or an accident anywhere in [ ].

GRAFFITTI AND CRIMINAL DAMAGE

Marking or defacing any wall, fence, window or other surface of any building, structure or vehicle.

Carrying any bladed or sharply pointed instrument, including but not limited to, knives, screwdrivers, drills or drill bits, power tools or similar instruments anywhere in [ ].

---

11   Approved in *Braxton (Curtis) (Application for Leave to Appeal)* also known as *R v Braxton (Curtis) (also known as Owodun (Kamorudeen))* [2004] EWCA Crim 1374, [2005] 1 Cr App R. (S) 36.
12   Approved in *R v Vittles (Anthony Malcolm)* [2004] EWCA Crim 1089, [2005] 1 Cr App R (S) 8.
13   Similar exclusion zone approved in *M v Director of Public Prosecutions* [2007] EWHC 1032 (Admin).
14   Approved in *R v McGrath (Jamie Paul)* [2005] EWCA Crim 353, [2005] 2 Cr App R (S) 85.
15   Approved by the High Court in *Kieron Stannard v CPS* [2019] EWHC 84 (Admin).
16   Approved by the High Court in *Kieron Stannard v CPS* [2019] EWHC 84 (Admin).

Touching or entering any unattended vehicle without the express permission of the owner.[17]

Carrying marker pens or aerosols in public places in [ ].

Purchasing or requesting to be purchased on their behalf any aerosol spray paint within [ ].

Carrying the following articles, in any public place, namely any form of liquid paint in any form of container, any form of permanent marker pen, any form of shoe dye or permanent ink in any form of container, any form of grinding stone, glass cutting equipment, glass etching solution or paste anywhere in [ ].

Travelling on the top deck of any public transport bus, anywhere in [ ].

Lighting fires in any public area or open space anywhere in [ ].

GROUPS

Joining or remaining in any group of [*insert number*] or more people (including himself) in a public place, which is acting in a manner likely to [harass, alarm or distress/cause nuisance and annoyance to] any person, anywhere in [ ].

Congregating in a public place in a group of [*insert number*] or more persons which is behaving in a manner causing or likely to cause any person to fear for their safety anywhere in [ ].[18]

Not to be in a group of more than 3 individuals including yourself.[19]

LOCAL AUTHORITY AND HOUSING

Abusing, insulting or using threatening behaviour towards employees, agents of contractors of the council.

Entering [*insert name and address*] Housing Office without a prior written appointment.

MOTOR VEHICLES

Sitting on, standing on, pushing, pulling or riding any mechanically-propelled 'Go-ped' (micro scooter), moped, quad bike, tricycle or motorcycle anywhere in [ ].

Being a passenger in or on any mechanically propelled vehicle other than public transport without the consent of the owner or registered keeper anywhere in [ ].

---

17   Approved in *R v Boness (Dean), R v Bebbington (Shaun Anthony)* [2005] EWCA Crim 2395, [2006] 1 Cr App R (S) 120; see also *R v Barnard (Lawrence)* [2006] EWCA Crim 2041, (2006) 150 SJLB 1056.

18   Approved in *N v Director of Public Prosecutions* [2007] EWHC 883 (Admin).

19   Approved by the High Court in *Kieron Stannard v CPS* [2019] EWHC 84 (Admin).

Sitting in the front seat of any motor vehicle, in [ ], whilst serving a period of disqualification from driving, imposed by a court.

Driving any mechanically propelled vehicle in a public place.

Washing any vehicle or part of a vehicle that is not registered to you in any public place in [ ].

NOISE

Making any noise or vibration or disturbance at [*insert address*], so as to cause nuisance to those living at [*insert address*].

Playing any music, shouting or banging, so as to cause [harassment, alarm or distress/nuisance or annoyance] to those living in nearby dwellings anywhere within [ ].

Making noise, shouting or using swear words within sight or hearing of any person or allowing anyone else within the boundaries of your property to do so.

Banging or striking any walls, doors, floors or ceilings such as to cause nuisance or annoyance to any occupants or visitors of any neighbouring properties.

NON-ASSOCIATION

Associate with [*a named individual*] in any public place.[20]

Associating with any female under the age of 16.[21]

Associating with [*insert names*] or be present on [*insert names of roads*] where these individuals live.

Visiting [*insert name*] unless accompanied by a [*insert name(s) of parent or legal guardian*].

PROSTITUTION

Engaging in any activity which amounts to the provision of, or offer to provide, any services for gain, either financial or otherwise, except for legitimate employment or business.

STREET DRINKING

Not to be in possession of an opened vessel containing or purporting to contain alcoholic liquor.

---

20   Approved in *Hills v Chief Constable of Essex* [2006] EWHC 2633 (Admin), (2007) 171 JP 14.
21   *R v Melvin Harris* [2006] EWCA Crim 1864 (history of sexual behaviour towards school girls).

Sitting on the bench/floor [insert location, eg outside XX supermarket on XX street, outside XX bank cash point marked on the attached map].

TRANSPORT

Entering any car park, which is provided for the use of persons travelling on London Underground, as per the attached list.

Entering any depot, siding or other part of London Underground property or railway property which is not expressly open to public whether on payment or otherwise anywhere in [ ].

Travelling on a London Underground train which is on or travelling within the LUL circle line, or being on any of the LUL stations which are on or within the LUL circle line. This includes all of the stations highlighted in yellow on the attached map.

Entering or alighting at [ ] London Underground station.

Travelling on the top deck of any public transport bus, anywhere in [ ].

Entering any tube station except to purchase valid tickets and to travel to your destination.

Causing harassment, nuisance or annoyance by seeking to transfer or receive or sell or offer for sale any partly used travel ticket.

Boarding any form of public transport between the hours of 08:00–09:00 and 15:00–16:30 unless with a letter of appointment for medical, court, probation or solicitors appointments.[22]

THEFT AND DECEPTION

Calling at any residential premises (by way of doorbell, knocking or telephone call) without the prior permission of an occupier anywhere in [ ].

Riding any pedal cycle belonging to any person other than the defendant in [ ].

Engaging in any activity which amounts to the provision of, or offer to provide, any services for gain, either financial or otherwise, except for legitimate employment or business anywhere in [ ].

Being in possession of a bank card, credit card or other identification belonging to another person, and acting in an anti-social manner in [ ].

---

22   To avoid known child sex offenders getting on public transport with school children.

TRESPASS

Remaining on any land or premises in England and Wales, after being asked to leave by a person or persons with authority or responsibility for those premises.[23]

Entering any car park which is owned, opened or leased by Network Rail, any train operating company or London Underground Ltd whether on payment or otherwise within the counties of Hertfordshire, Bedfordshire or Buckinghamshire.[24]

Climbing on roofs of property anywhere in [ ].

Entering the buildings or grounds of any National Health Service (NHS) or private hospital property at any time save for treatment for a medical emergency or by prior written appointment.

Entering the Bradford Royal Infirmary and its grounds, unless arriving in an ambulance or a police vehicle.

Entering any sheltered housing complex or supported living accommodation in [*insert address*].

VEHICLE REPAIR

Repairing or dismantling any mechanically propelled vehicle, or any electrical or mechanical machine or appliance in a public place, anywhere in [ ].

Having in your care or control, more than one mechanically propelled vehicle not lawfully registered to you, anywhere in [ ].

VICTIM AND WITNESS INTIMIDATION

Doing any act, including making a statement, whether by yourself or encouraging others to do so, which is likely to intimidate any named person who has provided information which might be used as evidence in these or other proceedings involving the Defendant, whether that person is a witness in the proceedings or not.

In any way, directly or through another, contacting, or interfering with property belonging to any person whose evidence is used at court during these [injunction/CBO (etc)] proceedings.

WEAPONS

Carrying any knife or bladed article in any public place in England and Wales.[25]

---

23   Approved in *R v Boness (Dean), R v Bebbington (Shaun Anthony)* [2005] EWCA Crim 2395, [2006] 1 Cr App R (S) 120.

24   Approved in *R v McGrath (Jamie Paul)* [2005] EWCA Crim 353, [2005] 2 Cr App R (S) 85.

25   Approved in *Joseph Daniel Hills v Chief Constable of Essex* [2006] EWHC 2633 (Admin).

Being in possession of a ball-bearing gun, soft air pellet gun, or any other imitation weapon in a public place anywhere in [ ].

MISCELLANEOUS

Inciting or encouraging others to commit any act prohibited by this Order.

Purchasing, carrying, setting off or throwing fireworks anywhere in [ ].

Owning, or having in his care and control any dog anywhere in [ ].

Being in possession of any mobile phone other than a single phone registered to your name and address.

Index

[References are to paragraph numbers]

485

492

Lightning Source UK Ltd.
Milton Keynes UK
UKHW032035030223
416453UK00007B/69